ALSO AVAILABLE FROM

MANGA

@LARGE (August 2003)
ANGELIC LAYER*
BABY BIRTH* (September 2003)
BATTLE ROYALE*
BRAIN POWERED*
BRIGADOON* (August 2003)
CARDCAPTOR SAKURA
CARDCAPTOR SAKURA: MASTER OF THE CLOW*
CHOBITS*
CHRONICLES OF THE CURSED SWORD
CLAMP SCHOOL DETECTIVES*
CLOVER
CONFIDENTIAL CONFESSIONS* (July 2003)
CORRECTOR YUI
COWBOY BEBOP*
COWBOY BEBOP: SHOOTING STAR*
DEMON DIARY
DIGIMON*
DRAGON HUNTER
DRAGON KNIGHTS*
DUKLYON: CLAMP SCHOOL DEFENDERS*
ERICA SAKURAZAWA*
ESCAFLOWNE* (July 2003)
FAKE*
FLCL* (September 2003)
FORBIDDEN DANCE* (August 2003)
GATE KEEPERS*
G GUNDAM*
GRAVITATION*
GTO*
GUNDAM WING
GUNDAM WING: BATTLEFIELD OF PACIFISTS
GUNDAM WING: ENDLESS WALTZ*
GUNDAM WING: THE LAST OUTPOST*
HAPPY MANIA*
HARLEM BEAT
I.N.V.U.
INITIAL D*
ISLAND
JING: KING OF BANDITS*
JULINE
KARE KANO*
KINDAICHI CASE FILES, THE*
KING OF HELL
KODOCHA: SANA'S STAGE*
LOVE HINA*
LUPIN III*
MAGIC KNIGHT RAYEARTH* (August 2003)

MAGIC KNIGHT RAYEARTH II* (COMING SOON)
MAN OF MANY FACES*
MARMALADE BOY*
MARS*
MIRACLE GIRLS
MIYUKI-CHAN IN WONDERLAND* (October 2003)
MONSTERS, INC.
NIEA_7* (August 2003)
PARADISE KISS*
PARASYTE
PEACH GIRL
PEACH GIRL: CHANGE OF HEART*
PET SHOP OF HORRORS*
PLANET LADDER*
PLANETES* (October 2003)
PRIEST
RAGNAROK
RAVE MASTER*
REALITY CHECK
REBIRTH
REBOUND*
RISING STARS OF MANGA
SABER MARIONETTE J* (July 2003)
SAILOR MOON
SAINT TAIL
SAMURAI DEEPER KYO* (August 2003)
SAMURAI GIRL: REAL BOUT HIGH SCHOOL*
SCRYED*
SHAOLIN SISTERS*
SHIRAHIME-SYO: SNOW GODDESS TALES* (Dec. 2003)
SHUTTERBOX (November 2003)
SORCERER HUNTERS
THE SKULL MAN*
TOKYO MEW MEW*
UNDER THE GLASS MOON
VAMPIRE GAME
WILD ACT* (July 2003)
WISH*
WORLD OF HARTZ (August 2003)
X-DAY* (August 2003)
ZODIAC P.I. * (July 2003)

*INDICATES 100% AUTHENTIC MANGA (RIGHT-TO-LEFT FORMAT)

CINE-MANGA™

CARDCAPTORS
JACKIE CHAN ADVENTURES (COMING SOON)
JIMMY NEUTRON (September 2003)
KIM POSSIBLE
LIZZIE MCGUIRE
POWER RANGERS: NINJA STORM (August 2003)
SPONGEBOB SQUAREPANTS (September 2003)
SPY KIDS 2

NOVELS

KARMA CLUB (July 2003)
SAILOR MOON

TOKYOPOP KIDS

STRAY SHEEP (September 2003)

ART BOOKS

CARDCAPTOR SAKURA*
MAGIC KNIGHT RAYEARTH*

ANIME GUIDES

COWBOY BEBOP ANIME GUIDES
GUNDAM TECHNICAL MANUALS
SAILOR MOON SCOUT GUIDES

Under the Glass Moon

VOLUME 1
BY
KO YA-SEONG

TOKYOPOP®

LOS ANGELES • TOKYO • LONDON

Translator - Lauren Na
English Adaptation - Paul Morrissey
Retouch & Lettering - Paul Morrissey
Cover Layout & Graphic Design - Patrick Hook

Senior Editor - Mark Paniccia
Managing Editor - Jill Freshney
Production Coordinator - Antonio DePietro
Production Manager - Jennifer Miller
Art Director - Matthew Alford
Director of Editorial - Jeremy Ross
VP of Production & Manufacturing - Ron Klamert
President & C.O.O. - John Parker
Publisher & C.E.O. - Stuart Levy

Email: editor@TOKYOPOP.com
Come visit us online at www.TOKYOPOP.com

A ⊙ **TOKYOPOP**® Manga
TOKYOPOP® is an imprint of Mixx Entertainment, Inc.
5900 Wilshire Blvd. Suite 2000, Los Angeles, CA 90036

ISBN: 1-59182-240-8

First TOKYOPOP® printing: June 2003

10 9 8 7 6 5 4 3 2 1
Printed in Canada

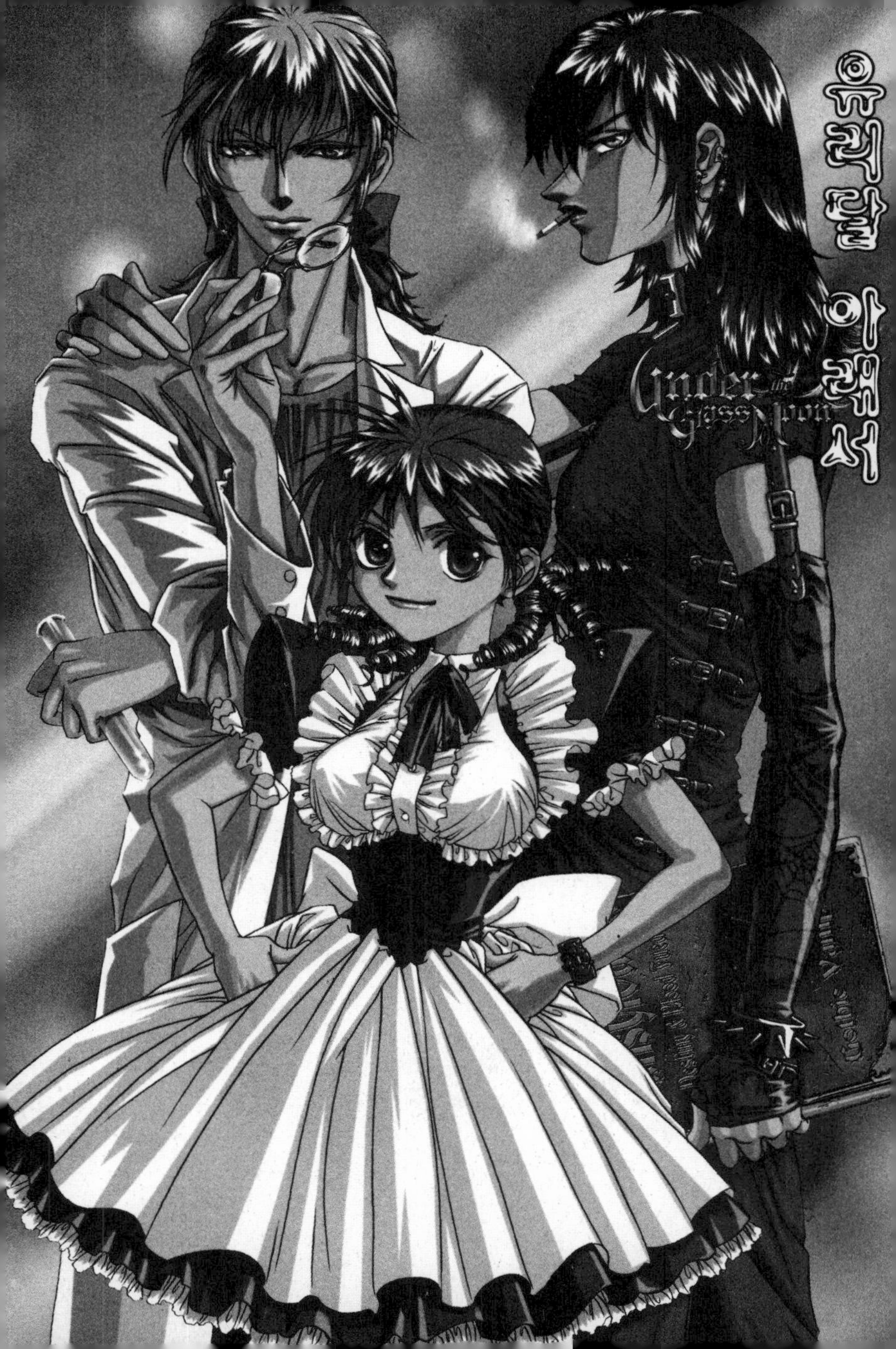
유리달 아래서
Under the Glass Moon

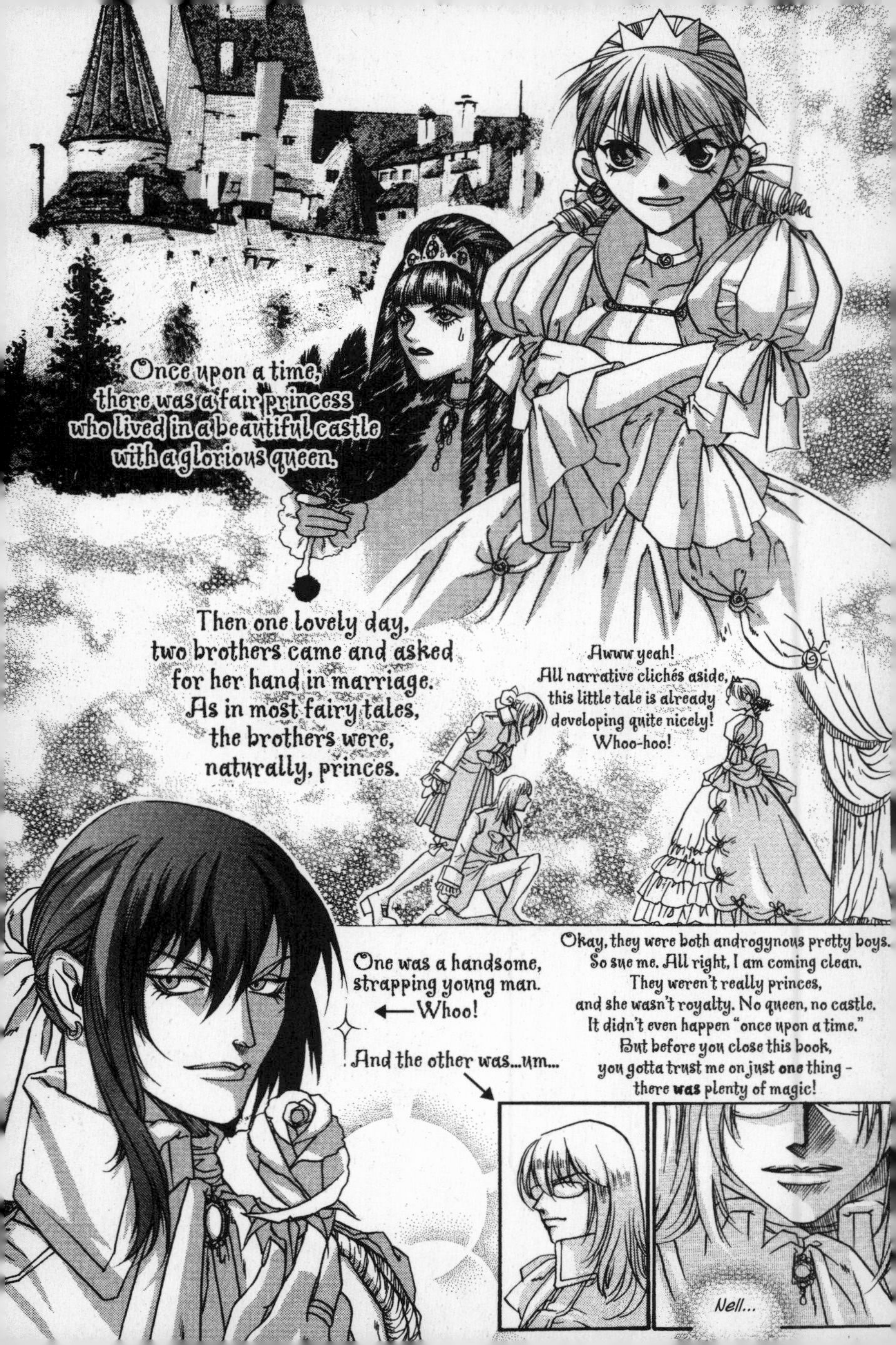
Once upon a time,
there was a fair princess
who lived in a beautiful castle
with a glorious queen.
Then one lovely day,
two brothers came and asked
for her hand in marriage.
As in most fairy tales,
the brothers were,
naturally, princes.
Awww yeah!
All narrative clichés aside,
this little tale is already
developing quite nicely!
Whoo-hoo!
One was a handsome,
strapping young man.
←Whoo!
And the other was...um...
Okay, they were both androgynous pretty boys.
So sue me. All right, I am coming clean.
They weren't really princes,
and she wasn't royalty. No queen, no castle.
It didn't even happen "once upon a time."
But before you close this book,
you gotta trust me on just one thing -
there **was** plenty of magic!
Nell...

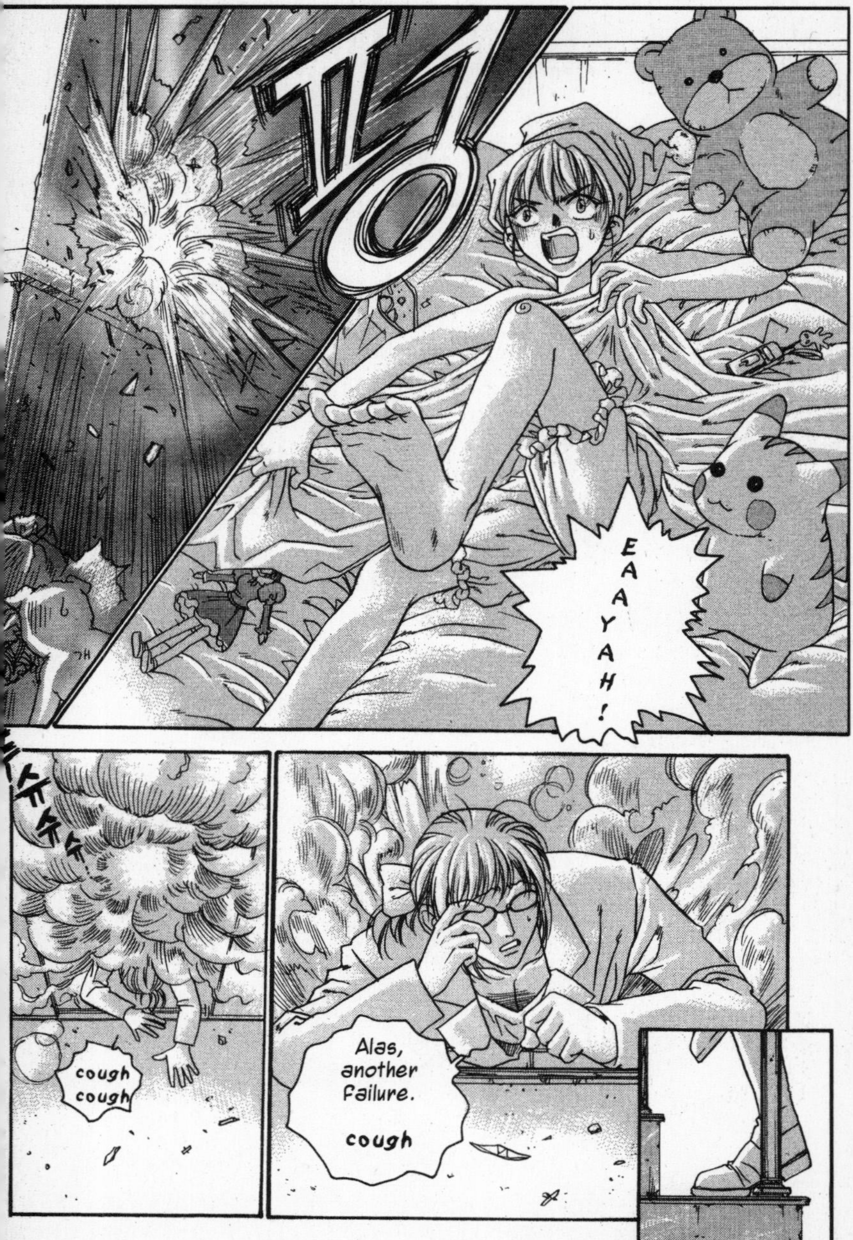
EAAAYAH!
cough cough
Alas, another failure.
cough

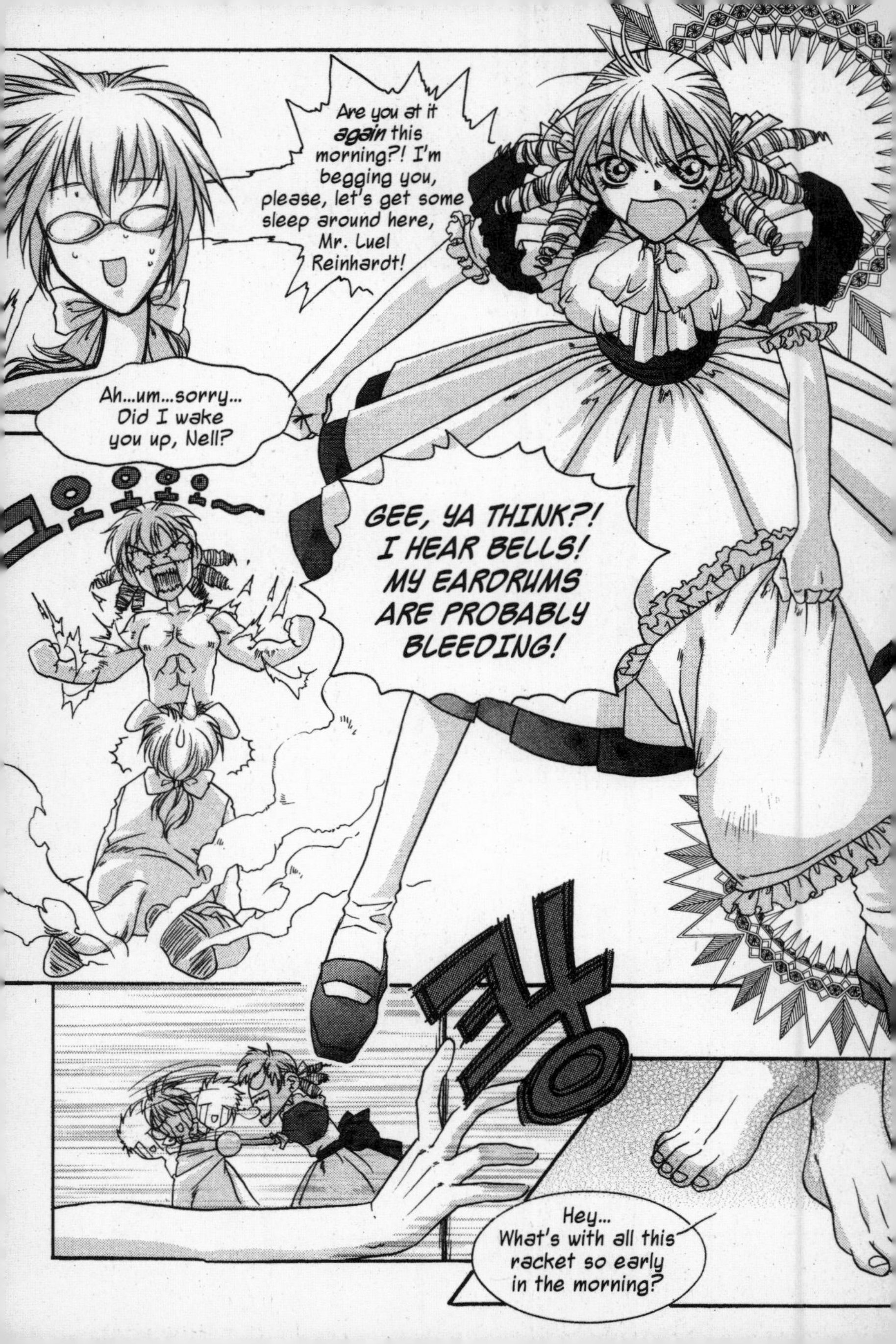
Are you at it *again* this morning?! I'm begging you, please, let's get some sleep around here, Mr. Luel Reinhardt!
Ah...um...sorry... Did I wake you up, Nell?
GEE, YA THINK?! I HEAR BELLS! MY EARDRUMS ARE PROBABLY BLEEDING!
Hey... What's with all this racket so early in the morning?

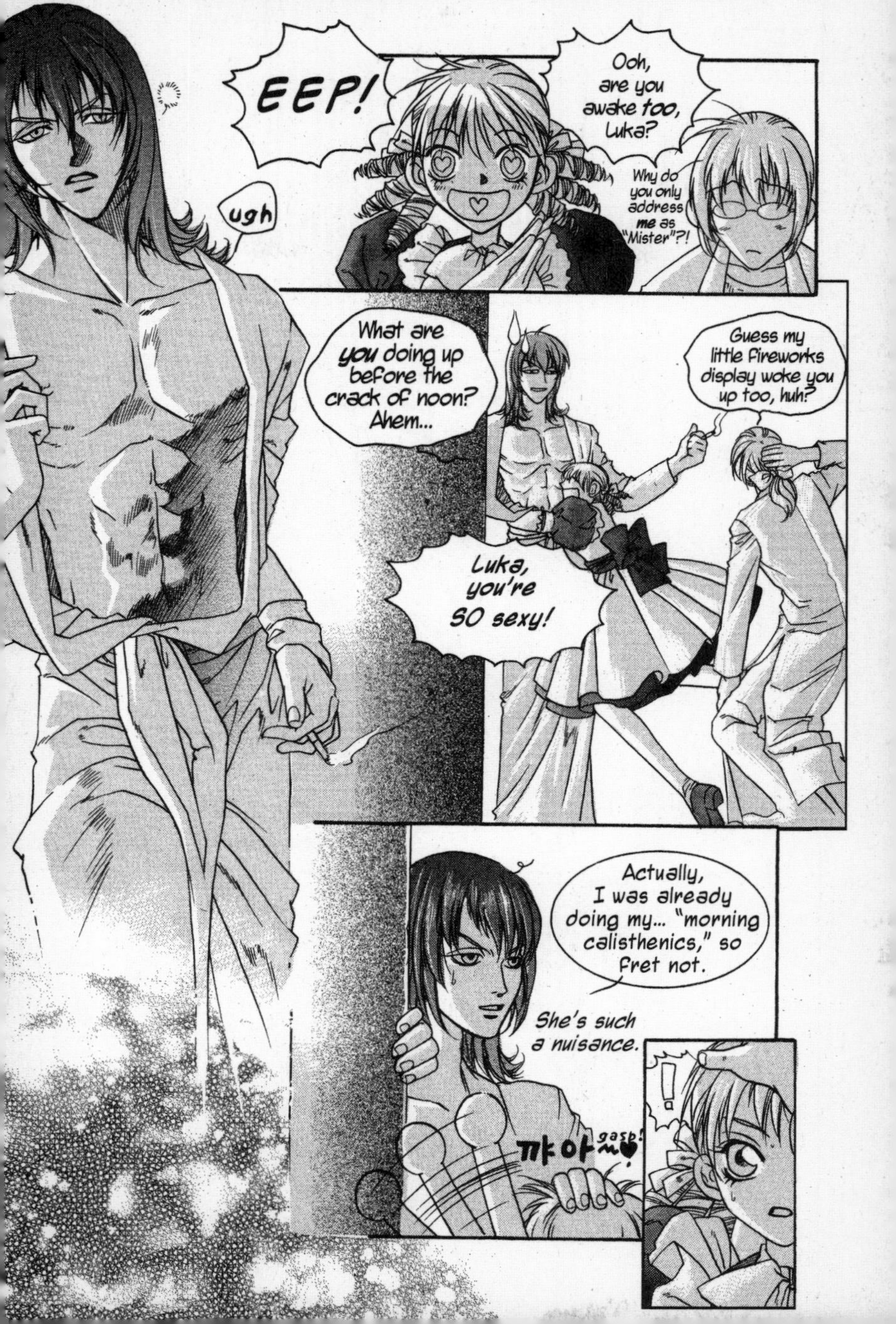
ugh
EEP!
Ooh, are you awake too, Luka?
Why do you only address me as "Mister"?!
What are you doing up before the crack of noon? Ahem...
Guess my little fireworks display woke you up too, huh?
Luka, you're SO sexy!
Actually, I was already doing my... "morning calisthenics," so fret not.
She's such a nuisance.
!
까아
gasp!

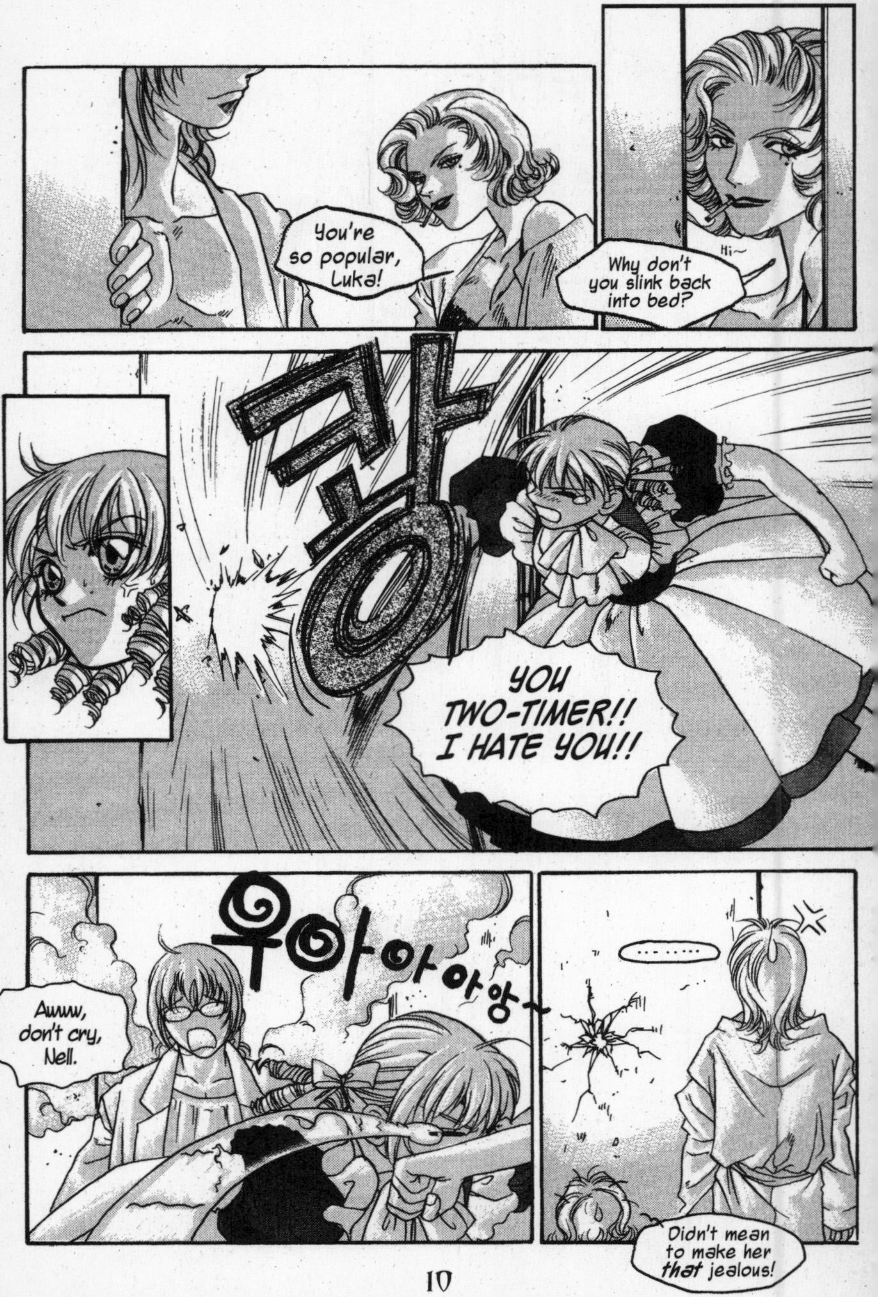
You're so popular, Luka!
Hi~
Why don't you slink back into bed?
광
YOU TWO-TIMER!! I HATE YOU!!
우아아아앙~
Awww, don't cry, Nell.
....
Didn't mean to make her *that* jealous!

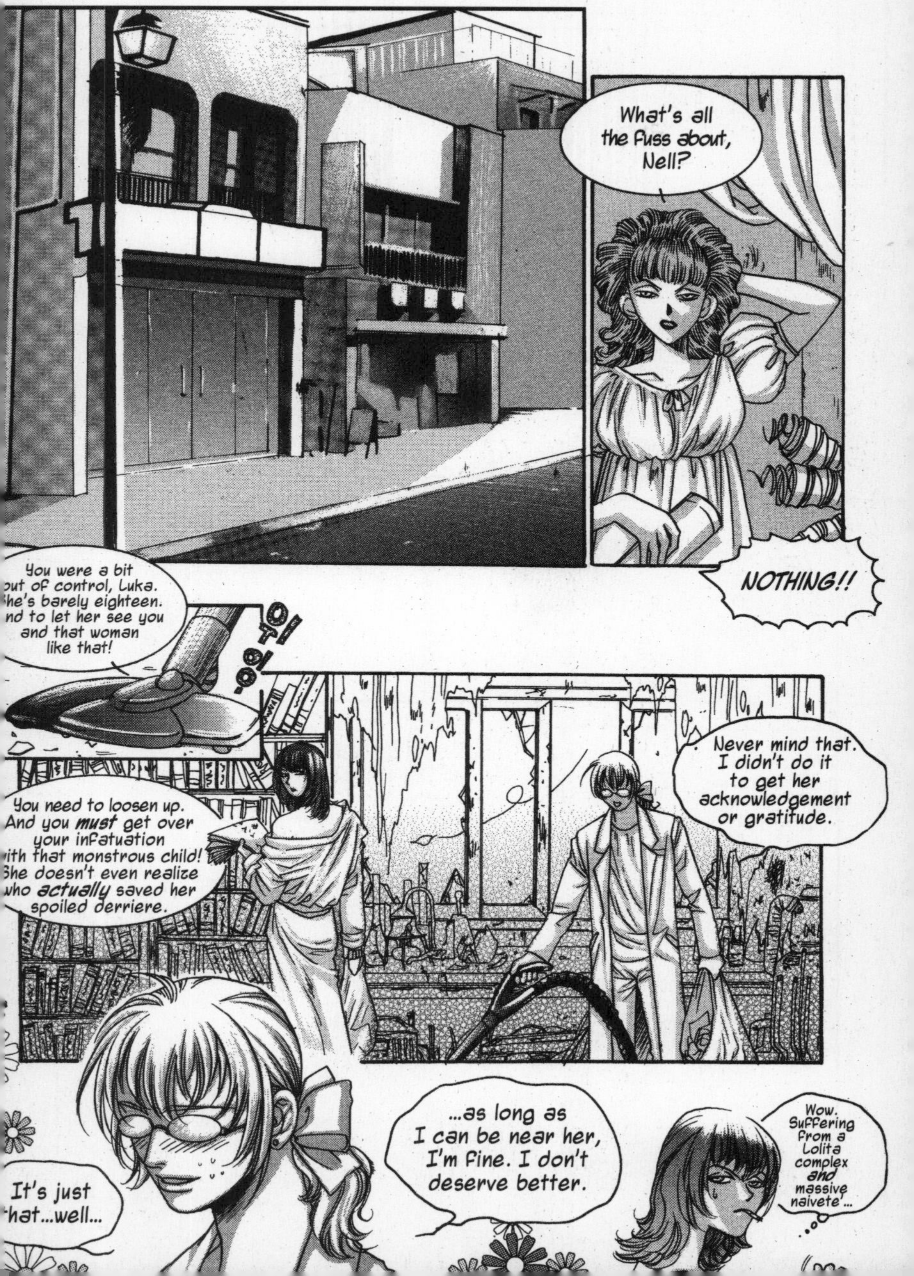

What's all the fuss about, Nell?
NOTHING!!
You were a bit out of control, Luka. he's barely eighteen. nd to let her see you and that woman like that!
위잉.
You need to loosen up. And you *must* get over your infatuation with that monstrous child! She doesn't even realize who *actually* saved her spoiled derriere.
Never mind that. I didn't do it to get her acknowledgement or gratitude.
It's just that...well...
...as long as I can be near her, I'm fine. I don't deserve better.
Wow. Suffering from a Lolita complex *and* massive naivete'...

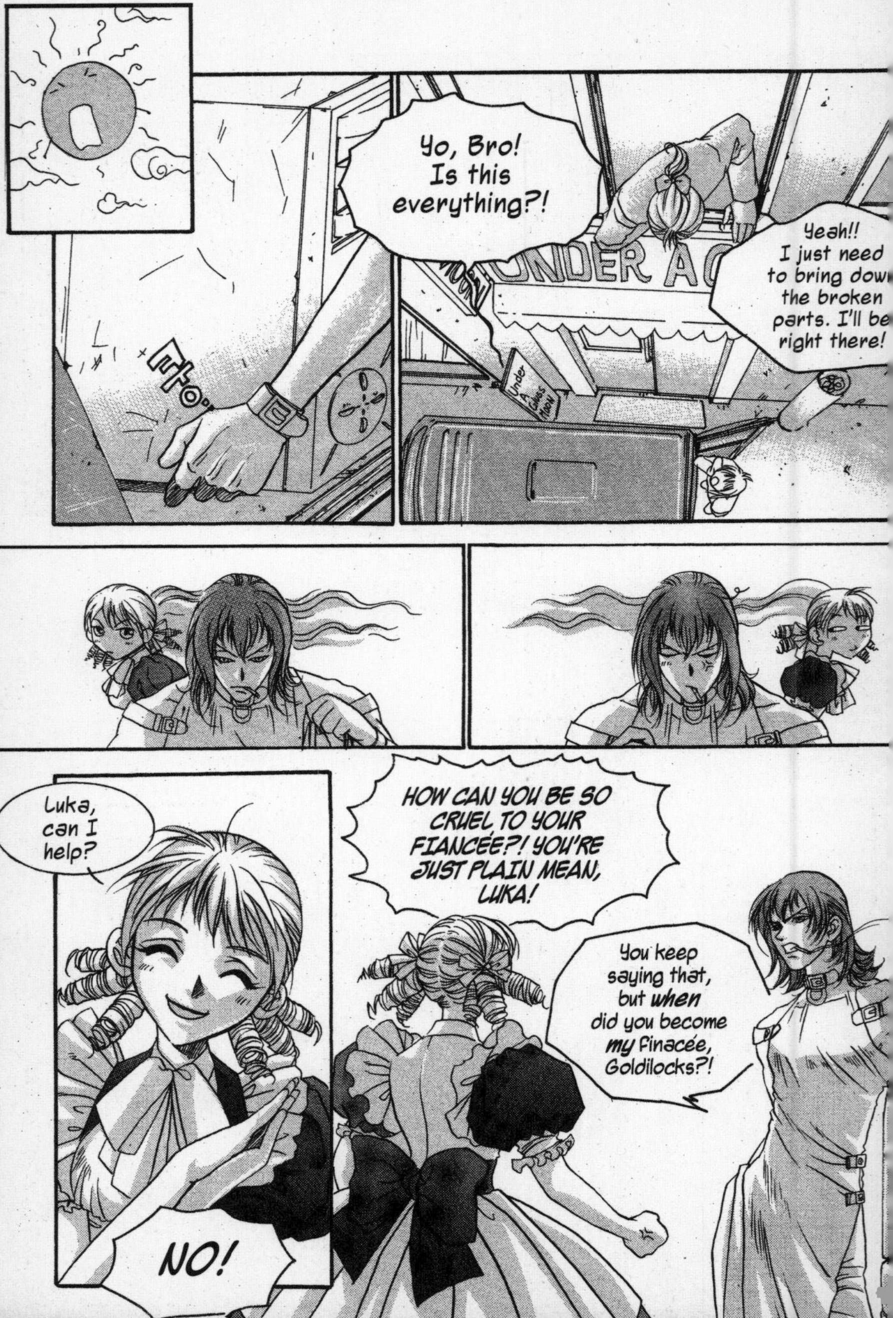
Yo, Bro! Is this everything?!
Yeah!! I just need to bring dow the broken parts. I'll be right there!
Luka, can I help?
NO!
HOW CAN YOU BE SO CRUEL TO YOUR FIANCÉE?! YOU'RE JUST PLAIN MEAN, LUKA!
You keep saying that, but *when* did you become *my* finacée, Goldilocks?!

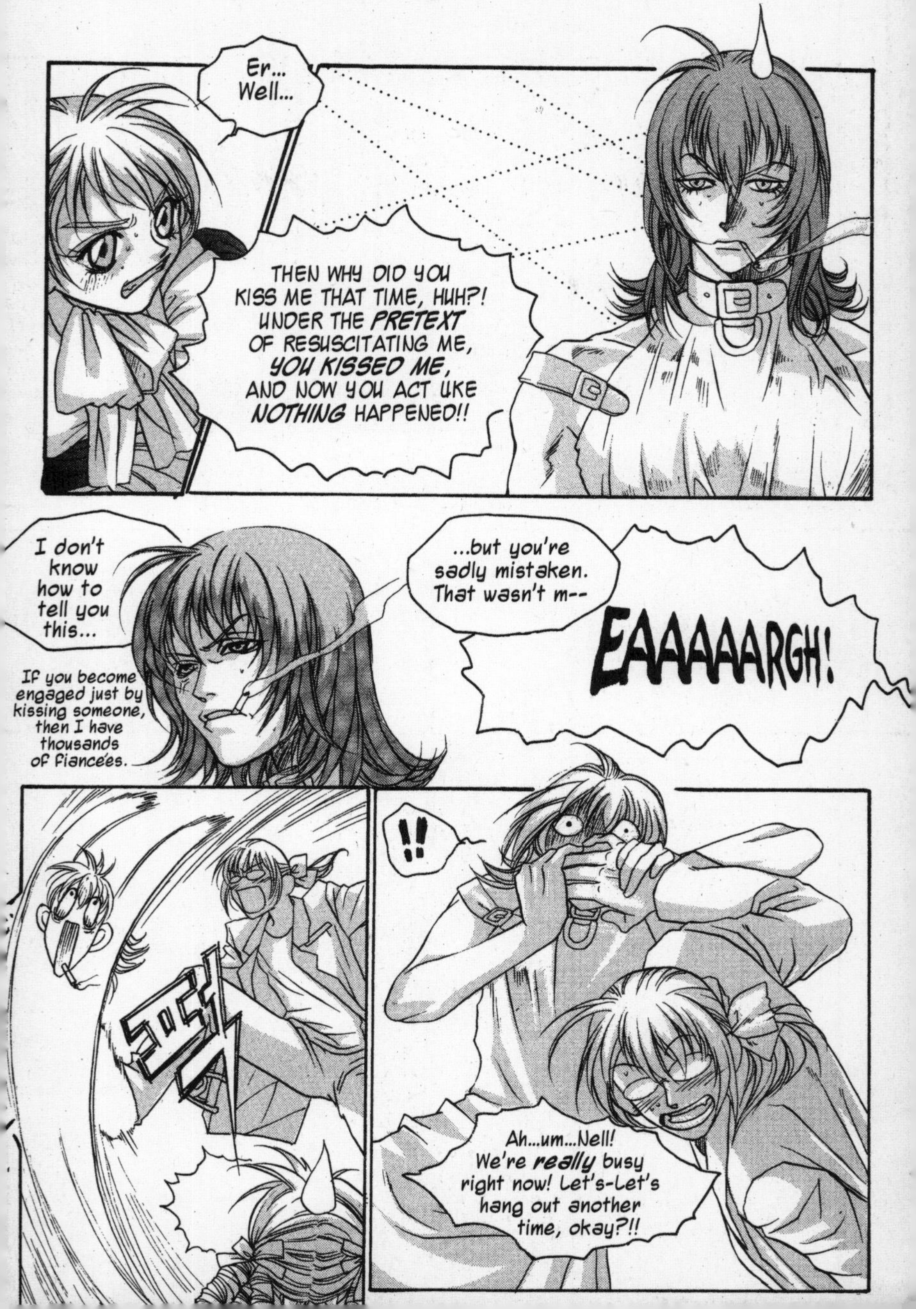
Er... Well...
THEN WHY DID YOU KISS ME THAT TIME, HUH?! UNDER THE *PRETEXT* OF RESUSCITATING ME, ***YOU KISSED ME***, AND NOW YOU ACT LIKE ***NOTHING*** HAPPENED!!
I don't know how to tell you this...
If you become engaged just by kissing someone, then I have thousands of fiancées.
...but you're sadly mistaken. That wasn't m--
EAAAAAARGH!
!!
Ah...um...Nell! We're ***really*** busy right now! Let's-Let's hang out another time, okay?!!

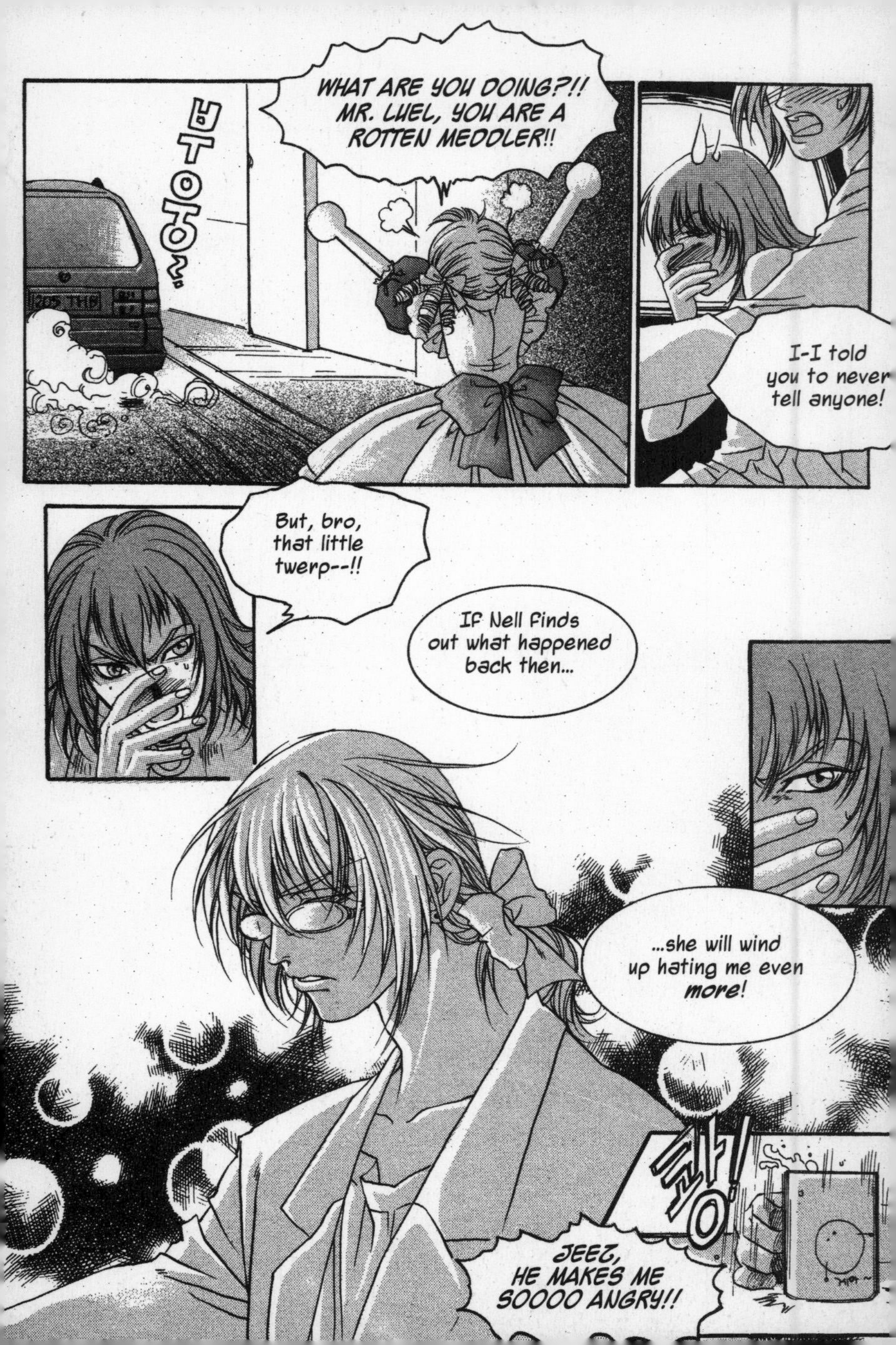
WHAT ARE YOU DOING?!! MR. LUEL, YOU ARE A ROTTEN MEDDLER!!
I-I told you to never tell anyone!
But, bro, that little twerp--!!
If Nell finds out what happened back then...
...she will wind up hating me even *more*!
JEEZ, HE MAKES ME SOOOO ANGRY!!

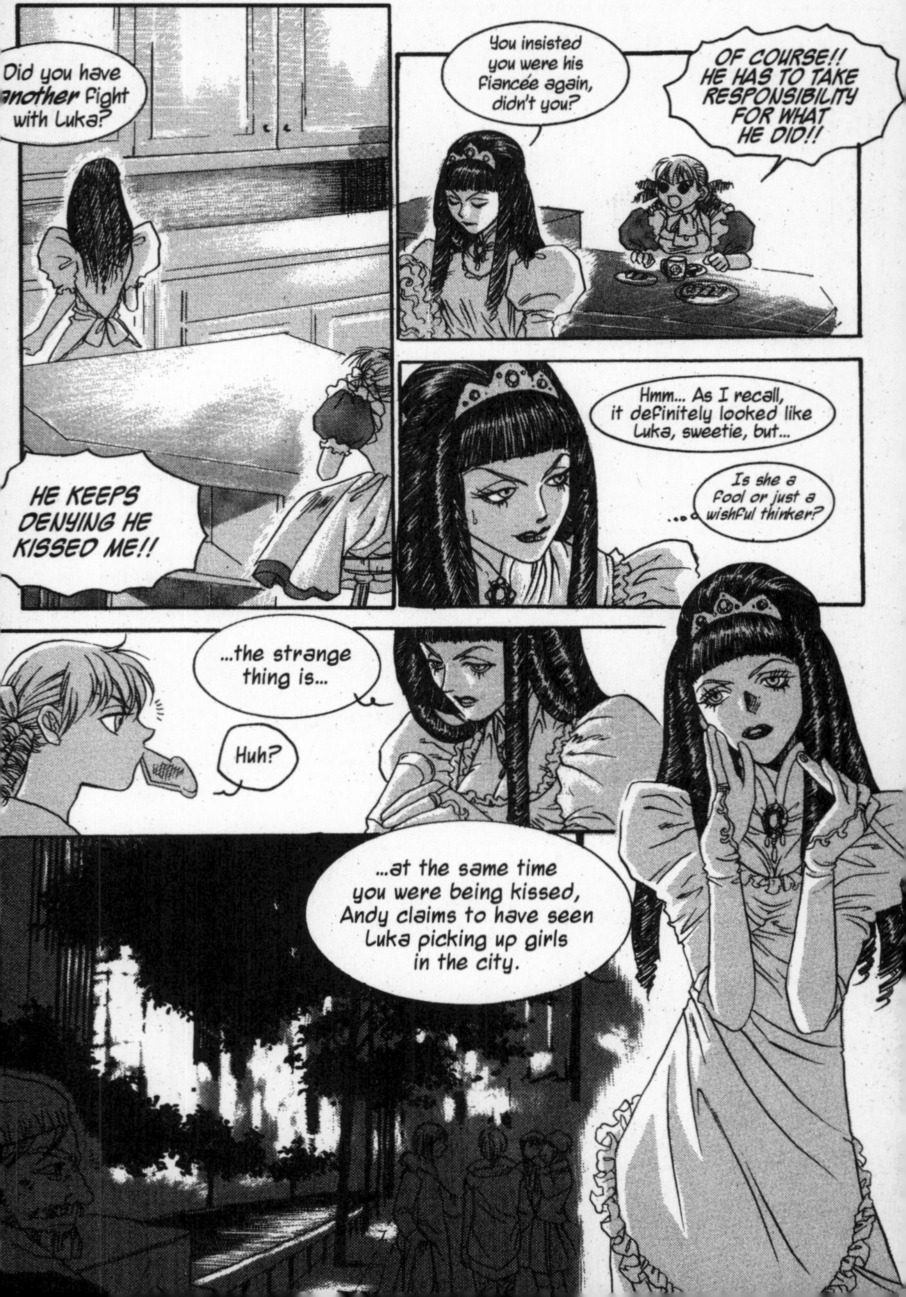
Did you have **another** fight with Luka?
HE KEEPS DENYING HE KISSED ME!!
You insisted you were his fiancée again, didn't you?
OF COURSE!! HE HAS TO TAKE RESPONSIBILITY FOR WHAT HE DID!!
Hmm... As I recall, it definitely looked like Luka, sweetie, but...
Is she a fool or just a wishful thinker?
...the strange thing is...
Huh?
...at the same time you were being kissed, Andy claims to have seen Luka picking up girls in the city.

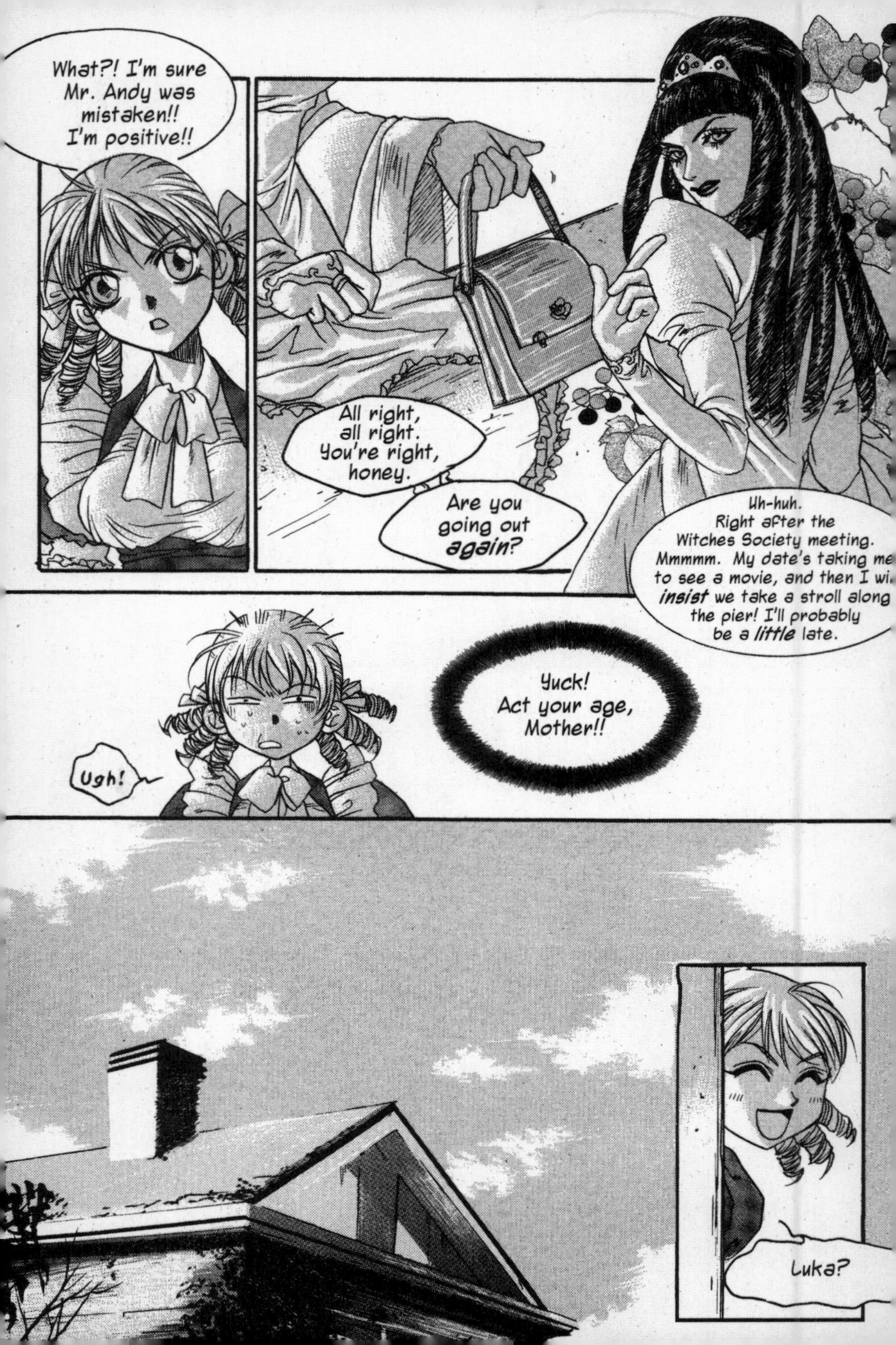
What?! I'm sure Mr. Andy was mistaken!! I'm positive!!
All right, all right. You're right, honey.
Are you going out *again*?
Uh-huh. Right after the Witches Society meeting. Mmmmm. My date's taking me to see a movie, and then I wi *insist* we take a stroll along the pier! I'll probably be a *little* late.
Ugh!
Yuck! Act your age, Mother!!
Luka?

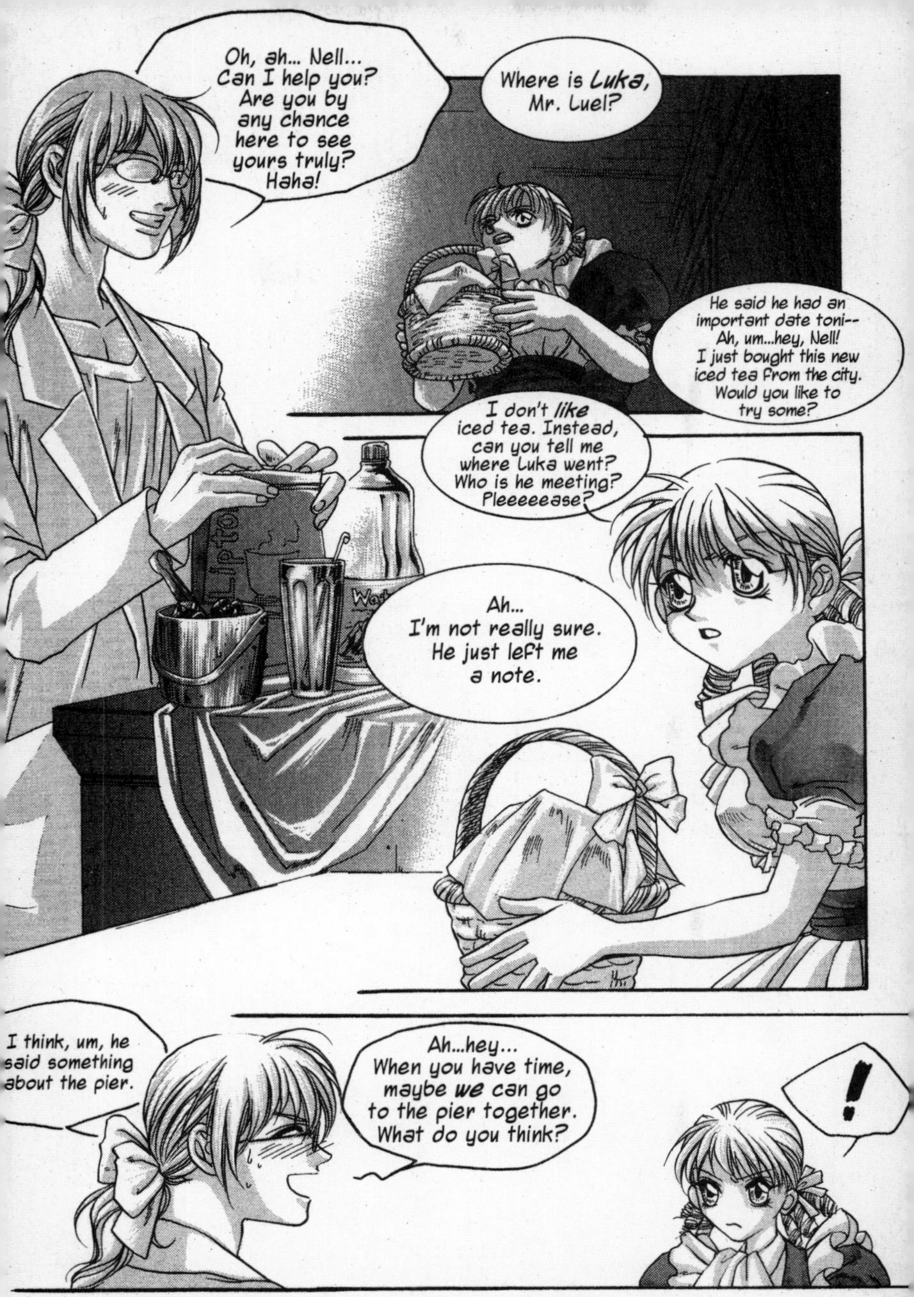
Oh, ah... Nell... Can I help you? Are you by any chance here to see yours truly? Haha!
Where is *Luka*, Mr. Luel?
He said he had an important date toni-- Ah, um...hey, Nell! I just bought this new iced tea from the city. Would you like to try some?
I don't *like* iced tea. Instead, can you tell me where Luka went? Who is he meeting? Pleeeeease?
Ah... I'm not really sure. He just left me a note.
I think, um, he said something about the pier.
Ah...hey... When you have time, maybe *we* can go to the pier together. What do you think?
!

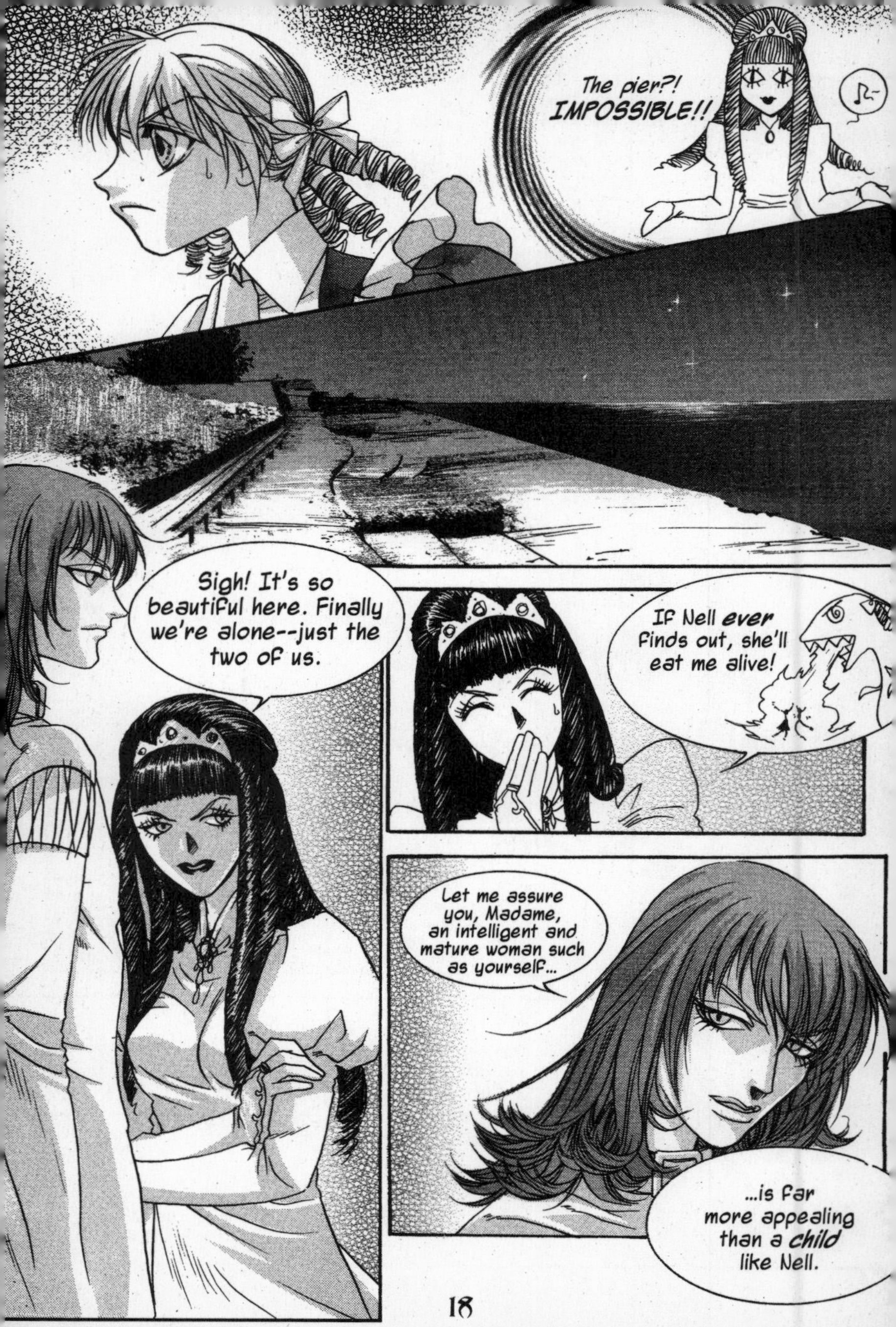
The pier?!
IMPOSSIBLE!!
♪~
Sigh! It's so beautiful here. Finally we're alone--just the two of us.
If Nell ever finds out, she'll eat me alive!
Let me assure you, Madame, an intelligent and mature woman such as yourself...
...is far more appealing than a child like Nell.

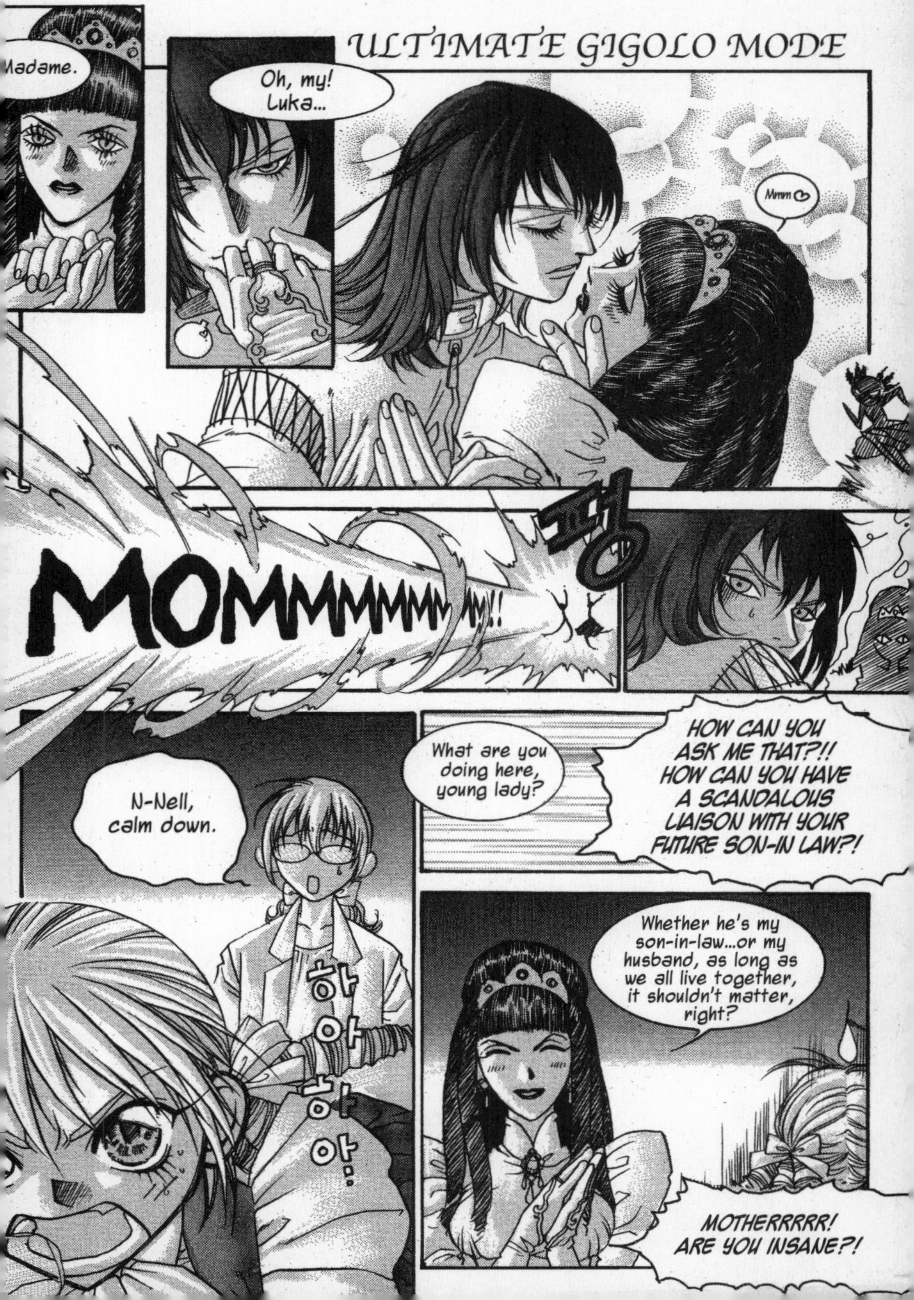
Madame.
Oh, my! Luka...
ULTIMATE GIGOLO MODE
Mmm ♡
MOMMMMMMMM!!
N-Nell, calm down.
What are you doing here, young lady?
HOW CAN YOU ASK ME THAT?!! HOW CAN YOU HAVE A SCANDALOUS LIAISON WITH YOUR FUTURE SON-IN LAW?!
하아 하아!!
Whether he's my son-in-law...or my husband, as long as we all live together, it shouldn't matter, right?
MOTHERRRRR! ARE YOU INSANE?!

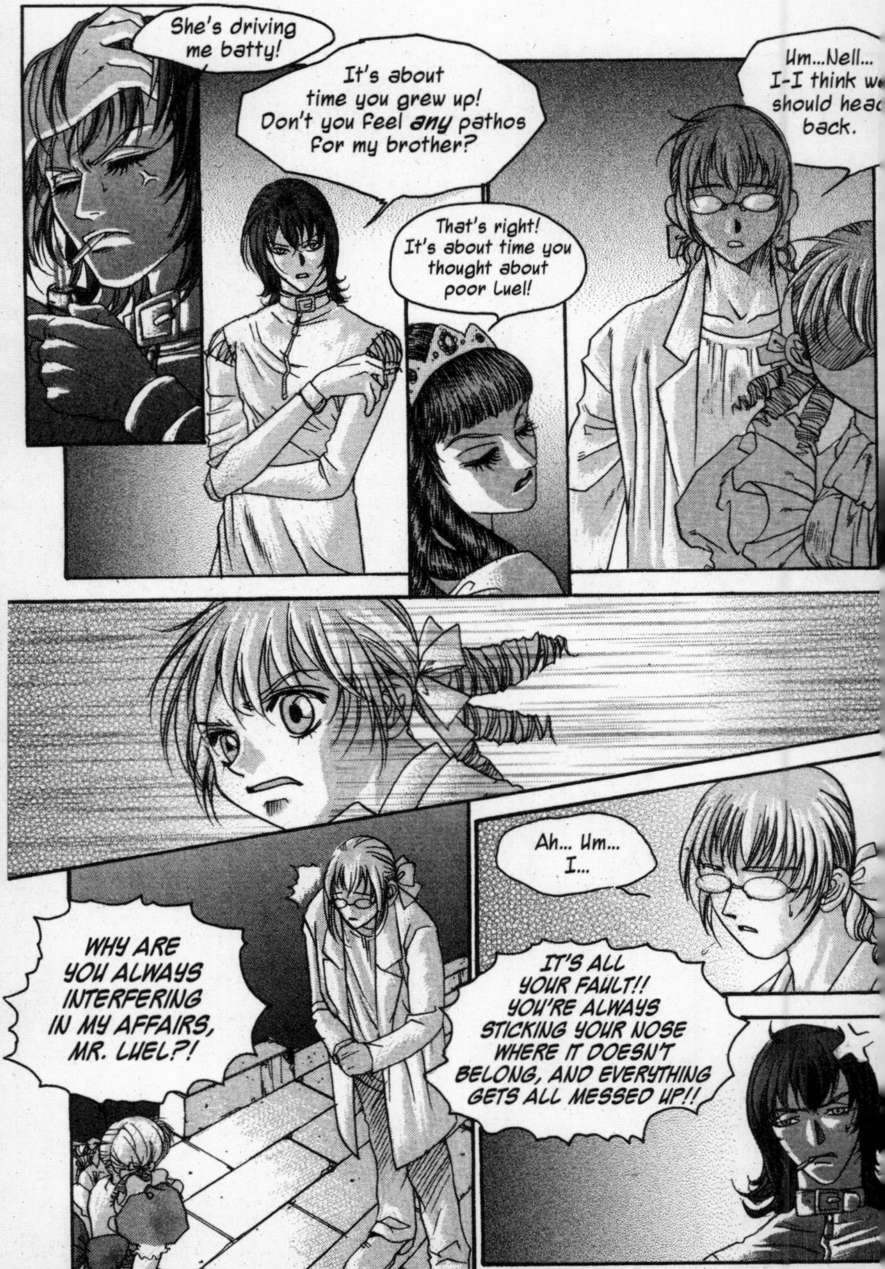
She's driving me batty!
It's about time you grew up! Don't you feel *any* pathos for my brother?
That's right! It's about time you thought about poor Luel!
Um...Nell... I-I think w should hea back.
Ah... Um... I...
WHY ARE YOU ALWAYS INTERFERING IN MY AFFAIRS, MR. LUEL?!
IT'S ALL YOUR FAULT!! YOU'RE ALWAYS STICKING YOUR NOSE WHERE IT DOESN'T BELONG, AND EVERYTHING GETS ALL MESSED UP!!

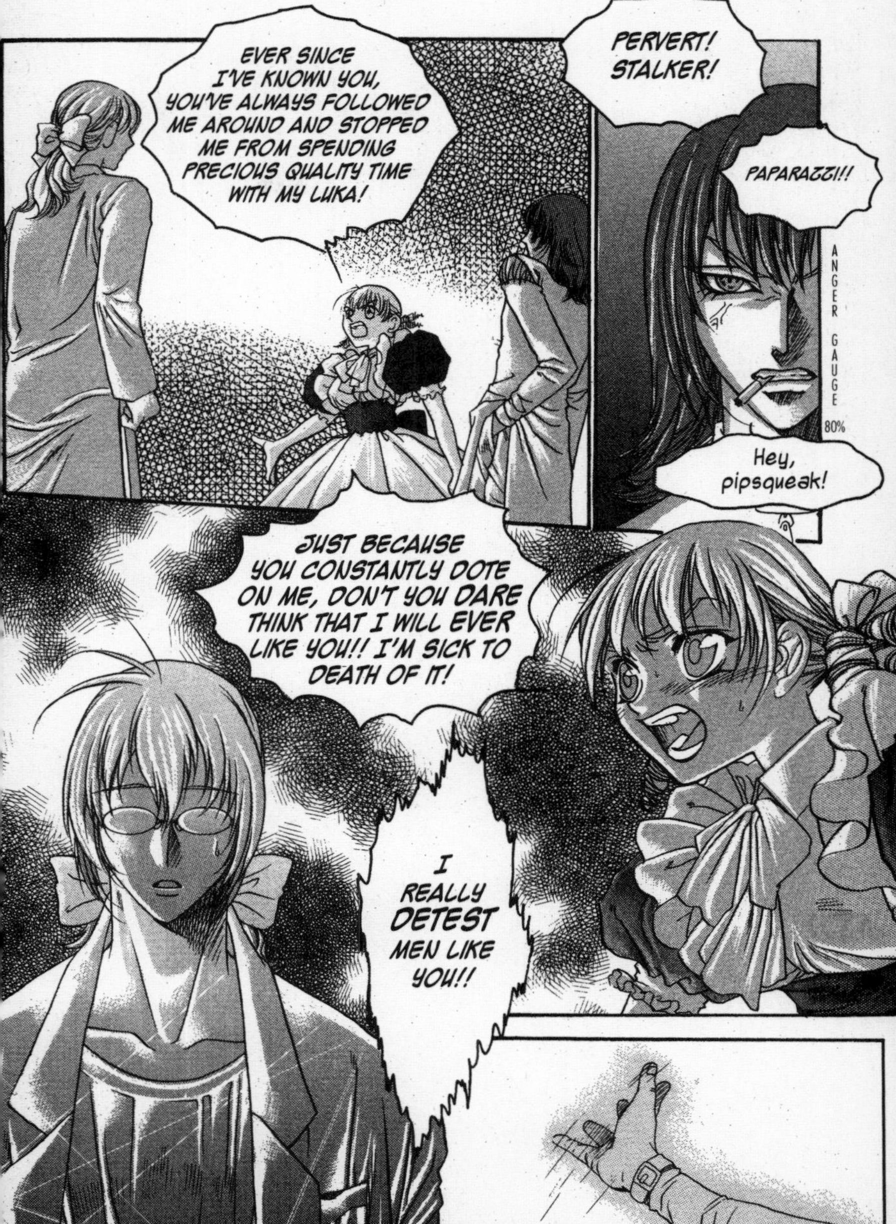
EVER SINCE I'VE KNOWN YOU, YOU'VE ALWAYS FOLLOWED ME AROUND AND STOPPED ME FROM SPENDING PRECIOUS QUALITY TIME WITH MY LUKA!
PERVERT! STALKER!
PAPARAZZI!!
ANGER GAUGE
80%
Hey, pipsqueak!
JUST BECAUSE YOU CONSTANTLY DOTE ON ME, DON'T YOU DARE THINK THAT I WILL EVER LIKE YOU!! I'M SICK TO DEATH OF IT!
I REALLY DETEST MEN LIKE YOU!!

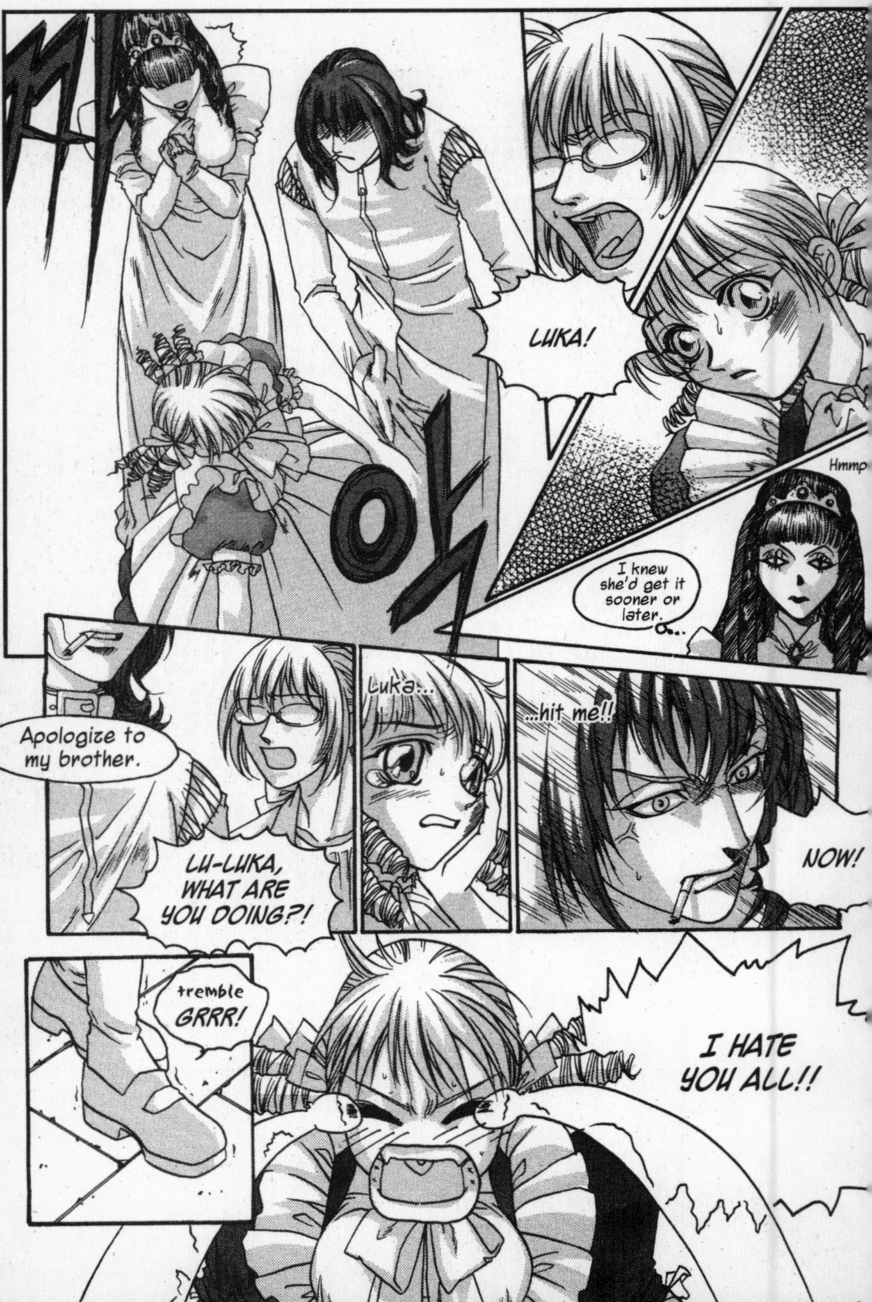
LUKA!
Hmmp
I knew she'd get it sooner or later...
Apologize to my brother.
LU-LUKA, WHAT ARE YOU DOING?!
Luka...
...hit me!!
NOW!
tremble
GRRR!
I HATE YOU ALL!!

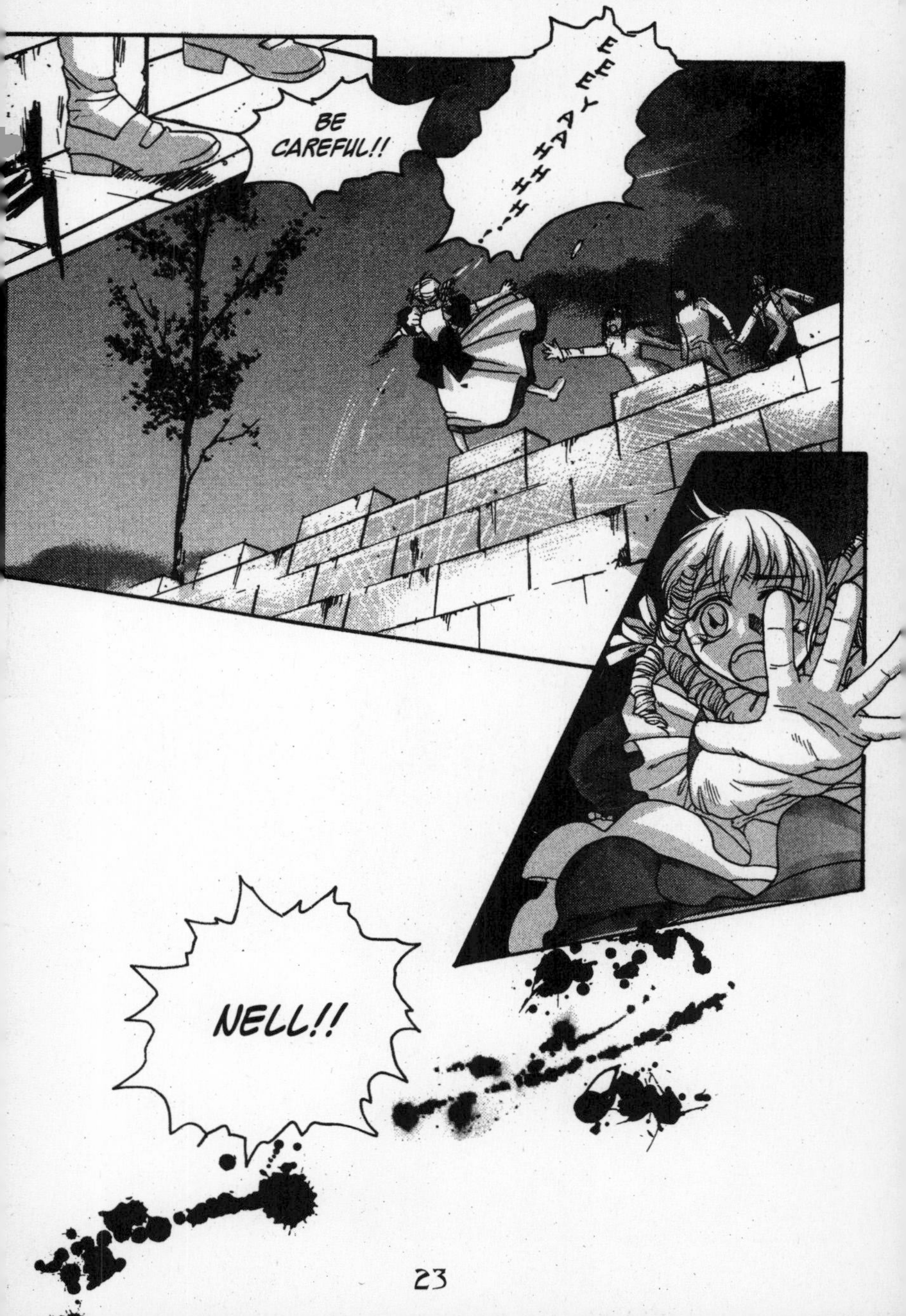
BE CAREFUL!!
EEEYAAHHHH!!..
NELL!!

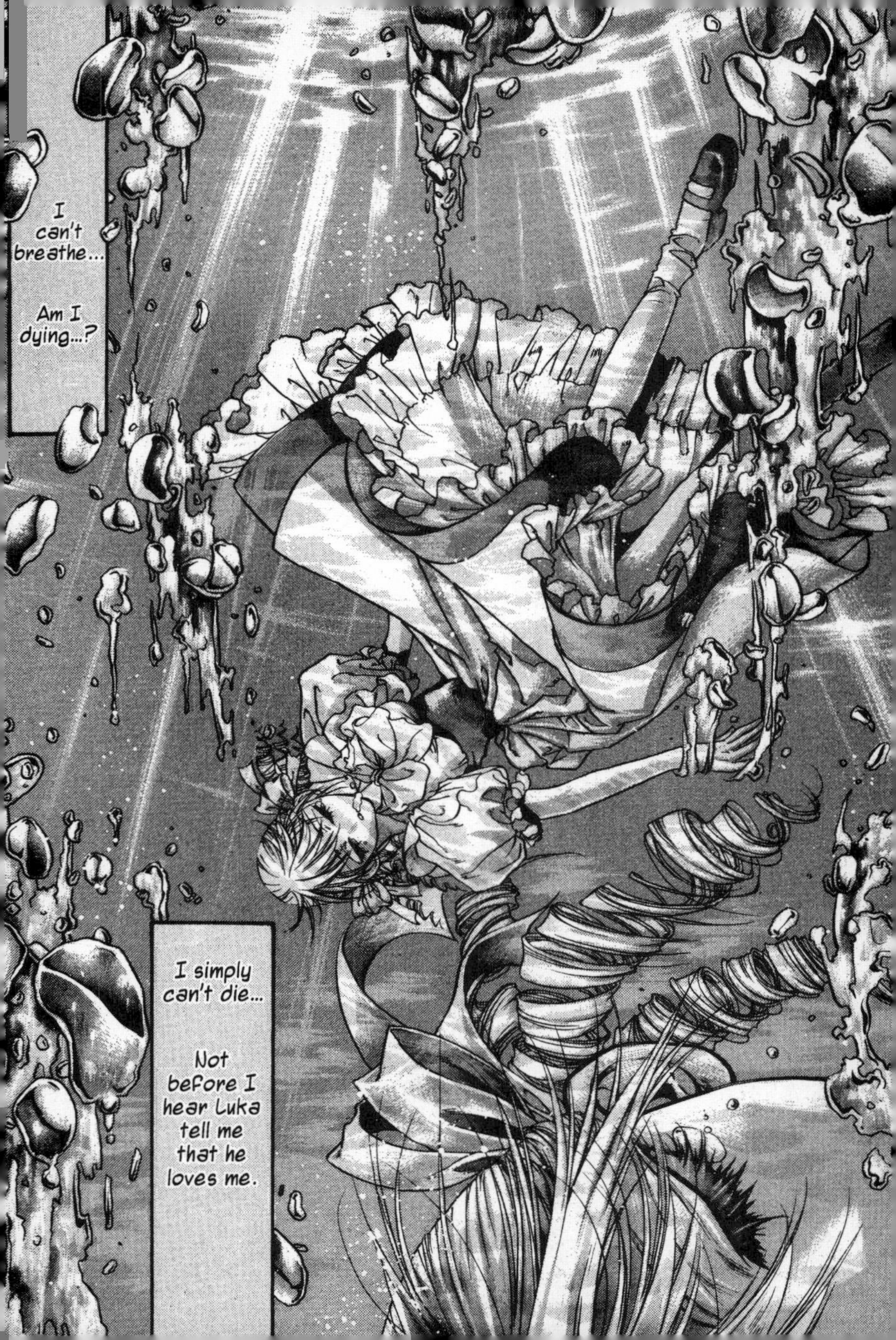
I can't breathe... Am I dying...?
I simply can't die... Not before I hear Luka tell me that he loves me.

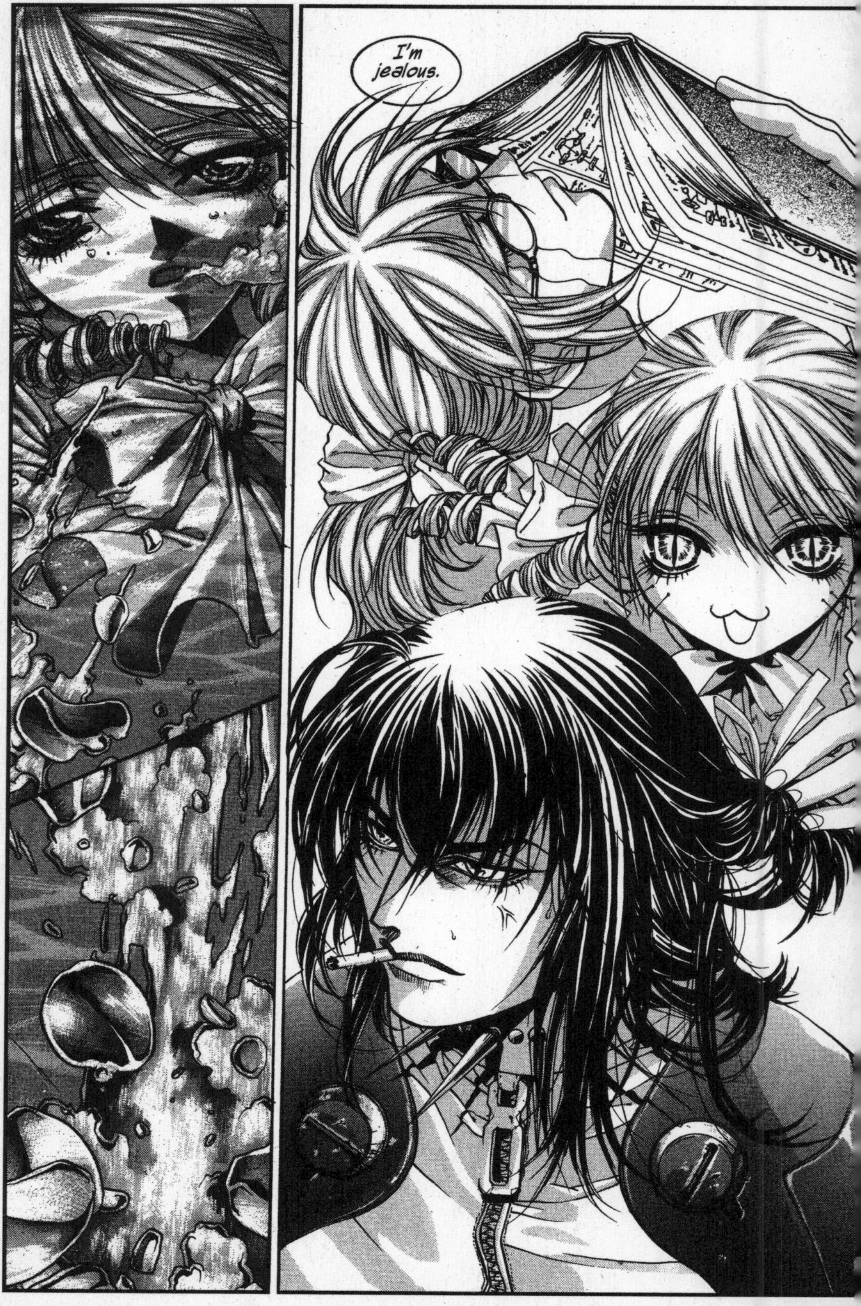
I'm jealous.

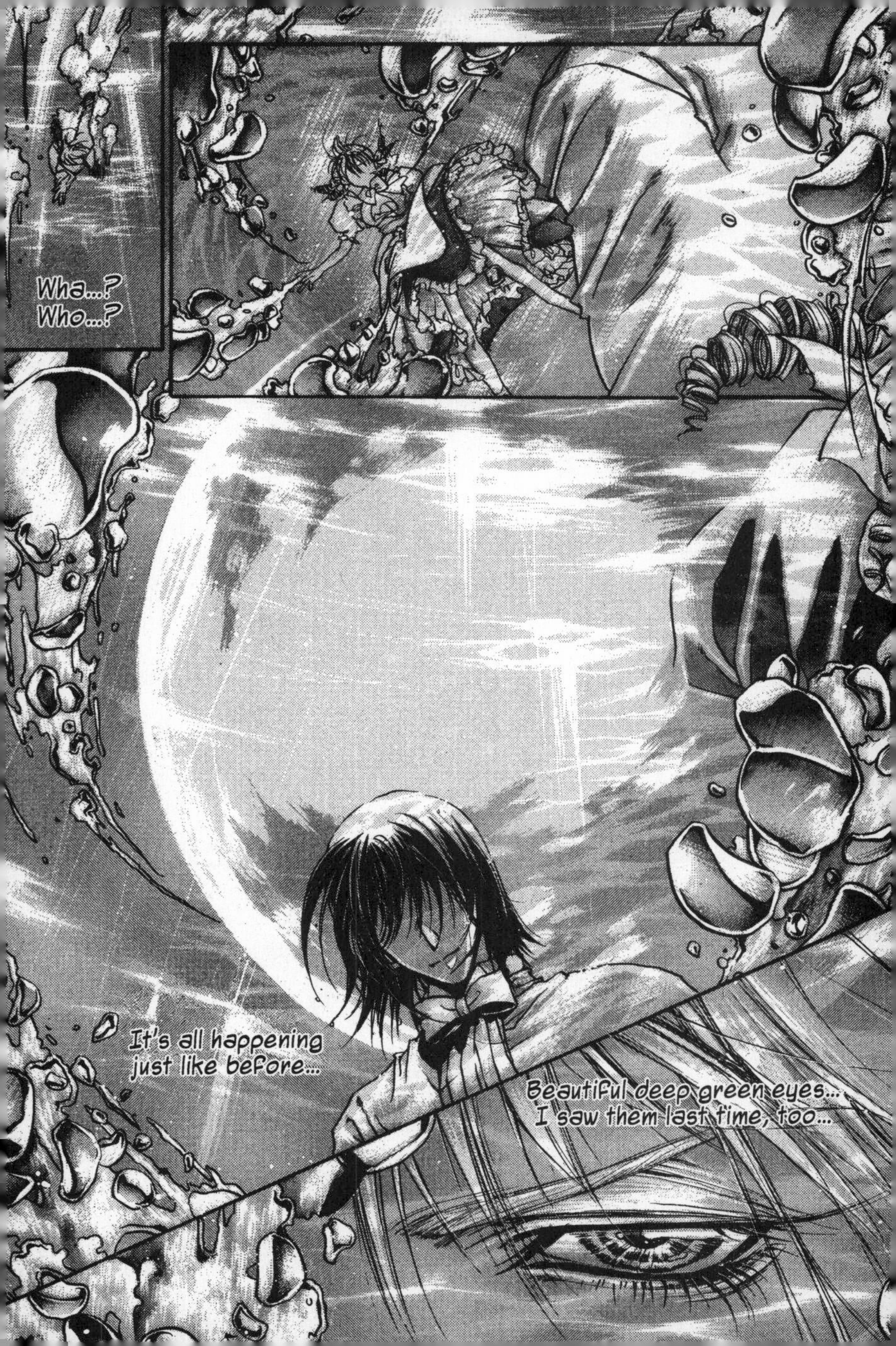
Wha...?
Who...?
It's all happening just like before...
Beautiful deep green eyes... I saw them last time, too...

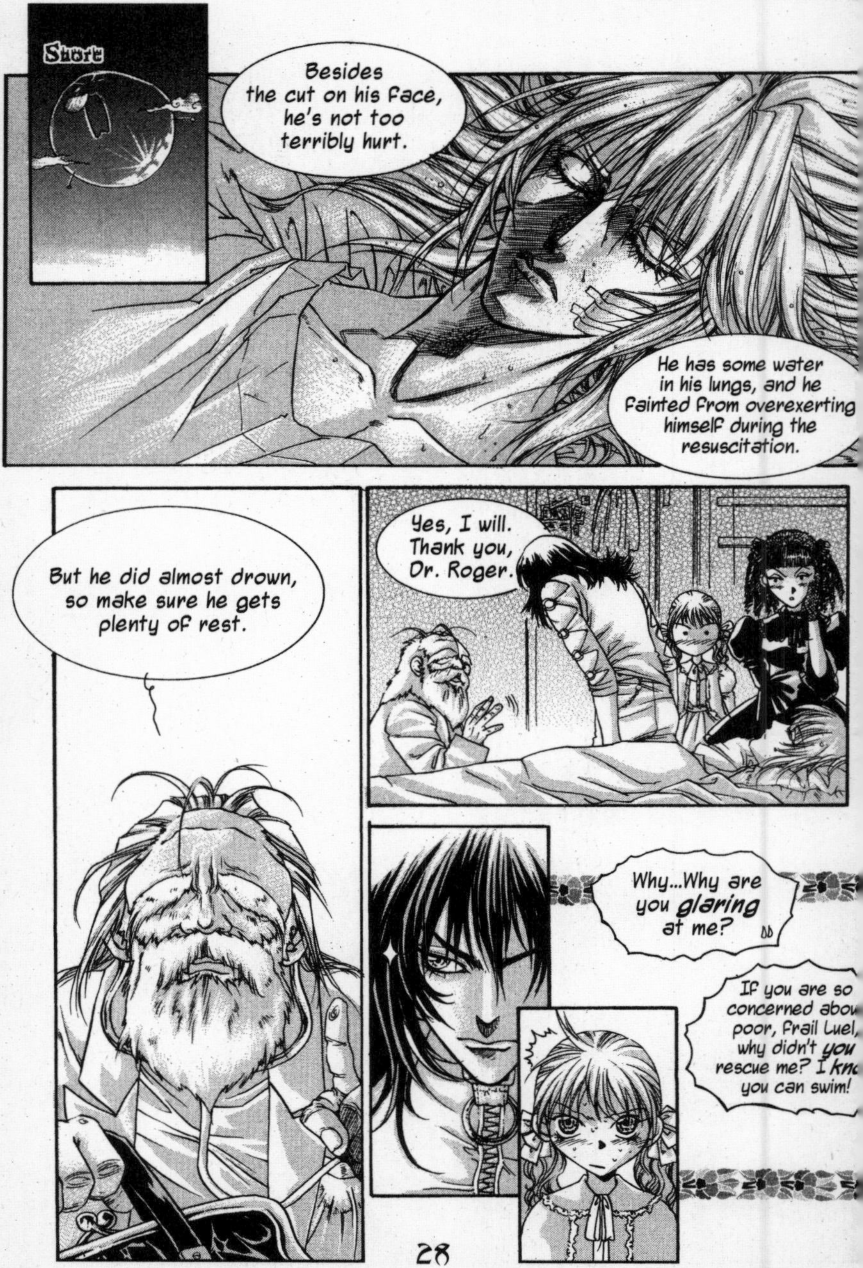
Short
Besides the cut on his face, he's not too terribly hurt.
He has some water in his lungs, and he fainted from overexerting himself during the resuscitation.
But he did almost drown, so make sure he gets plenty of rest.
Yes, I will. Thank you, Dr. Roger.
Why...Why are you glaring at me?
If you are so concerned abou poor, frail Luel, why didn't you rescue me? I kn you can swim!

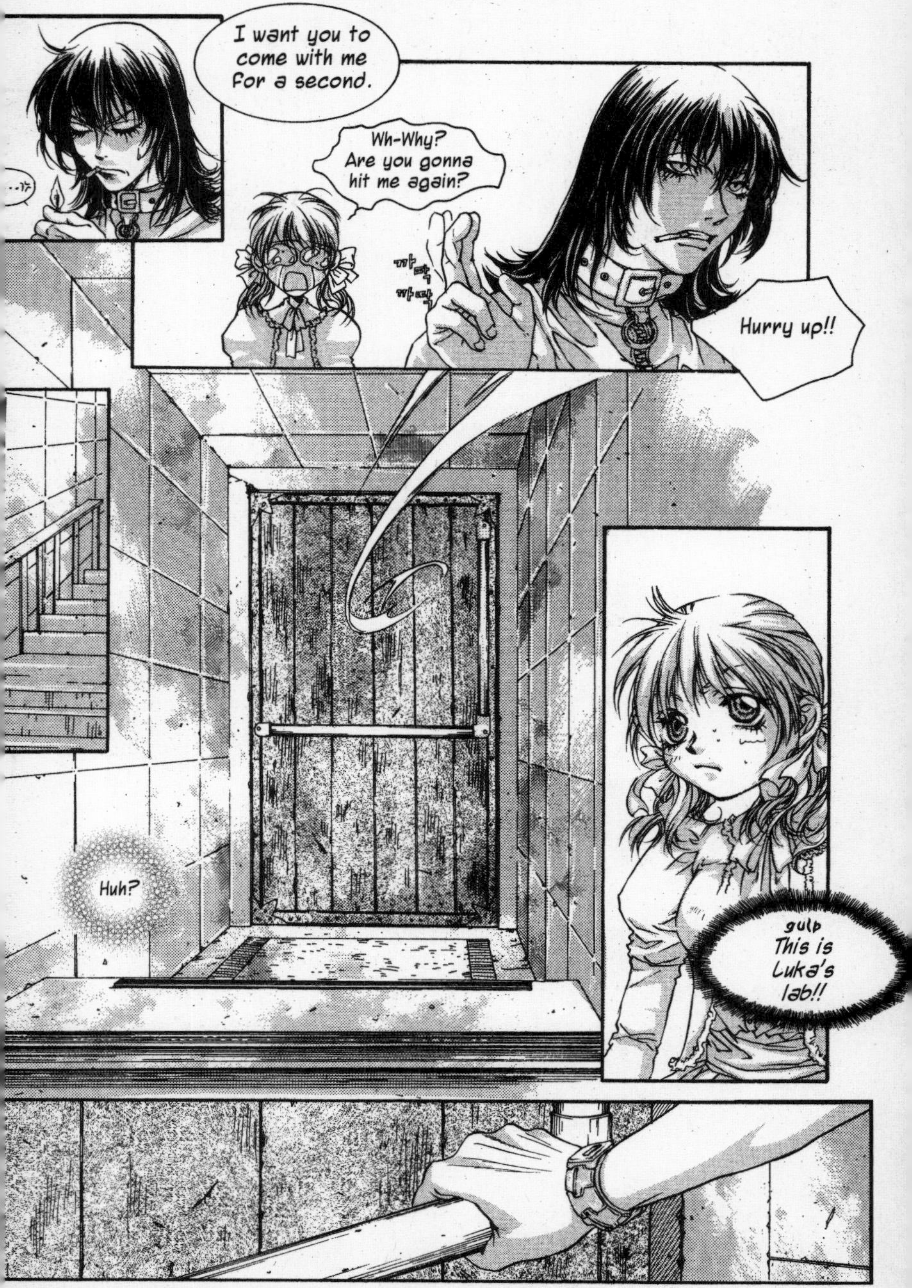

...가
I want you to come with me for a second.
Wh-Why? Are you gonna hit me again?
까딱 까딱
Hurry up!!
Huh?
gulp
This is Luka's lab!!

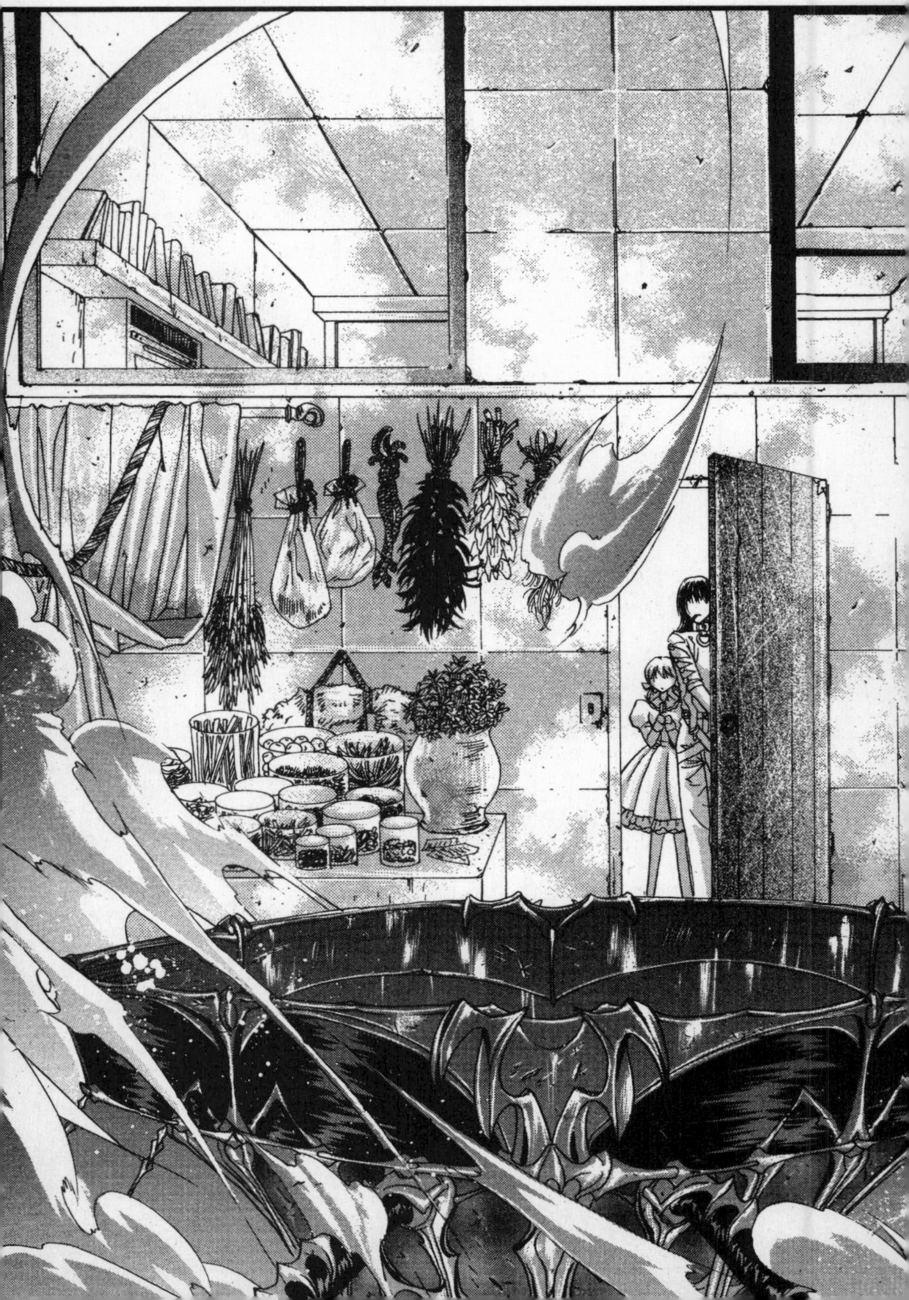

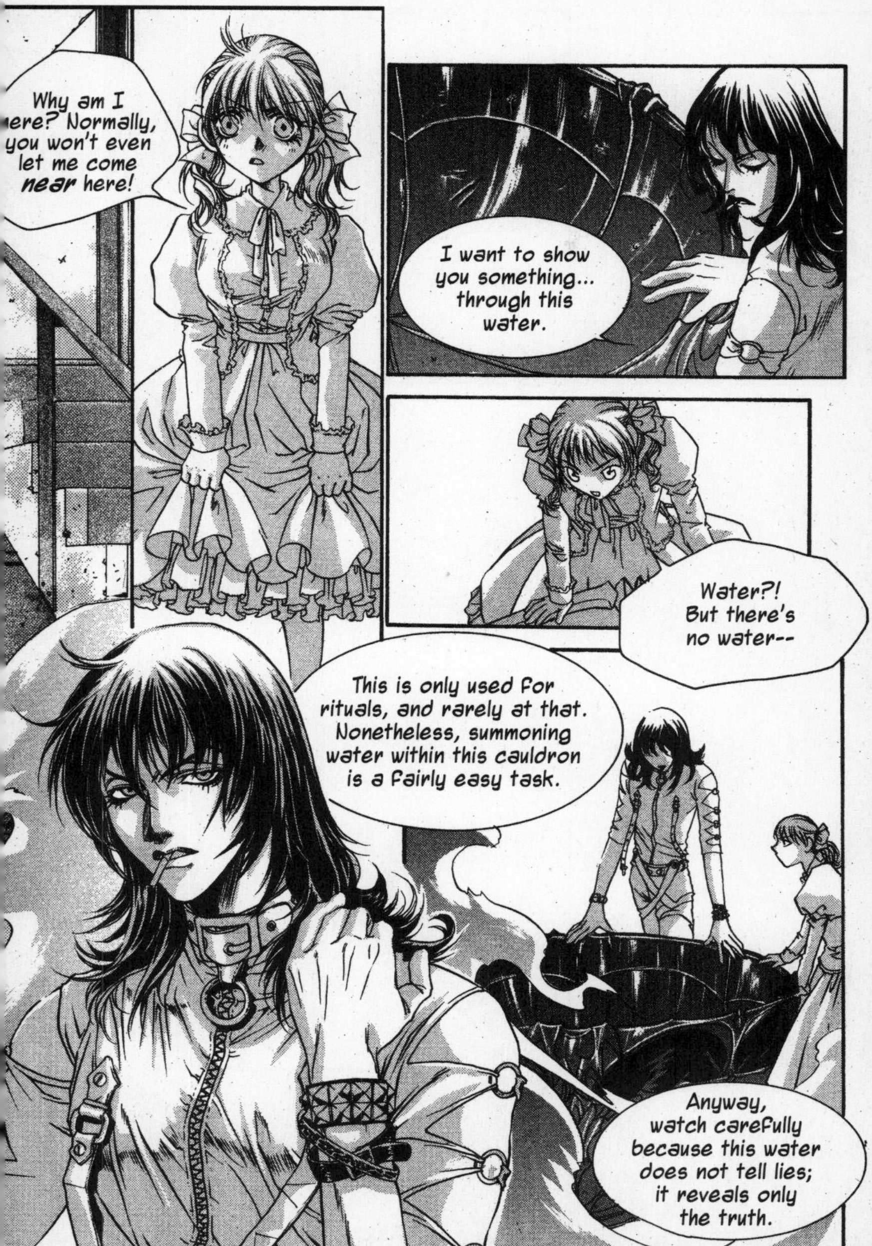
Why am I ere? Normally, you won't even let me come ***near*** here!
I want to show you something... through this water.
Water?! But there's no water--
This is only used for rituals, and rarely at that. Nonetheless, summoning water within this cauldron is a fairly easy task.
Anyway, watch carefully because this water does not tell lies; it reveals only the truth.

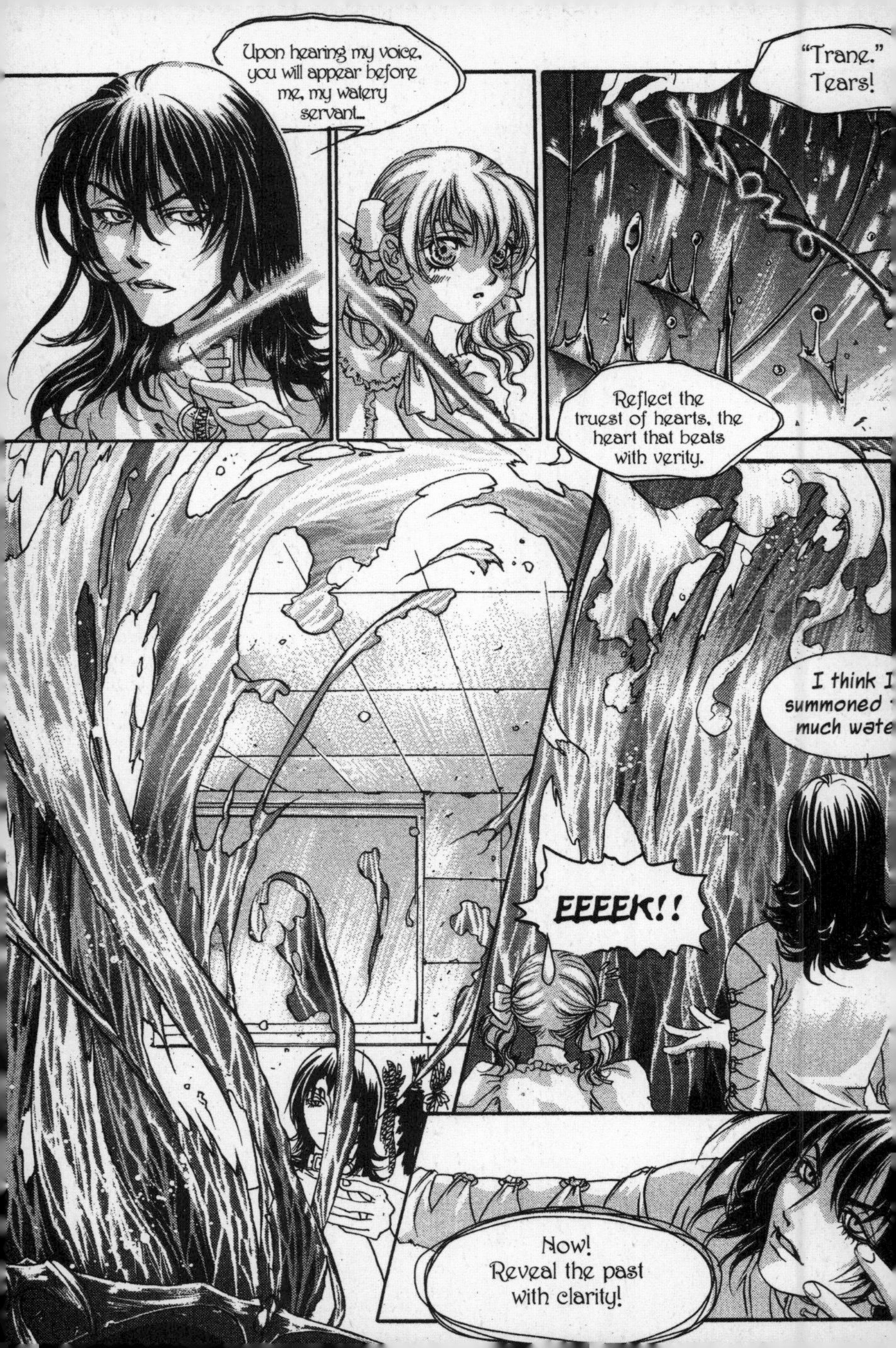
Upon hearing my voice, you will appear before me, my watery servant...
"Trane." Tears!
Reflect the truest of hearts, the heart that beats with verity.
I think I summoned much wate
EEEEK!!
Now! Reveal the past with clarity!

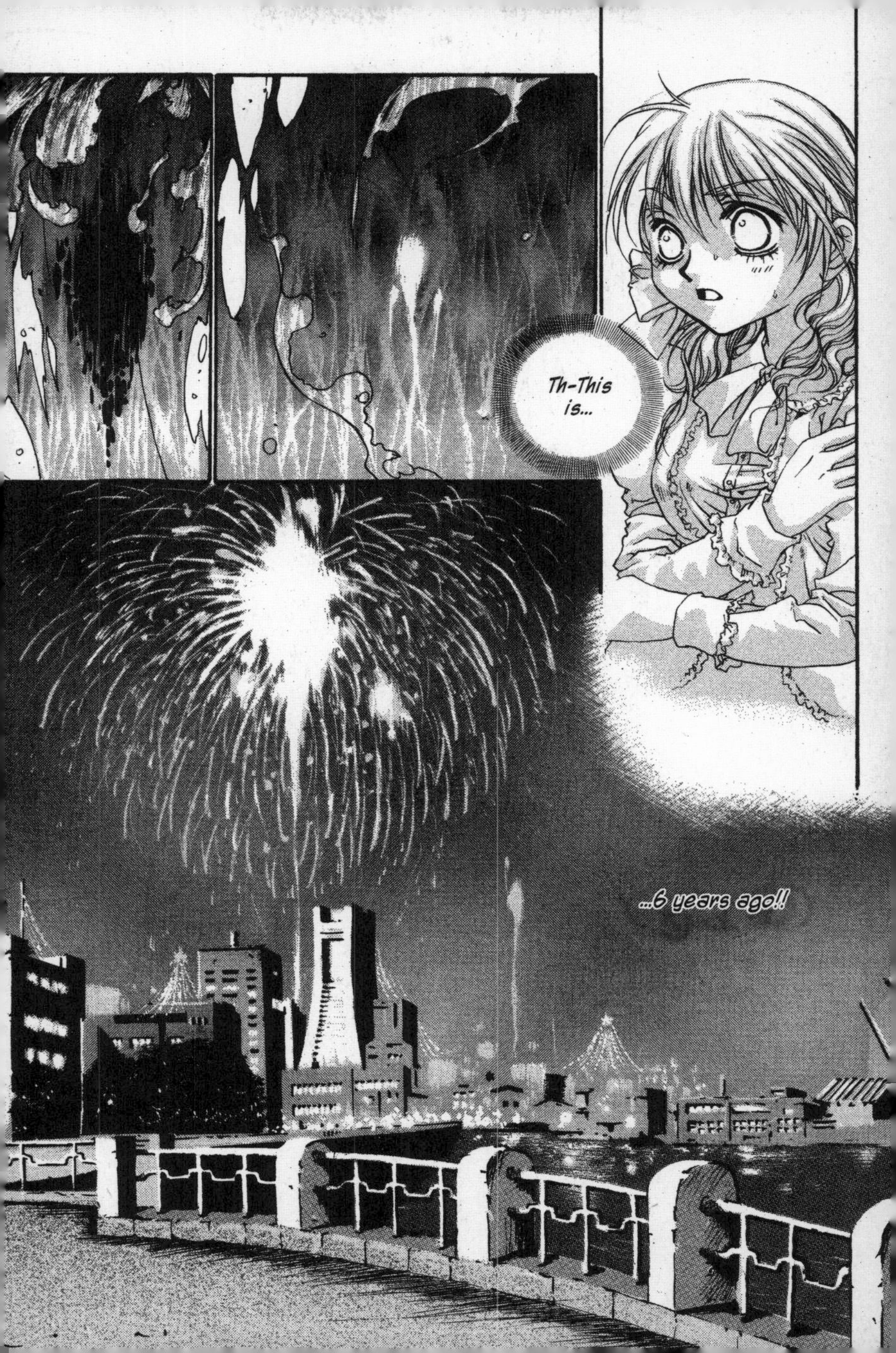
Th-This is...
...6 years ago!!

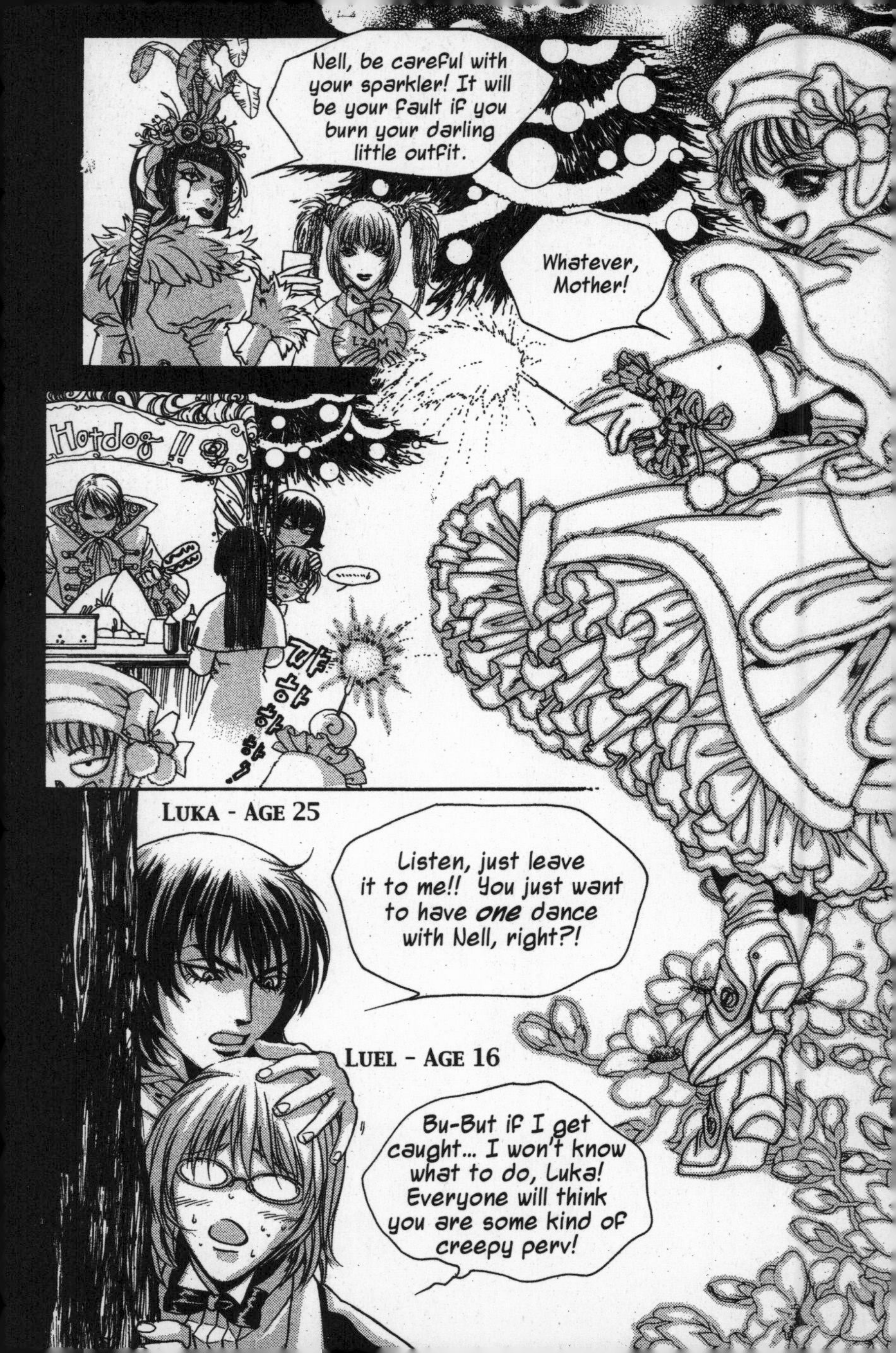
Nell, be careful with your sparkler! It will be your fault if you burn your darling little outfit.
Whatever, Mother!
Hotdog !!
까하하하
LUKA - AGE 25
Listen, just leave it to me!! You just want to have *one* dance with Nell, right?!
LUEL - AGE 16
Bu-But if I get caught... I won't know what to do, Luka! Everyone will think you are some kind of creepy perv!

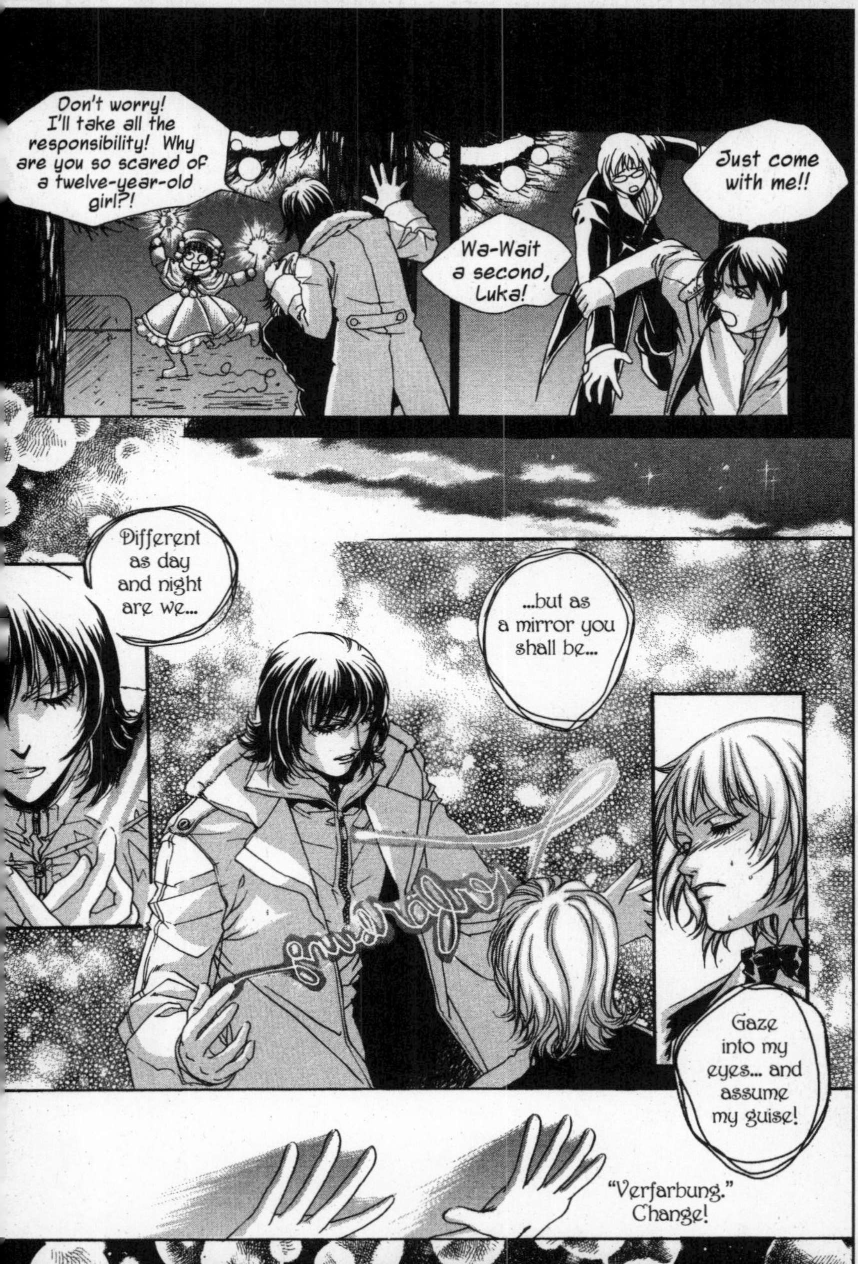

Don't worry! I'll take all the responsibility! Why are you so scared of a twelve-year-old girl?!
Wa-Wait a second, Luka!
Just come with me!!
Different as day and night are we...
...but as a mirror you shall be...
Gaze into my eyes... and assume my guise!
"Verfarbung." Change!

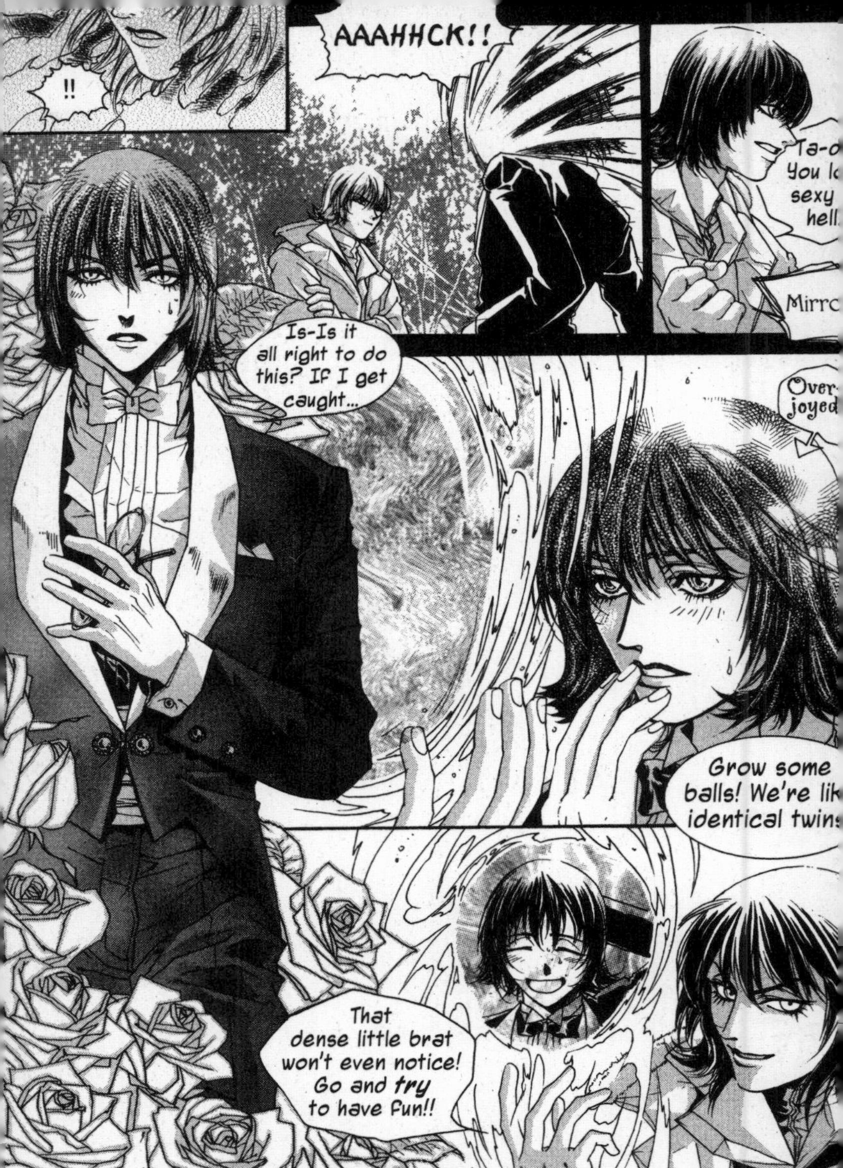
!!
AAAHHCK!!
Ta-o You lo sexy hell.
Mirro
Is-Is it all right to do this? If I get caught...
Over-joyed
Grow some balls! We're lik identical twin
That dense little brat won't even notice! Go and *try* to have fun!!

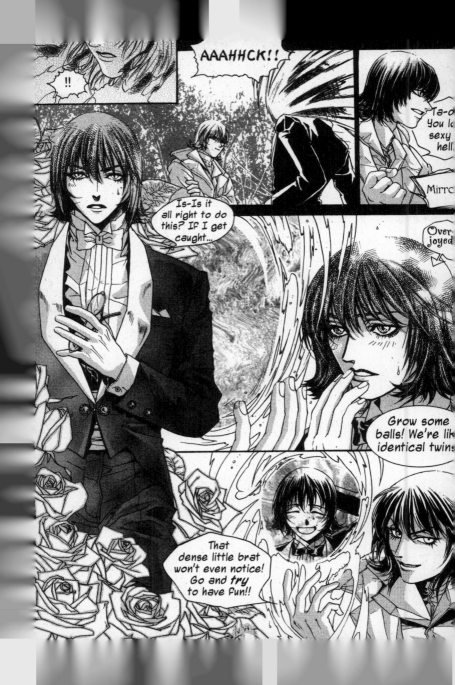

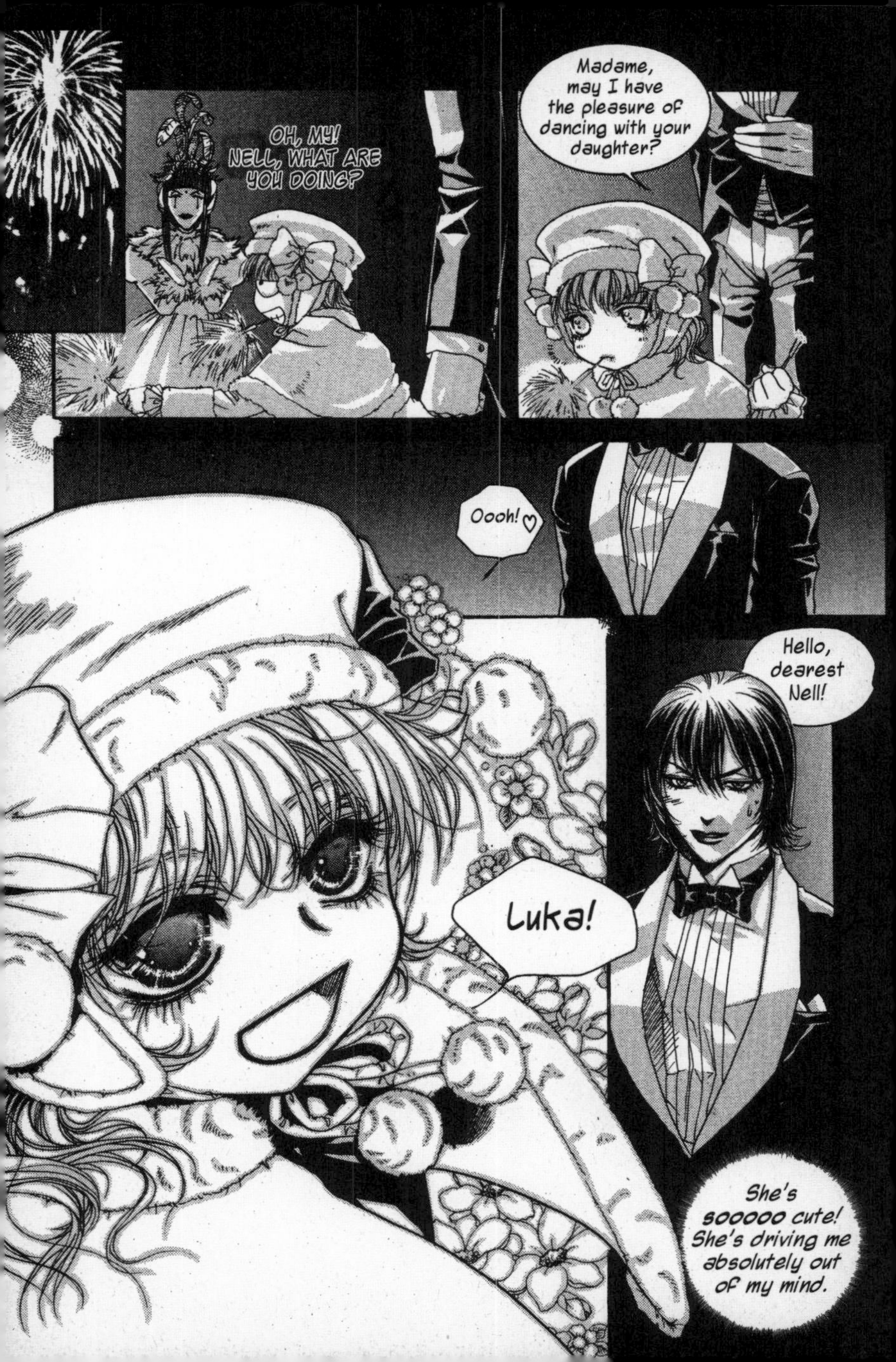
OH, MY! NELL, WHAT ARE YOU DOING?
Madame, may I have the pleasure of dancing with your daughter?
Oooh! ♡
Luka!
Hello, dearest Nell!
She's sooooo cute! She's driving me absolutely out of my mind.

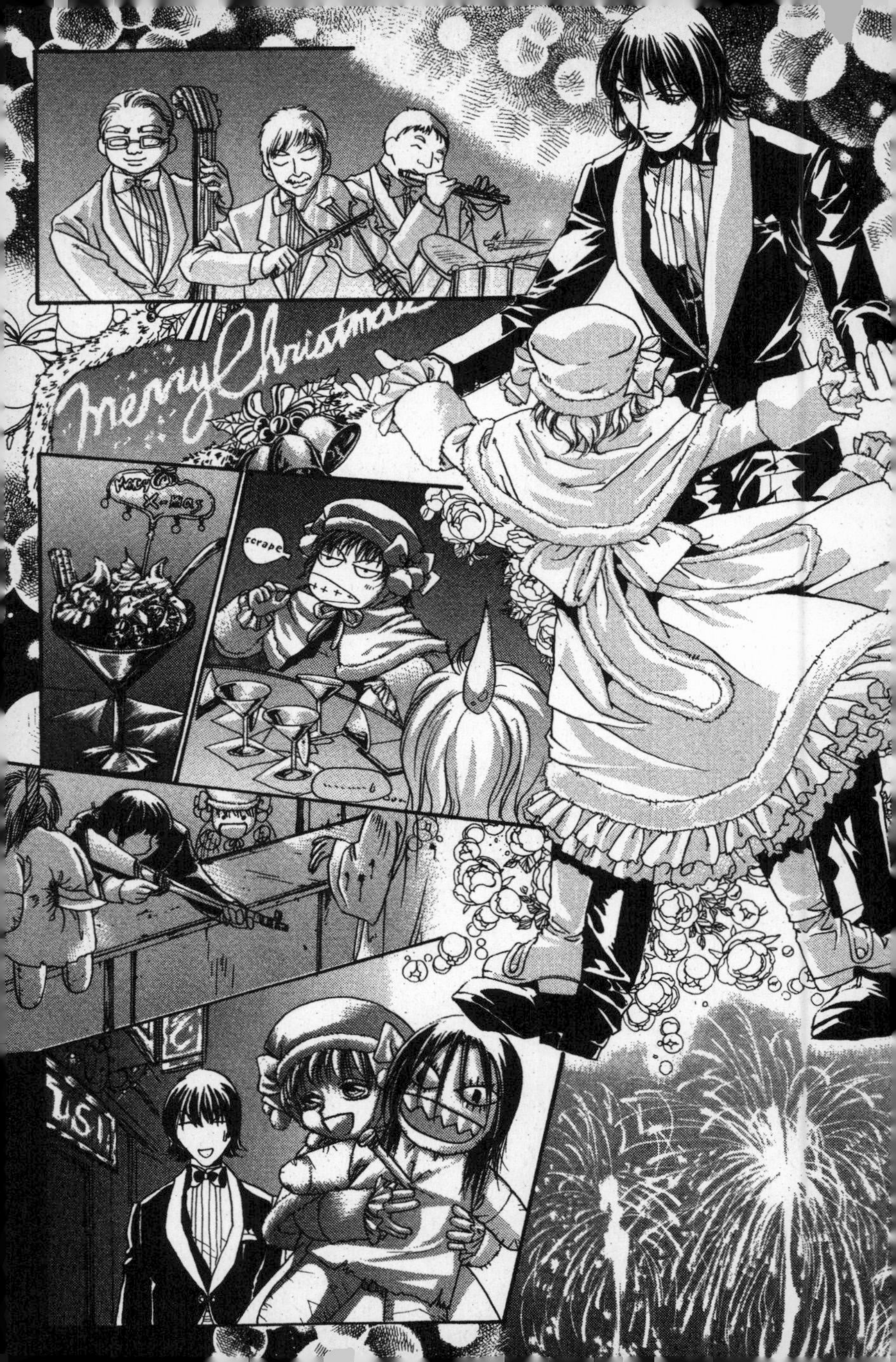
Merry Christmas
scrape
....

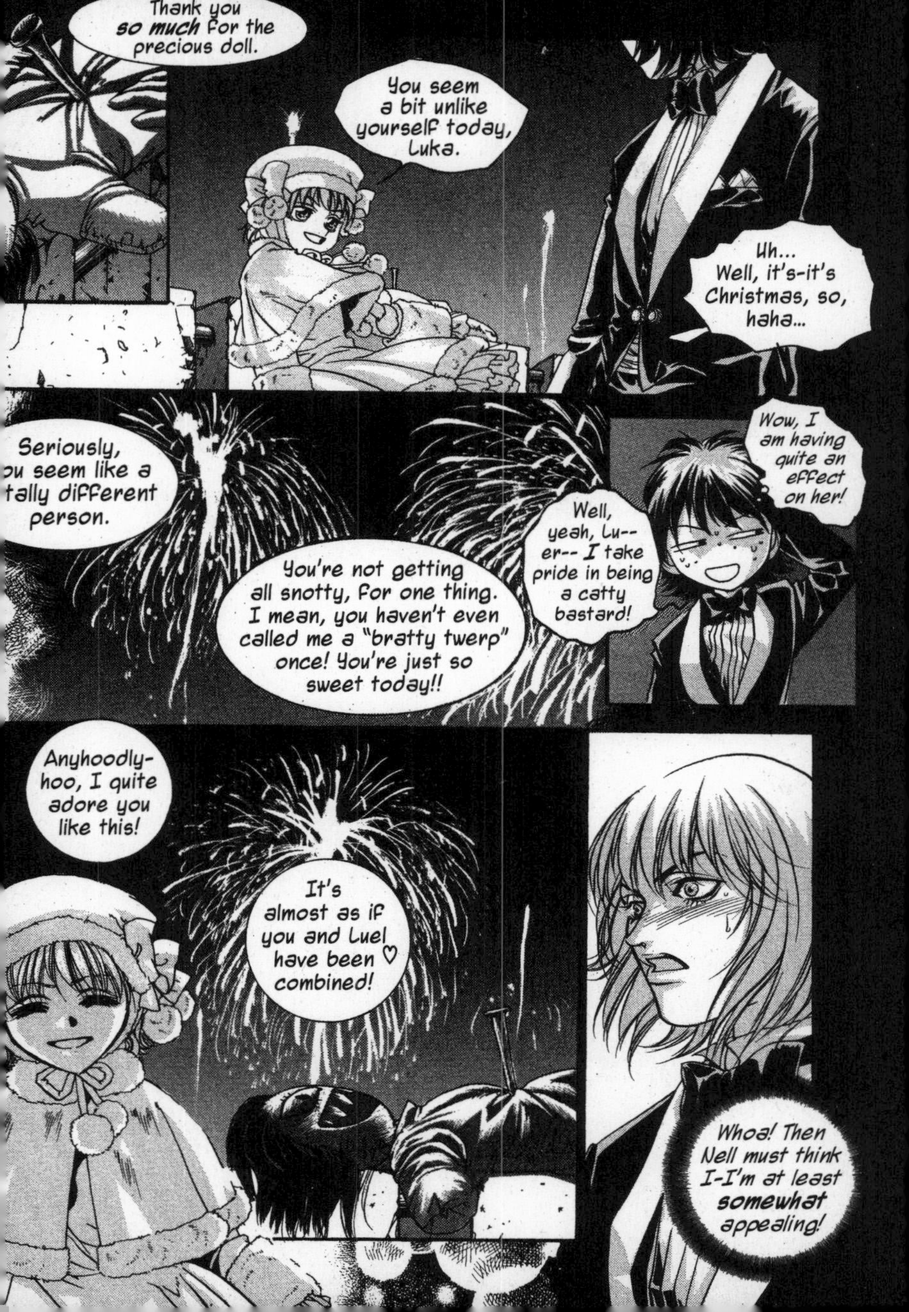
Thank you **so much** for the precious doll.
You seem a bit unlike yourself today, Luka.
Uh... Well, it's-it's Christmas, so, haha...
Seriously, ou seem like a tally different person.
You're not getting all snotty, for one thing. I mean, you haven't even called me a "bratty twerp" once! You're just so sweet today!!
Well, yeah, Lu-- er-- *I* take pride in being a catty bastard!
Wow, I am having quite an effect on her!
Anyhoodly-hoo, I quite adore you like this!
It's almost as if you and Luel have been combined! ♡
*Whoa! Then Nell must think I-I'm at least **somewhat** appealing!*

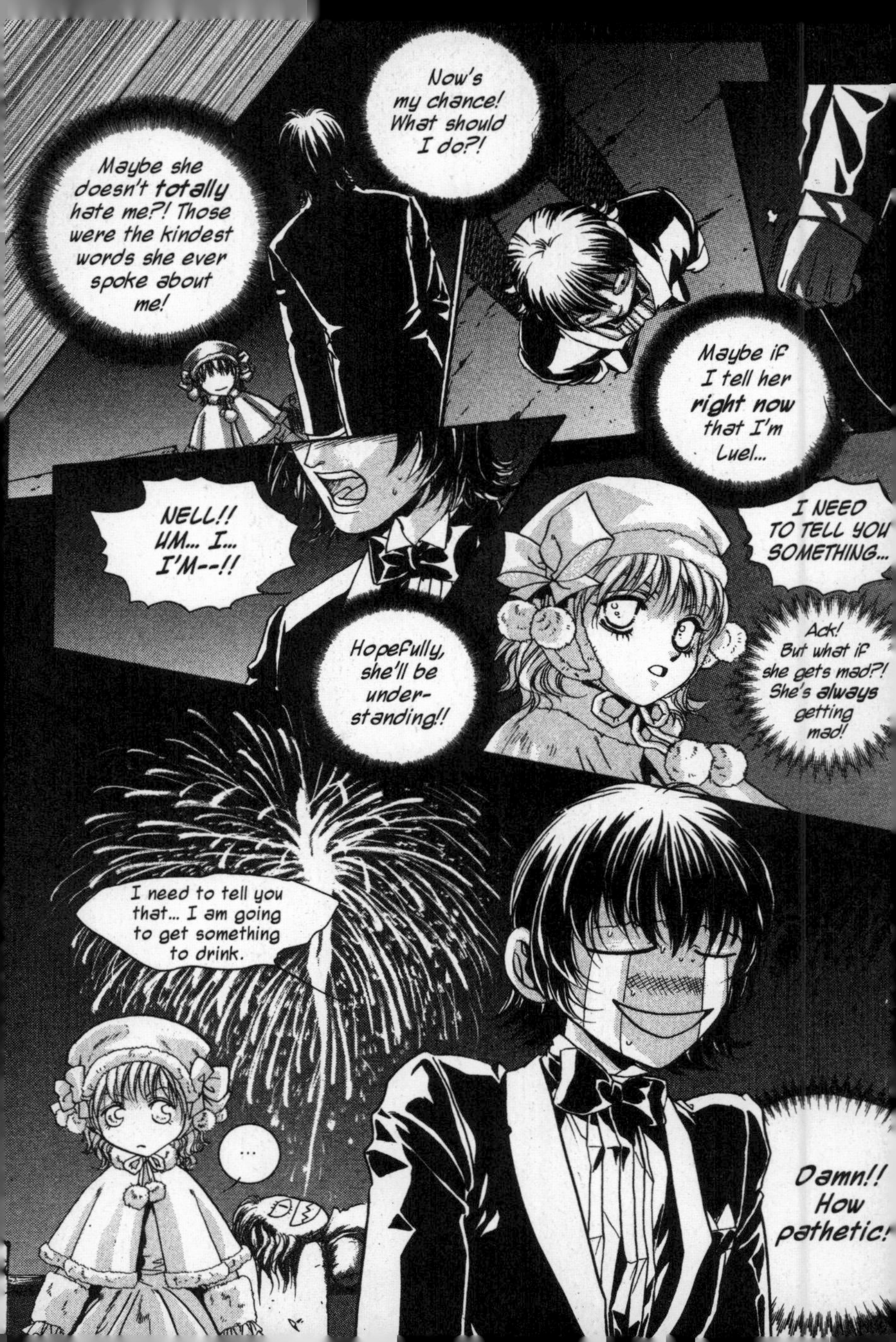

Maybe she doesn't totally hate me?! Those were the kindest words she ever spoke about me!
Now's my chance! What should I do?!
Maybe if I tell her right now that I'm Luel...
NELL!! UM... I... I'M--!!
Hopefully, she'll be under-standing!!
I NEED TO TELL YOU SOMETHING...
Ack! But what if she gets mad?! She's always getting mad!
I need to tell you that... I am going to get something to drink.
...
Damn!! How pathetic!

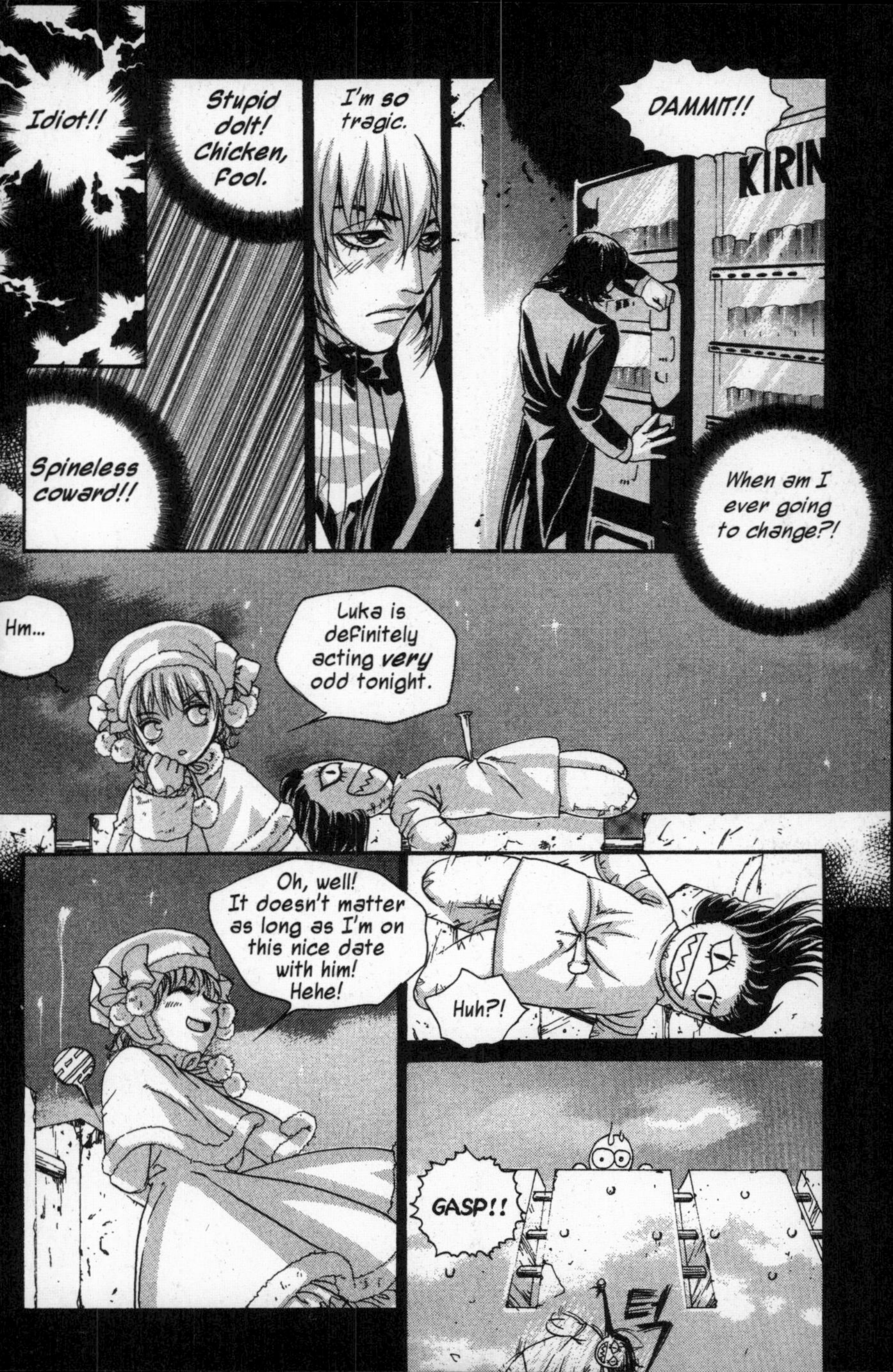
Idiot!!
Stupid dolt! Chicken, fool.
Spineless coward!!
I'm so tragic.
DAMMIT!!
KIRIN
When am I ever going to change?!
Hm...
Luka is definitely acting *very* odd tonight.
Oh, well! It doesn't matter as long as I'm on this nice date with him! Hehe!
Huh?!
GASP!!

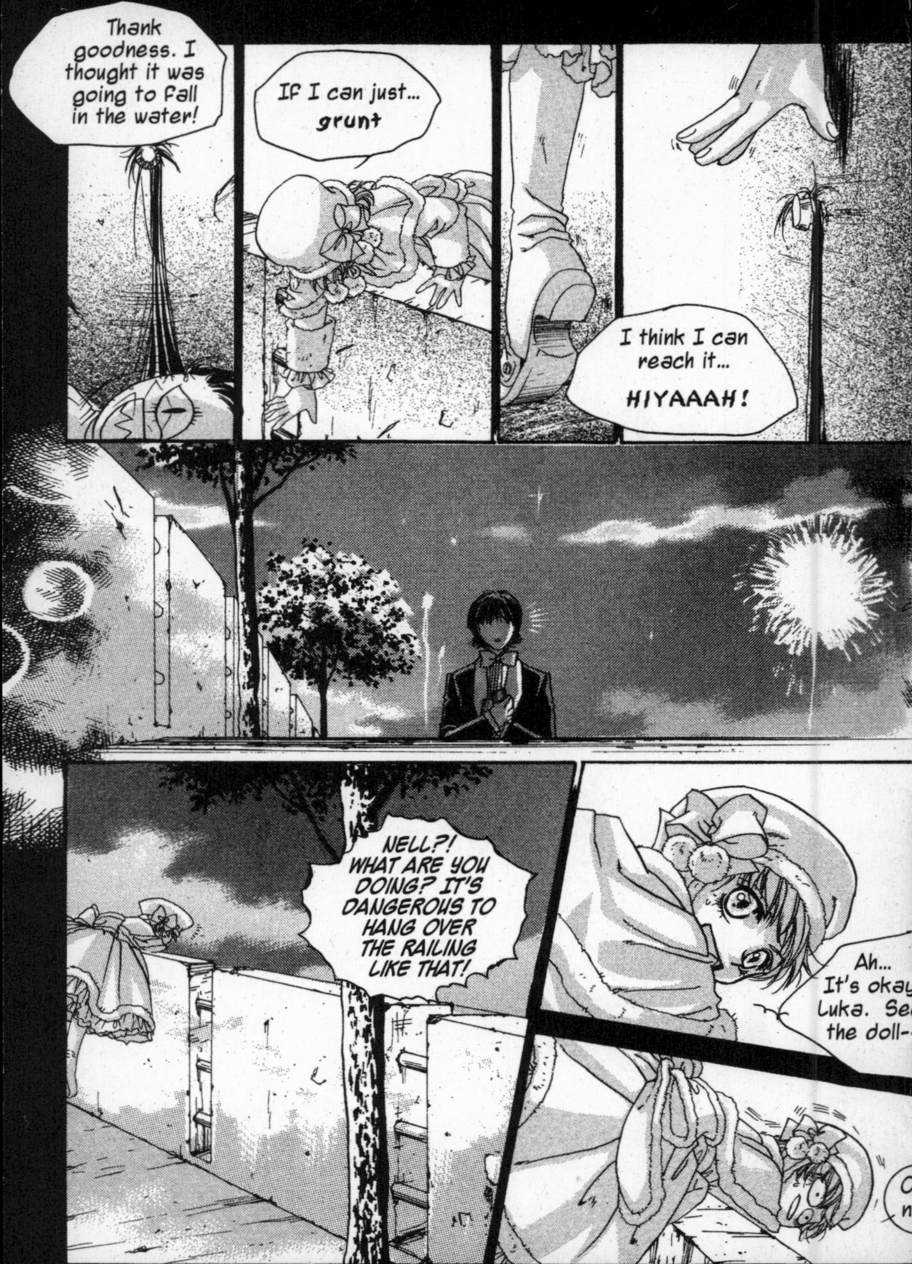
Thank goodness. I thought it was going to fall in the water!
If I can just... grunt
I think I can reach it... HIYAAAH!
NELL?! WHAT ARE YOU DOING? IT'S DANGEROUS TO HANG OVER THE RAILING LIKE THAT!
Ah... It's oka
Luka. Se
the doll-

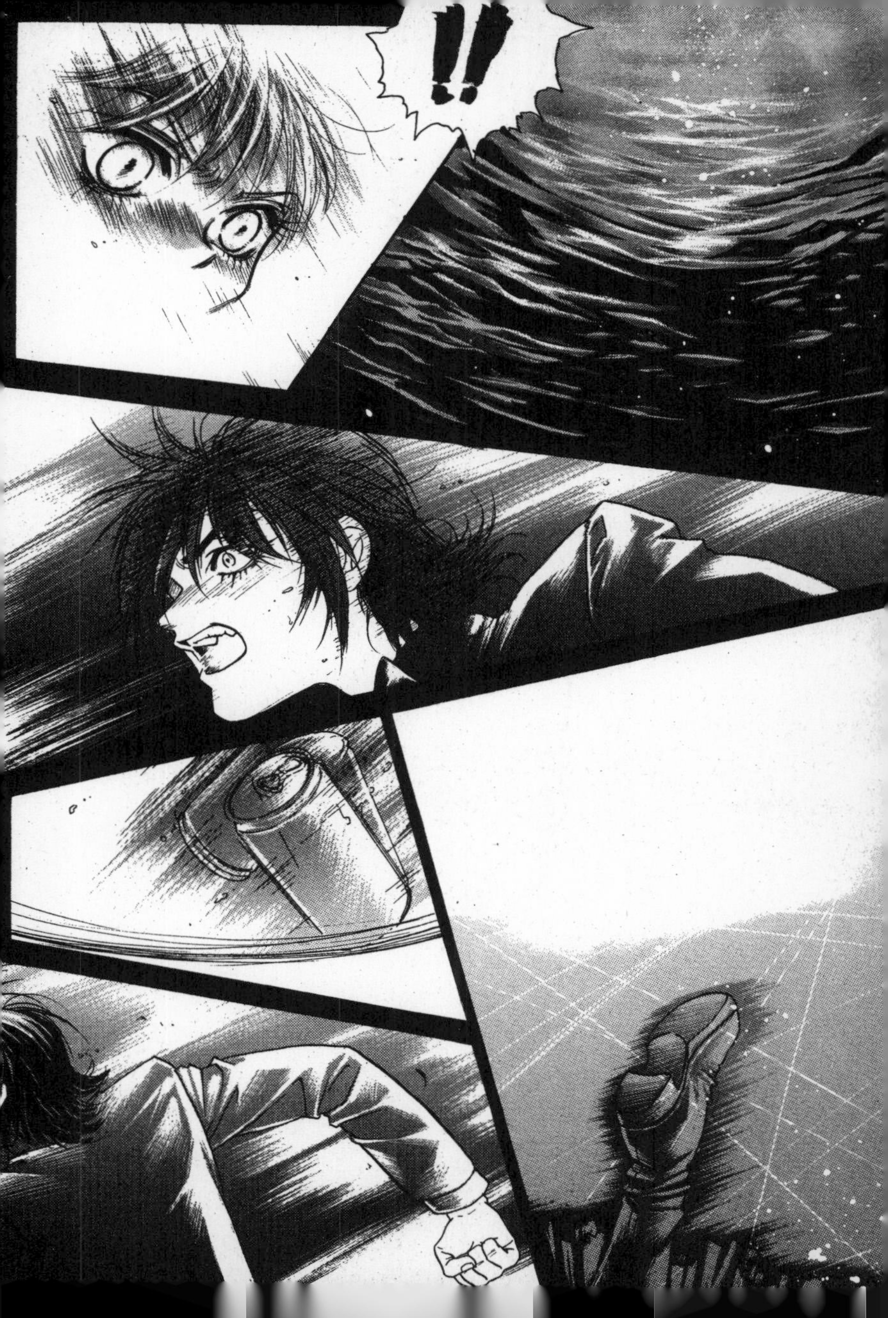
!!

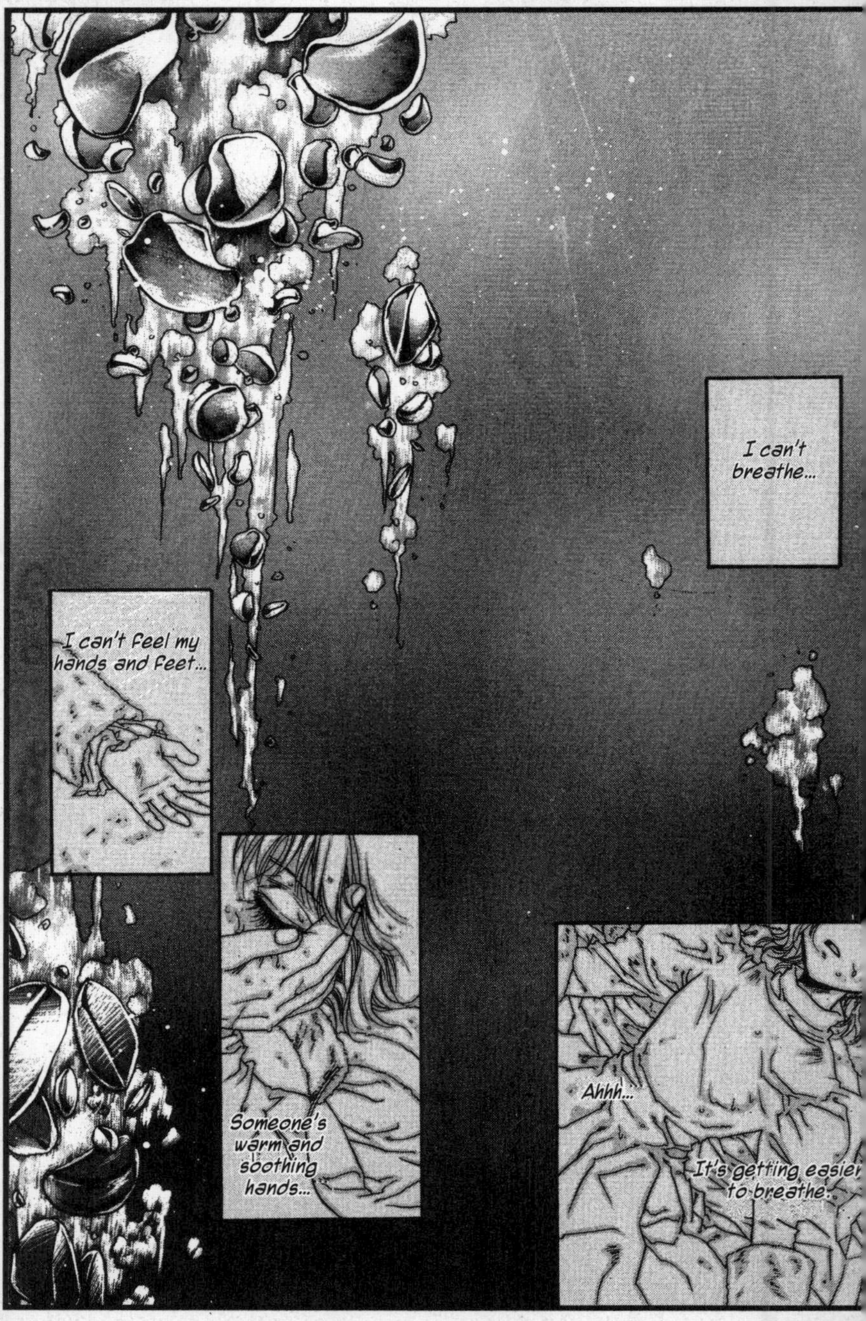
I can't breathe...
I can't feel my hands and feet...
Someone's warm and soothing hands...
Ahhh...
It's getting easier to breathe.

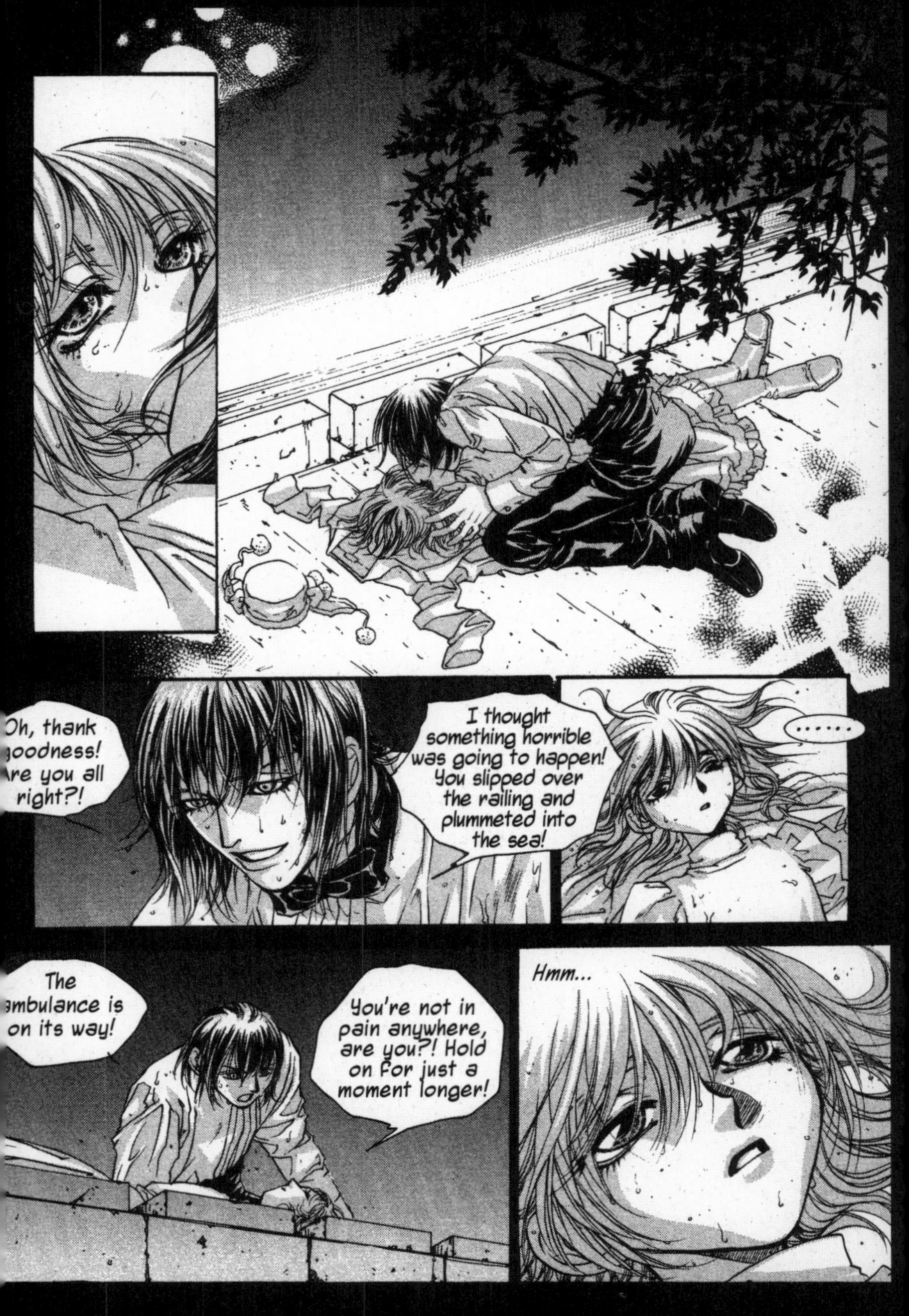
Oh, thank goodness! Are you all right?!
I thought something horrible was going to happen! You slipped over the railing and plummeted into the sea!
......
The ambulance is on its way!
You're not in pain anywhere, are you?! Hold on for just a moment longer!
Hmm...

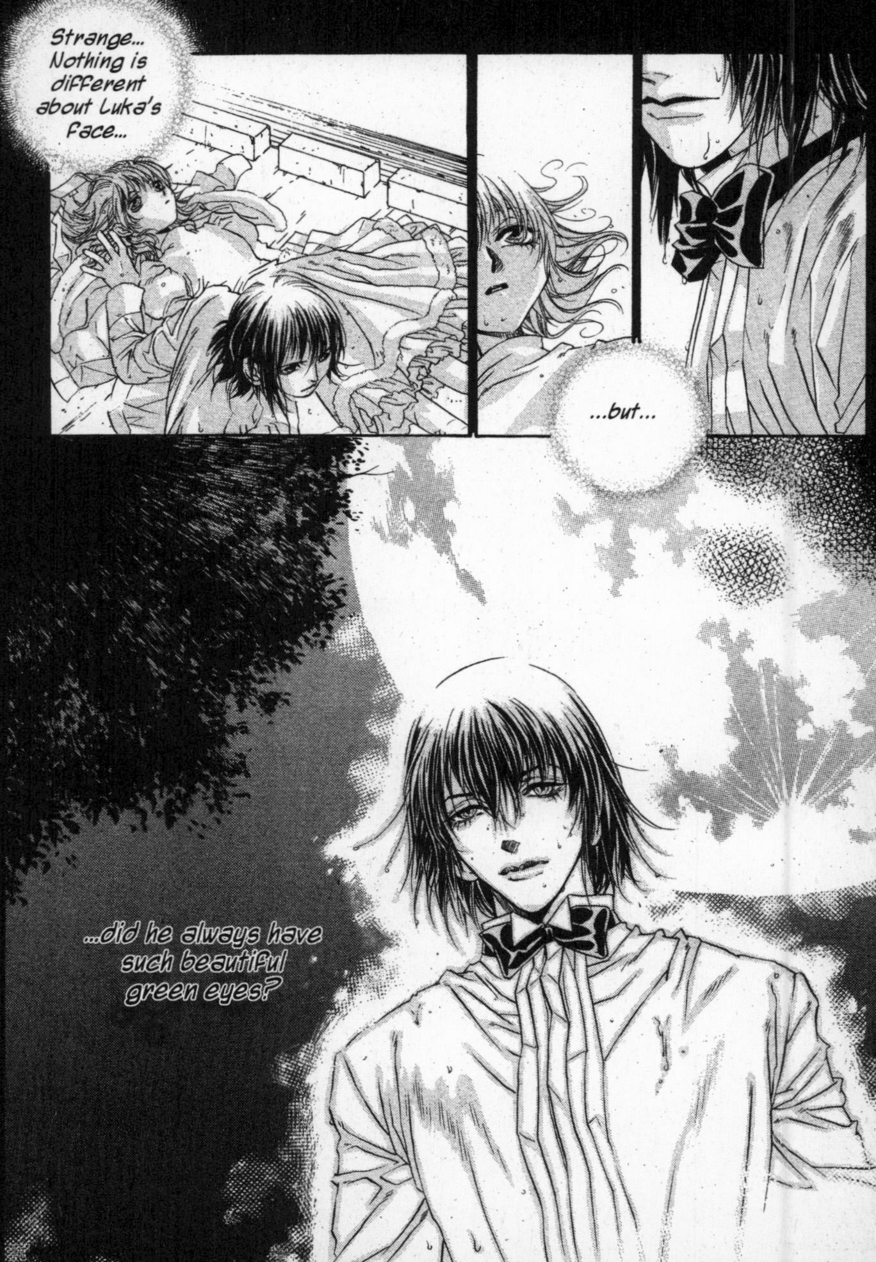

Strange... Nothing is different about Luka's face...
...but...
...did he always have such beautiful green eyes?

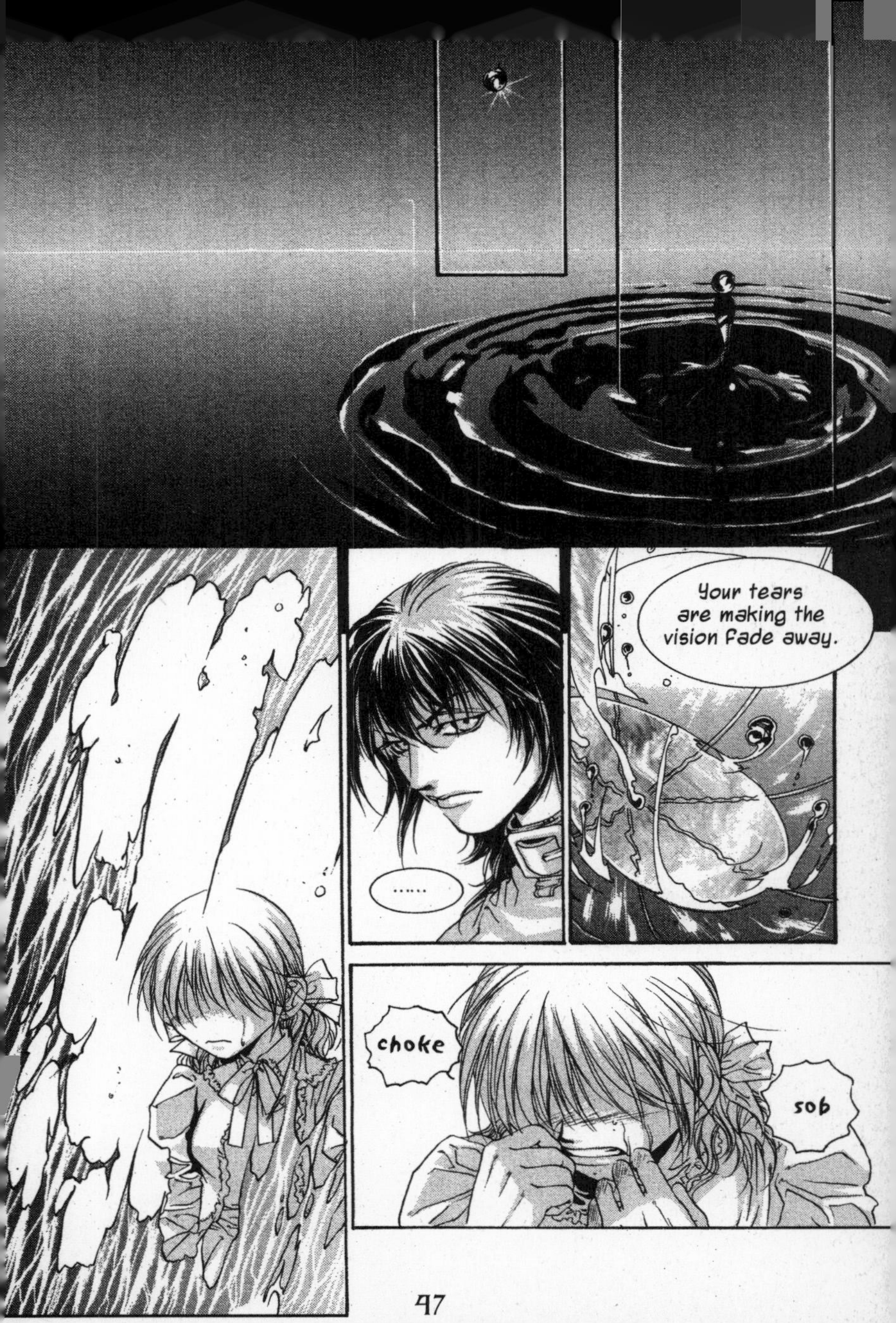
......
Your tears are making the vision fade away.
choke
sob

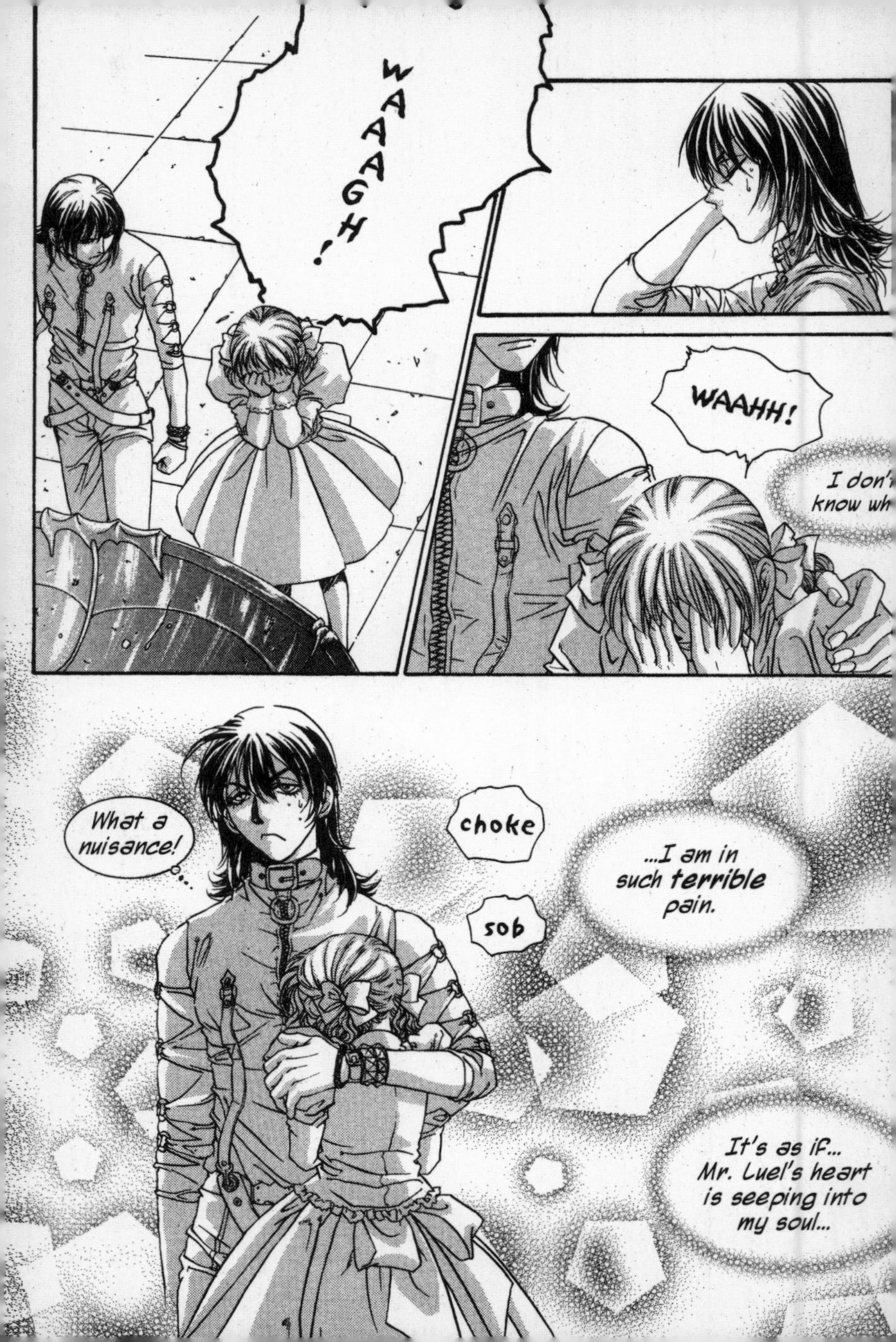
WAAAAGH!
WAAHH!
I don't know wh
What a nuisance!
choke
sob
...I am in such terrible pain.
It's as if... Mr. Luel's heart is seeping into my soul...

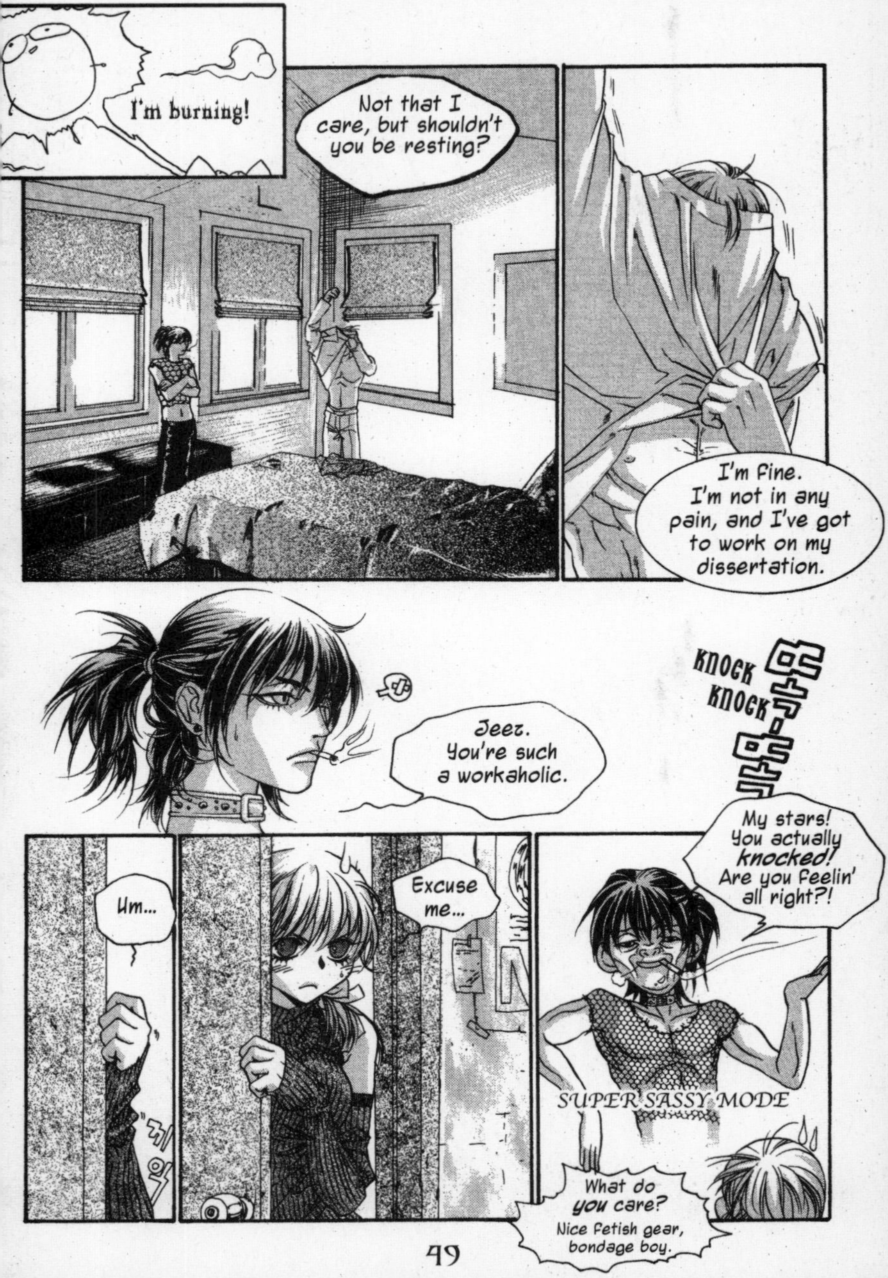
I'm burning!
Not that I care, but shouldn't you be resting?
I'm fine. I'm not in any pain, and I've got to work on my dissertation.
Jeez. You're such a workaholic.
KNOCK KNOCK
Um...
Excuse me...
My stars! You actually *knocked!* Are you feelin' all right?!
SUPER SASSY MODE
What do *you* care? Nice fetish gear, bondage boy.

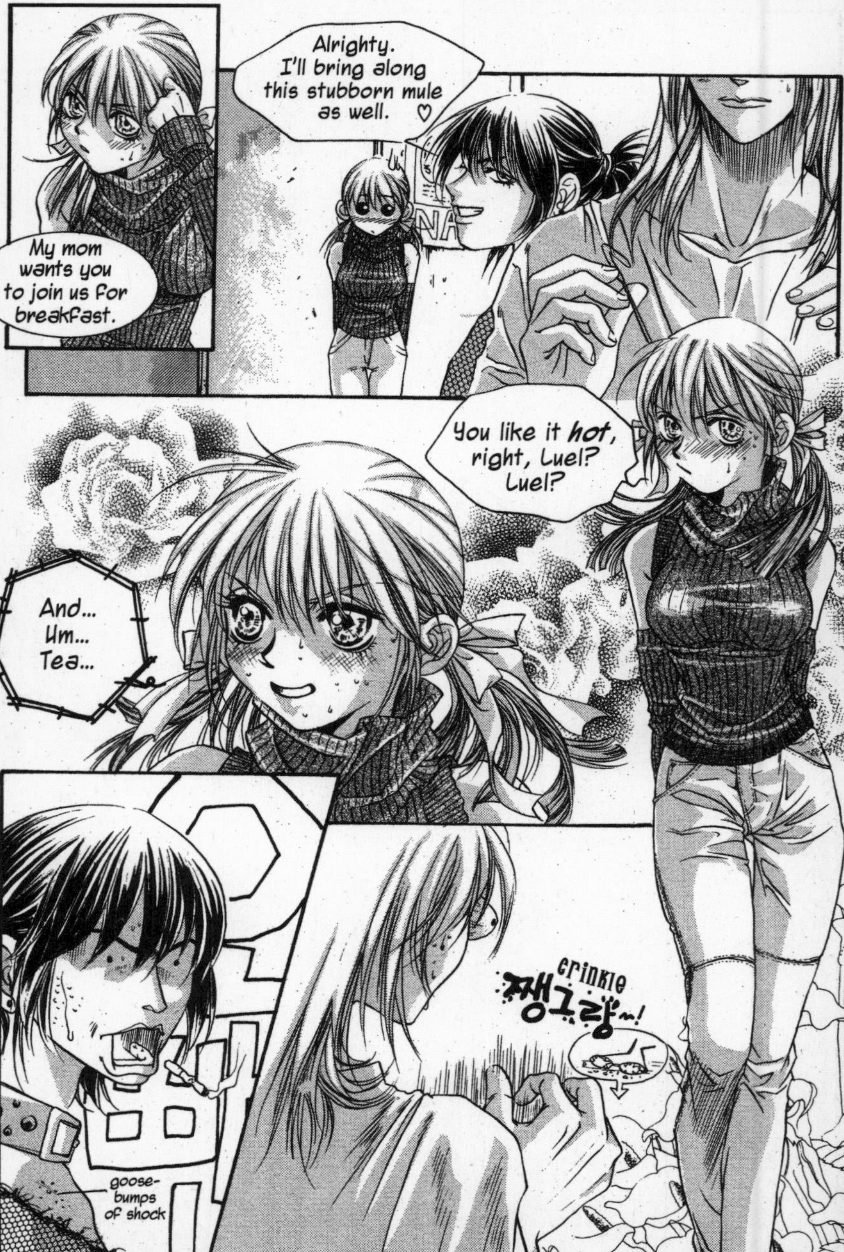
My mom wants you to join us for breakfast.
Alrighty. I'll bring along this stubborn mule as well. ♡
And... Um... Tea...
You like it *hot*, right, Luel? Luel?
goose-bumps of shock
crinkle
쨍그랑~!

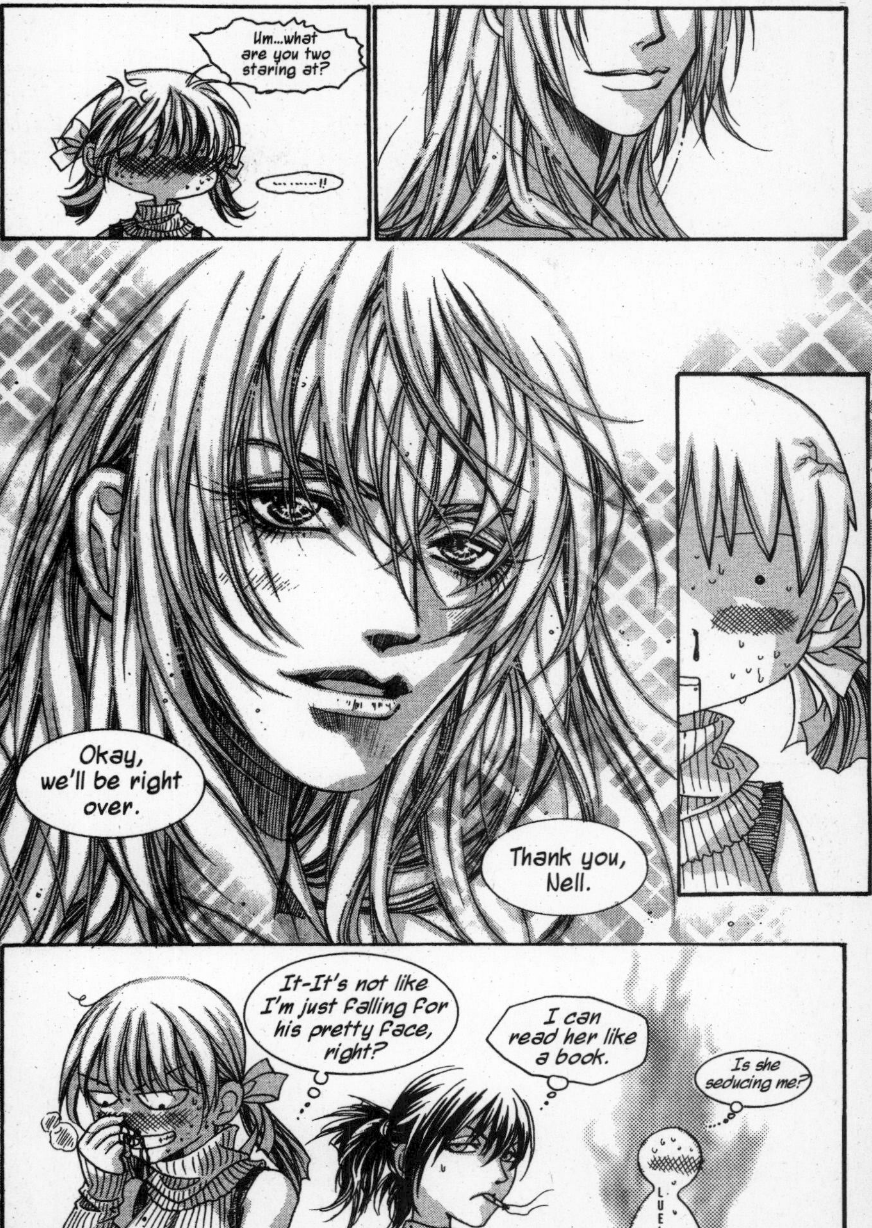
Um...what are you two staring at?
........!!
Okay, we'll be right over.
Thank you, Nell.
It-It's not like I'm just falling for his pretty face, right?
I can read her like a book.
Is she seducing me?
LUEL

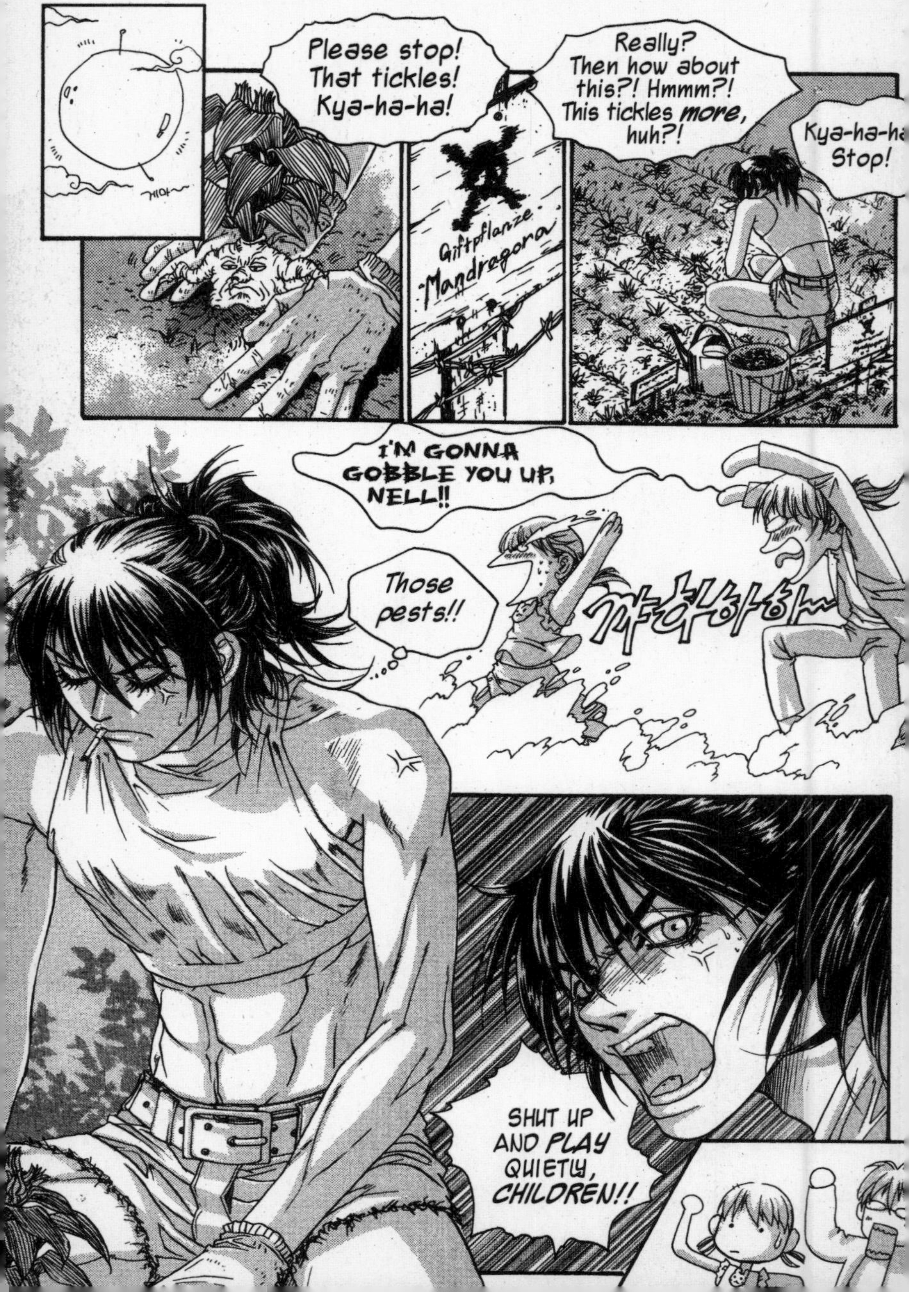
Please stop! That tickles! Kya-ha-ha!
Giftpflanze
Mandragora
Really? Then how about this?! Hmmm?! This tickles *more*, huh?!
Kya-ha-ha Stop!
I'M GONNA GOBBLE YOU UP, NELL!!
Those pests!!
꺄하하하~
SHUT UP AND *PLAY* QUIETLY, *CHILDREN*!!

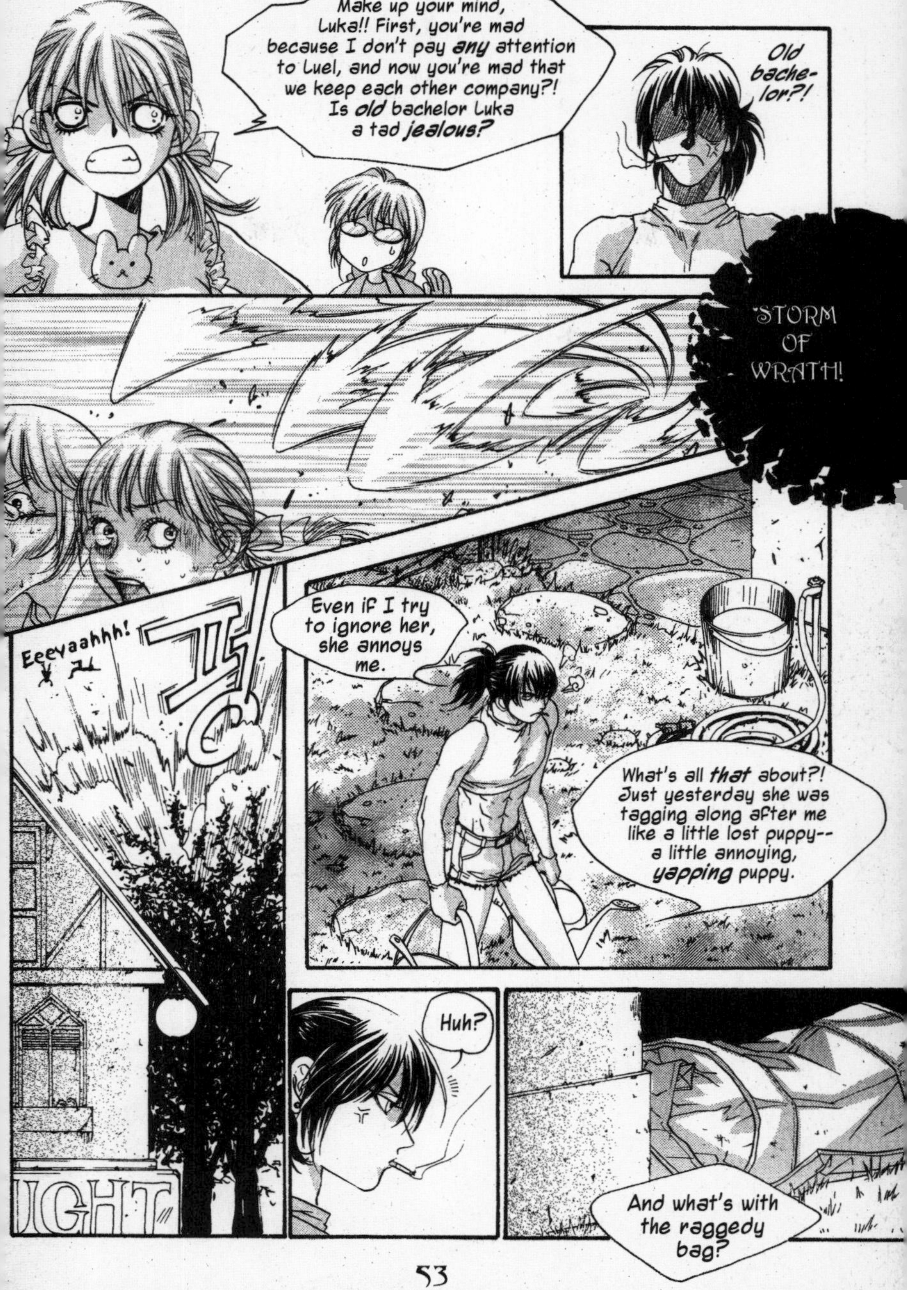
Make up your mind, Luka!! First, you're mad because I don't pay *any* attention to Luel, and now you're mad that we keep each other company?! Is *old* bachelor Luka a tad *jealous?*
Old bache-lor?!
STORM OF WRATH!
Eeevaahhh!
Even if I try to ignore her, she annoys me.
What's all *that* about?! Just yesterday she was tagging along after me like a little lost puppy-- a little annoying, *yapping* puppy.
IGHT
Huh?
And what's with the raggedy bag?

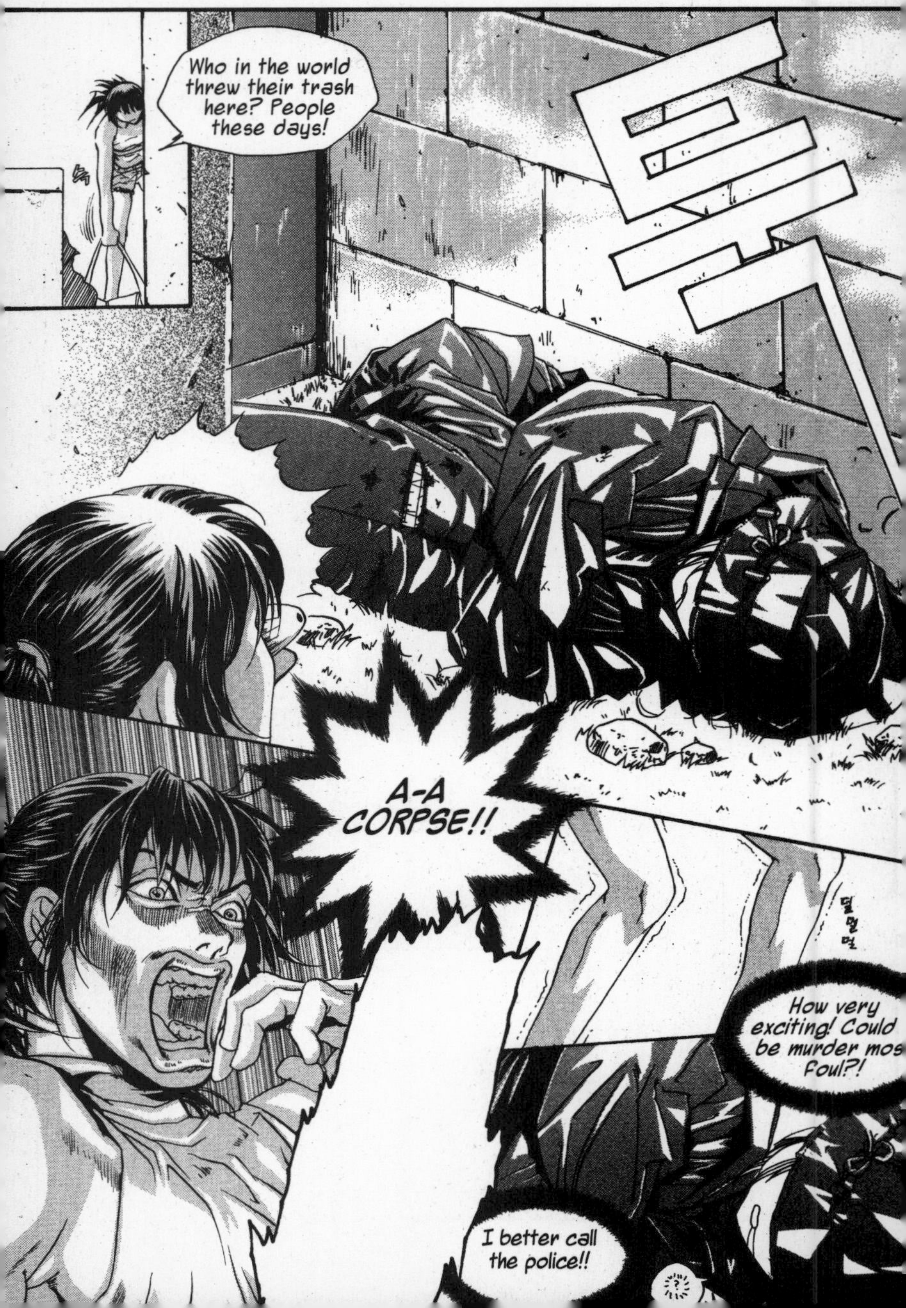
Who in the world threw their trash here? People these days!
A-A CORPSE!!
덜덜덜
How very exciting! Could be murder mos foul?!
I better call the police!!

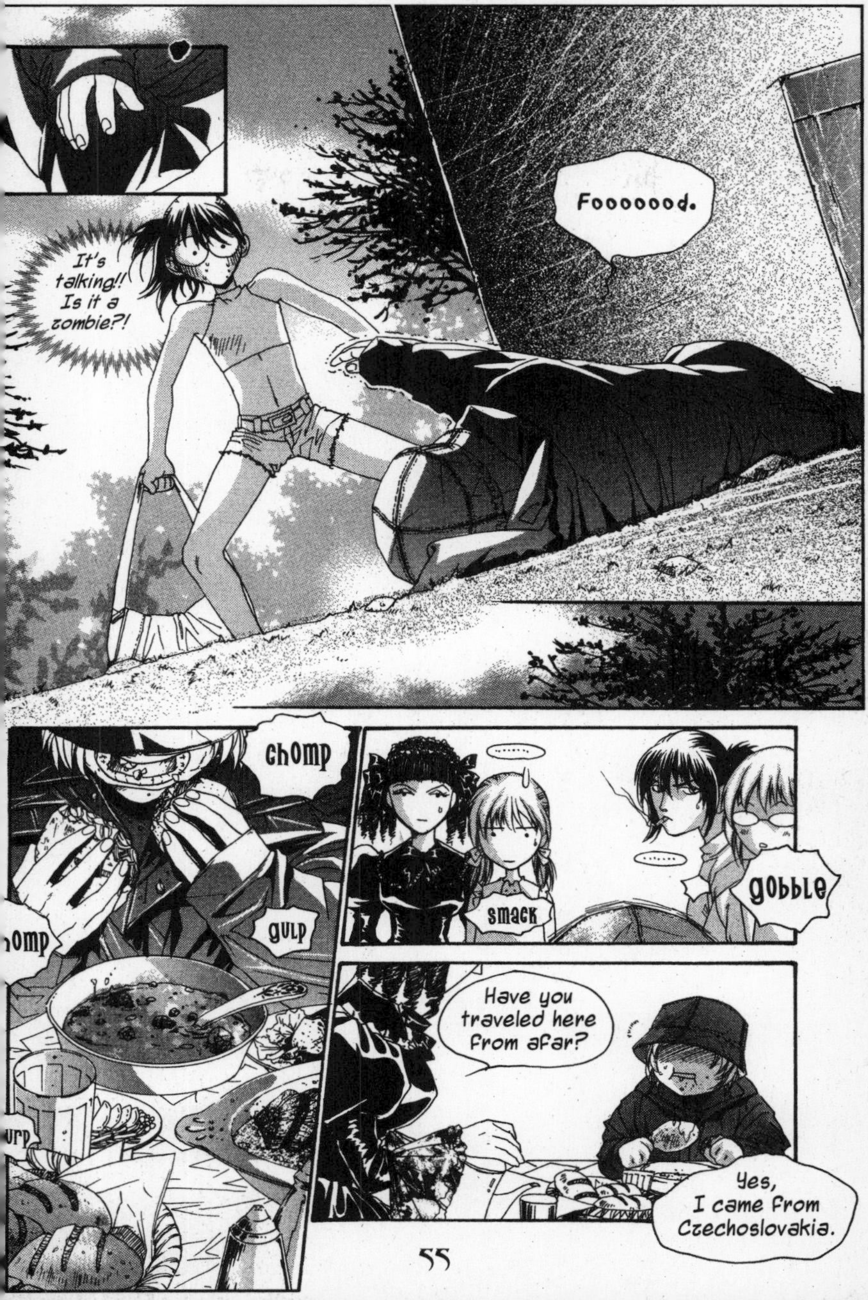
Foooooood.
It's talking!! Is it a zombie?!
chomp
gulp
homp
urp
......
......
smack
gobble
Have you traveled here from afar?
Yes, I came from Czechoslovakia.

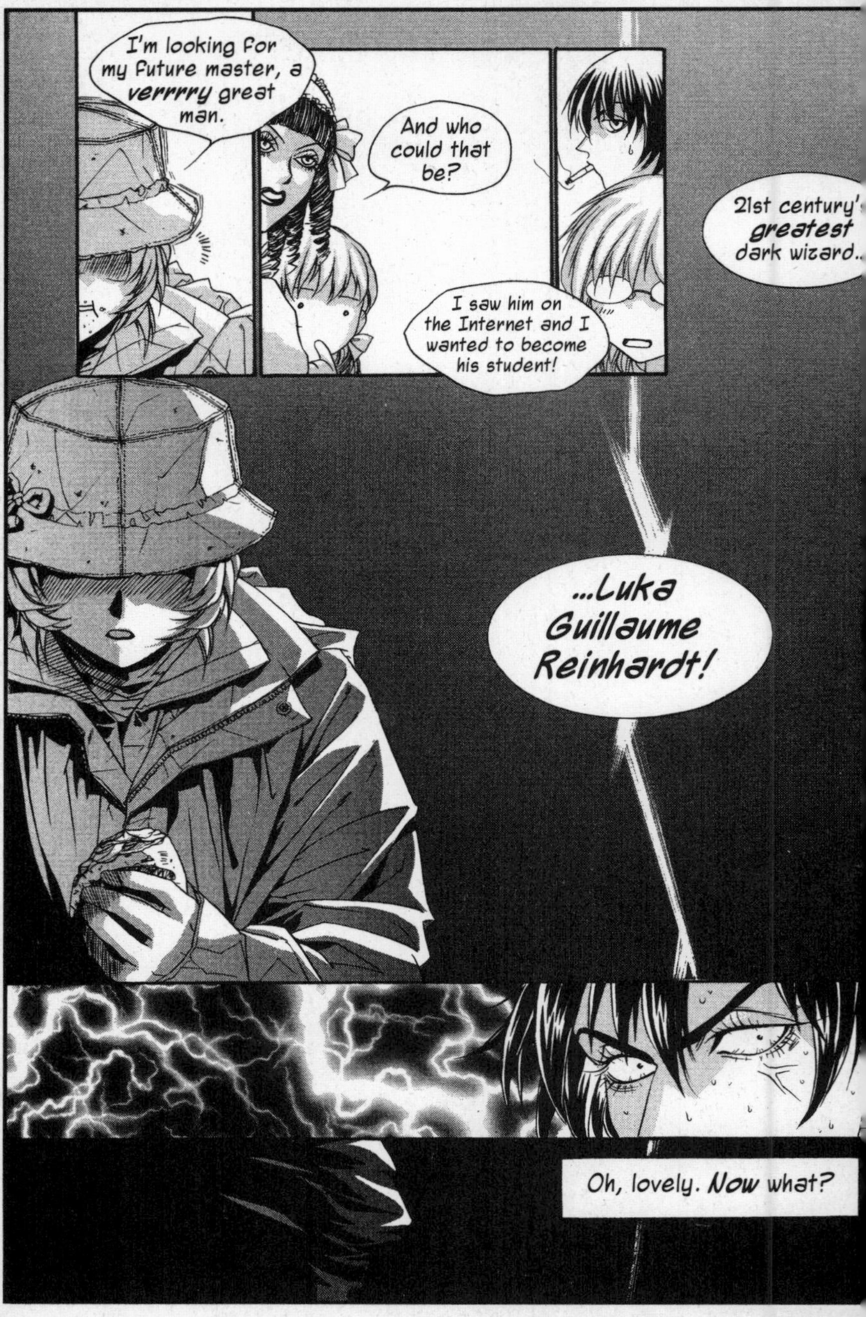
I'm looking for my future master, a verrrry great man.
And who could that be?
I saw him on the Internet and I wanted to become his student!
21st century's greatest dark wizard...
...Luka Guillaume Reinhardt!
Oh, lovely. Now what?

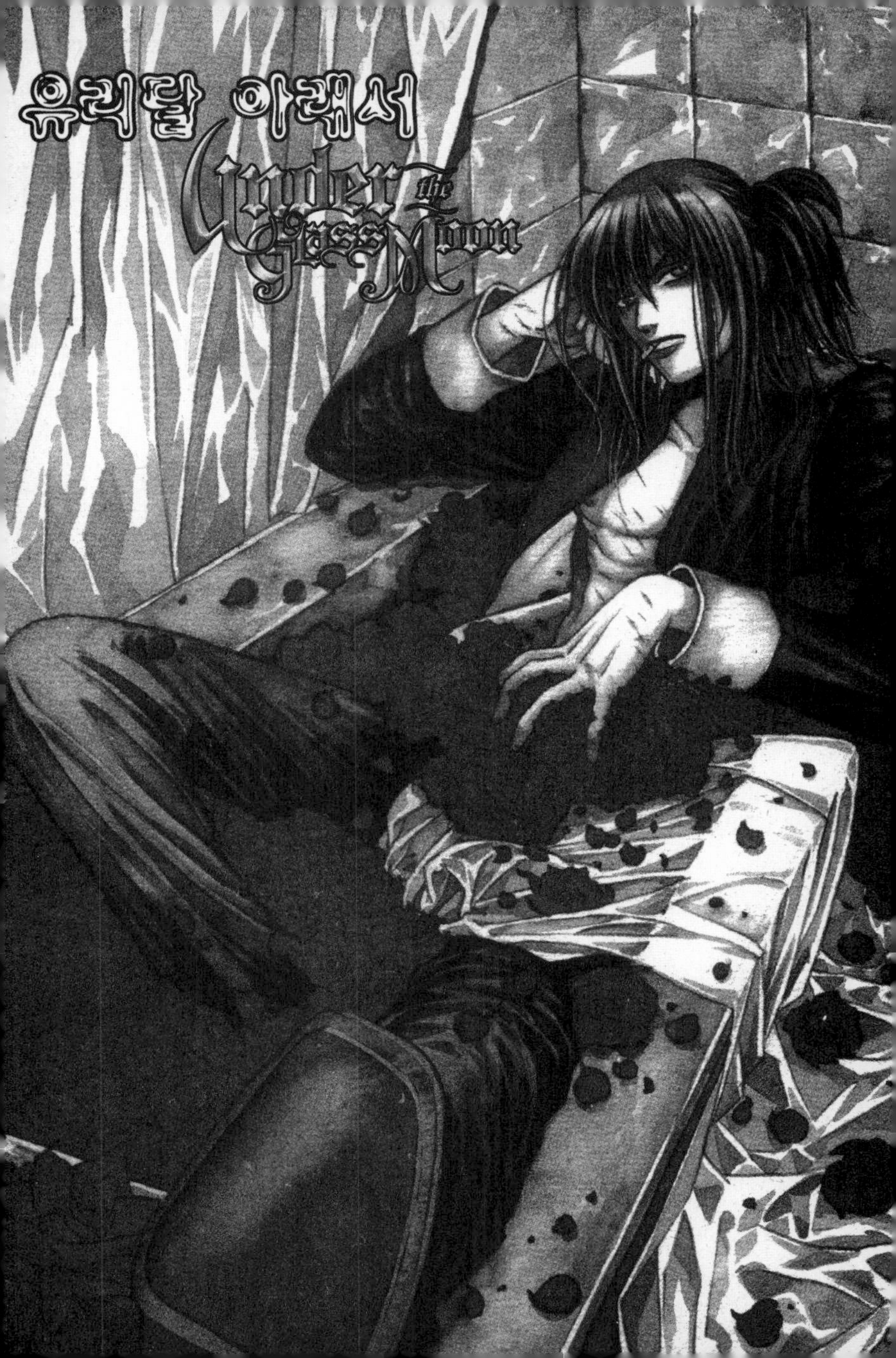
유리달 아래서
Under the Glass Moon

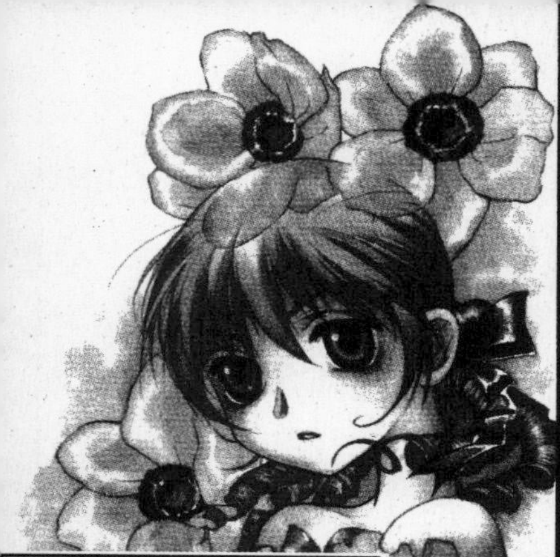

NELL

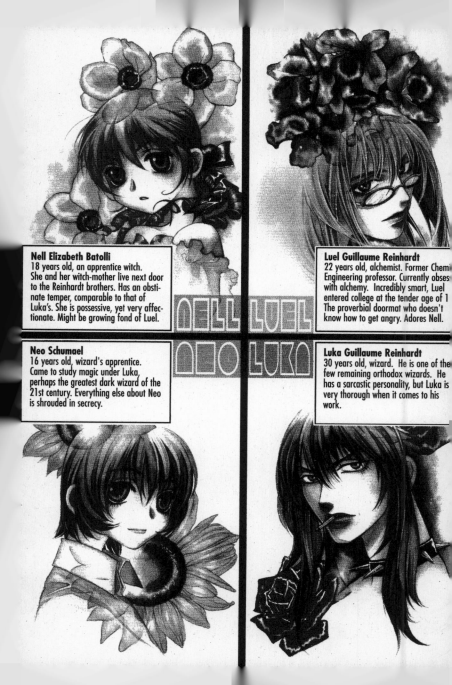

Nell Elizabeth Batolli
18 years old, an apprentice witch. She and her witch-mother live next door to the Reinhardt brothers. Has an obstinate temper, comparable to that of Luka's. She is possessive, yet very affectionate. Might be growing fond of Luel.

NEO

Neo Schumael
16 years old, wizard's apprentice. Came to study magic under Luka, perhaps the greatest dark wizard of the 21st century. Everything else about Neo is shrouded in secrecy.

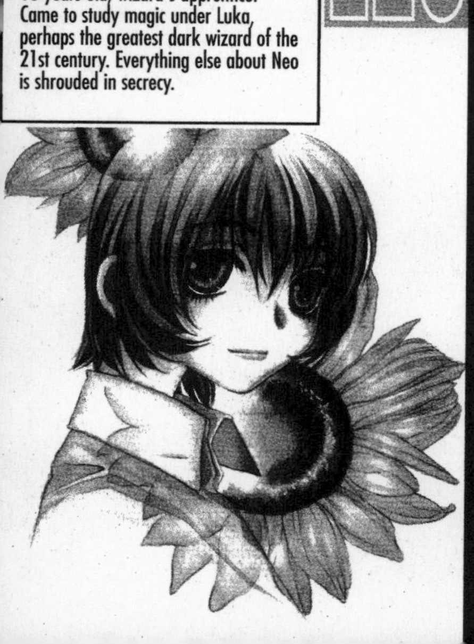

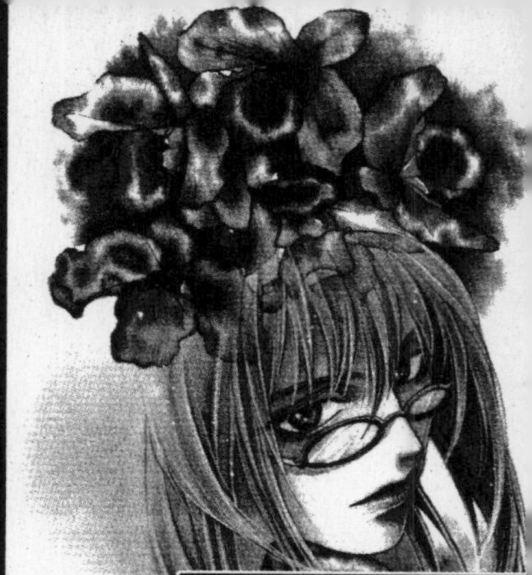

LUEL

Luel Guillaume Reinhardt
22 years old, alchemist. Former Chemi Engineering professor. Currently obses with alchemy. Incredibly smart, Luel entered college at the tender age of 1 The proverbial doormat who doesn't know how to get angry. Adores Nell.

LUKA

Luka Guillaume Reinhardt
30 years old, wizard. He is one of the few remaining orthodox wizards. He has a sarcastic personality, but Luka is very thorough when it comes to his work.

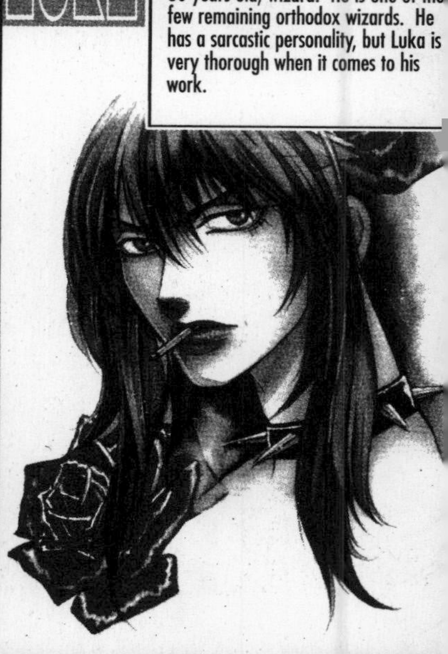

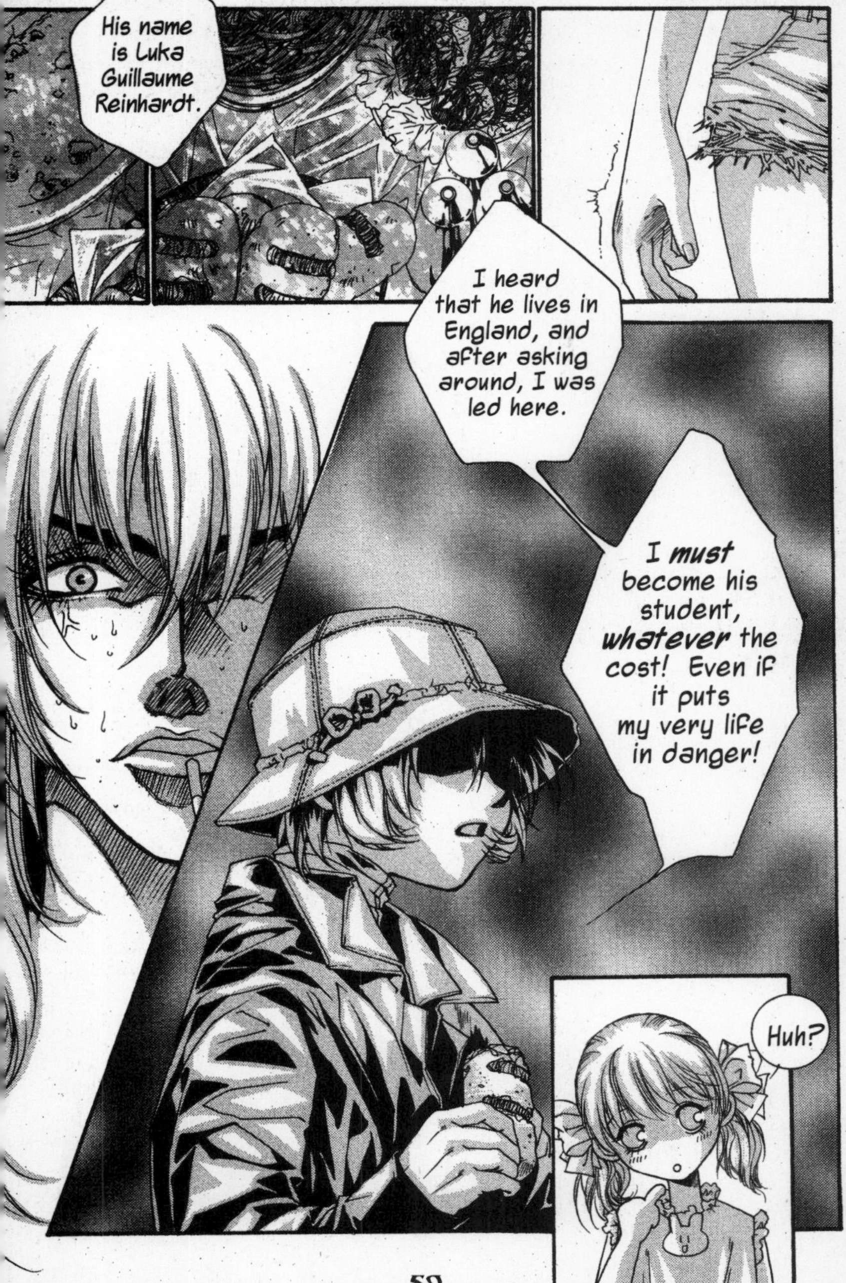
His name is Luka Guillaume Reinhardt.
I heard that he lives in England, and after asking around, I was led here.
I *must* become his student, *whatever* the cost! Even if it puts my very life in danger!
Huh?

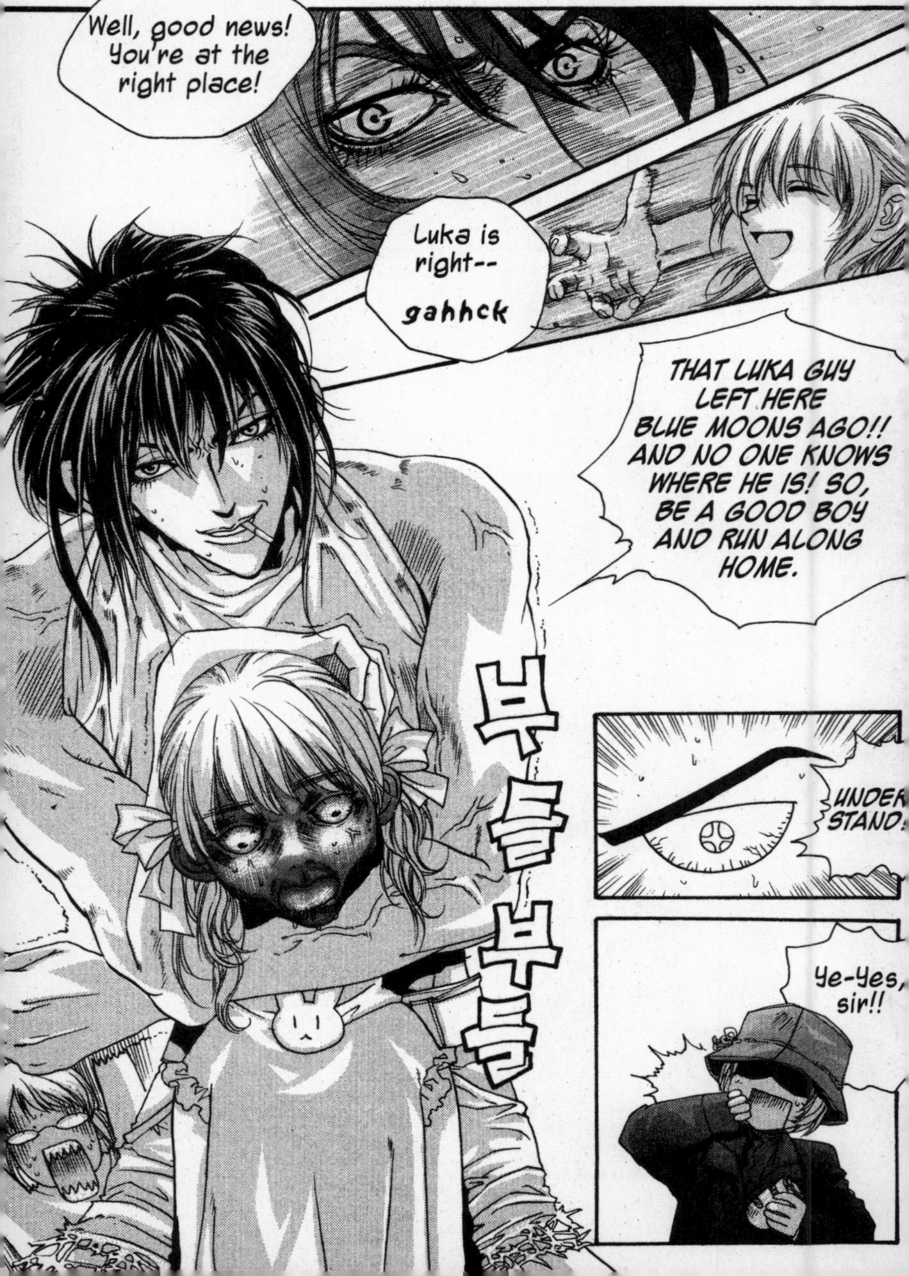
Well, good news! You're at the right place!
Luka is right--
gahhck
THAT LUKA GUY LEFT HERE BLUE MOONS AGO!! AND NO ONE KNOWS WHERE HE IS! SO, BE A GOOD BOY AND RUN ALONG HOME.
부들부들
UNDER STAND!
Ye-Yes, sir!!

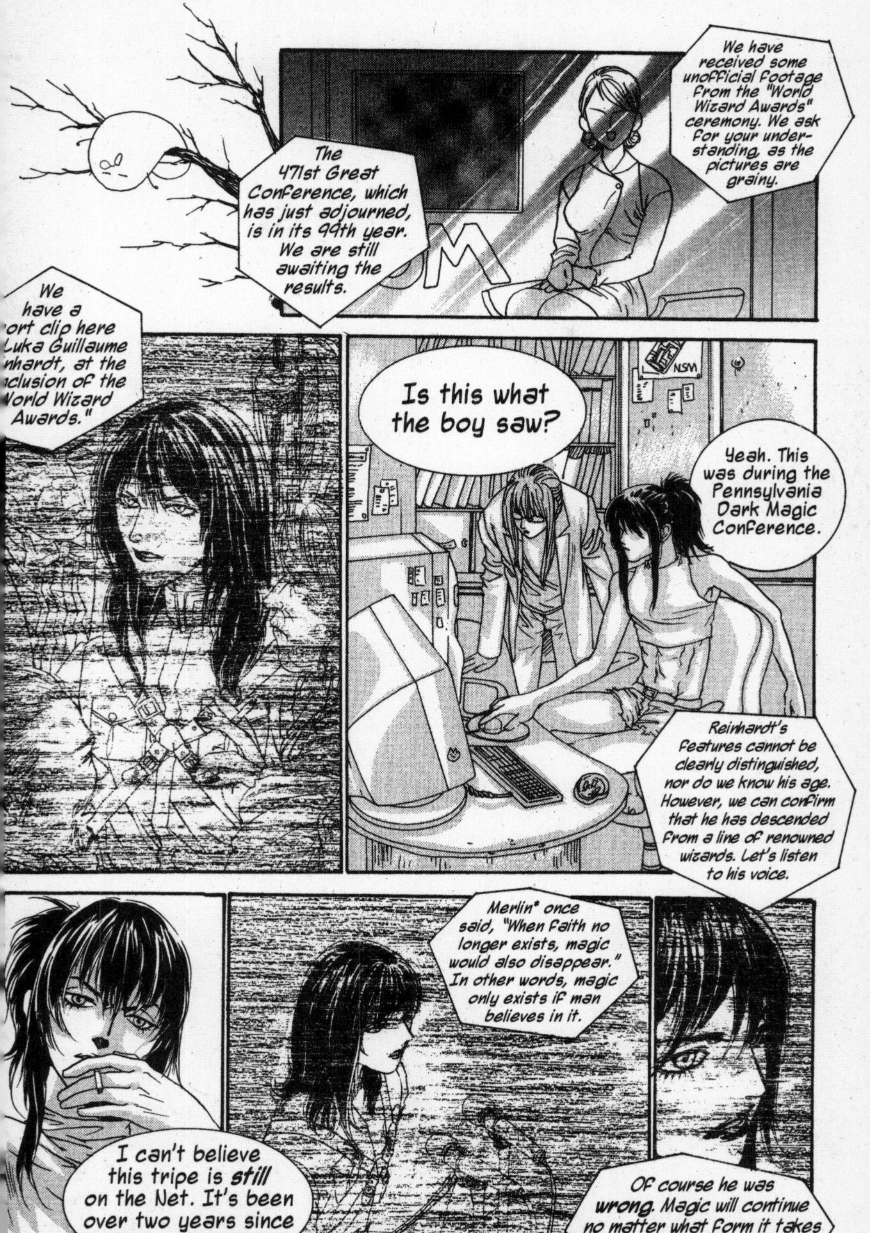
The 471st Great Conference, which has just adjourned, is in its 99th year. We are still awaiting the results.
We have received some unofficial footage from the "World Wizard Awards" ceremony. We ask for your understanding, as the pictures are grainy.
We have a ort clip here Luka Guillaume nhardt, at the nclusion of the World Wizard Awards."
Is this what the boy saw?
Yeah. This was during the Pennsylvania Dark Magic Conference.
Reinhardt's features cannot be clearly distinguished, nor do we know his age. However, we can confirm that he has descended from a line of renowned wizards. Let's listen to his voice.
I can't believe this tripe is *still* on the Net. It's been over two years since the conference.
Merlin* once said, "When faith no longer exists, magic would also disappear." In other words, magic only exists if man believes in it.
Of course he was **wrong**. Magic will continue no matter what form it takes or what era it is in. Magic is **immortal**.

*Merlin: A great wizard and teacher of King Arthur of Camelot.

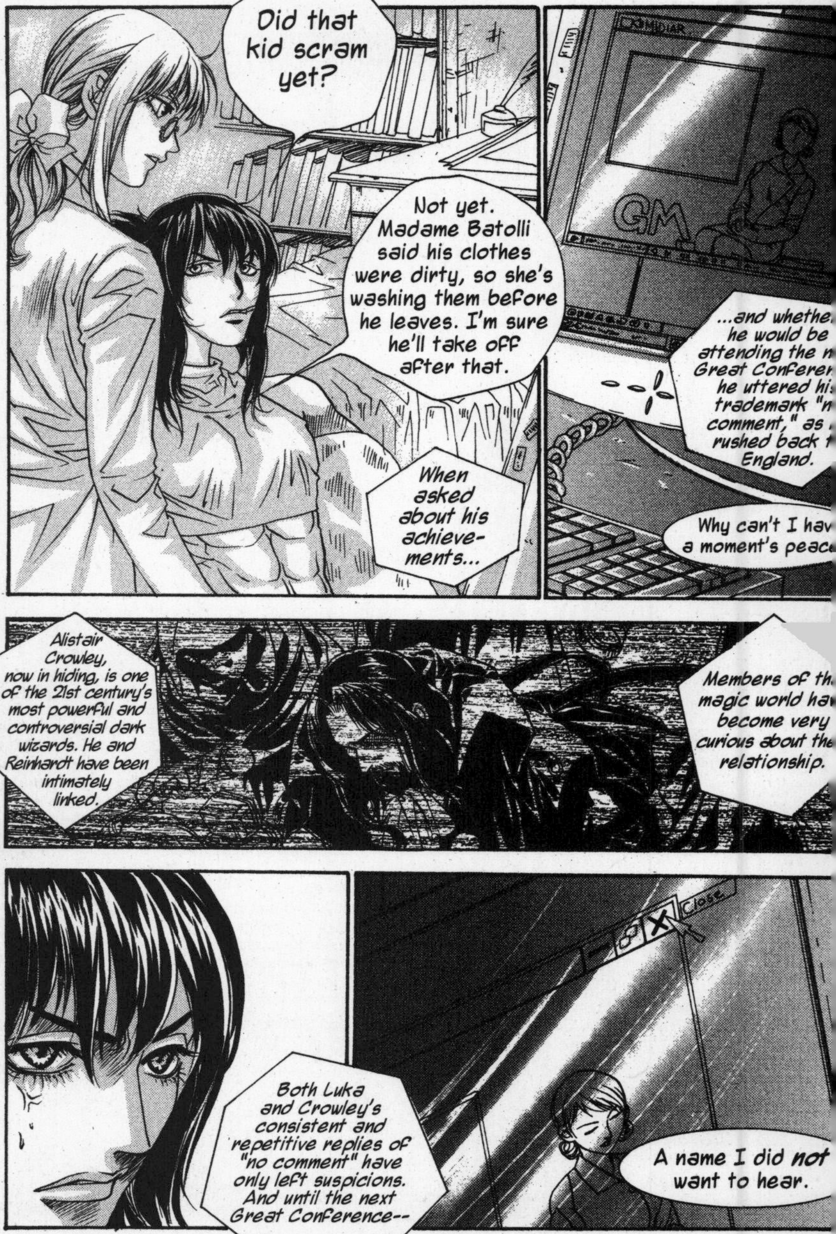
Did that kid scram yet?
Not yet. Madame Batolli said his clothes were dirty, so she's washing them before he leaves. I'm sure he'll take off after that.
When asked about his achieve-ments...
...and whethe he would be attending the n Great Conferen he uttered hi trademark "n comment," as rushed back t England.
Why can't I hav a moment's peac
Alistair Crowley, now in hiding, is one of the 21st century's most powerful and controversial dark wizards. He and Reinhardt have been intimately linked.
Members of th magic world ha become very curious about the relationship.
Both Luka and Crowley's consistent and repetitive replies of "no comment" have only left suspicions. And until the next Great Conference--
Close
A name I did *not* want to hear.

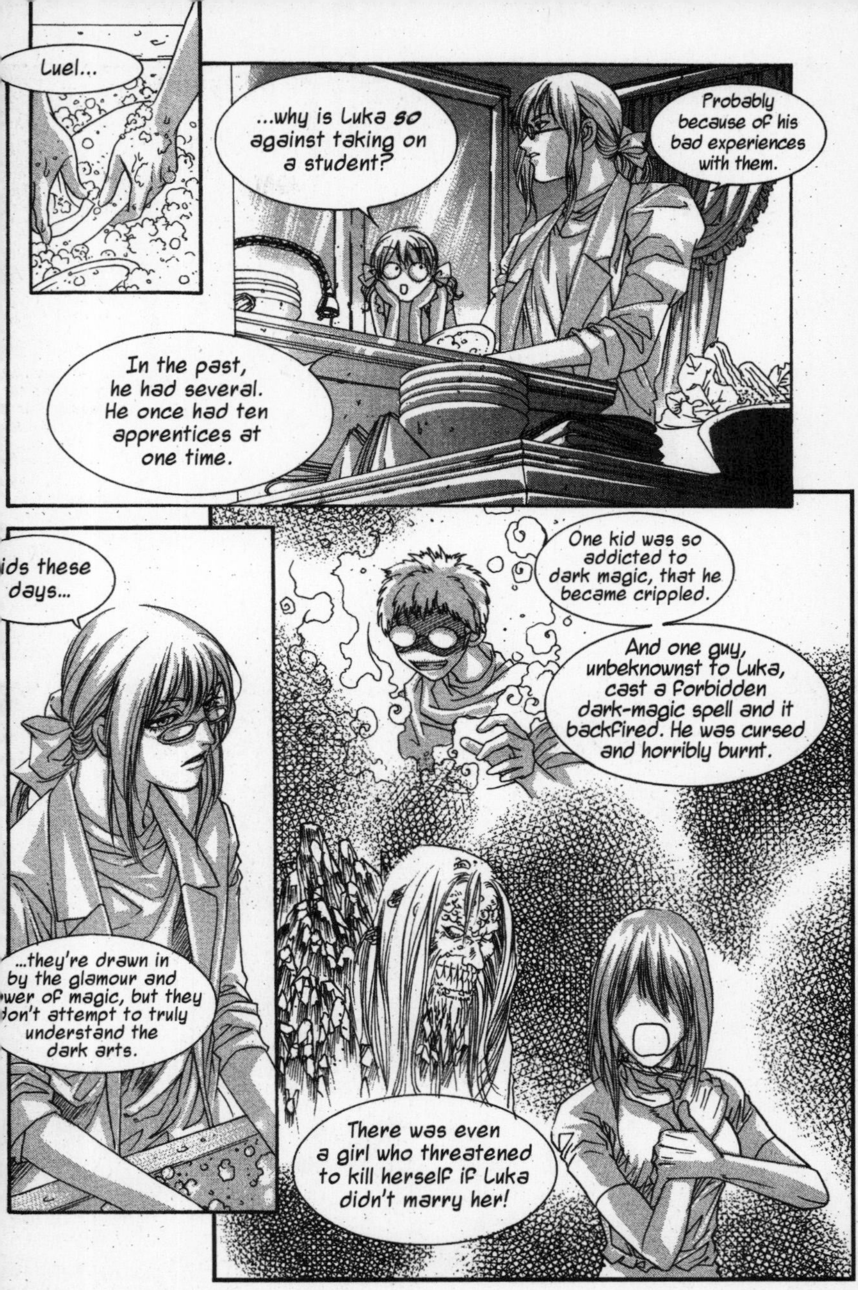

Luel...
...why is Luka so against taking on a student?
Probably because of his bad experiences with them.
In the past, he had several. He once had ten apprentices at one time.
ids these days...
...they're drawn in by the glamour and wer of magic, but they don't attempt to truly understand the dark arts.
One kid was so addicted to dark magic, that he became crippled.
And one guy, unbeknownst to Luka, cast a forbidden dark-magic spell and it backfired. He was cursed and horribly burnt.
There was even a girl who threatened to kill herself if Luka didn't marry her!

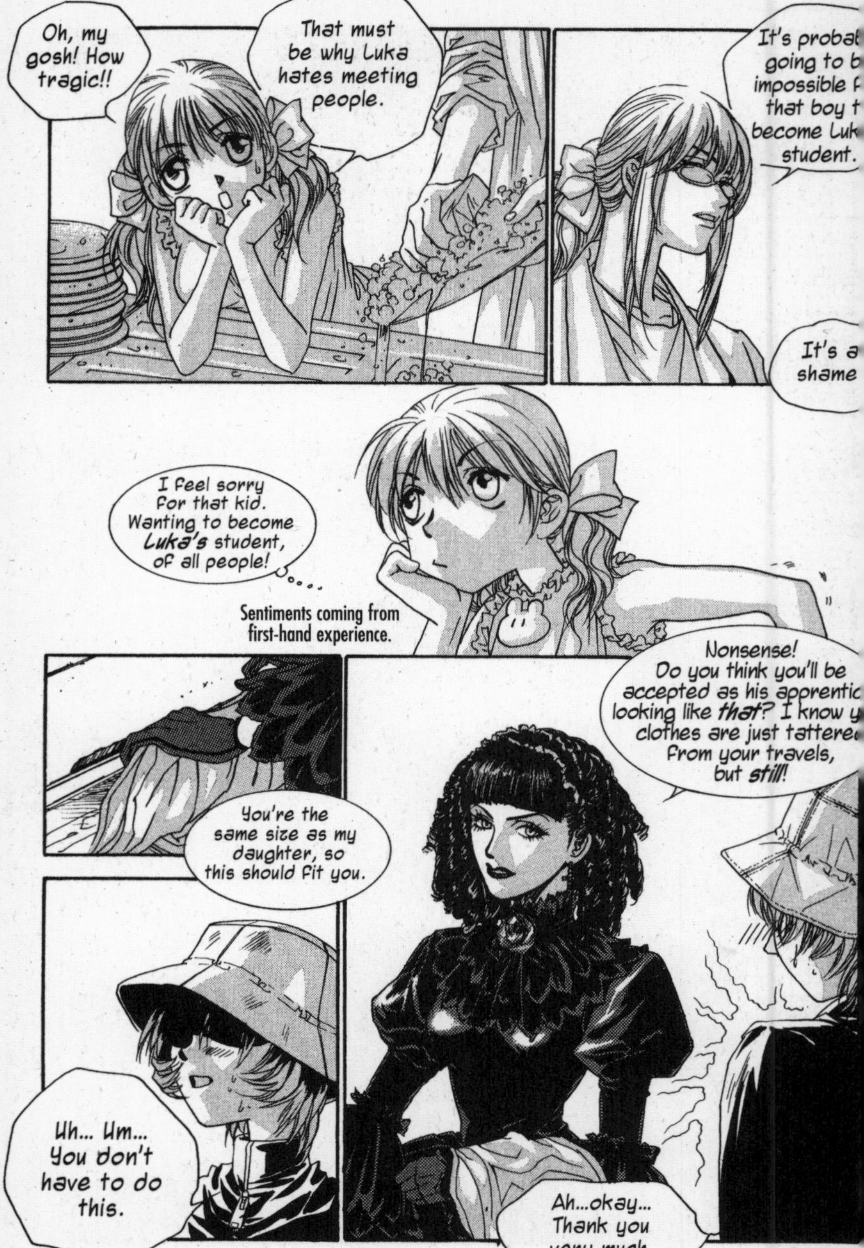
Oh, my gosh! How tragic!!
That must be why Luka hates meeting people.
It's probab going to b impossible f that boy t become Luk student.
It's a shame
I feel sorry for that kid. Wanting to become *Luka's* student, of all people!
Sentiments coming from first-hand experience.
You're the same size as my daughter, so this should fit you.
Uh... Um... You don't have to do this.
Nonsense! Do you think you'll be accepted as his apprentic looking like *that*? I know y clothes are just tattere from your travels, but *still*!
Ah...okay... Thank you very much.

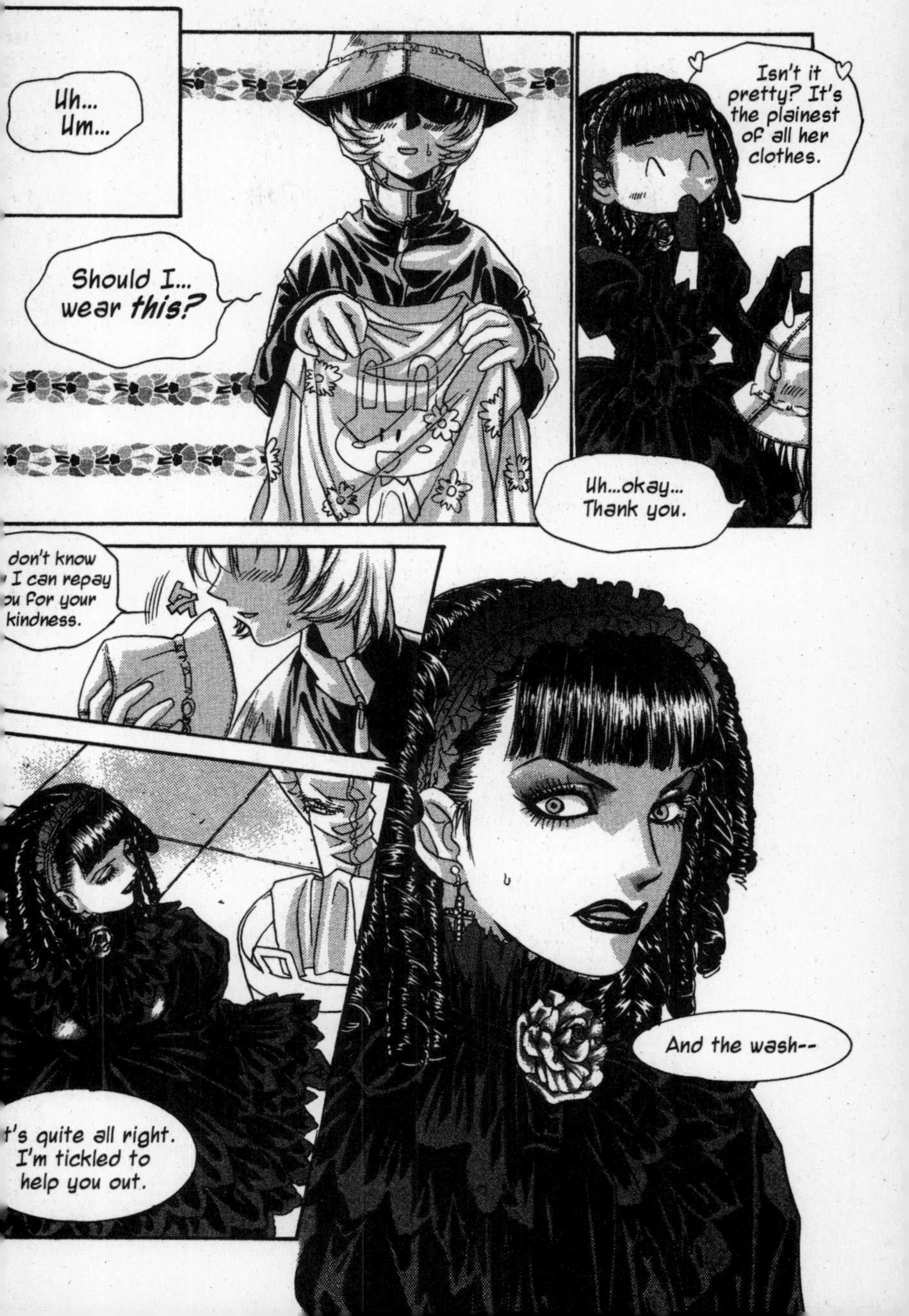
Uh...
Um...
Should I... wear this?
Isn't it pretty? It's the plainest of all her clothes.
Uh...okay... Thank you.
don't know
I can repay
ou for your
kindness.
And the wash--
t's quite all right. I'm tickled to help you out.

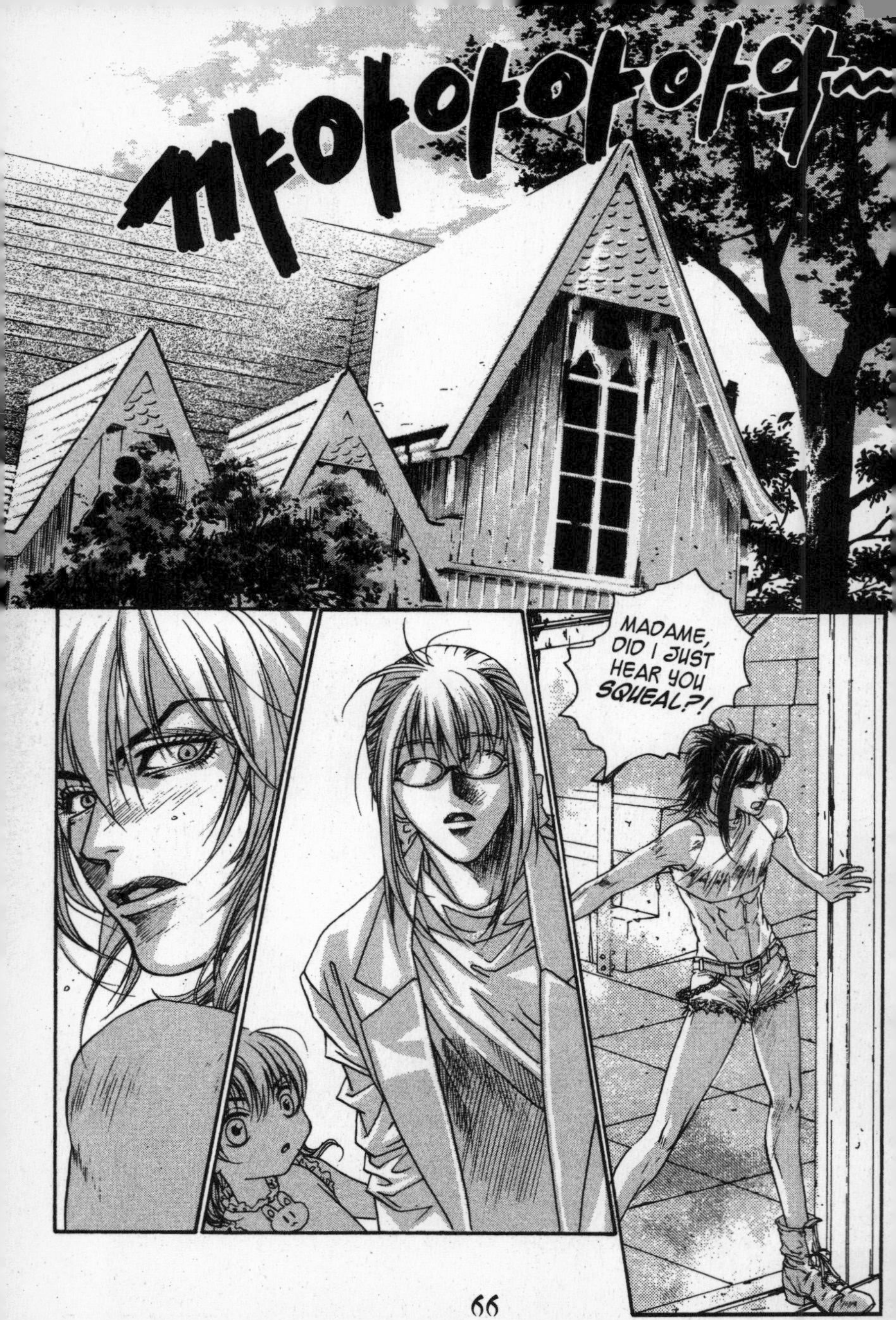
꺄아아아아악~
MADAME, DID I JUST HEAR YOU SQUEAL?!

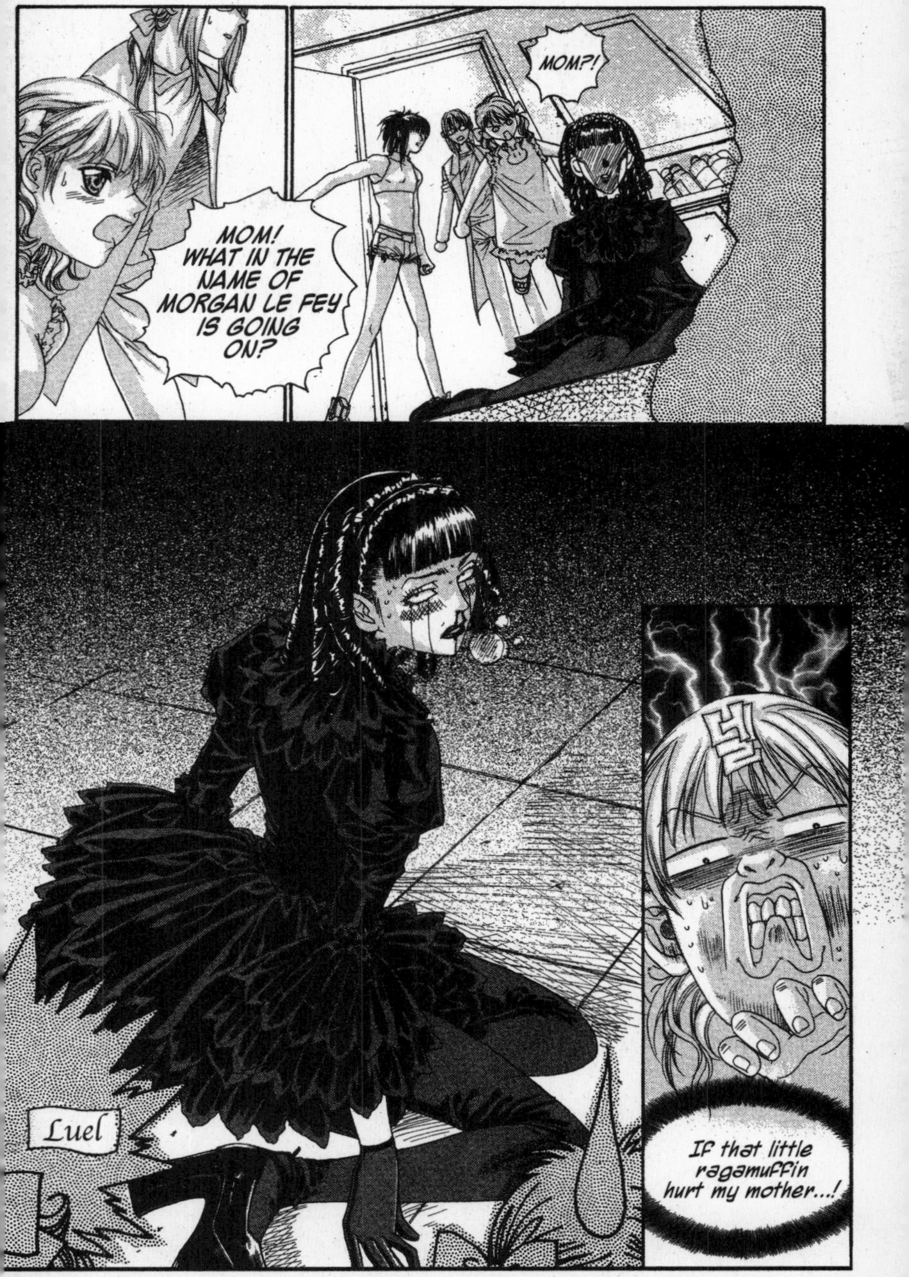
MOM! WHAT IN THE NAME OF MORGAN LE FEY IS GOING ON?
MOM?!
Luel
If that little ragamuffin hurt my mother...!

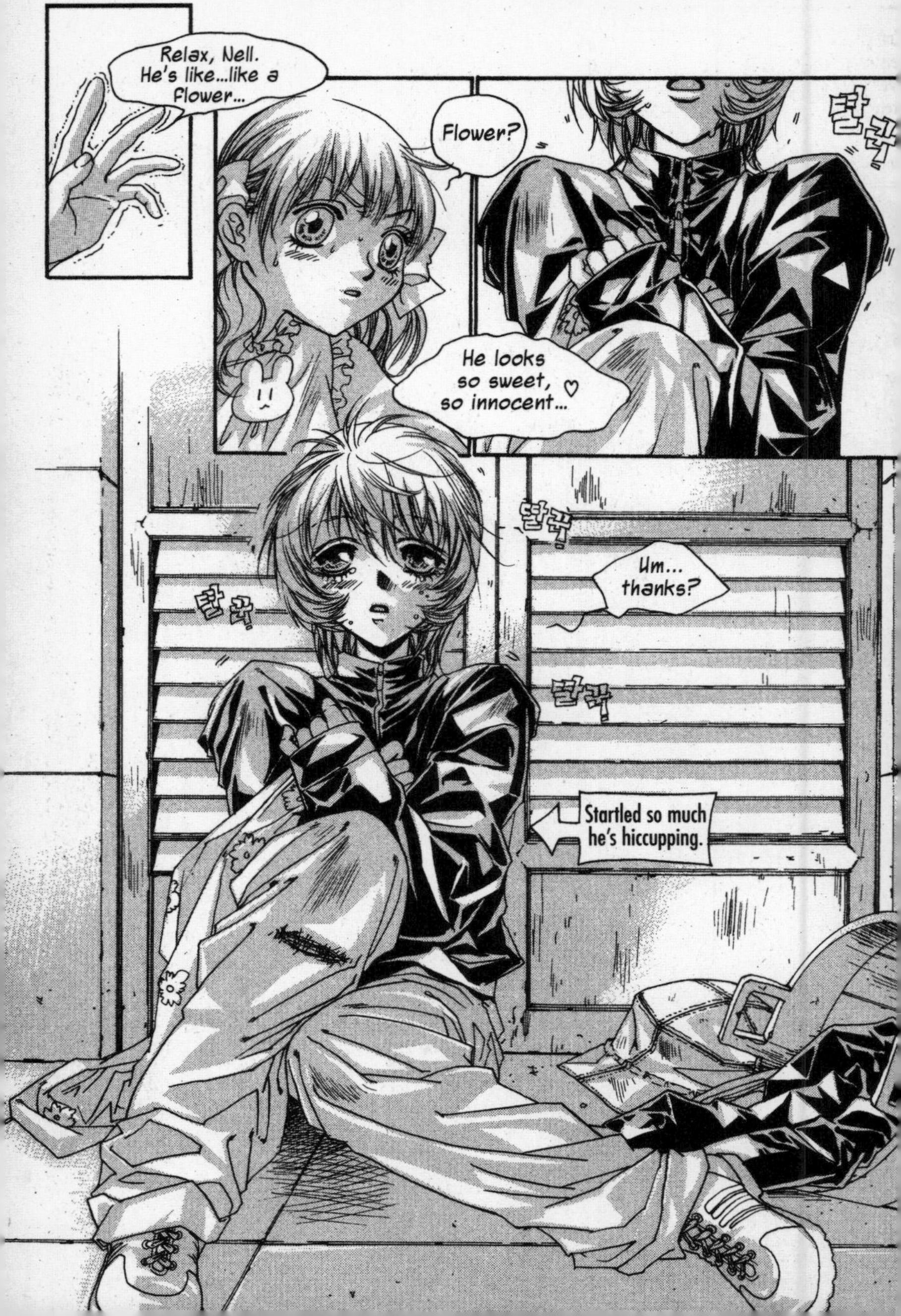
Relax, Nell. He's like...like a flower...
Flower?
He looks so sweet, so innocent... ♡
딸꾹
딸꾹
딸꾹
딸꾹
Um... thanks?
Startled so much he's hiccupping.

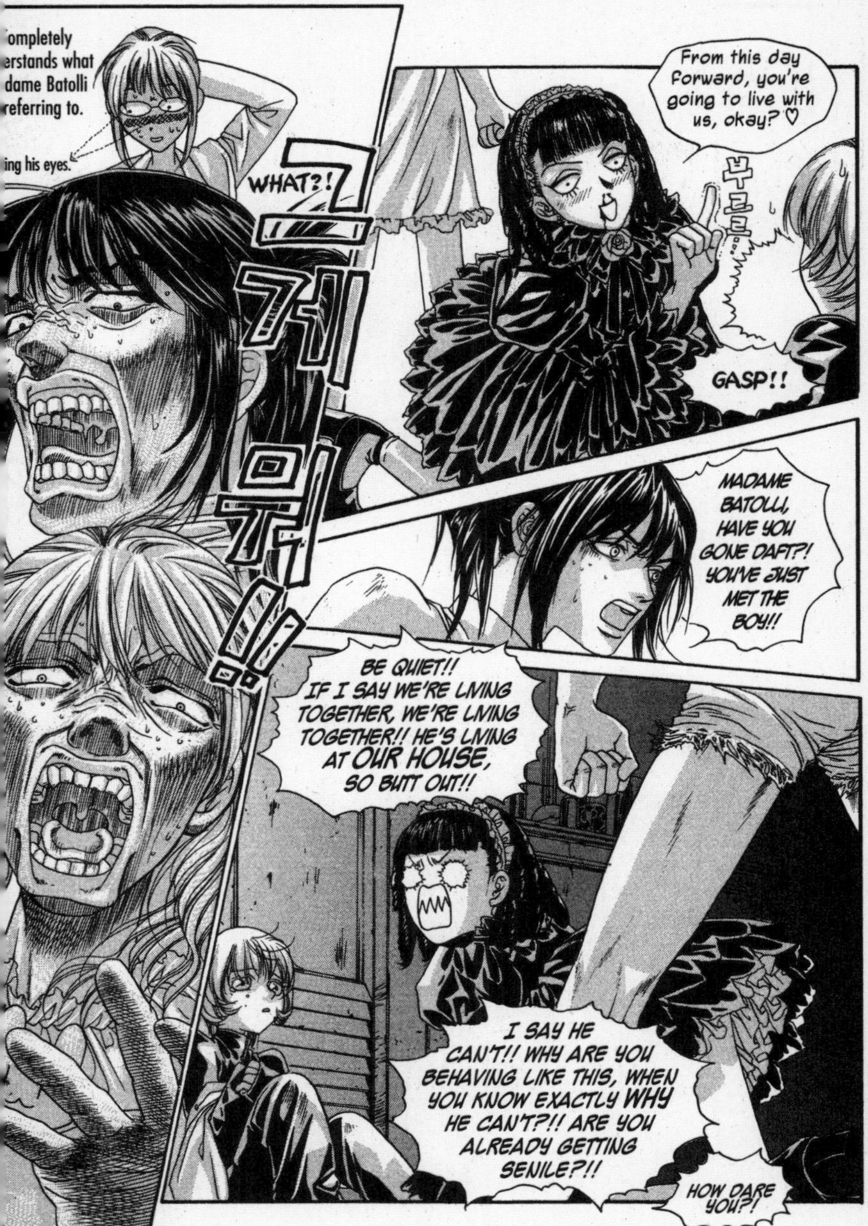
(C)ompletely (und)erstands what (Ma)dame Batolli (is) referring to.
(Roll)ing his eyes.
WHAT?!
그게 뭐!!
From this day forward, you're going to live with us, okay? ♡
부르르..
GASP!!
MADAME BATOLLI, HAVE YOU GONE DAFT?! YOU'VE JUST MET THE BOY!!
BE QUIET!! IF I SAY WE'RE LIVING TOGETHER, WE'RE LIVING TOGETHER!! HE'S LIVING AT OUR HOUSE, SO BUTT OUT!!
I SAY HE CAN'T!! WHY ARE YOU BEHAVING LIKE THIS, WHEN YOU KNOW EXACTLY WHY HE CAN'T?!! ARE YOU ALREADY GETTING SENILE?!!
HOW DARE YOU?!

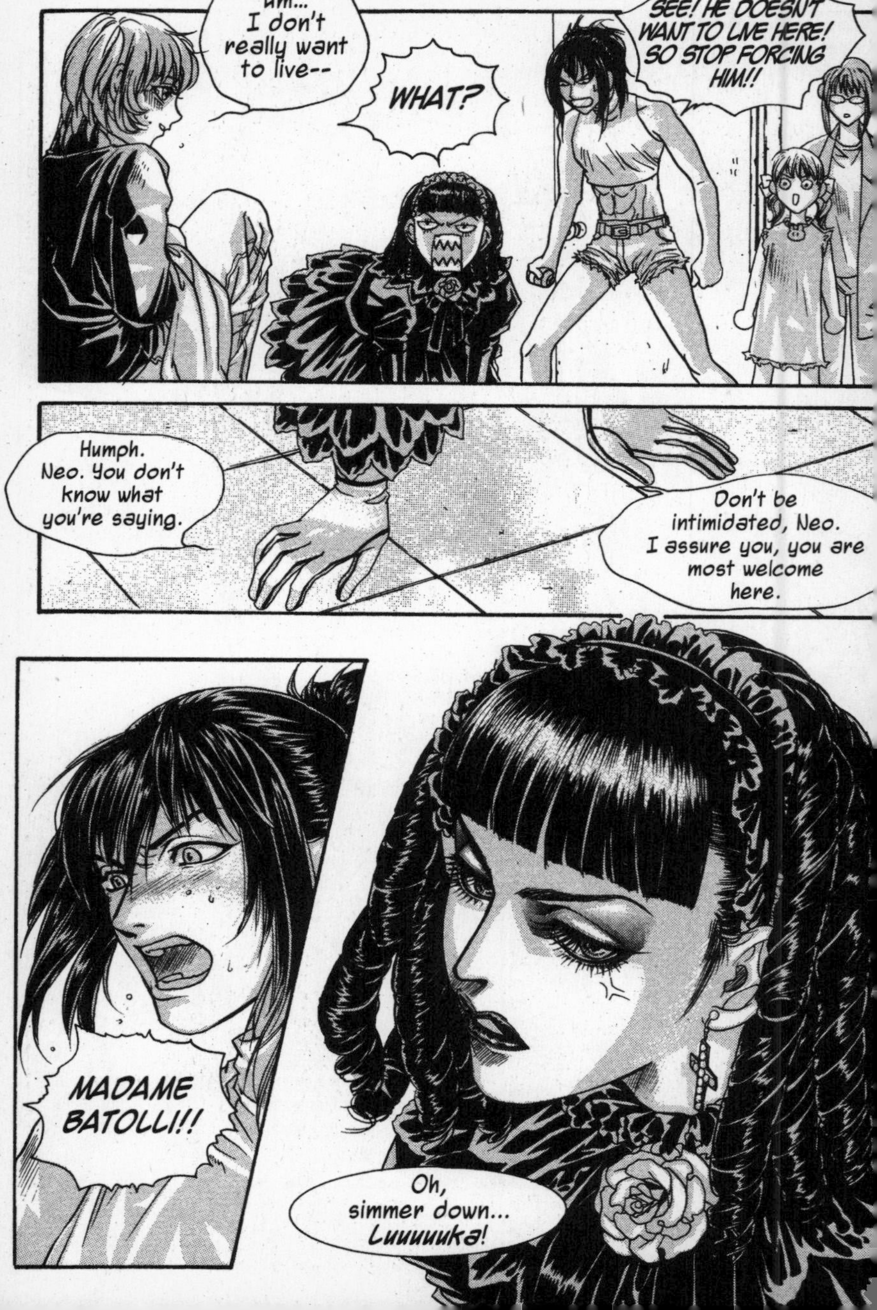
Um... I don't really want to live--
WHAT?
SEE! HE DOESN'T WANT TO LIVE HERE! SO STOP FORCING HIM!!
Humph. Neo. You don't know what you're saying.
Don't be intimidated, Neo. I assure you, you are most welcome here.
MADAME BATOLLI!!
Oh, simmer down... Luuuuuka!

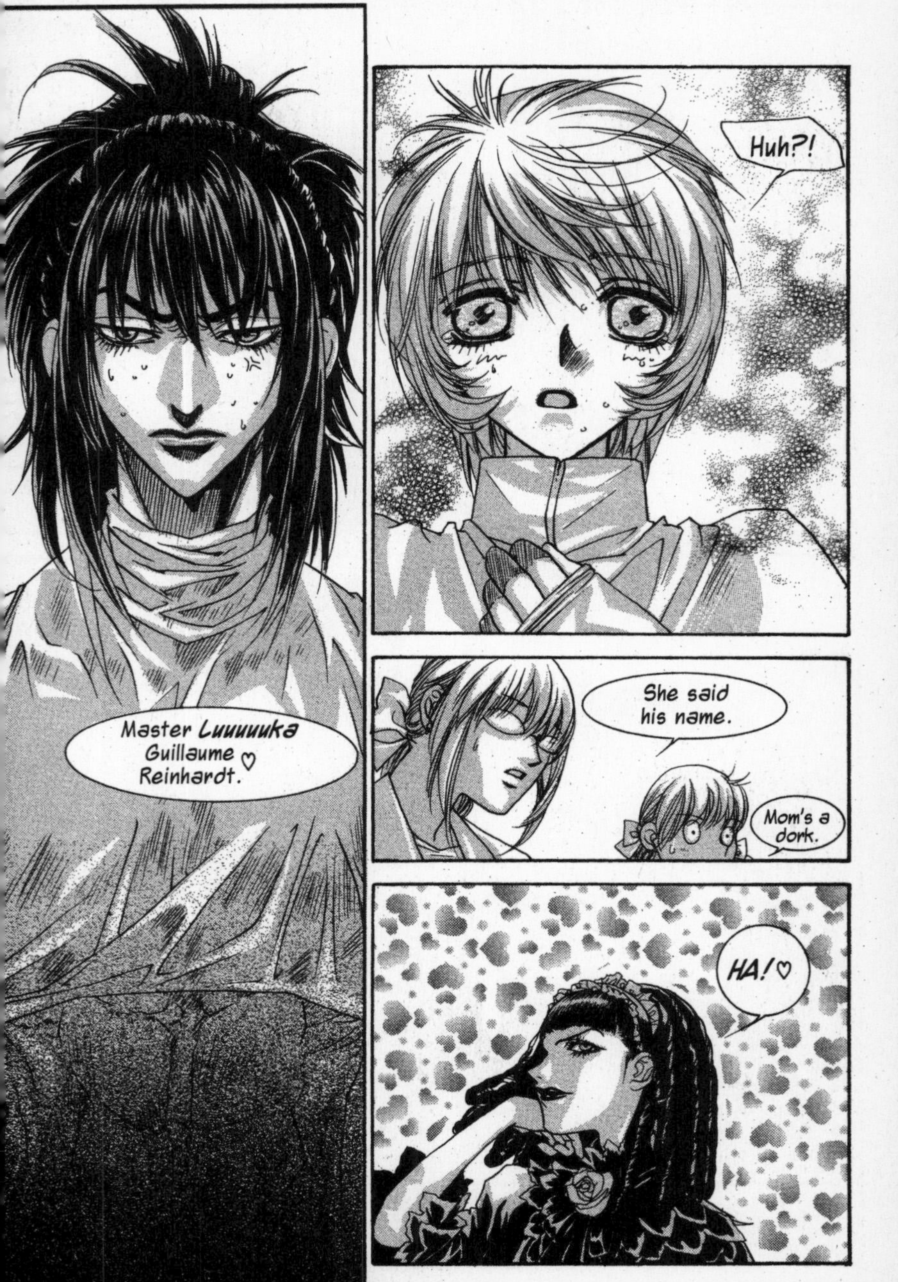
Master Luuuuuka Guillaume Reinhardt. ♡
Huh?!
She said his name.
Mom's a dork.
HA! ♡

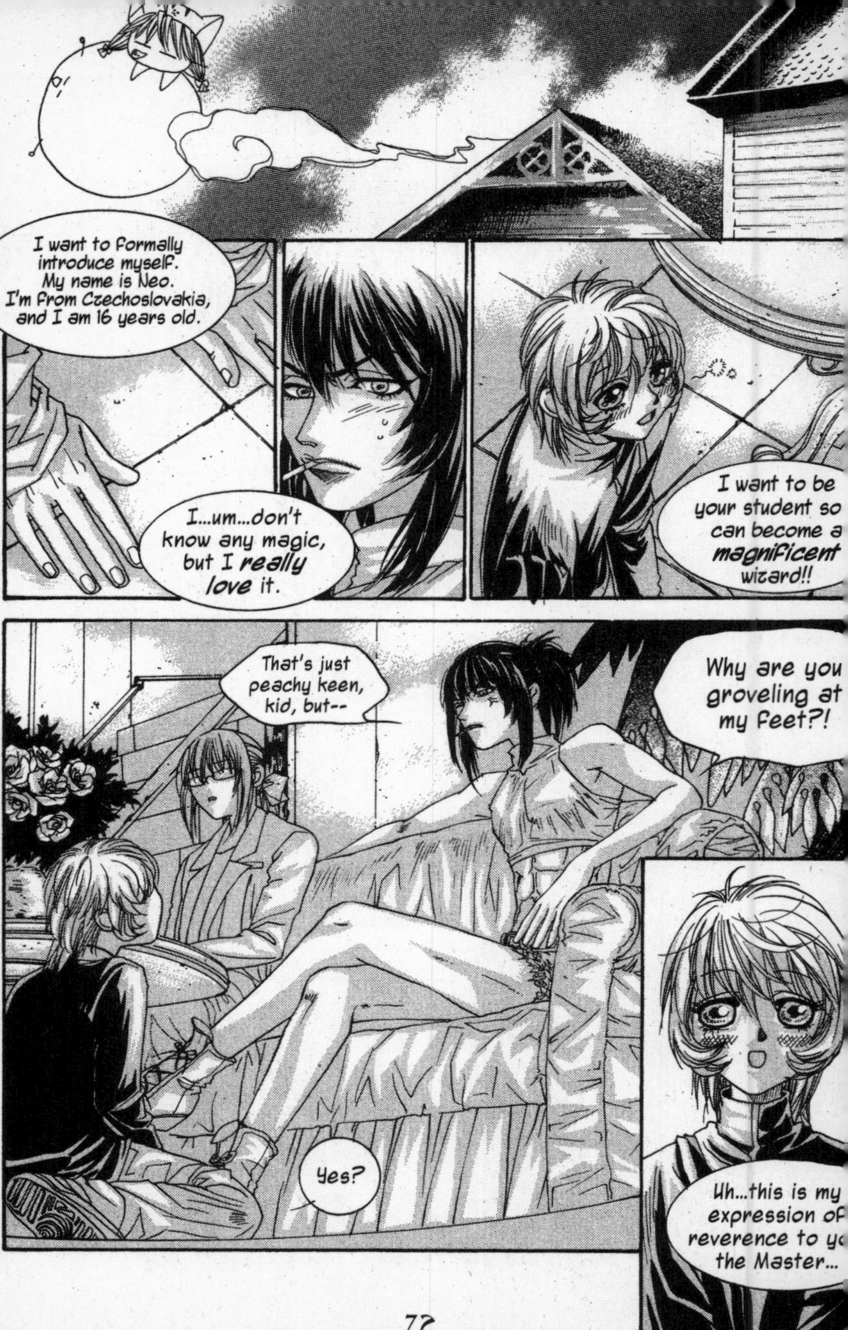
I want to formally introduce myself. My name is Neo. I'm from Czechoslovakia, and I am 16 years old.
I...um...don't know any magic, but I *really love* it.
I want to be your student so can become a *magnificent* wizard!!
That's just peachy keen, kid, but--
Why are you groveling at my feet?!
Yes?
Uh...this is my expression of reverence to y the Master...

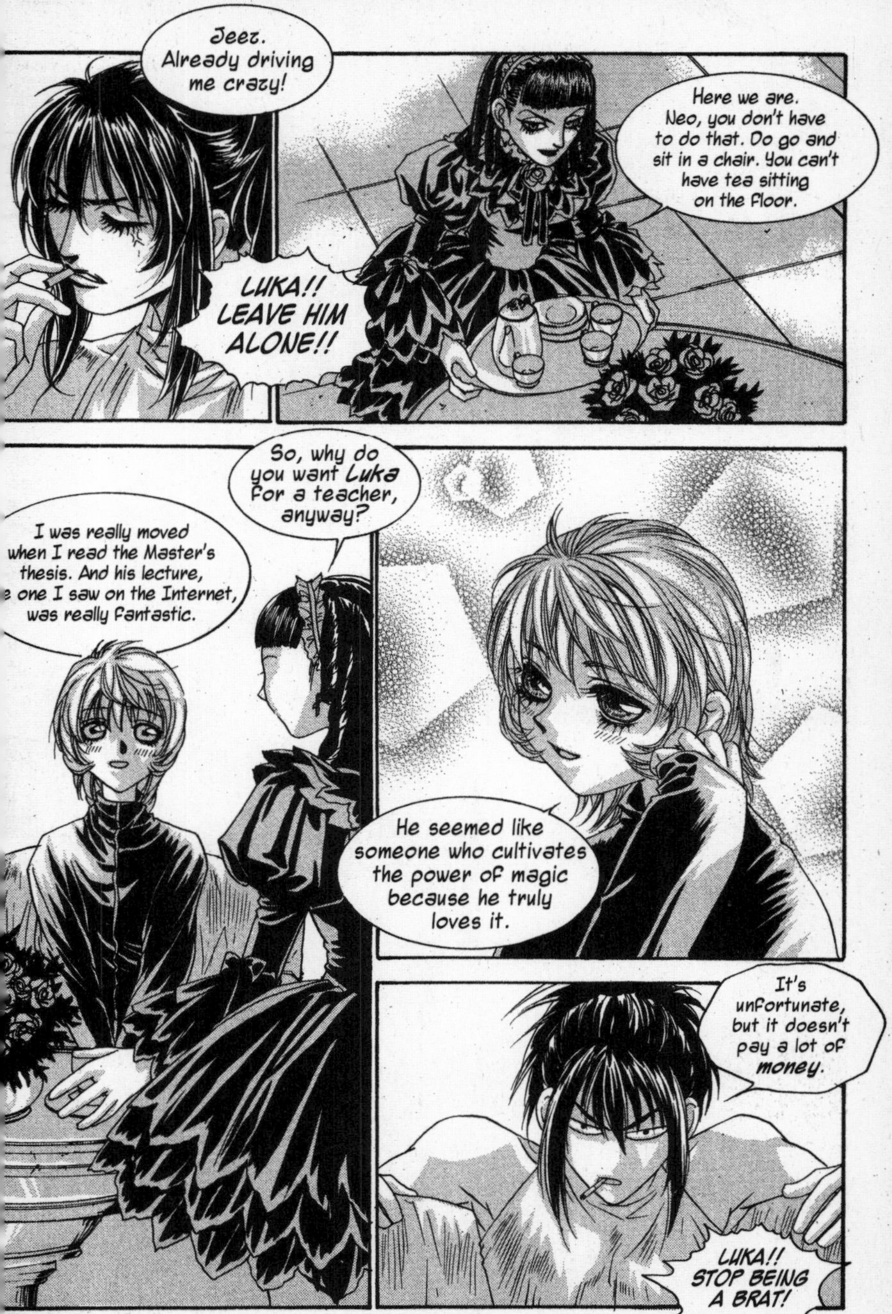
Jeez. Already driving me crazy!
LUKA!! LEAVE HIM ALONE!!
Here we are. Neo, you don't have to do that. Do go and sit in a chair. You can't have tea sitting on the floor.
So, why do you want *Luka* for a teacher, anyway?
I was really moved when I read the Master's thesis. And his lecture, e one I saw on the Internet, was really fantastic.
He seemed like someone who cultivates the power of magic because he truly loves it.
It's unfortunate, but it doesn't pay a lot of ***money***.
LUKA!! STOP BEING A BRAT!

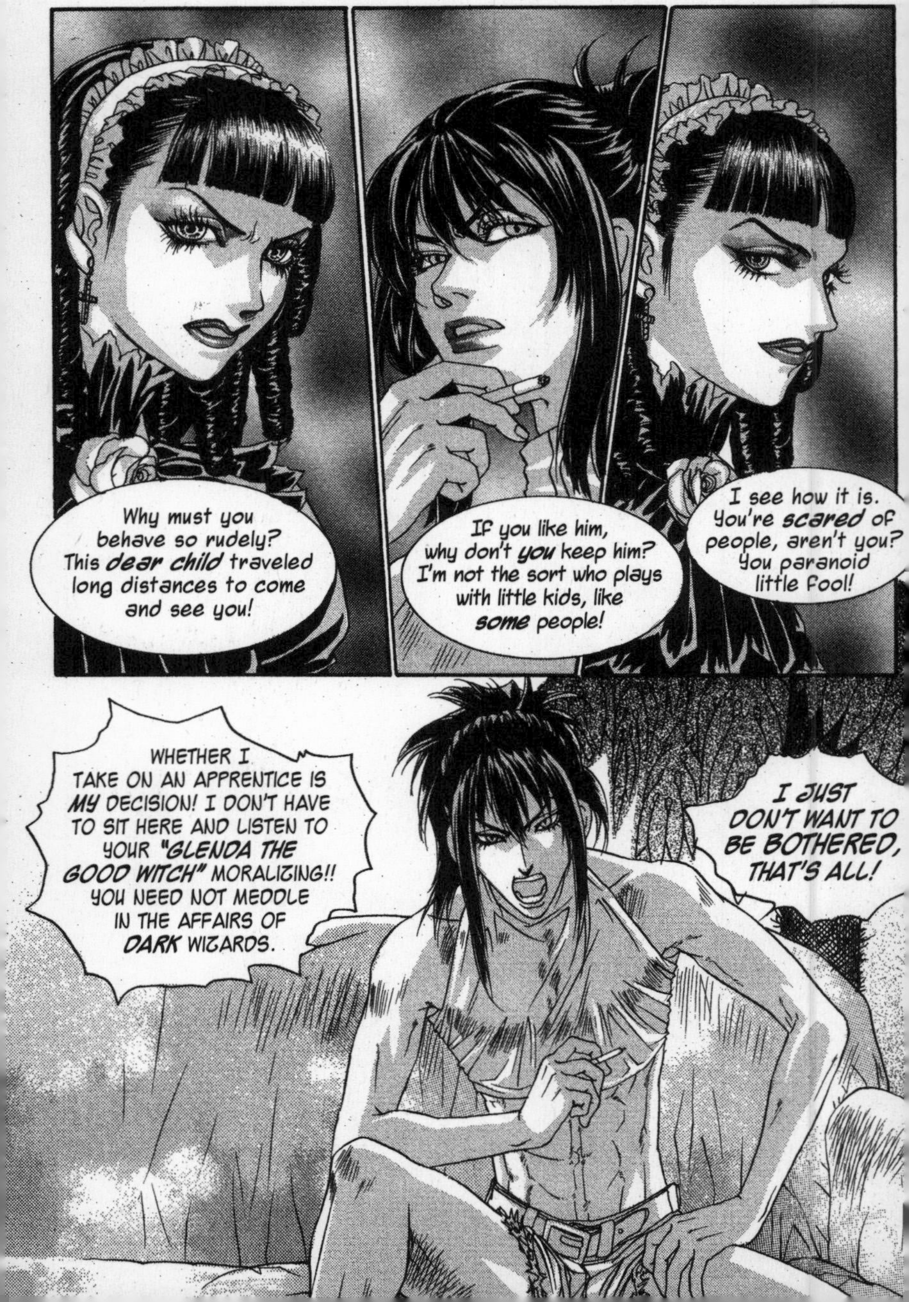

Why must you behave so rudely? This *dear child* traveled long distances to come and see you!
If you like him, why don't *you* keep him? I'm not the sort who plays with little kids, like *some* people!
I see how it is. You're *scared* of people, aren't you? You paranoid little fool!
WHETHER I TAKE ON AN APPRENTICE IS *MY* DECISION! I DON'T HAVE TO SIT HERE AND LISTEN TO YOUR *"GLENDA THE GOOD WITCH"* MORALIZING!! YOU NEED NOT MEDDLE IN THE AFFAIRS OF *DARK* WIZARDS.
I JUST DON'T WANT TO BE BOTHERED, THAT'S ALL!

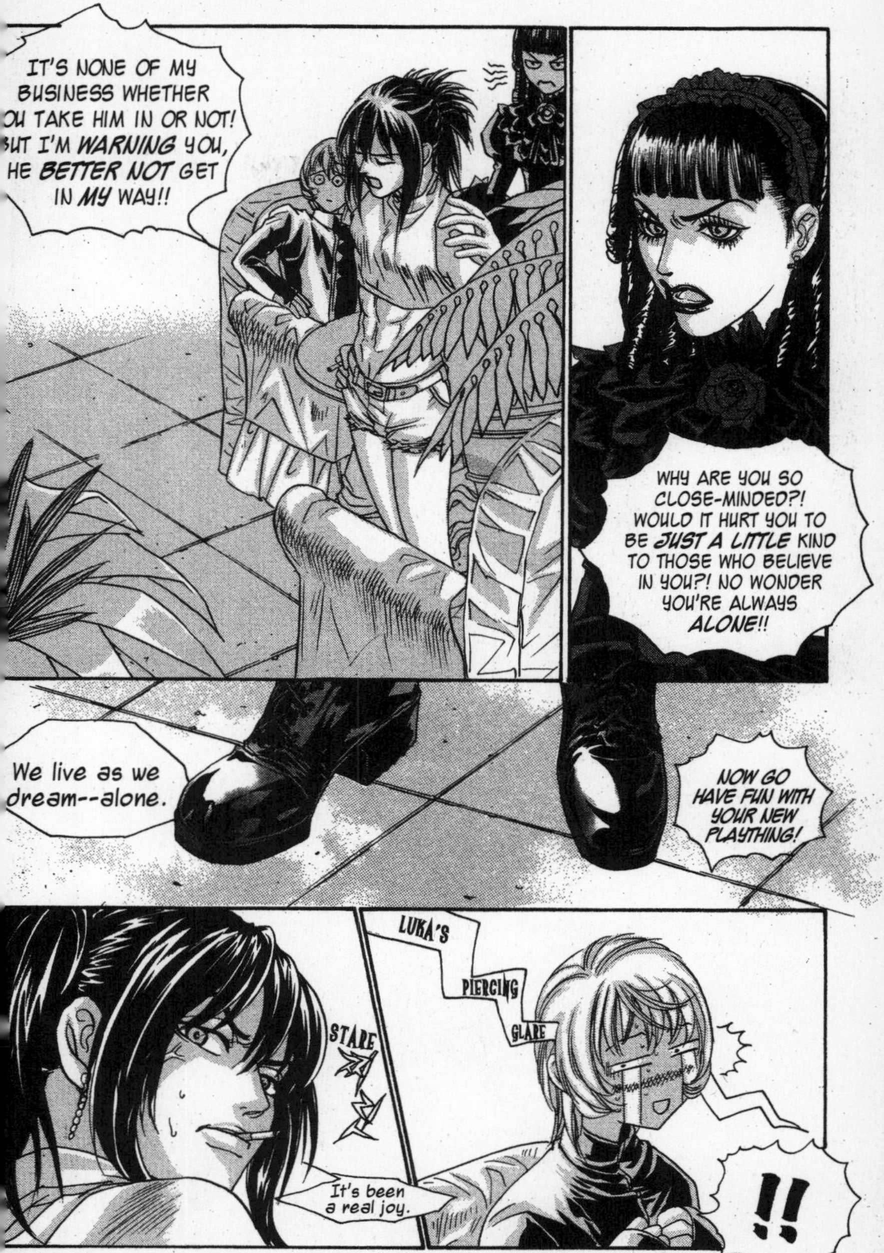
IT'S NONE OF MY BUSINESS WHETHER OU TAKE HIM IN OR NOT! UT I'M WARNING YOU, HE BETTER NOT GET IN MY WAY!!
WHY ARE YOU SO CLOSE-MINDED?! WOULD IT HURT YOU TO BE JUST A LITTLE KIND TO THOSE WHO BELIEVE IN YOU?! NO WONDER YOU'RE ALWAYS ALONE!!
We live as we dream--alone.
NOW GO HAVE FUN WITH YOUR NEW PLAYTHING!
STARE
It's been a real joy.
LUKA'S
PIERCING
GLARE
!!

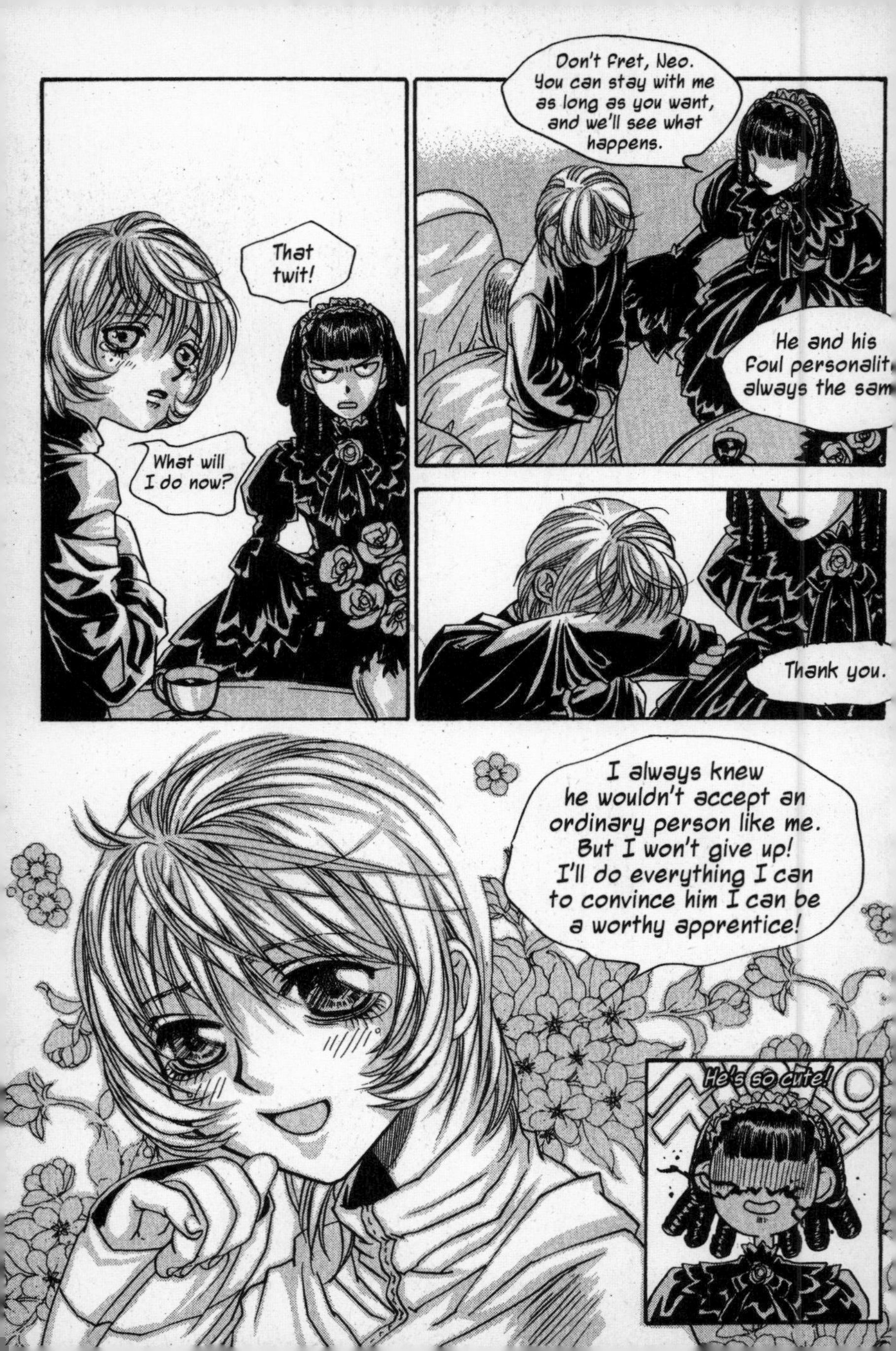
That twit!
What will I do now?
Don't fret, Neo. You can stay with me as long as you want, and we'll see what happens.
He and his foul personalit always the sam
Thank you.
I always knew he wouldn't accept an ordinary person like me. But I won't give up! I'll do everything I can to convince him I can be a worthy apprentice!
He's so cute!

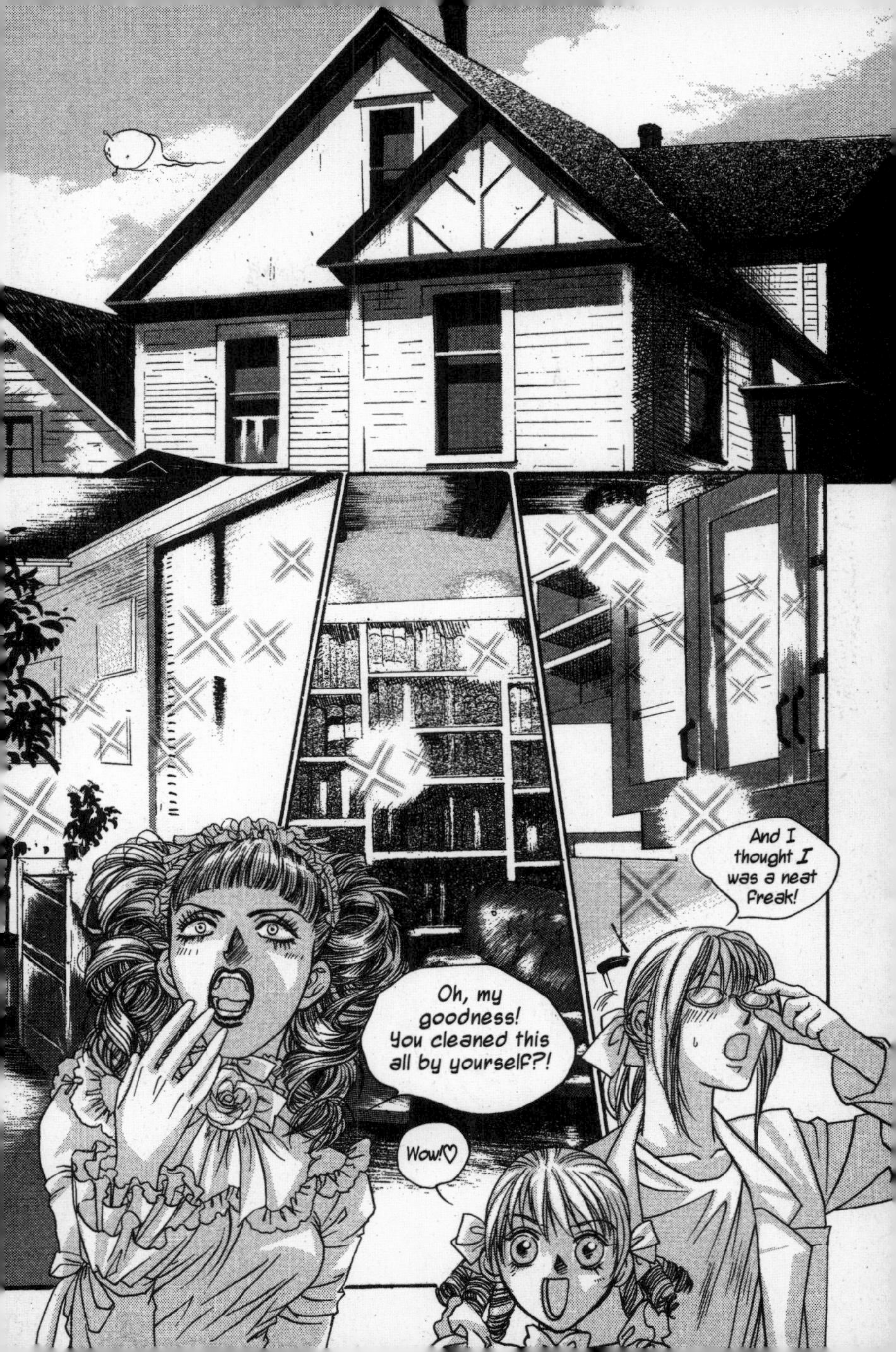
Oh, my goodness! You cleaned this all by yourself?!
Wow!♡
And I thought *I* was a neat freak!

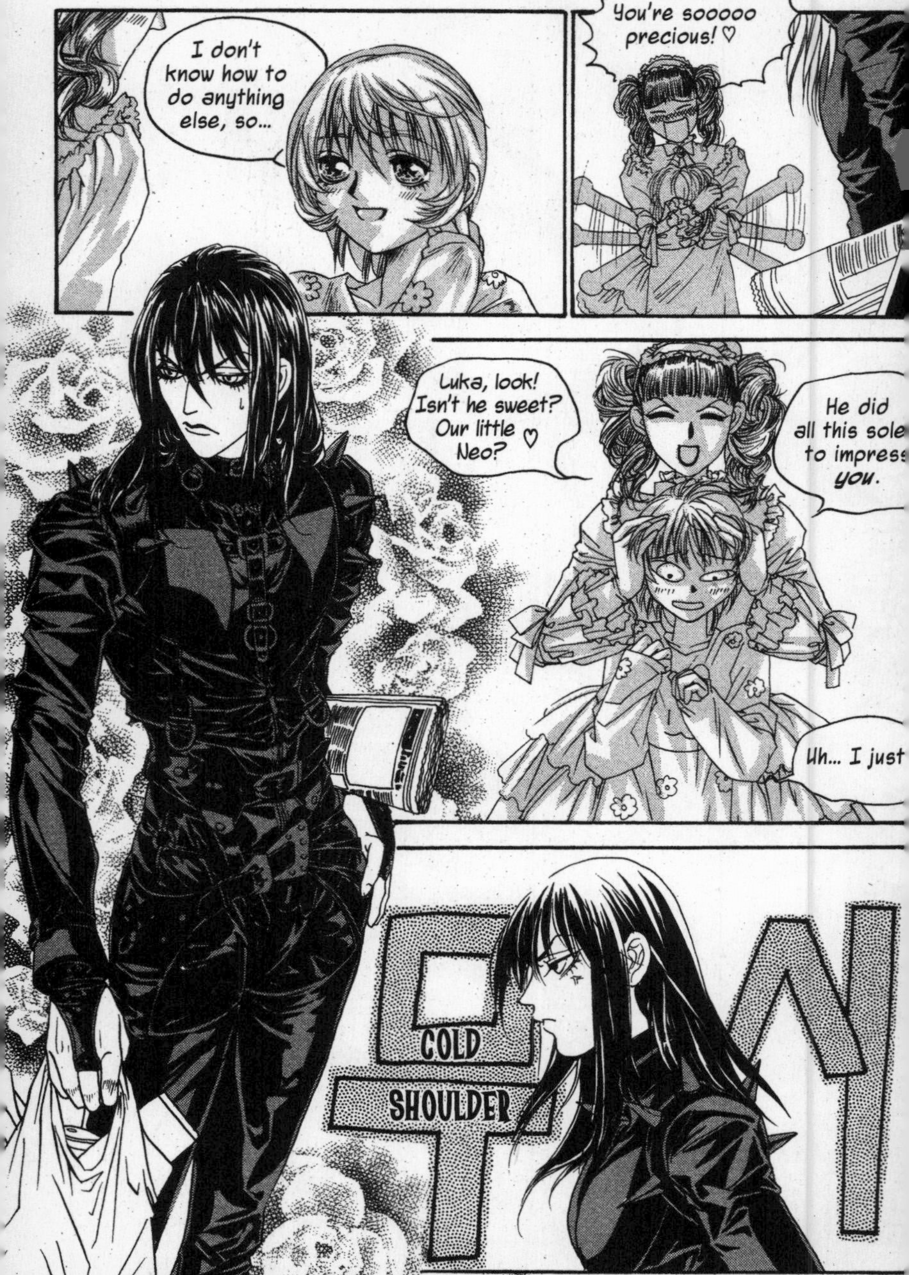

I don't know how to do anything else, so...
You're sooooo precious! ♡
Luka, look! Isn't he sweet? Our little Neo? ♡
He did all this sole to impress you.
Uh... I just
COLD SHOULDER

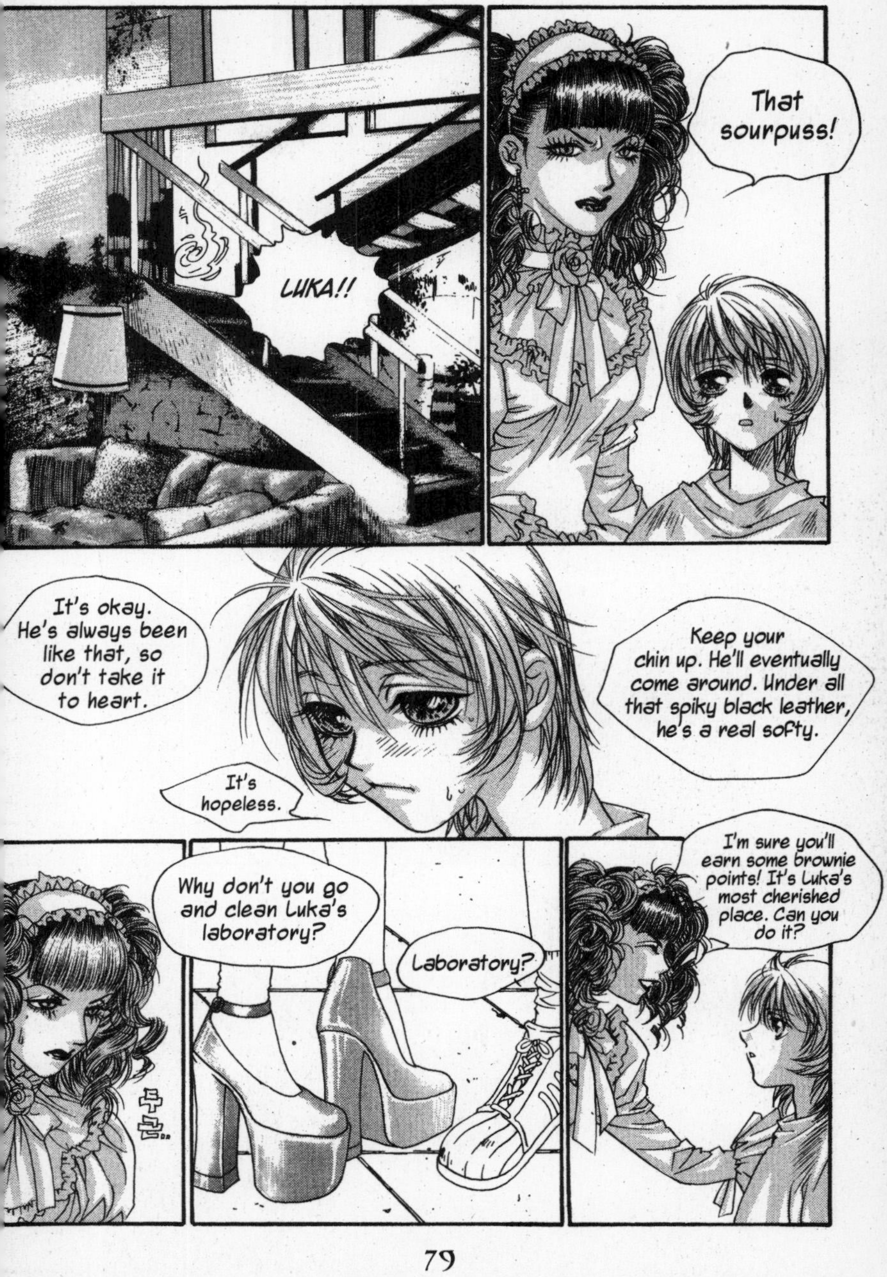
LUKA!!
That sourpuss!
It's okay. He's always been like that, so don't take it to heart.
It's hopeless.
Keep your chin up. He'll eventually come around. Under all that spiky black leather, he's a real softy.
Why don't you go and clean Luka's laboratory?
Laboratory?
I'm sure you'll earn some brownie points! It's Luka's most cherished place. Can you do it?

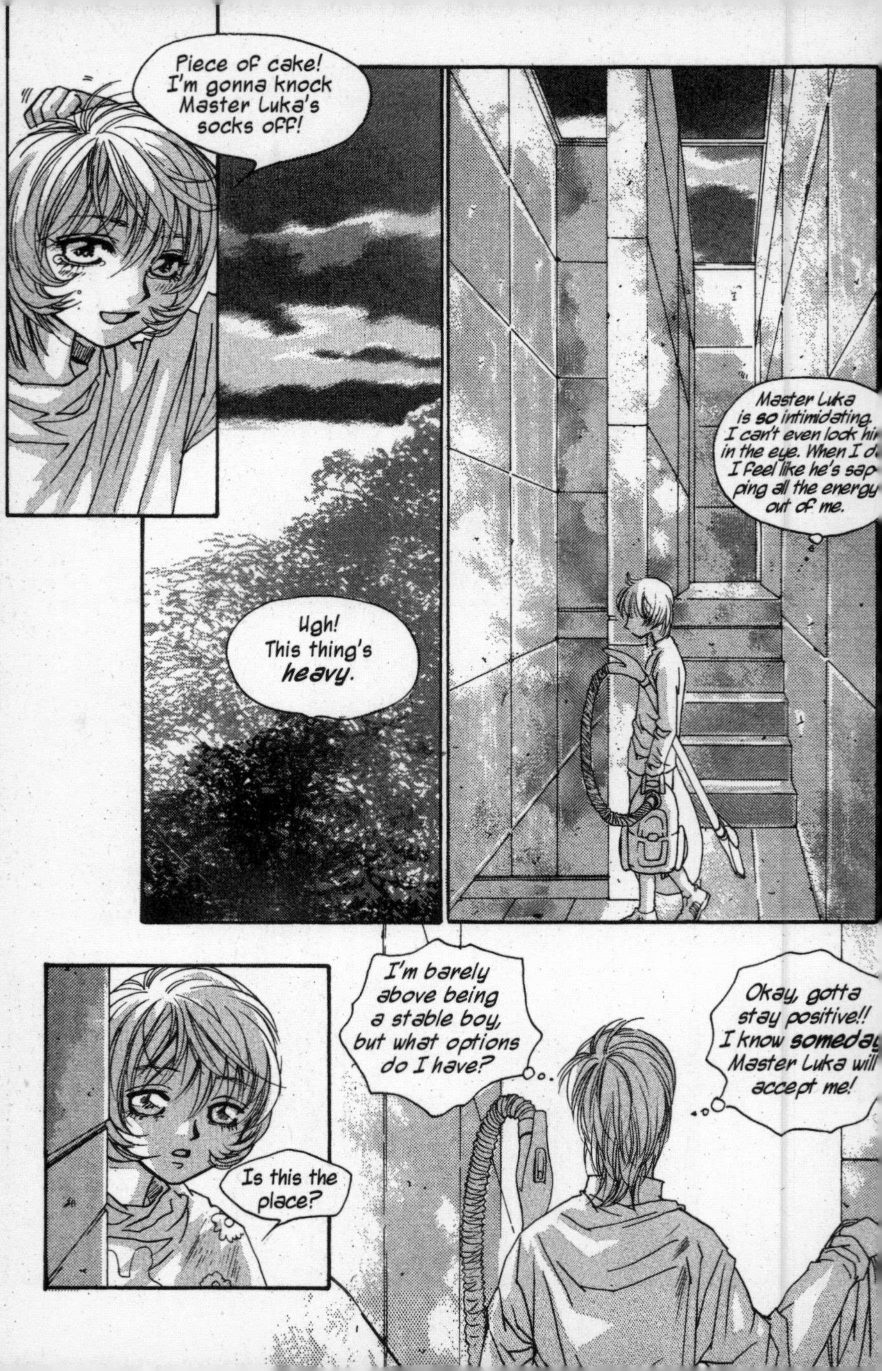

Piece of cake! I'm gonna knock Master Luka's socks off!
Ugh! This thing's *heavy*.
Master Luka is **so** intimidating. I can't even look hi in the eye. When I d I feel like he's sap ping all the energy out of me.
Is this the place?
I'm barely above being a stable boy, but what options do I have?
Okay, gotta stay positive!! I know **someda** Master Luka will accept me!

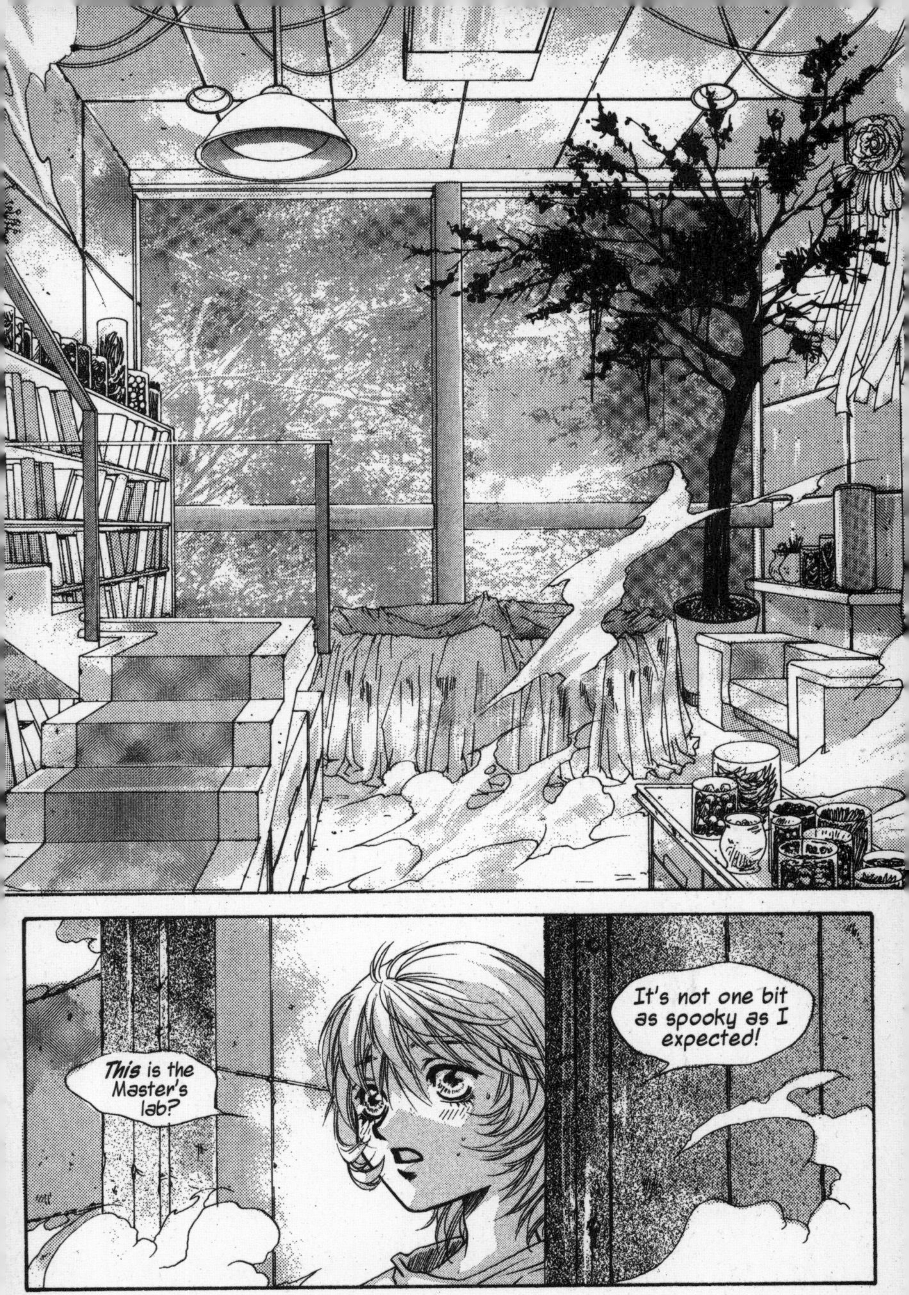
This is the Master's lab?
It's not one bit as spooky as I expected!

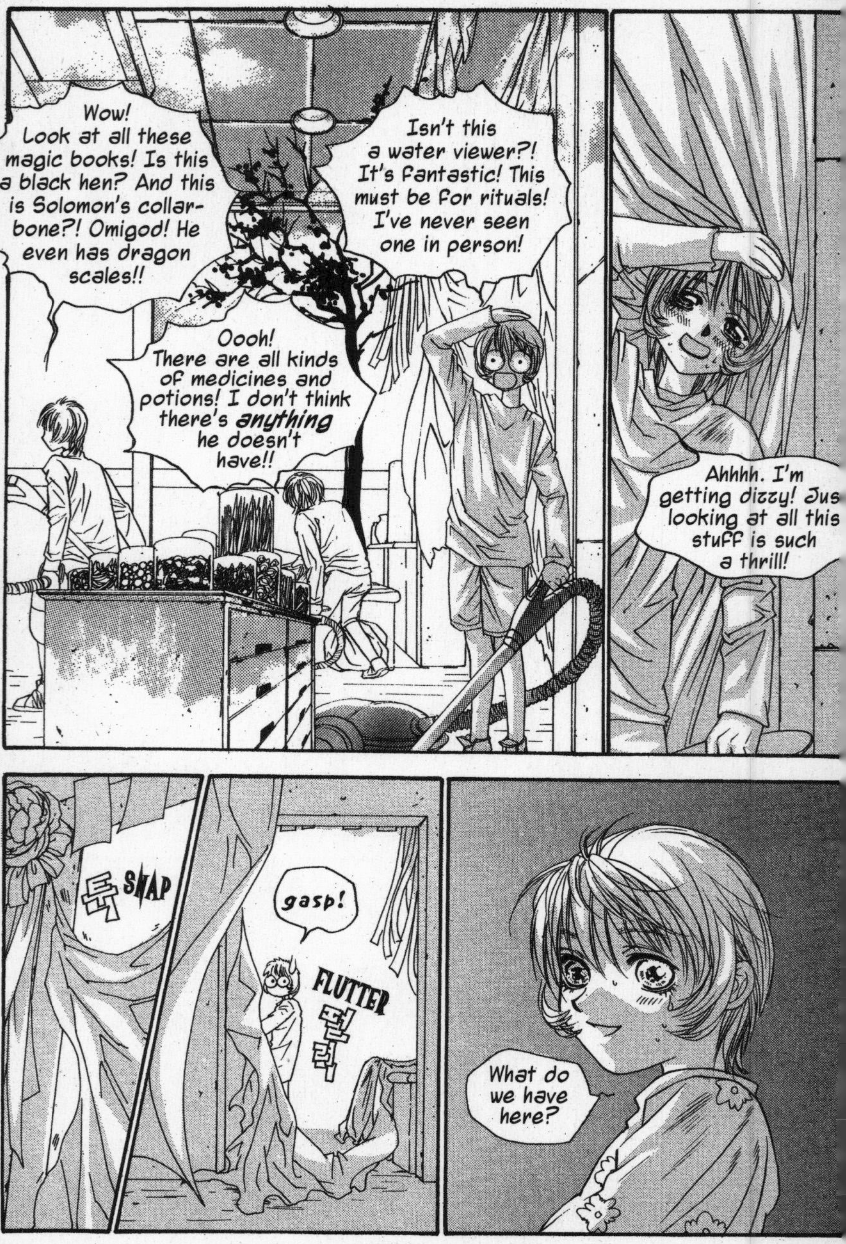
Wow! Look at all these magic books! Is this a black hen? And this is Solomon's collar-bone?! Omigod! He even has dragon scales!!
Isn't this a water viewer?! It's fantastic! This must be for rituals! I've never seen one in person!
Oooh! There are all kinds of medicines and potions! I don't think there's ***anything*** he doesn't have!!
Ahhhh. I'm getting dizzy! Jus looking at all this stuff is such a thrill!
툭 SNAP
gasp!
FLUTTER 펄럭
What do we have here?

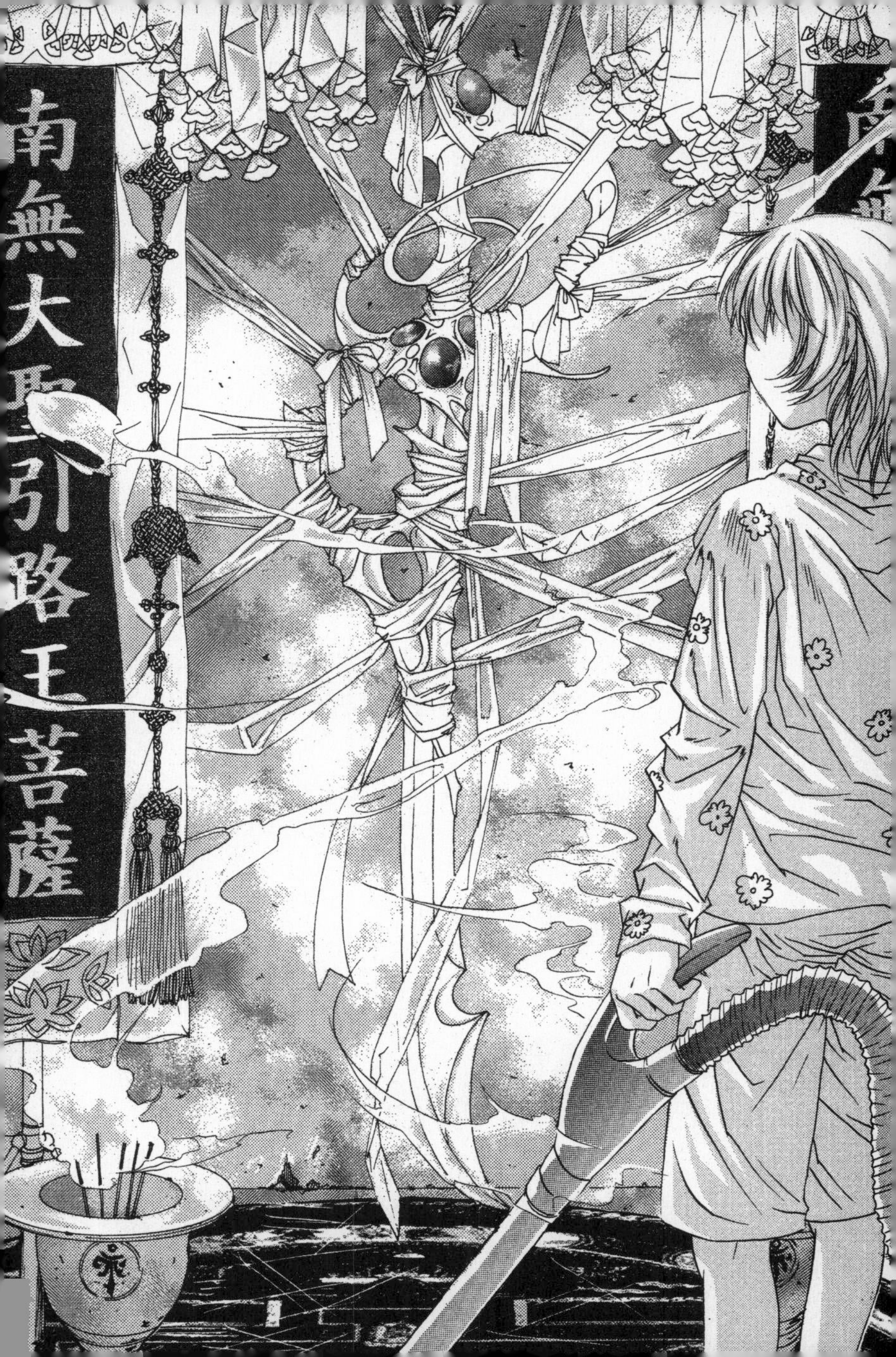
南無大聖引路王菩薩

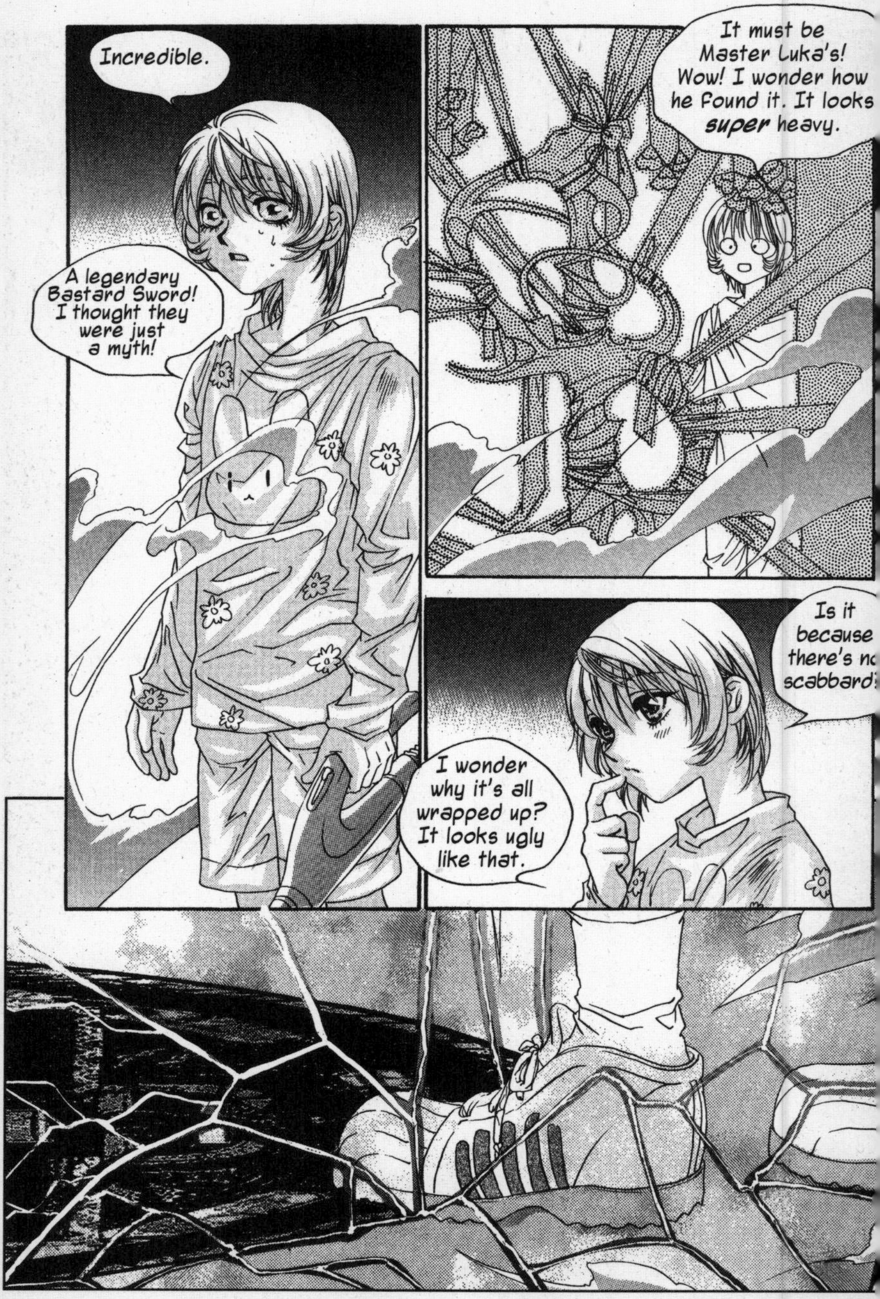

Incredible.
A legendary Bastard Sword! I thought they were just a myth!
It must be Master Luka's! Wow! I wonder how he found it. It looks **super** heavy.
I wonder why it's all wrapped up? It looks ugly like that.
Is it because there's n scabbard

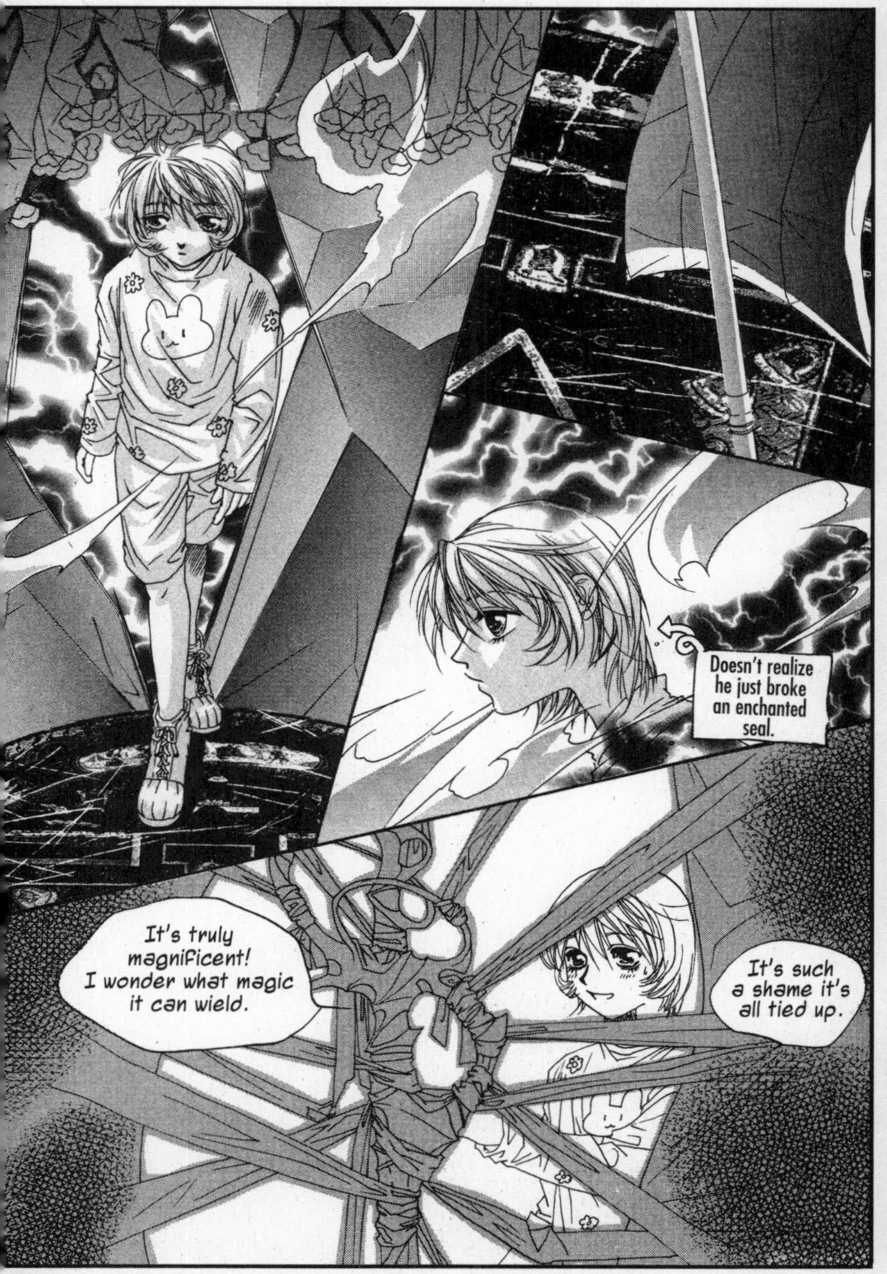
Doesn't realize he just broke an enchanted seal.
It's truly magnificent! I wonder what magic it can wield.
It's such a shame it's all tied up.

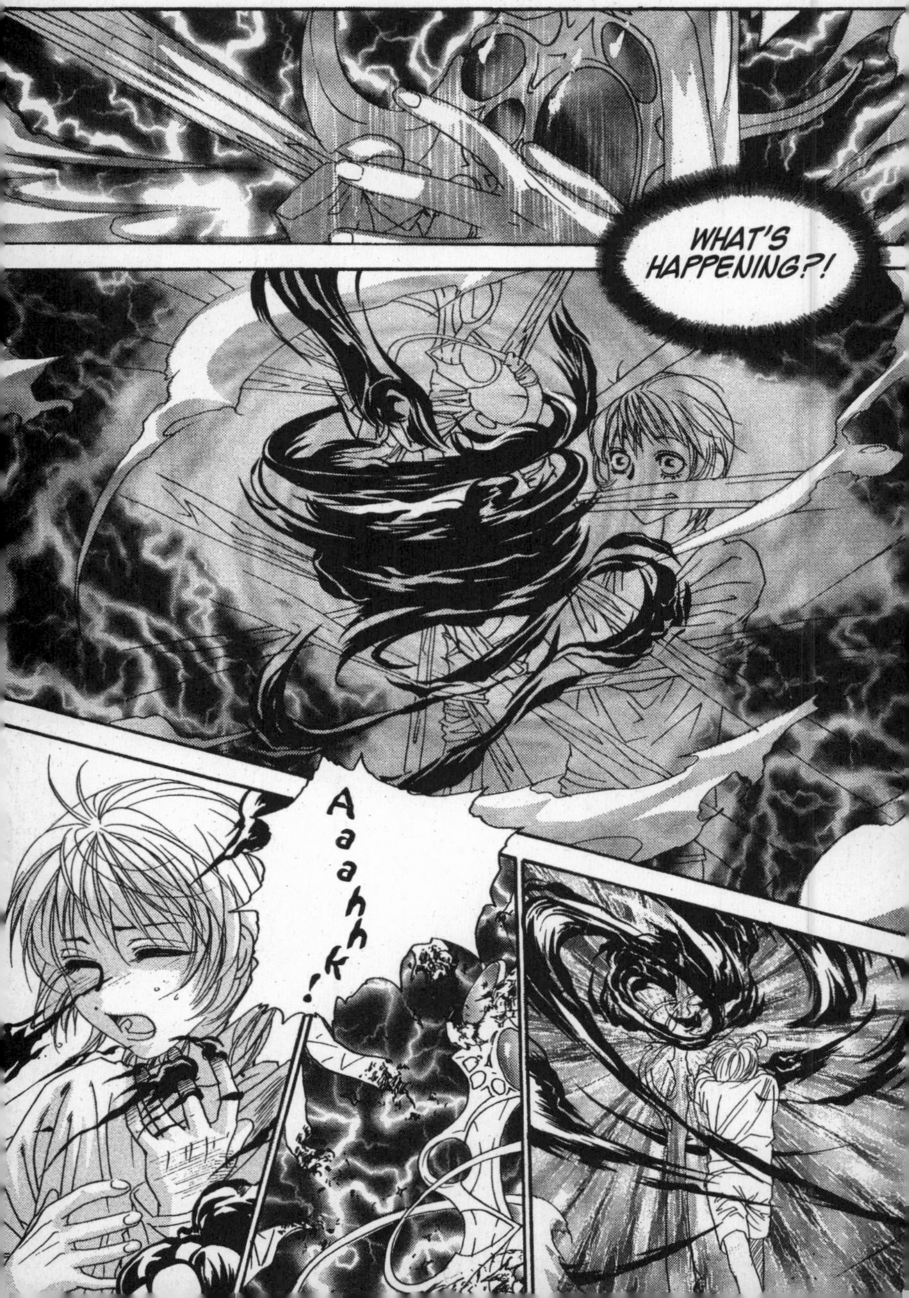

WHAT'S HAPPENING?!
Aaahhhk!

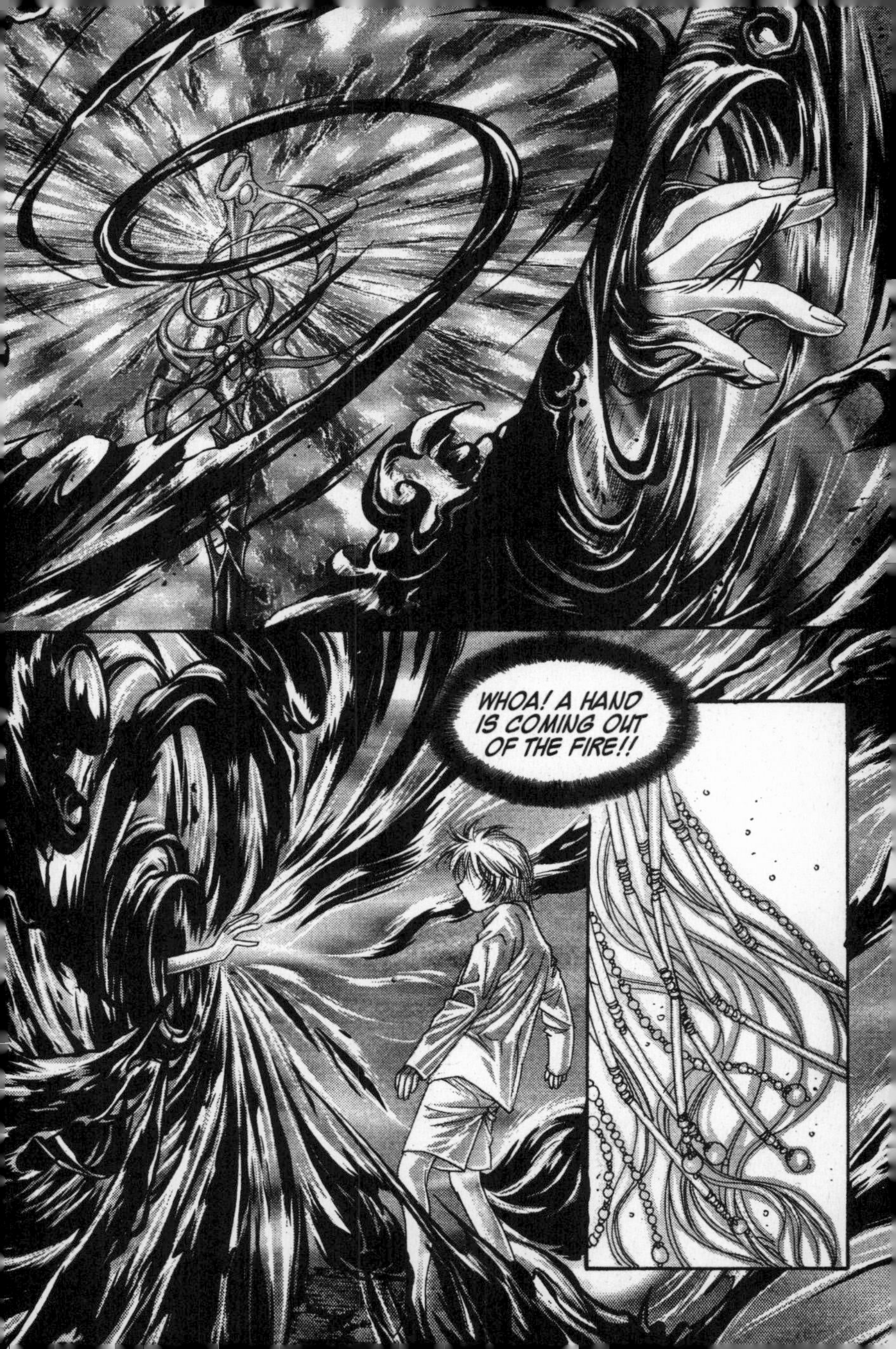
WHOA! A HAND IS COMING OUT OF THE FIRE!!

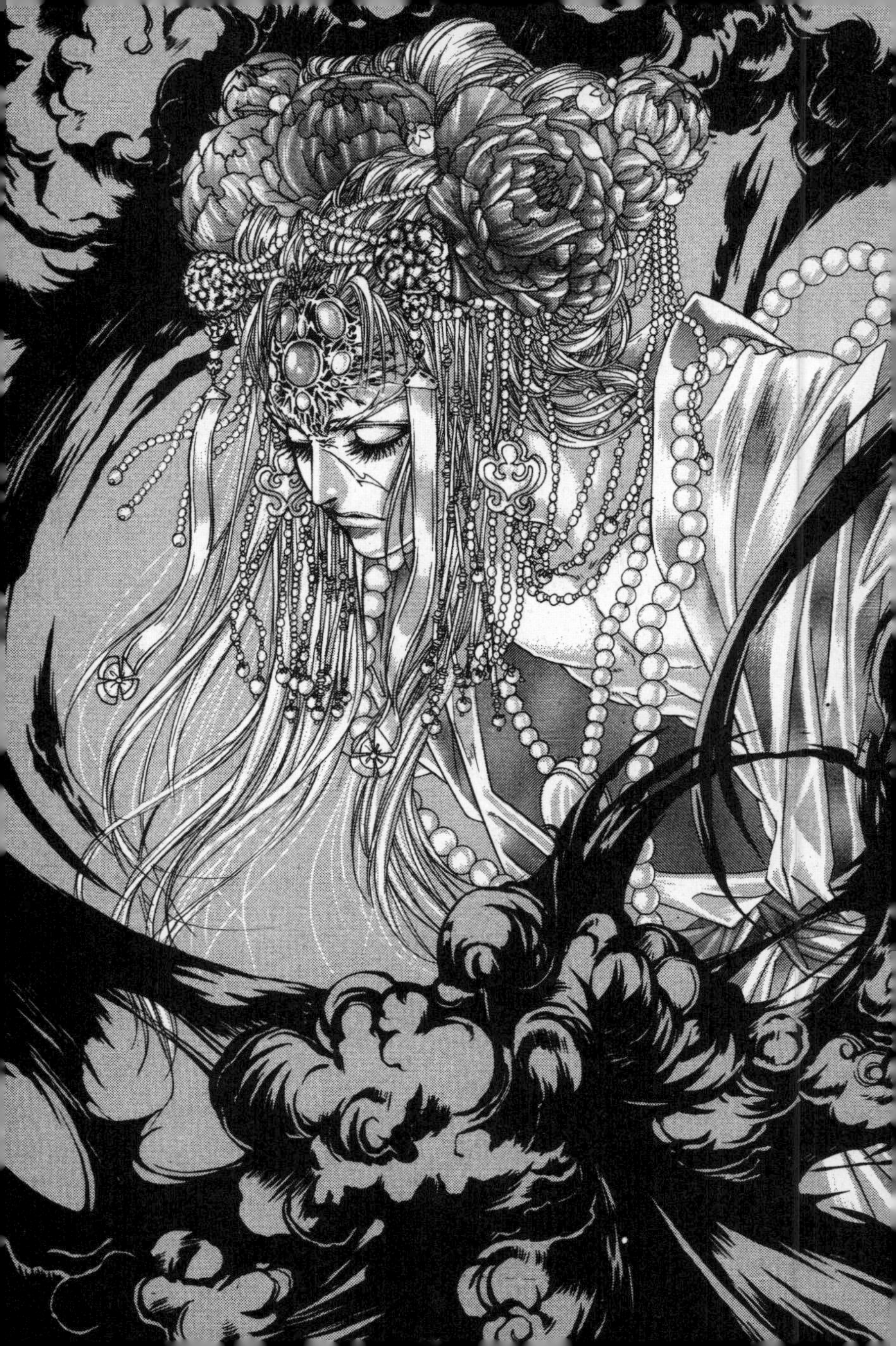

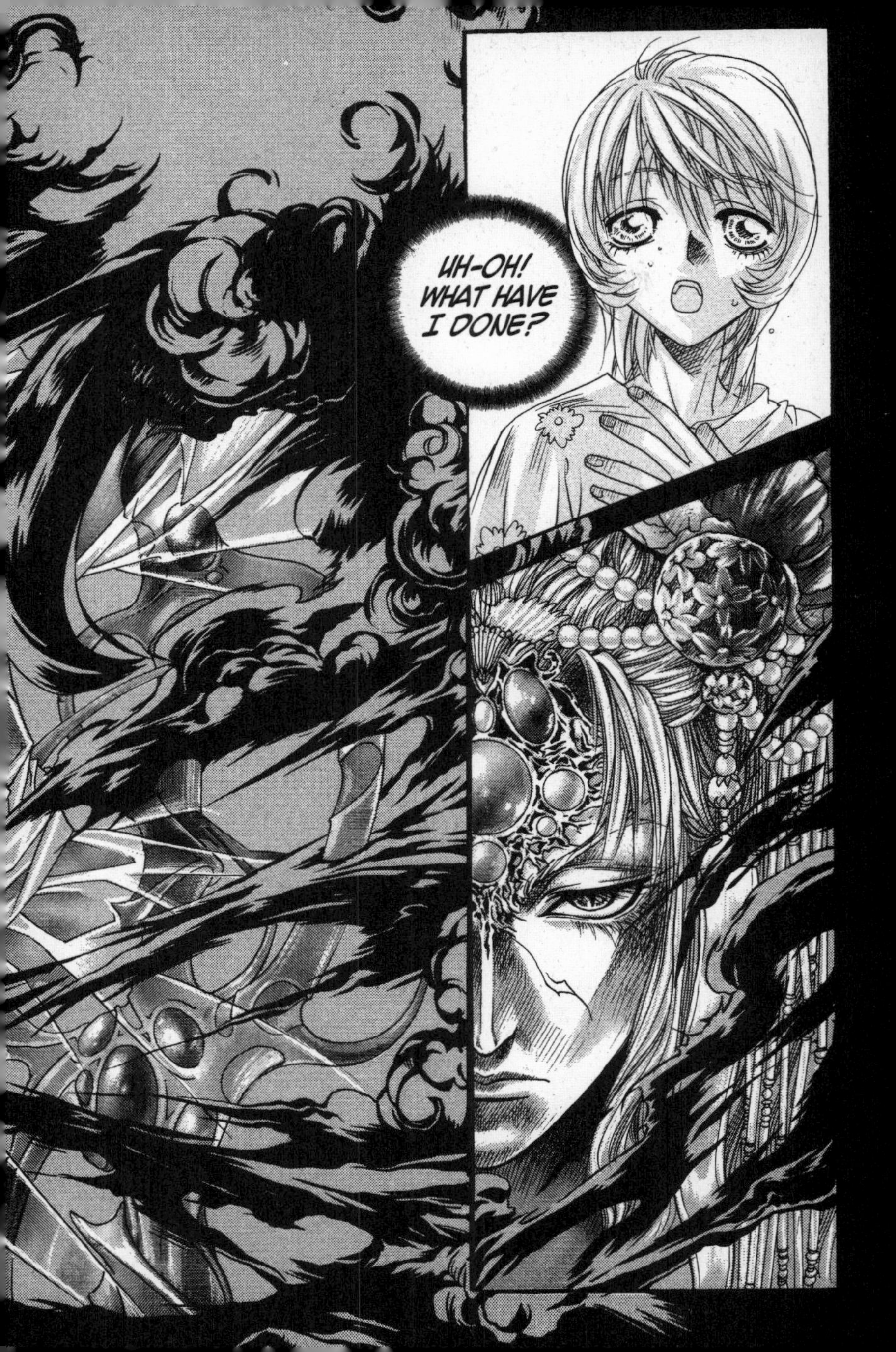
UH-OH! WHAT HAVE I DONE?

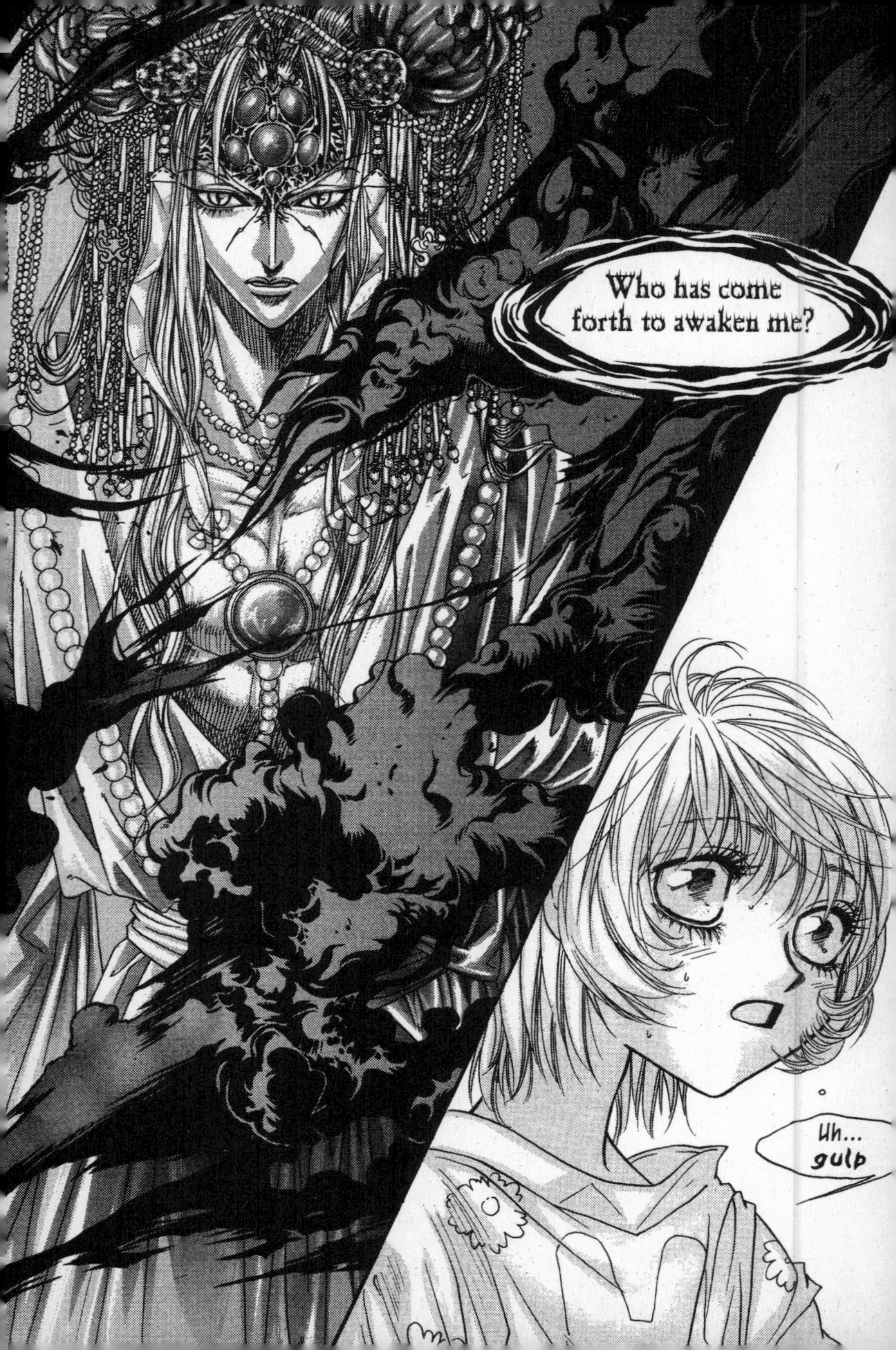
Who has come forth to awaken me?
Uh... gulp

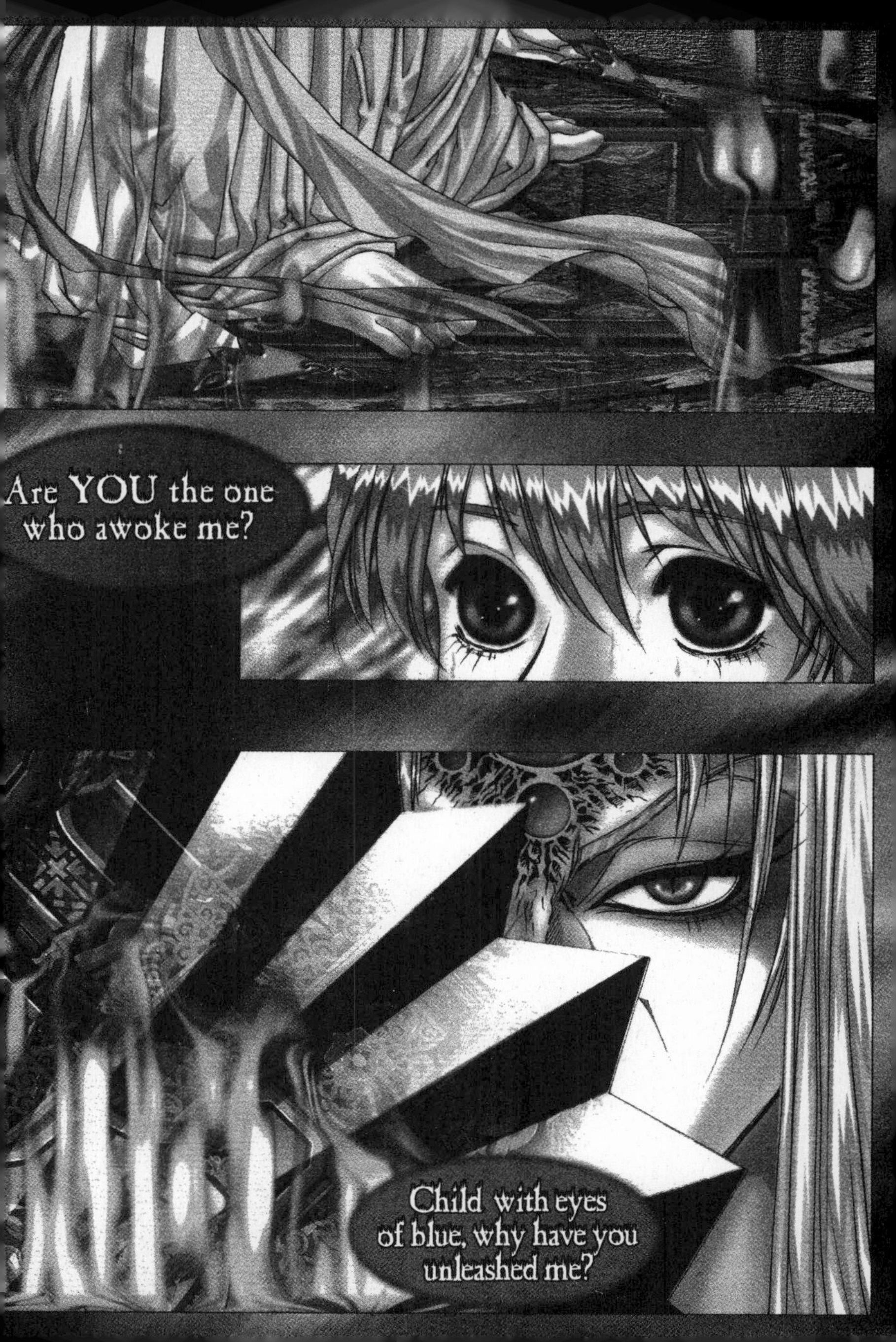

Are YOU the one who awoke me?
Child with eyes of blue, why have you unleashed me?

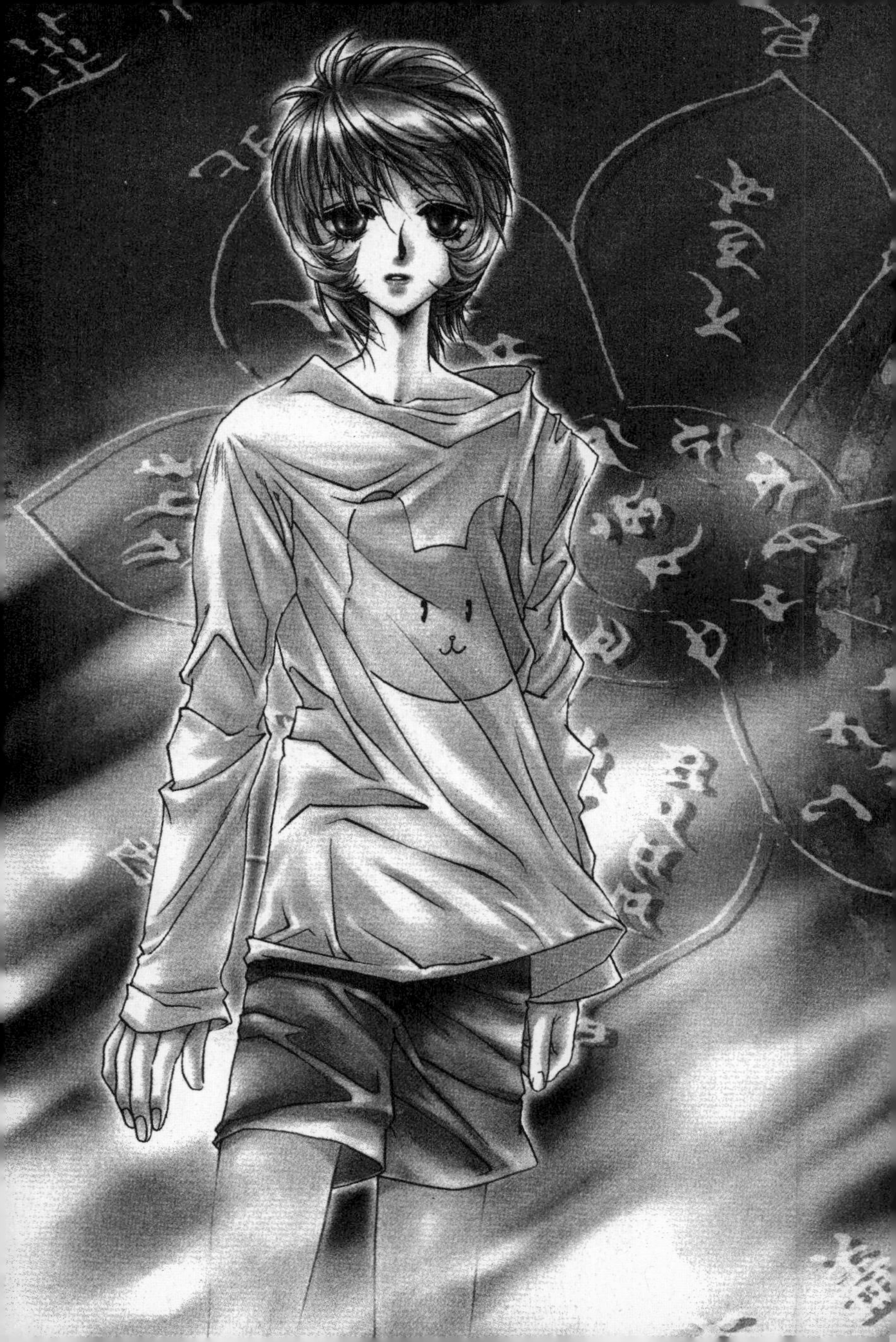

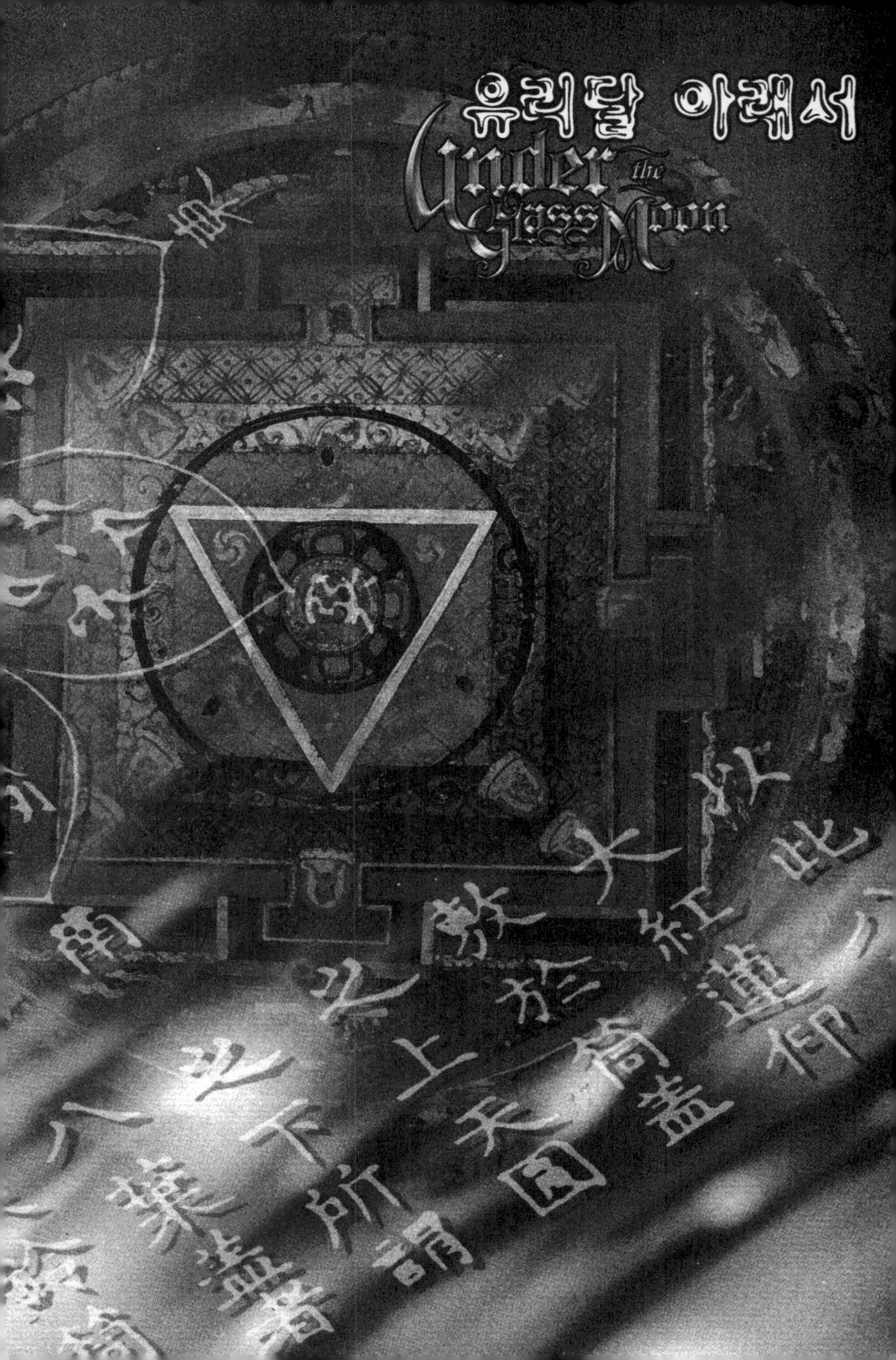
유리달 아래서
Under the Glass Moon

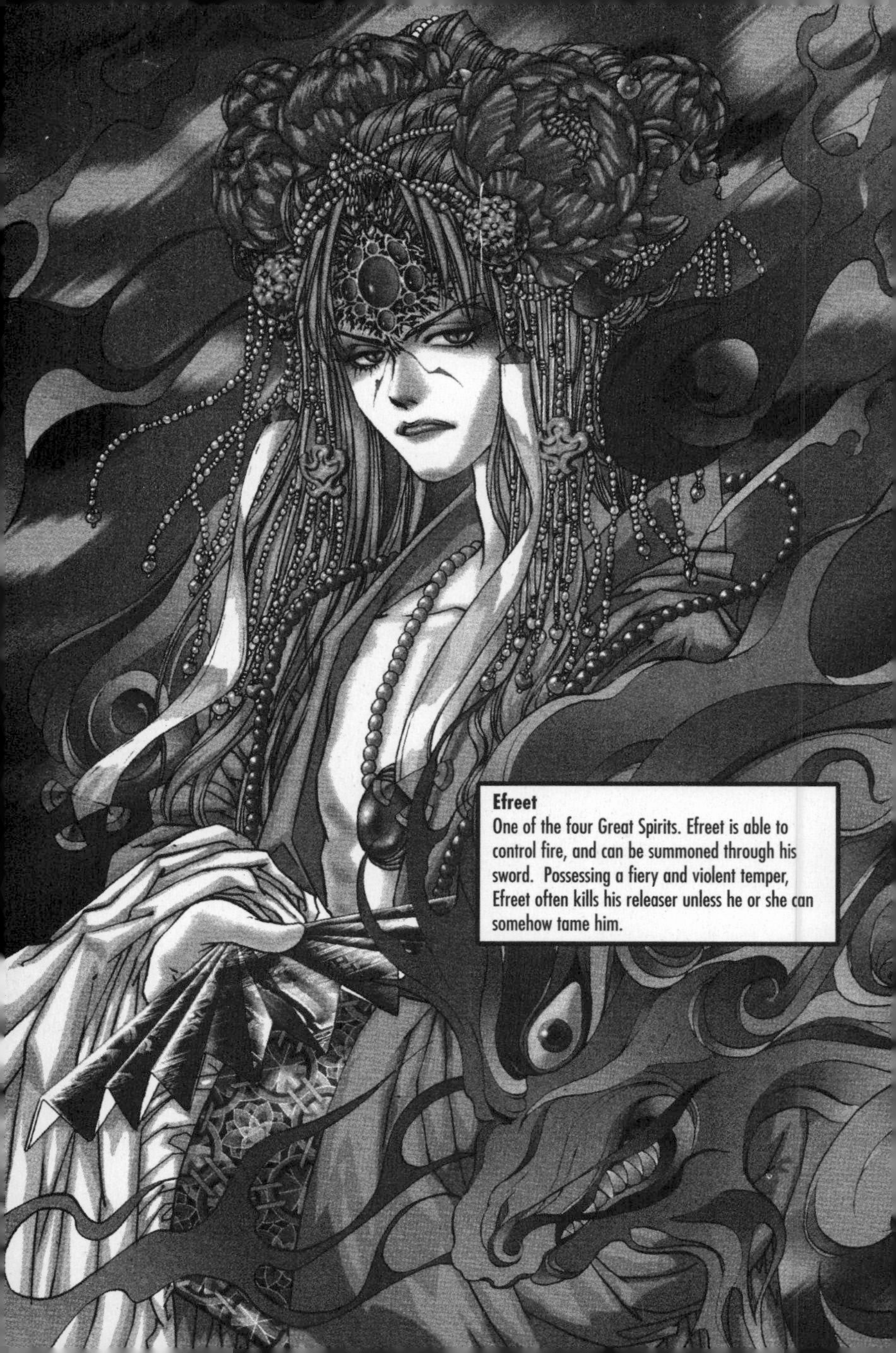
Efreet
One of the four Great Spirits. Efreet is able to control fire, and can be summoned through his sword. Possessing a fiery and violent temper, Efreet often kills his releaser unless he or she can somehow tame him.

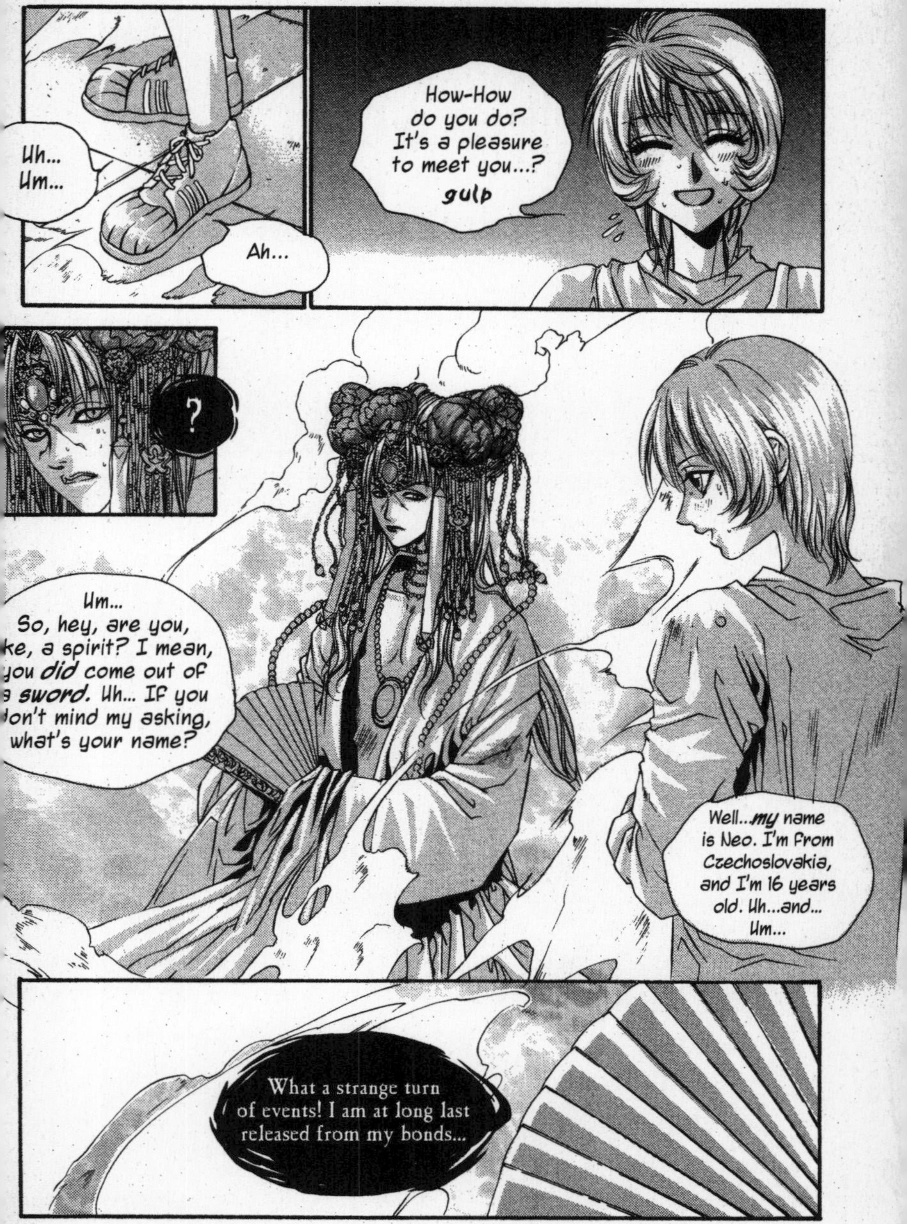
Uh... Um...
Ah...
How-How do you do? It's a pleasure to meet you...?
gulp
?
Um... So, hey, are you, ke, a spirit? I mean, you *did* come out of sword. Uh... If you don't mind my asking, what's your name?
Well...*my* name is Neo. I'm from Czechoslovakia, and I'm 16 years old. Uh...and... Um...
What a strange turn of events! I am at long last released from my bonds...

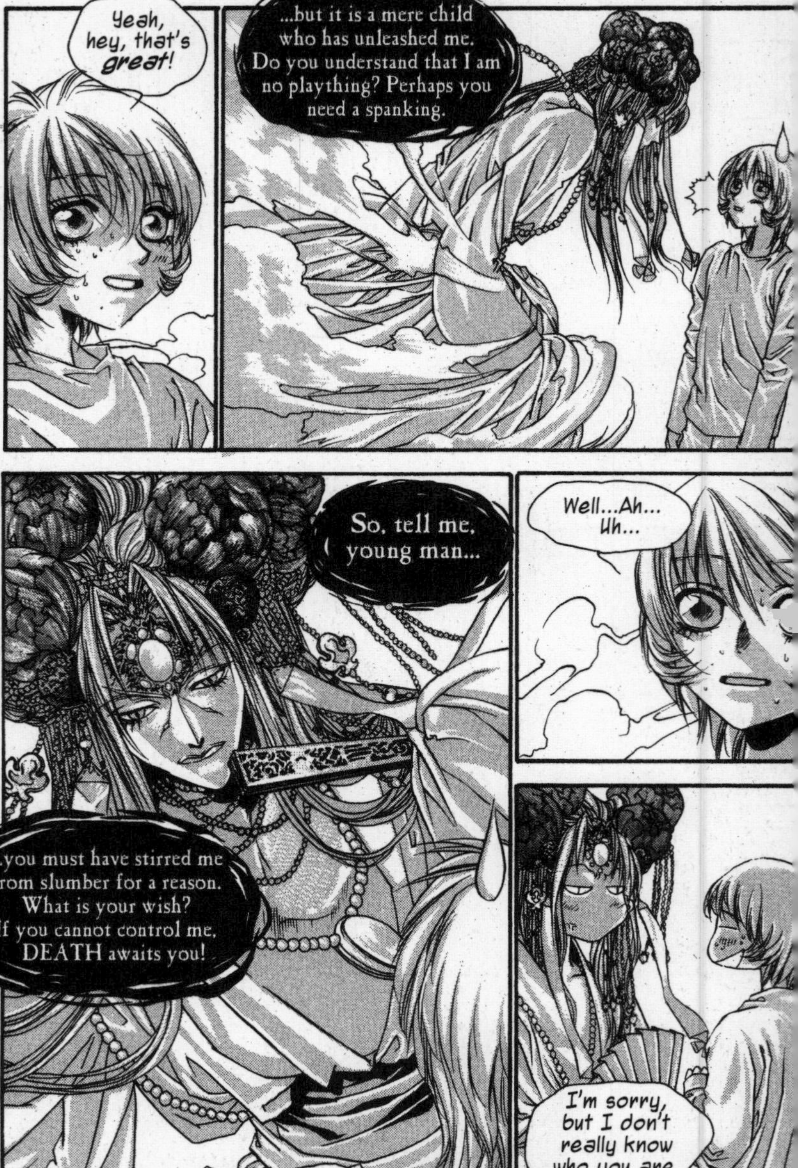

Yeah, hey, that's great!
...but it is a mere child who has unleashed me. Do you understand that I am no plaything? Perhaps you need a spanking.
So, tell me, young man...
...you must have stirred me from slumber for a reason. What is your wish? If you cannot control me, DEATH awaits you!
Well...Ah... Uh...
I'm sorry, but I don't really know who you are.

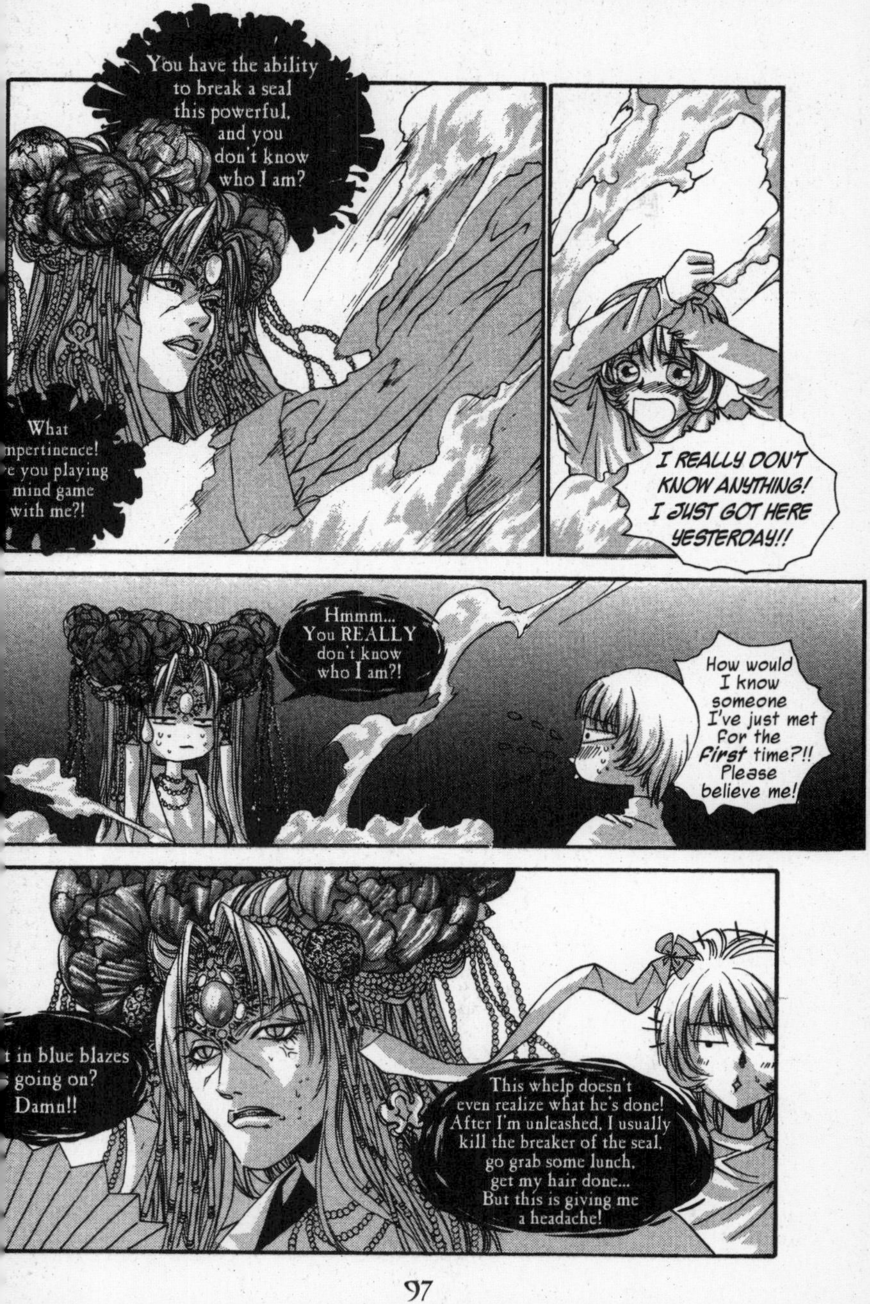

You have the ability to break a seal this powerful, and you don't know who I am?
What mpertinence! e you playing mind game with me?!
I REALLY DON'T KNOW ANYTHING! I JUST GOT HERE YESTERDAY!!
Hmmm... You REALLY don't know who I am?!
How would I know someone I've just met for the first time?!! Please believe me!
t in blue blazes going on? Damn!!
This whelp doesn't even realize what he's done! After I'm unleashed, I usually kill the breaker of the seal, go grab some lunch, get my hair done... But this is giving me a headache!

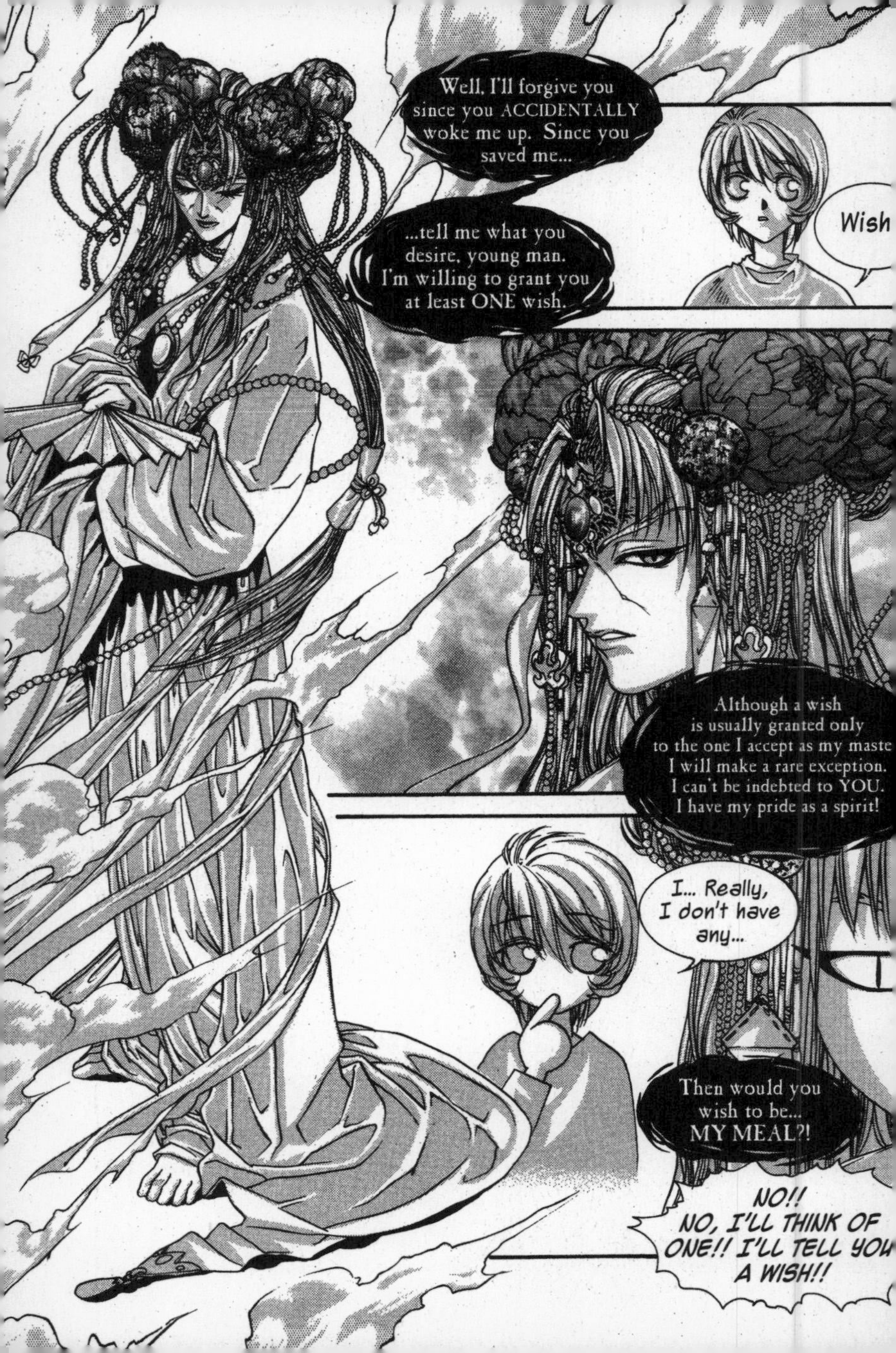

Well, I'll forgive you since you ACCIDENTALLY woke me up. Since you saved me...
...tell me what you desire, young man. I'm willing to grant you at least ONE wish.
Wish
Although a wish is usually granted only to the one I accept as my maste I will make a rare exception. I can't be indebted to YOU. I have my pride as a spirit!
I... Really, I don't have any...
Then would you wish to be... MY MEAL?!
NO!! NO, I'LL THINK OF ONE!! I'LL TELL YOU A WISH!!

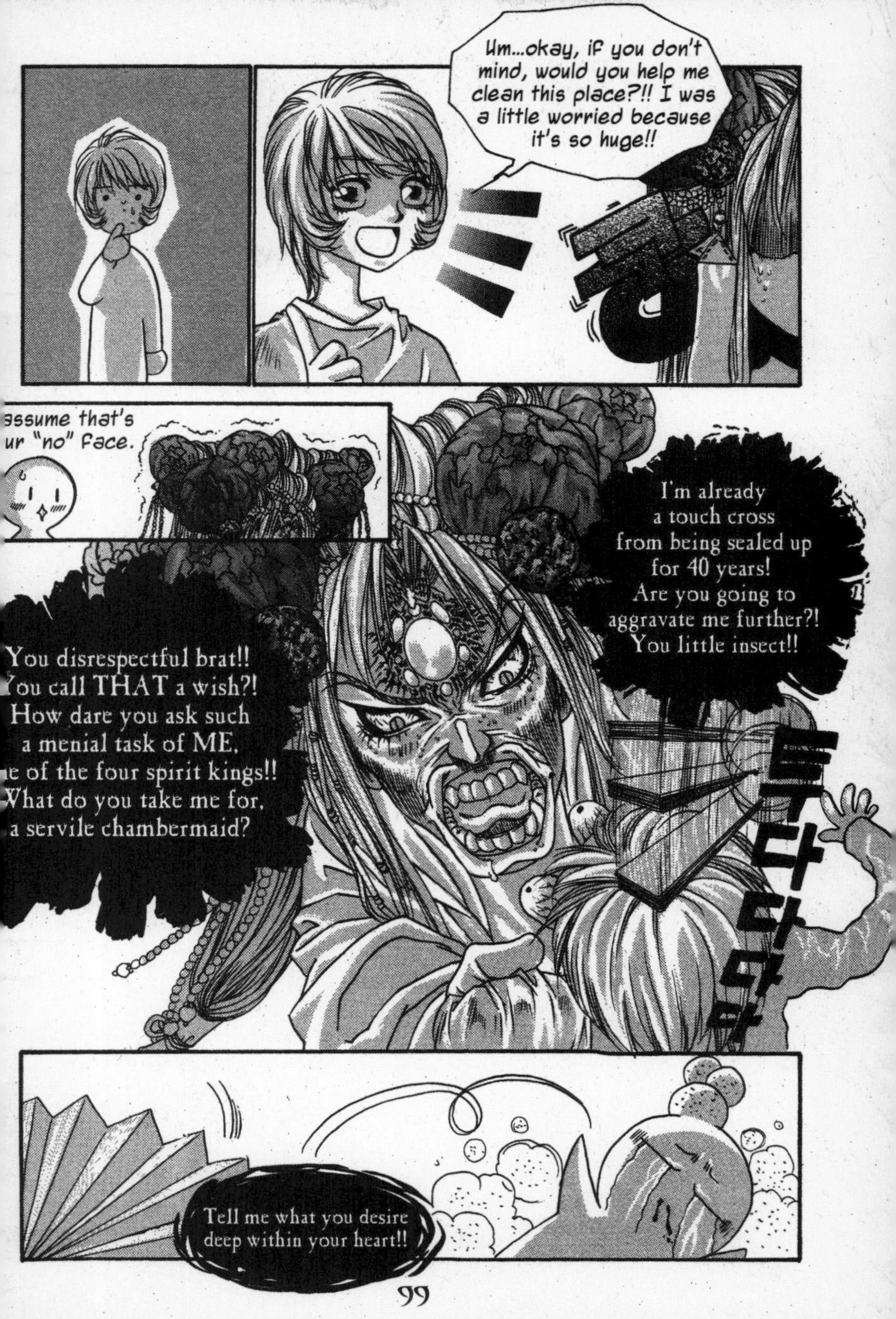
Um...okay, if you don't mind, would you help me clean this place?!! I was a little worried because it's so huge!!
assume that's
ur "no" face.
You disrespectful brat!!
ou call THAT a wish?!
How dare you ask such
a menial task of ME,
e of the four spirit kings!!
hat do you take me for,
a servile chambermaid?
I'm already a touch cross from being sealed up for 40 years! Are you going to aggravate me further?! You little insect!!
두다다다다
Tell me what you desire deep within your heart!!

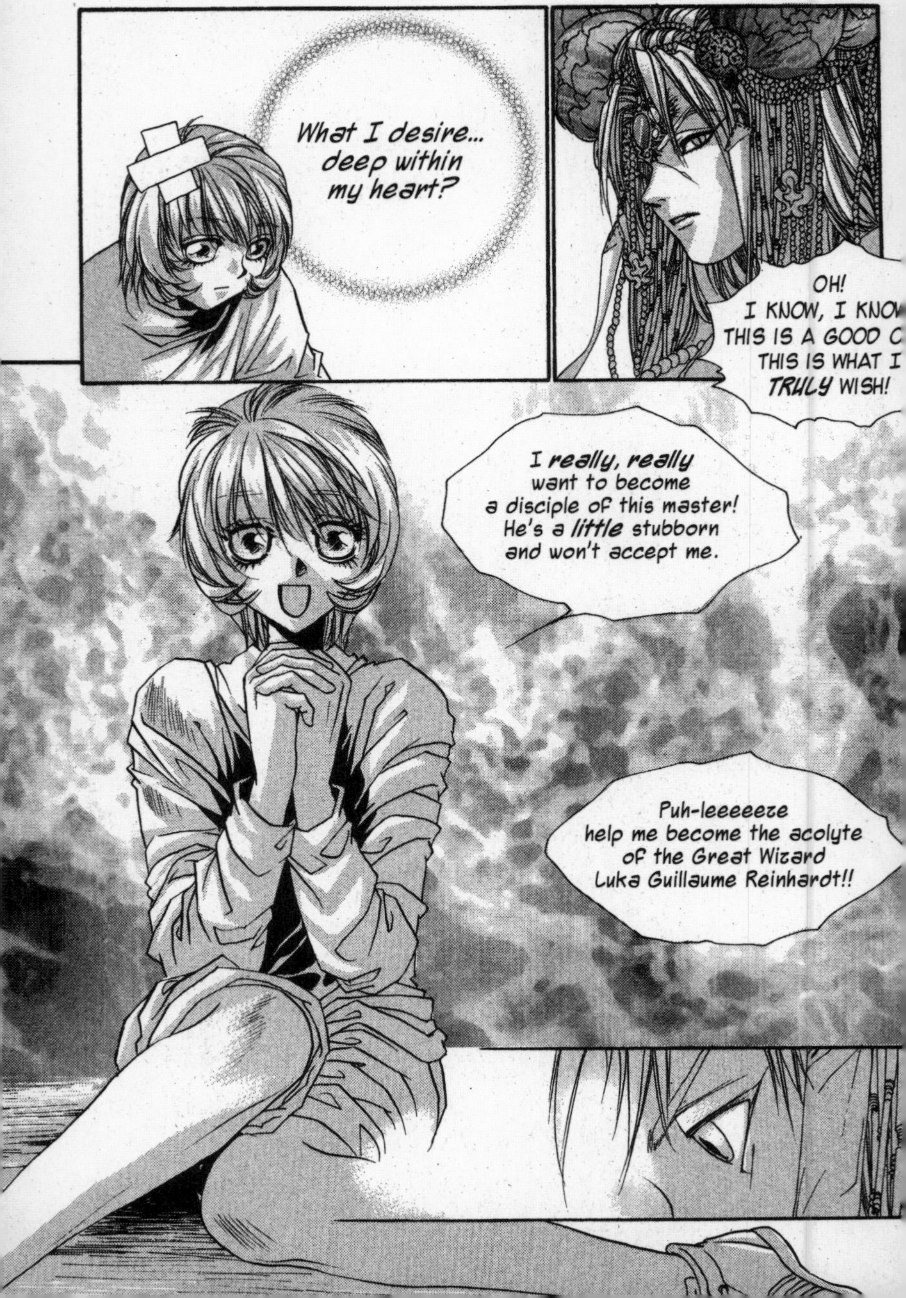
What I desire... deep within my heart?
OH! I KNOW, I KNO THIS IS A GOOD C THIS IS WHAT I *TRULY* WISH!
I *really, really* want to become a disciple of this master! He's a *little* stubborn and won't accept me.
Puh-leeeeeze help me become the acolyte of the Great Wizard Luka Guillaume Reinhardt!!

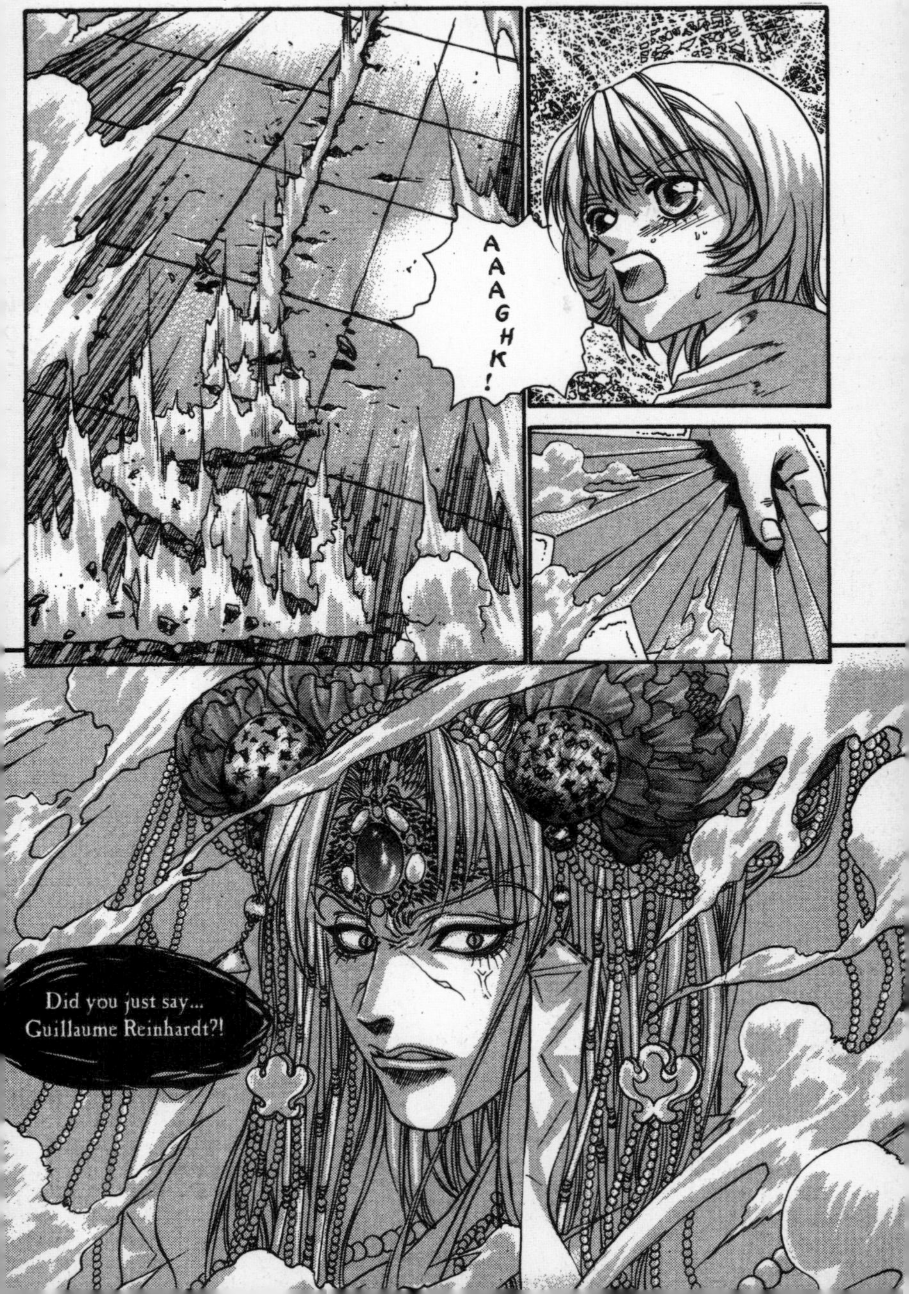
AAAGHK!
Did you just say...
Guillaume Reinhardt?!

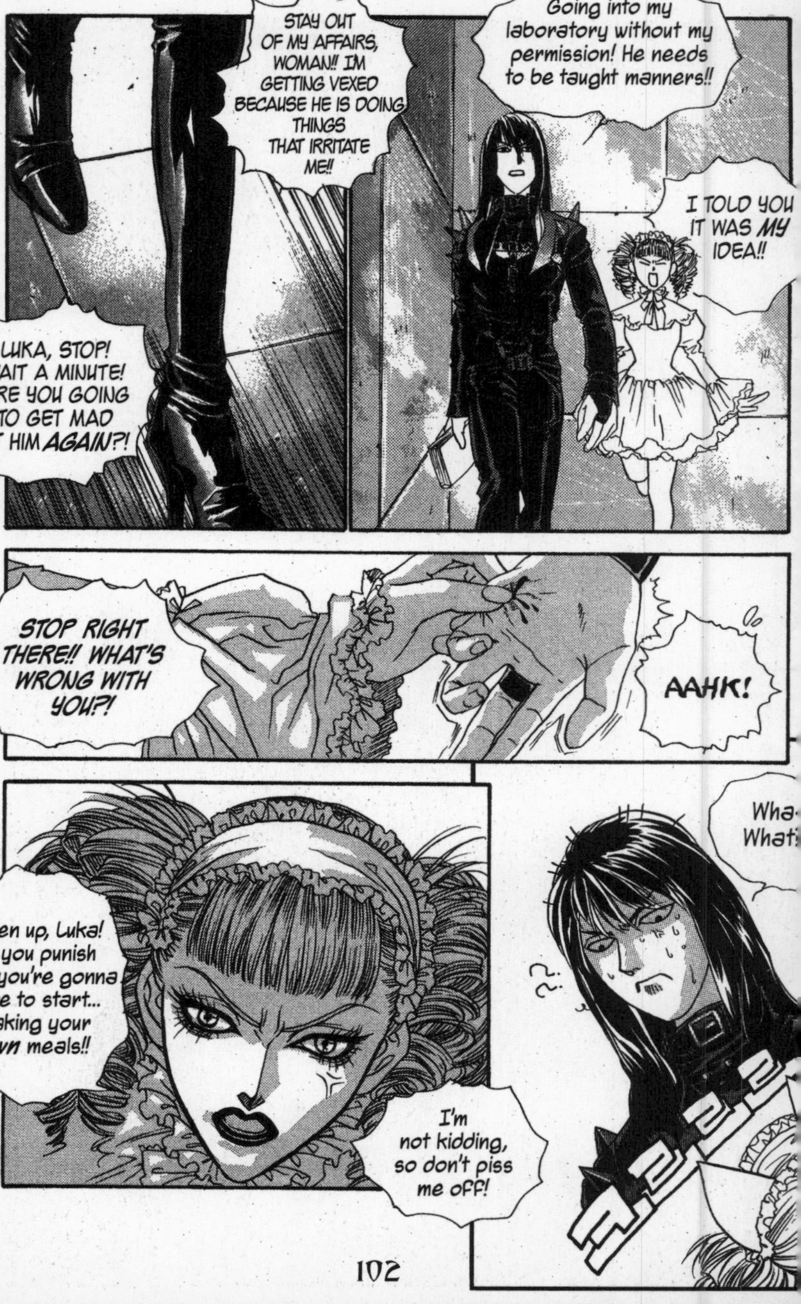
STAY OUT OF MY AFFAIRS, WOMAN!! I'M GETTING VEXED BECAUSE HE IS DOING THINGS THAT IRRITATE ME!!
LUKA, STOP! WAIT A MINUTE! ARE YOU GOING TO GET MAD AT HIM AGAIN?!
Going into my laboratory without my permission! He needs to be taught manners!!
I TOLD YOU IT WAS MY IDEA!!
STOP RIGHT THERE!! WHAT'S WRONG WITH YOU?!
AAHK!
Listen up, Luka! If you punish Neo, you're gonna have to start... making your own meals!!
I'm not kidding, so don't piss me off!
Wha-
What

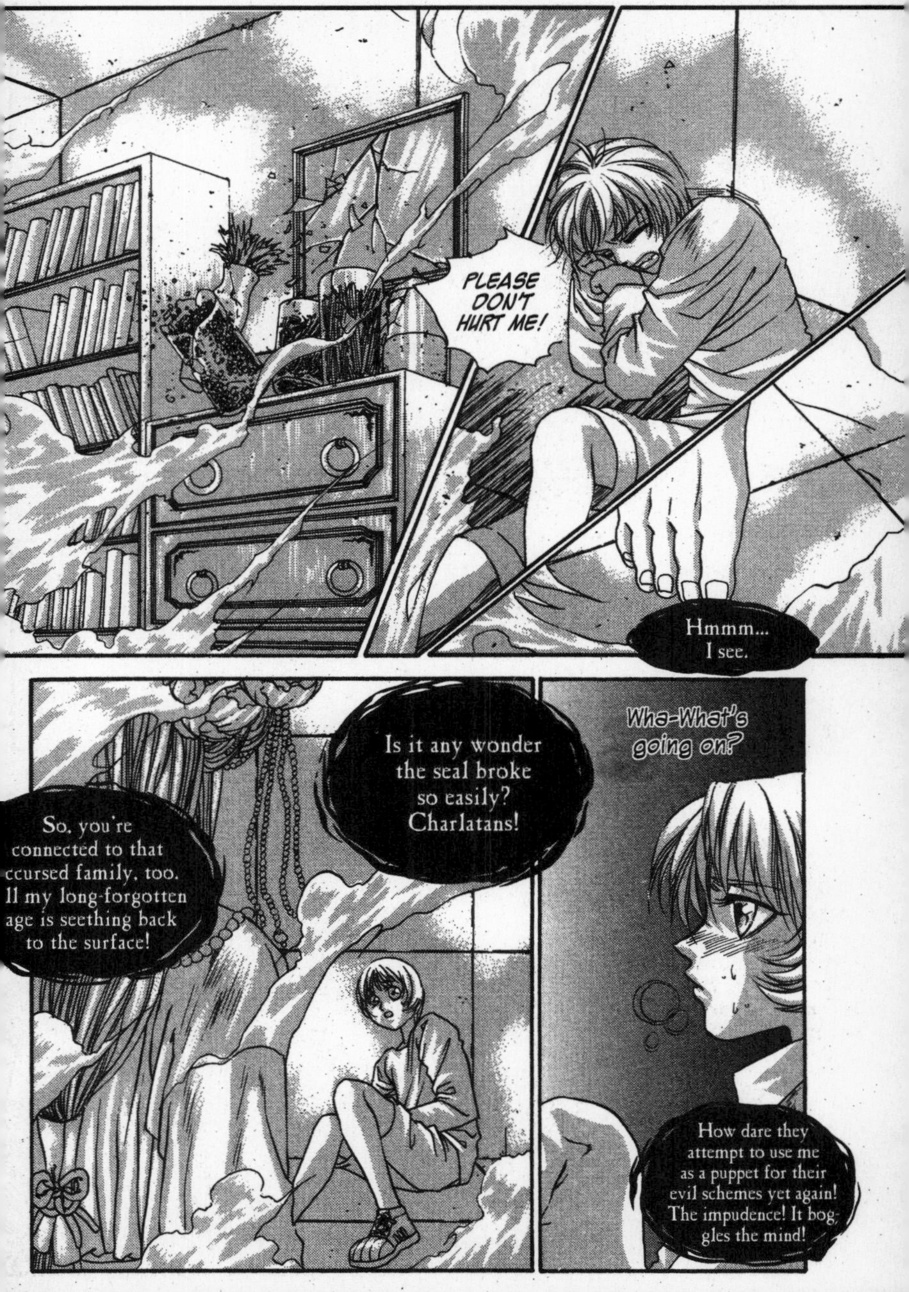
PLEASE DON'T HURT ME!
Hmmm... I see.
Is it any wonder the seal broke so easily? Charlatans!
So, you're connected to that ccursed family, too. ll my long-forgotten age is seething back to the surface!
Wha-What's going on?
How dare they attempt to use me as a puppet for their evil schemes yet again! The impudence! It boggles the mind!

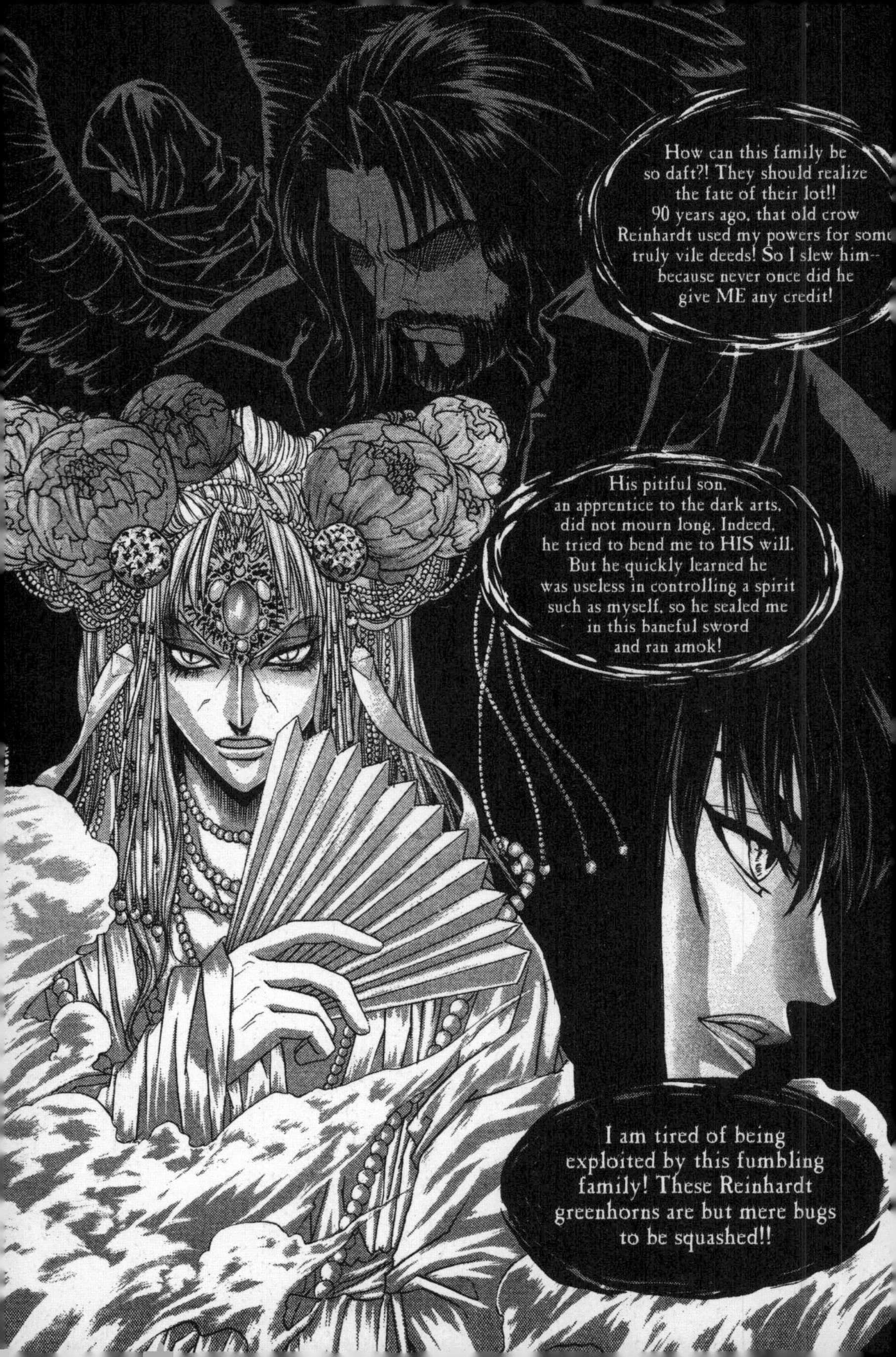
How can this family be so daft?! They should realize the fate of their lot!! 90 years ago, that old crow Reinhardt used my powers for some truly vile deeds! So I slew him--because never once did he give ME any credit!
His pitiful son, an apprentice to the dark arts, did not mourn long. Indeed, he tried to bend me to HIS will. But he quickly learned he was useless in controlling a spirit such as myself, so he sealed me in this baneful sword and ran amok!
I am tired of being exploited by this fumbling family! These Reinhardt greenhorns are but mere bugs to be squashed!!

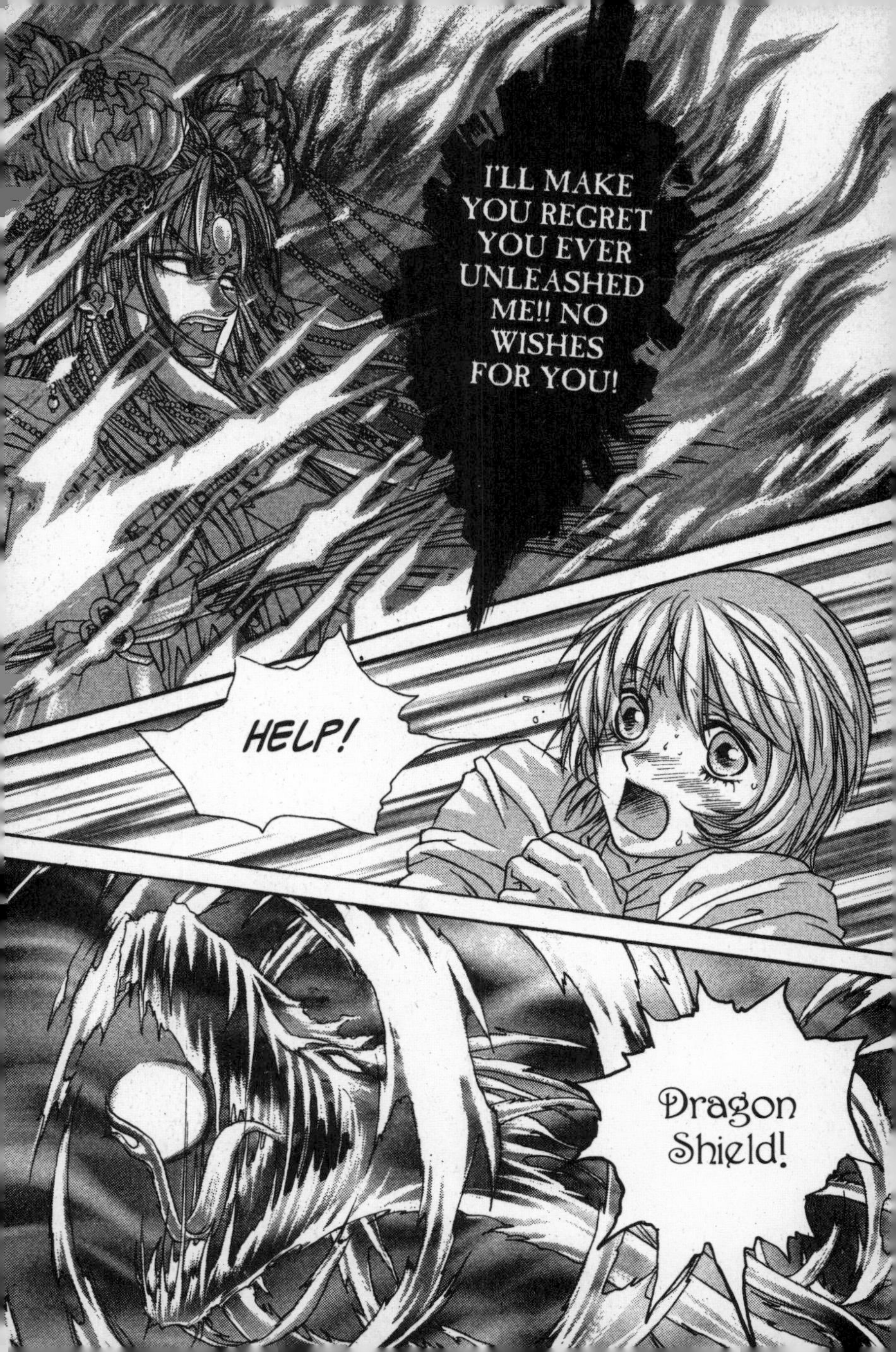
I'LL MAKE YOU REGRET YOU EVER UNLEASHED ME!! NO WISHES FOR YOU!
HELP!
Dragon Shield!

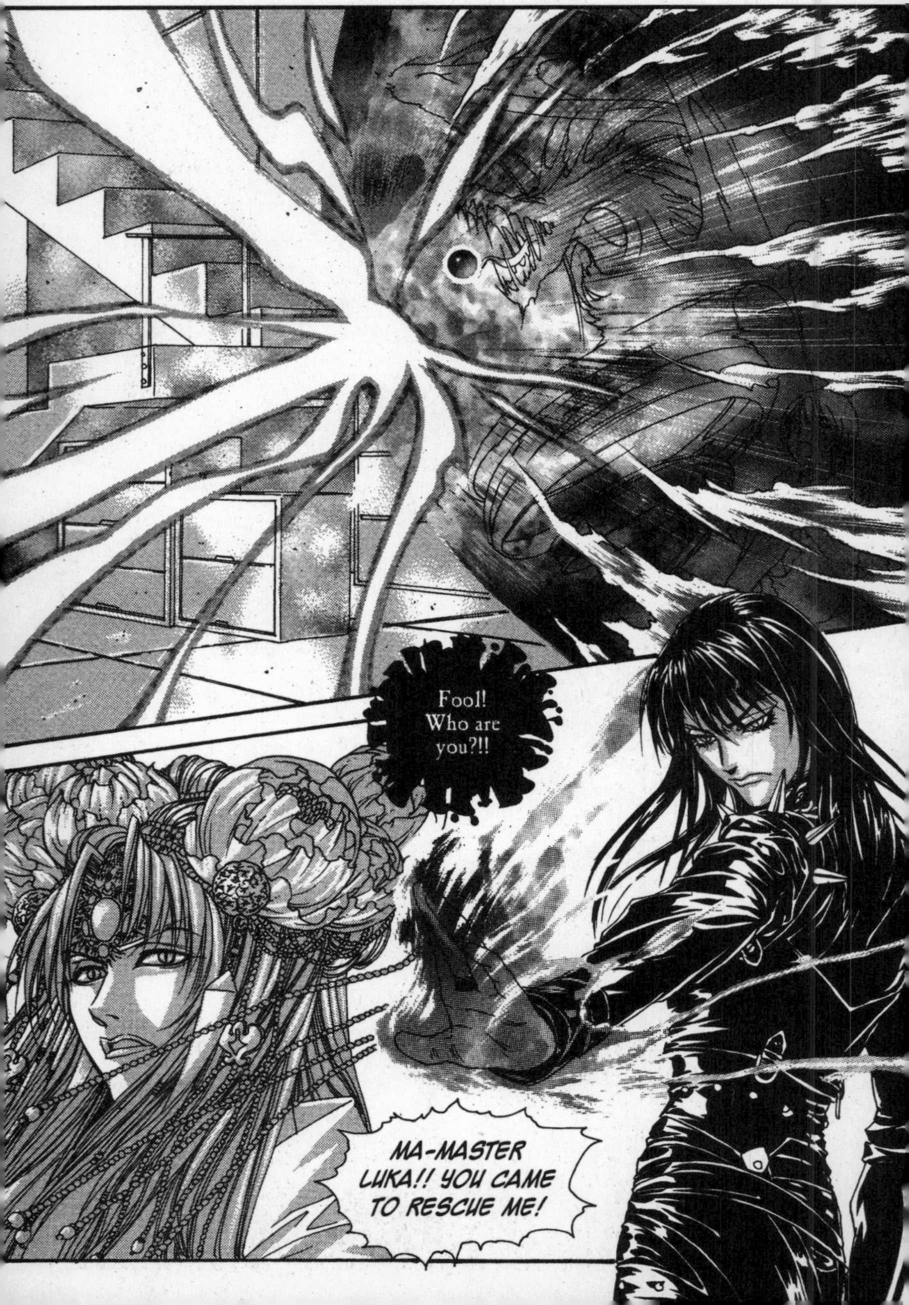
Fool! Who are you?!!
MA-MASTER LUKA!! YOU CAME TO RESCUE ME!

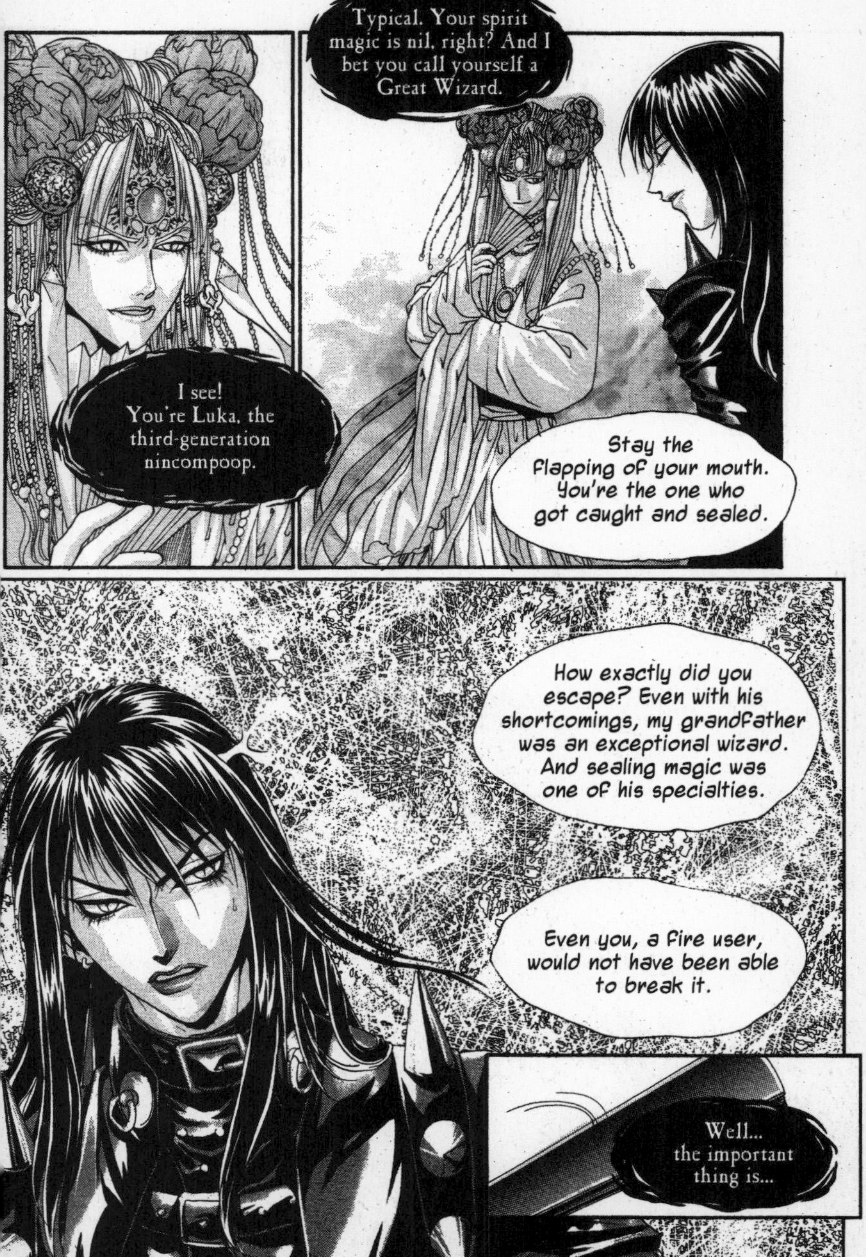
I see!
You're Luka, the third-generation nincompoop.
Typical. Your spirit magic is nil, right? And I bet you call yourself a Great Wizard.
Stay the flapping of your mouth. You're the one who got caught and sealed.
How exactly did you escape? Even with his shortcomings, my grandfather was an exceptional wizard. And sealing magic was one of his specialties.
Even you, a fire user, would not have been able to break it.
Well... the important thing is...

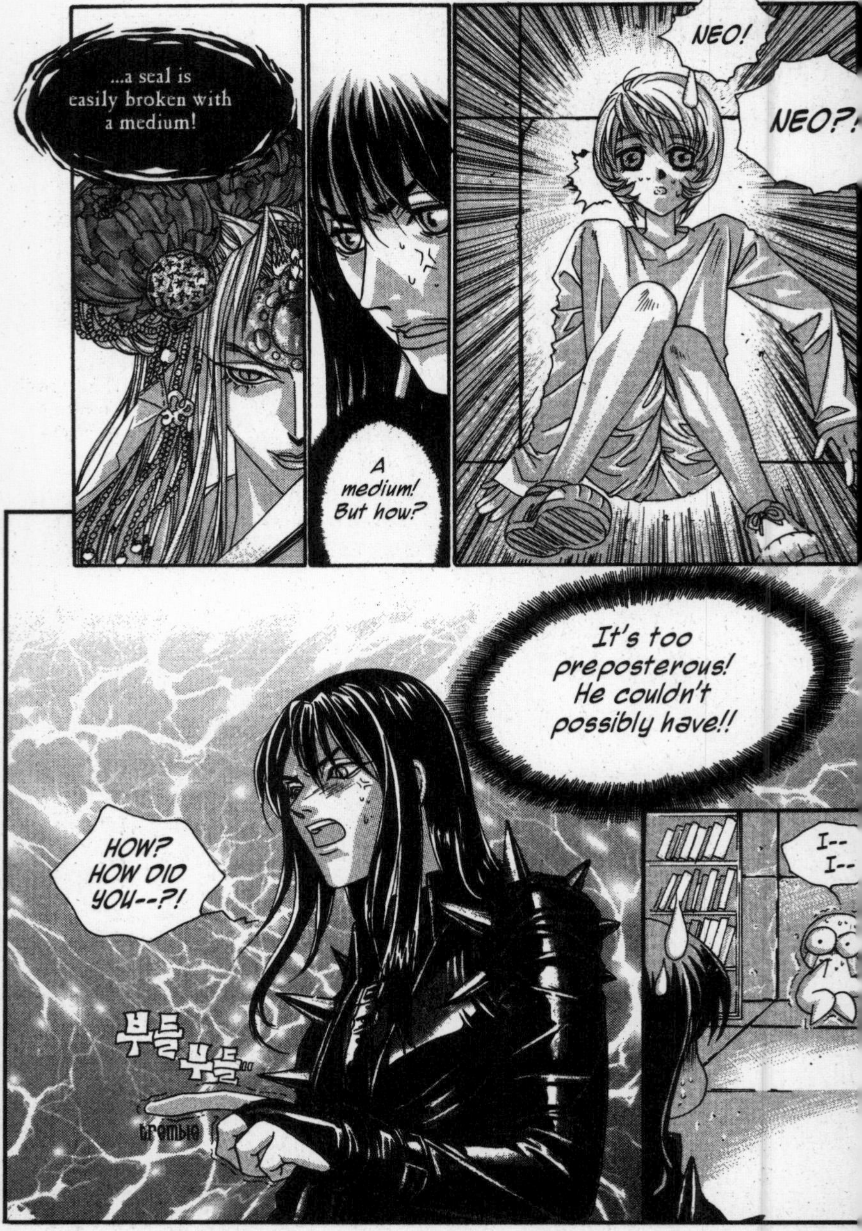
...a seal is easily broken with a medium!
A medium! But how?
NEO!
NEO?!
It's too preposterous! He couldn't possibly have!!
HOW? HOW DID YOU--?!
부들부들...
tremble
I-- I--

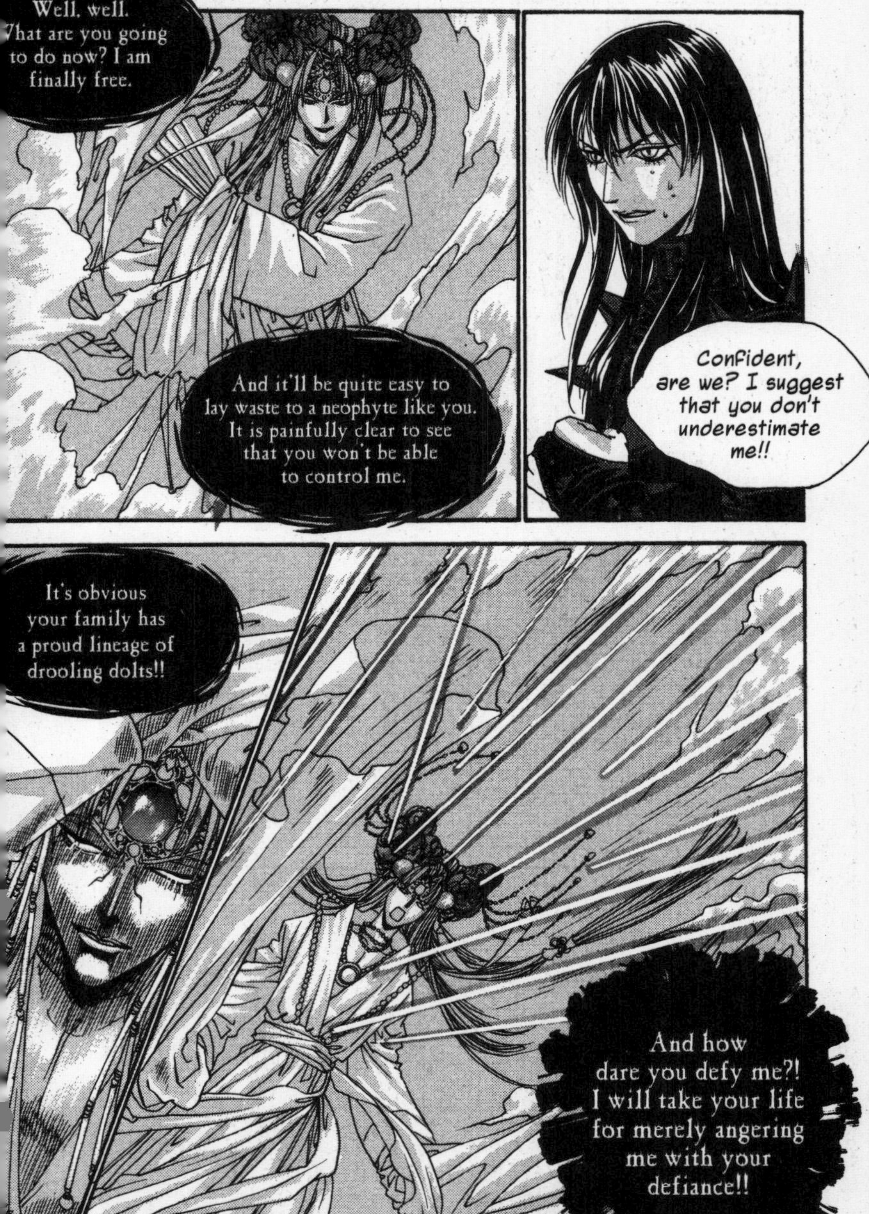
Well, well. What are you going to do now? I am finally free.
And it'll be quite easy to lay waste to a neophyte like you. It is painfully clear to see that you won't be able to control me.
Confident, are we? I suggest that you don't underestimate me!!
It's obvious your family has a proud lineage of drooling dolts!!
And how dare you defy me?! I will take your life for merely angering me with your defiance!!

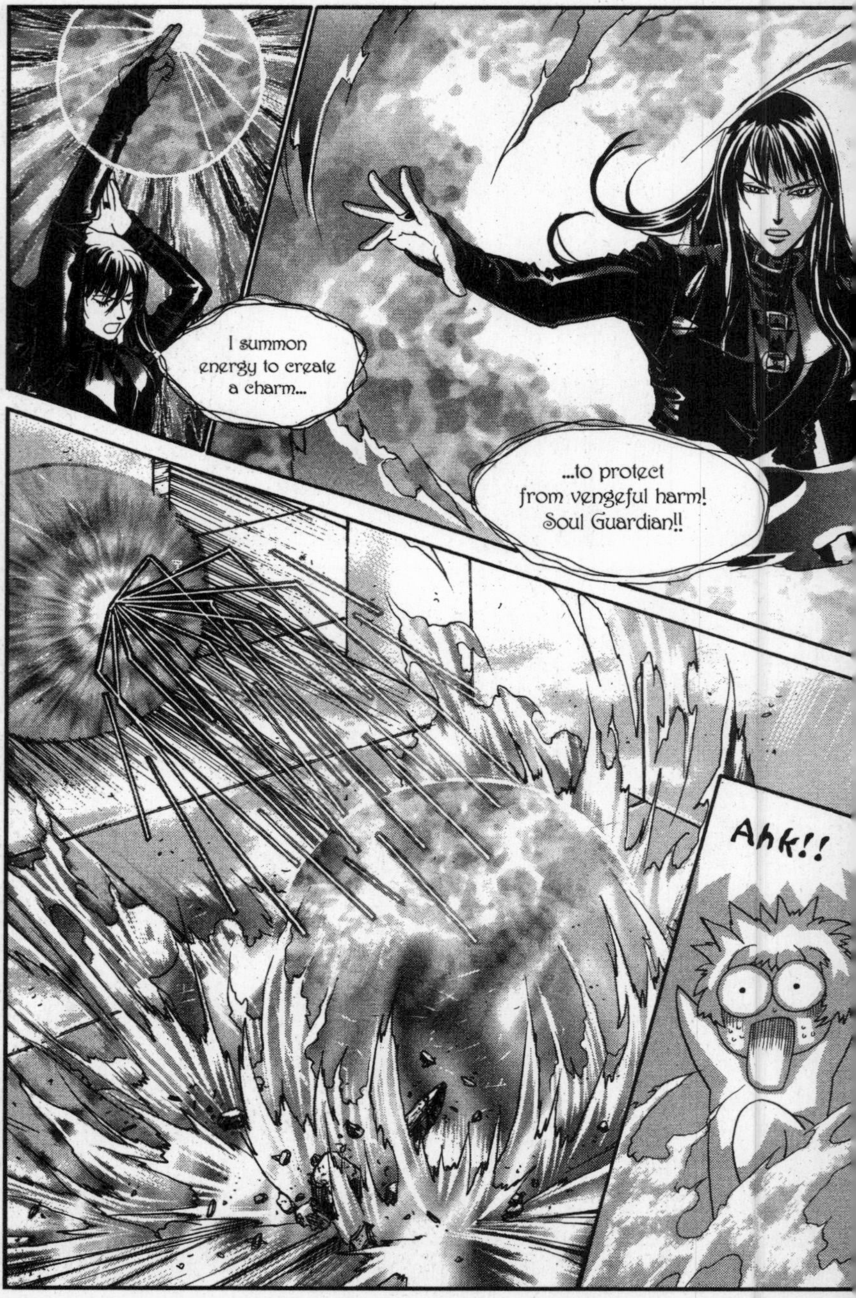
I summon energy to create a charm...
...to protect from vengeful harm! Soul Guardian!!
Ahk!!

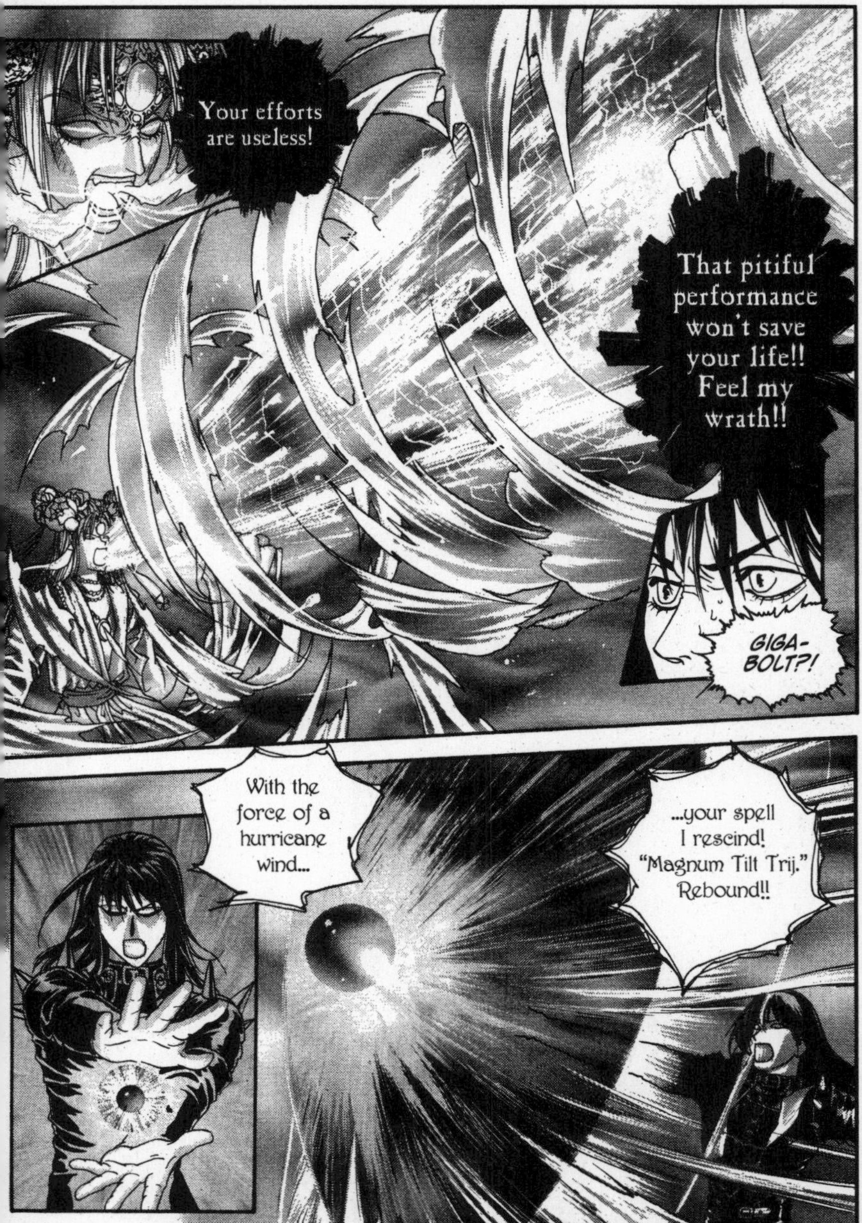
Your efforts are useless!
That pitiful performance won't save your life!! Feel my wrath!!
GIGA-BOLT?!
With the force of a hurricane wind...
...your spell I rescind! "Magnum Tilt Trij." Rebound!!

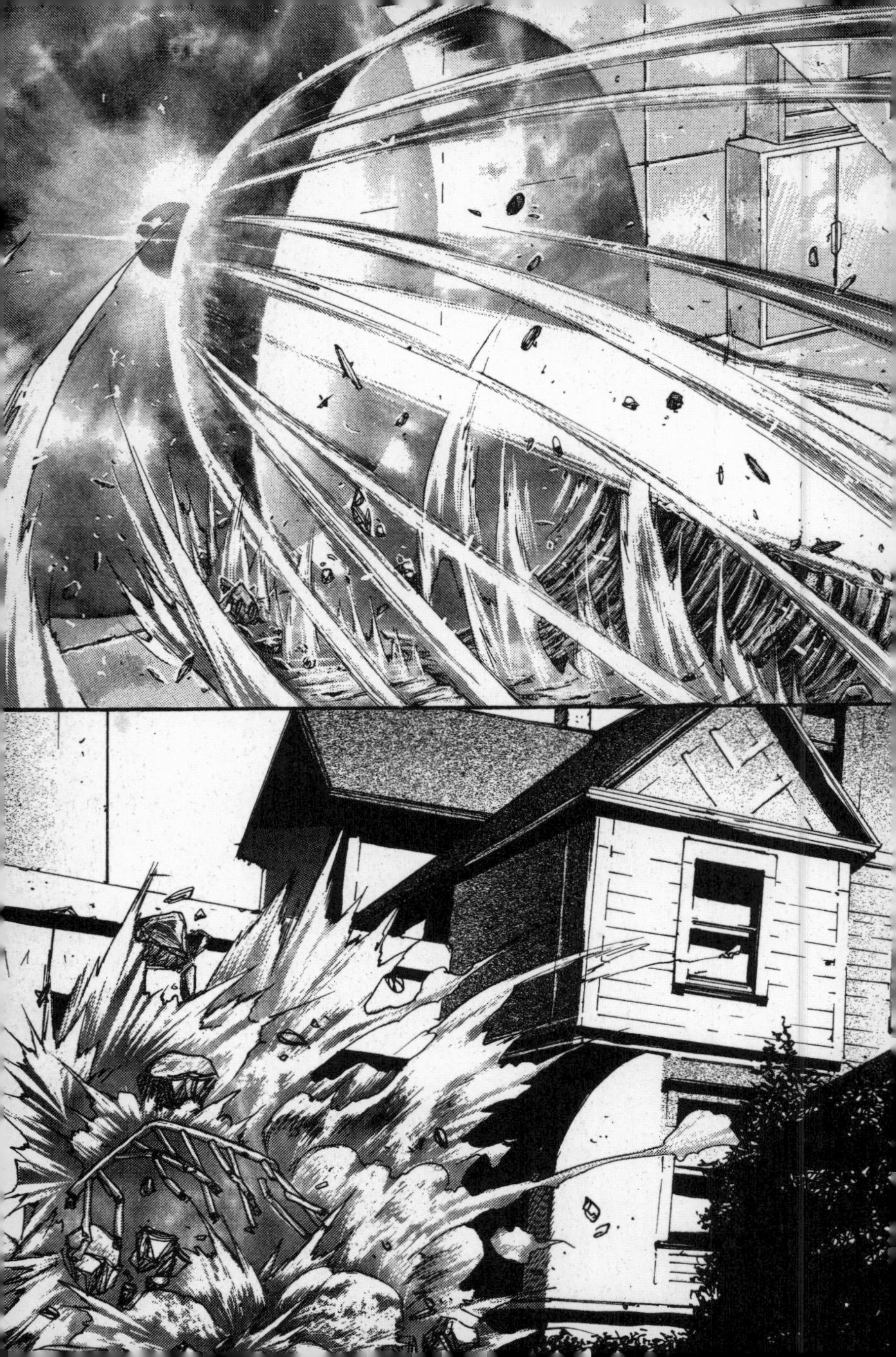

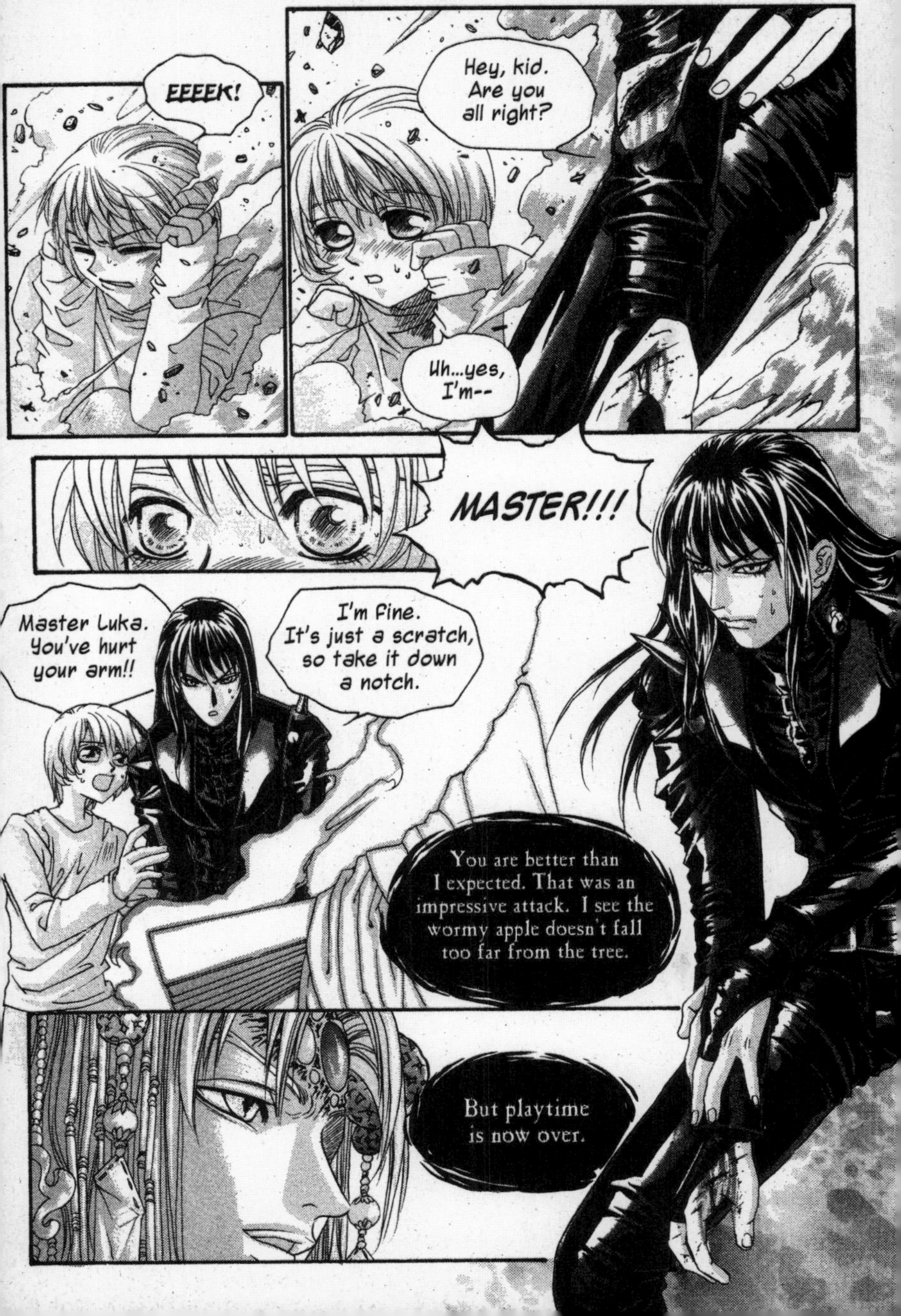
EEEEK!
Hey, kid. Are you all right?
Uh...yes, I'm--
MASTER!!!
Master Luka. You've hurt your arm!!
I'm fine. It's just a scratch, so take it down a notch.
You are better than I expected. That was an impressive attack. I see the wormy apple doesn't fall too far from the tree.
But playtime is now over.

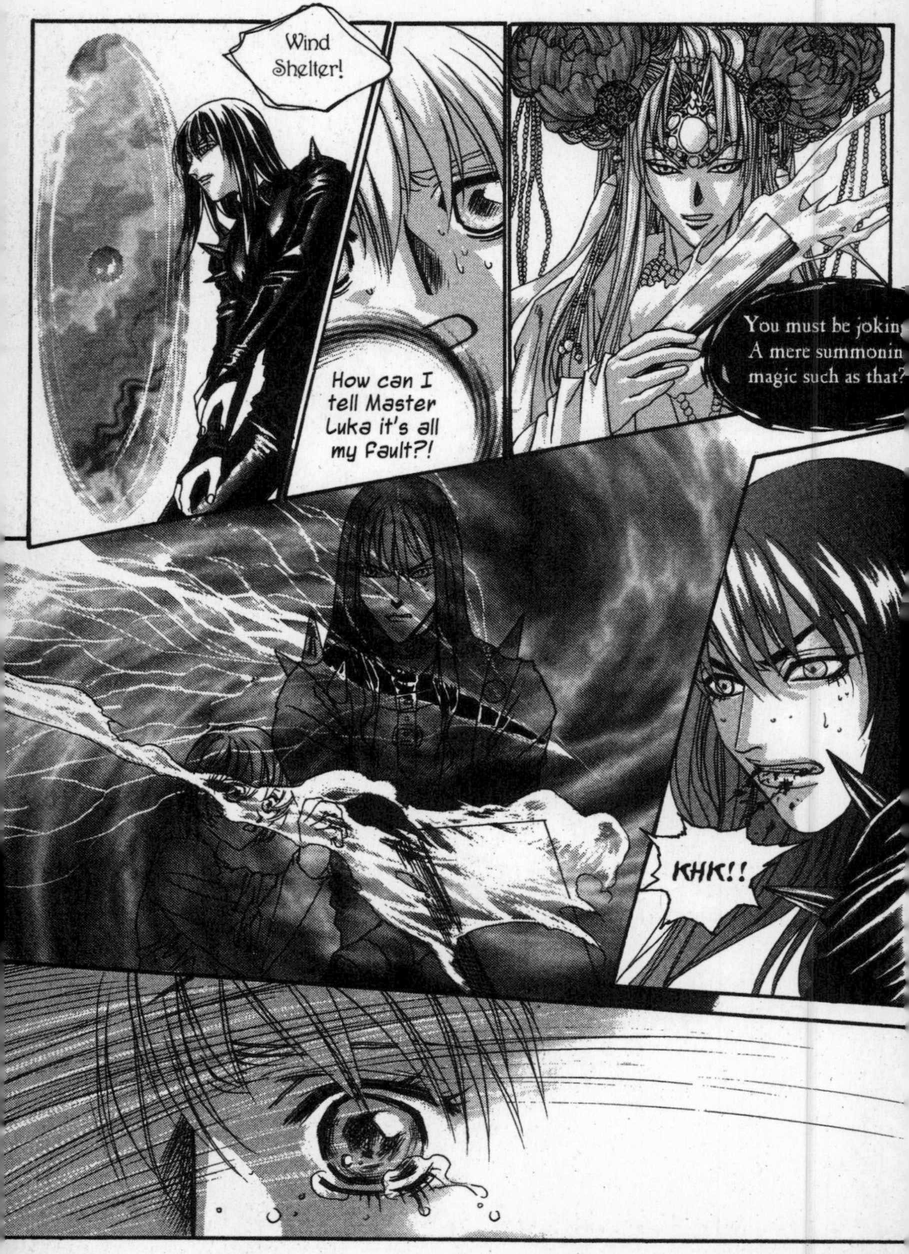
Wind Shelter!
How can I tell Master Luka it's all my fault?!
You must be jokin
A mere summonin
magic such as that?
KHK!!

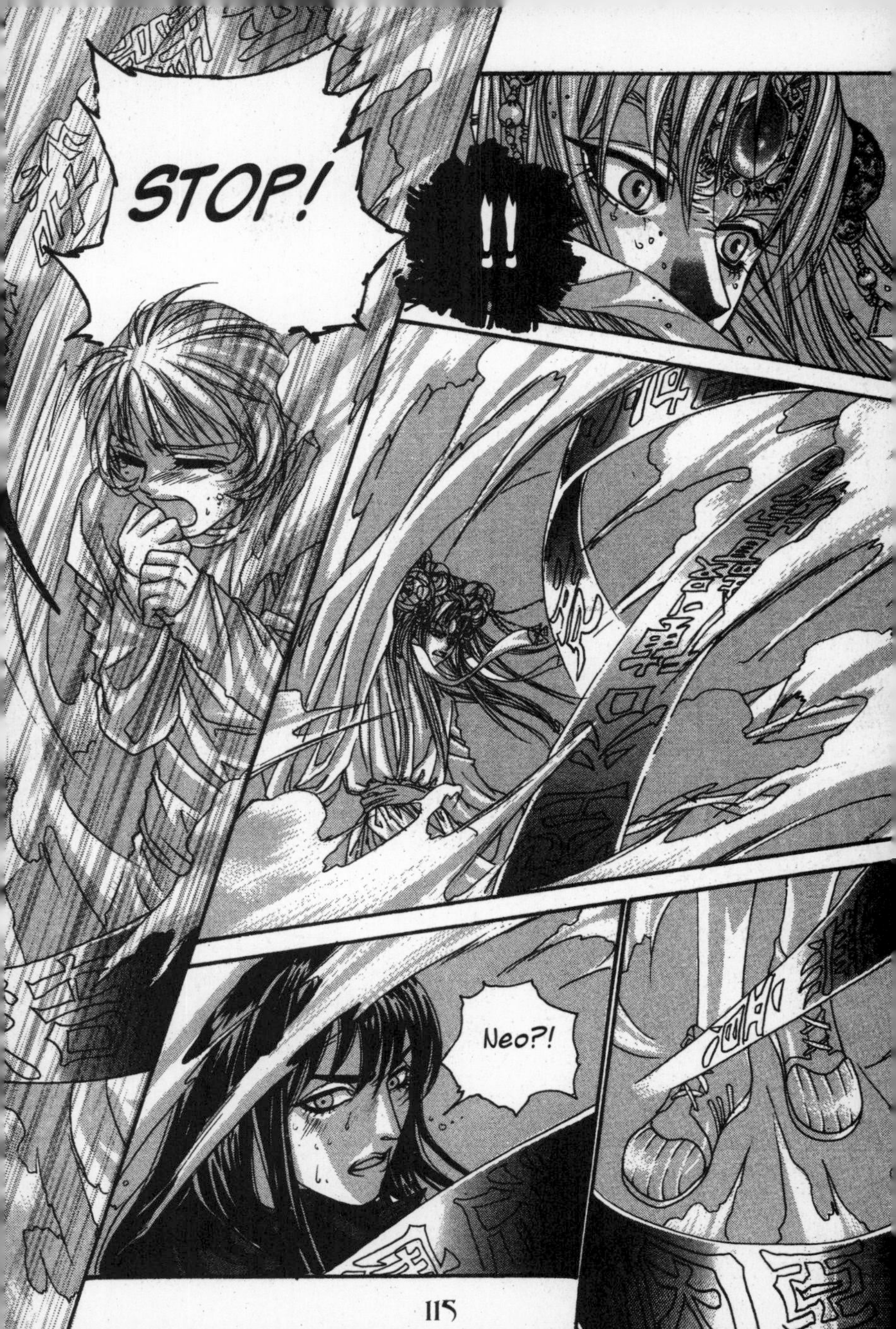
STOP!
!!
Neo?!

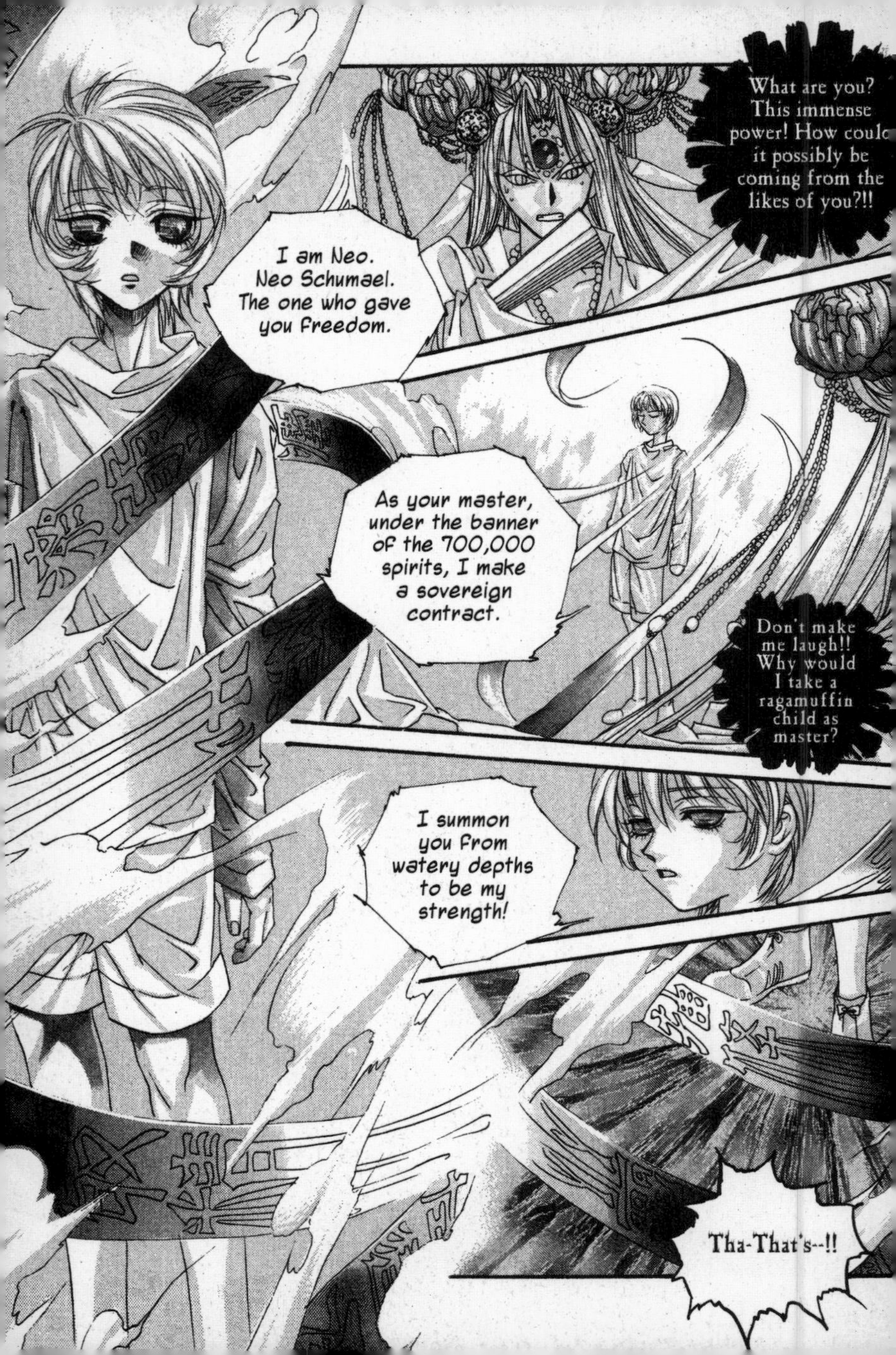
I am Neo. Neo Schumael. The one who gave you freedom.
What are you? This immense power! How could it possibly be coming from the likes of you?!!
As your master, under the banner of the 700,000 spirits, I make a sovereign contract.
Don't make me laugh!! Why would I take a ragamuffin child as master?
I summon you from watery depths to be my strength!
Tha-That's--!!

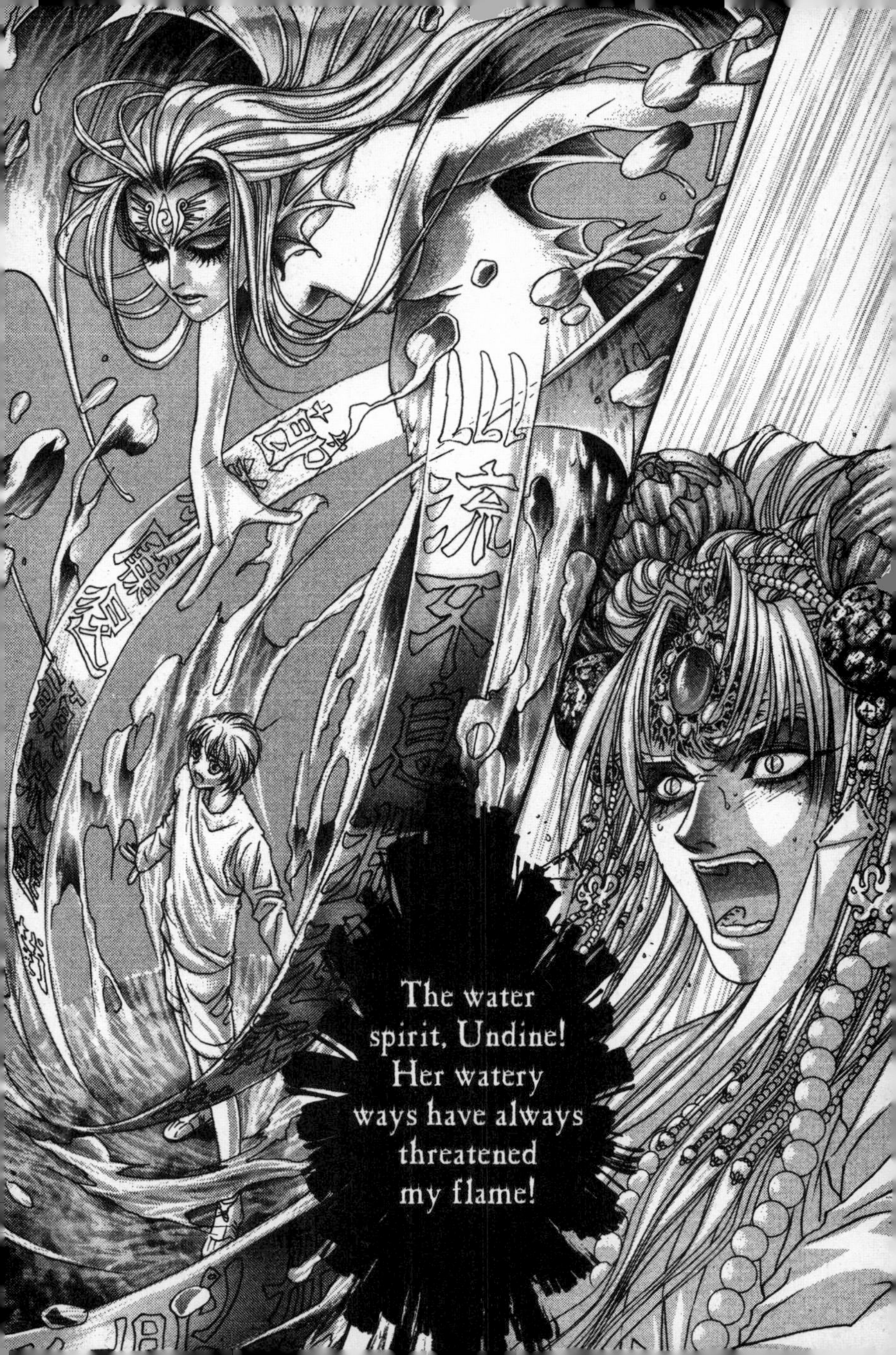
The water spirit, Undine! Her watery ways have always threatened my flame!

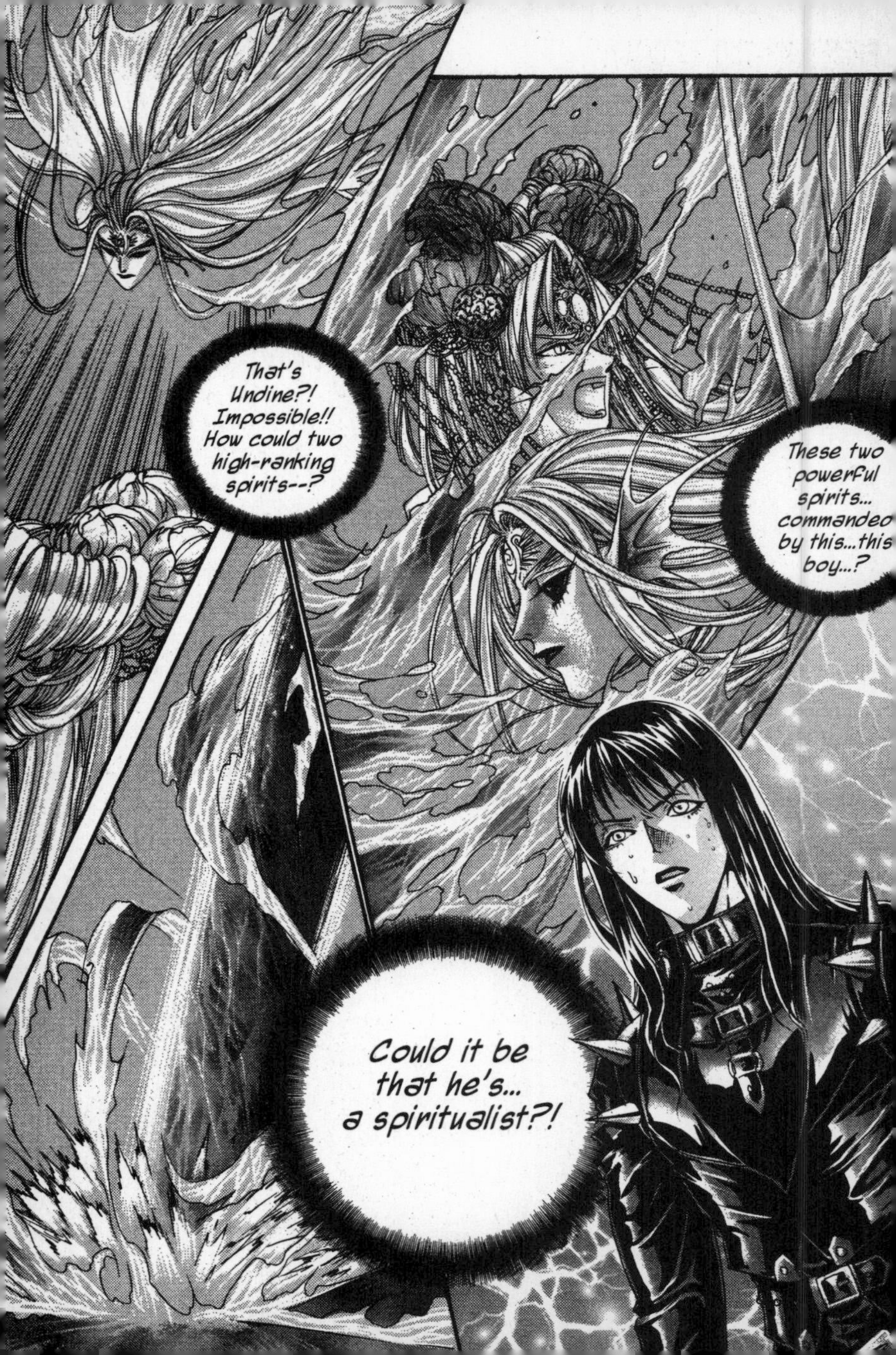
That's Undine?! Impossible!! How could two high-ranking spirits--?
These two powerful spirits... commanded by this...this boy...?
Could it be that he's... a spiritualist?!

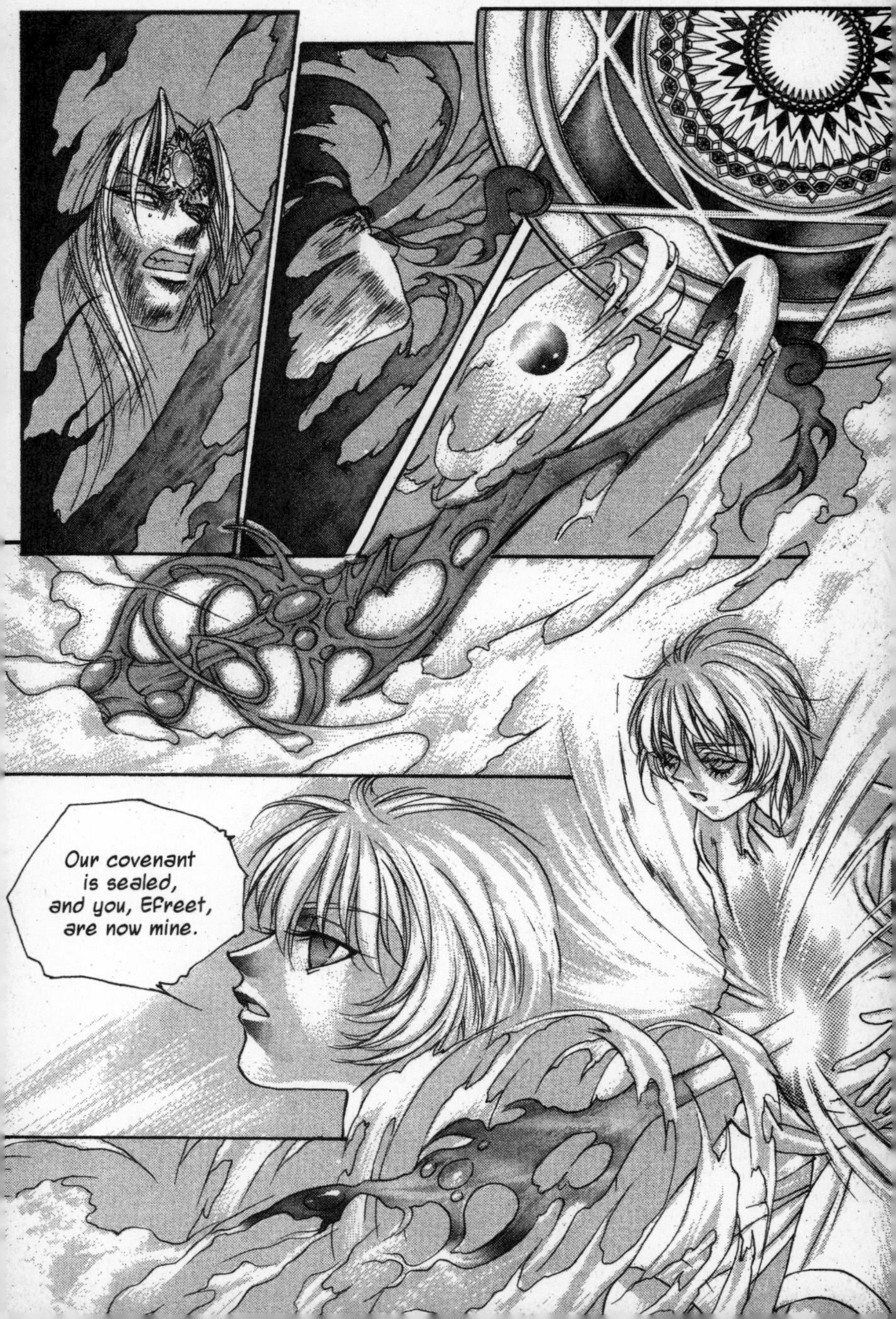
Our covenant is sealed, and you, Efreet, are now mine.

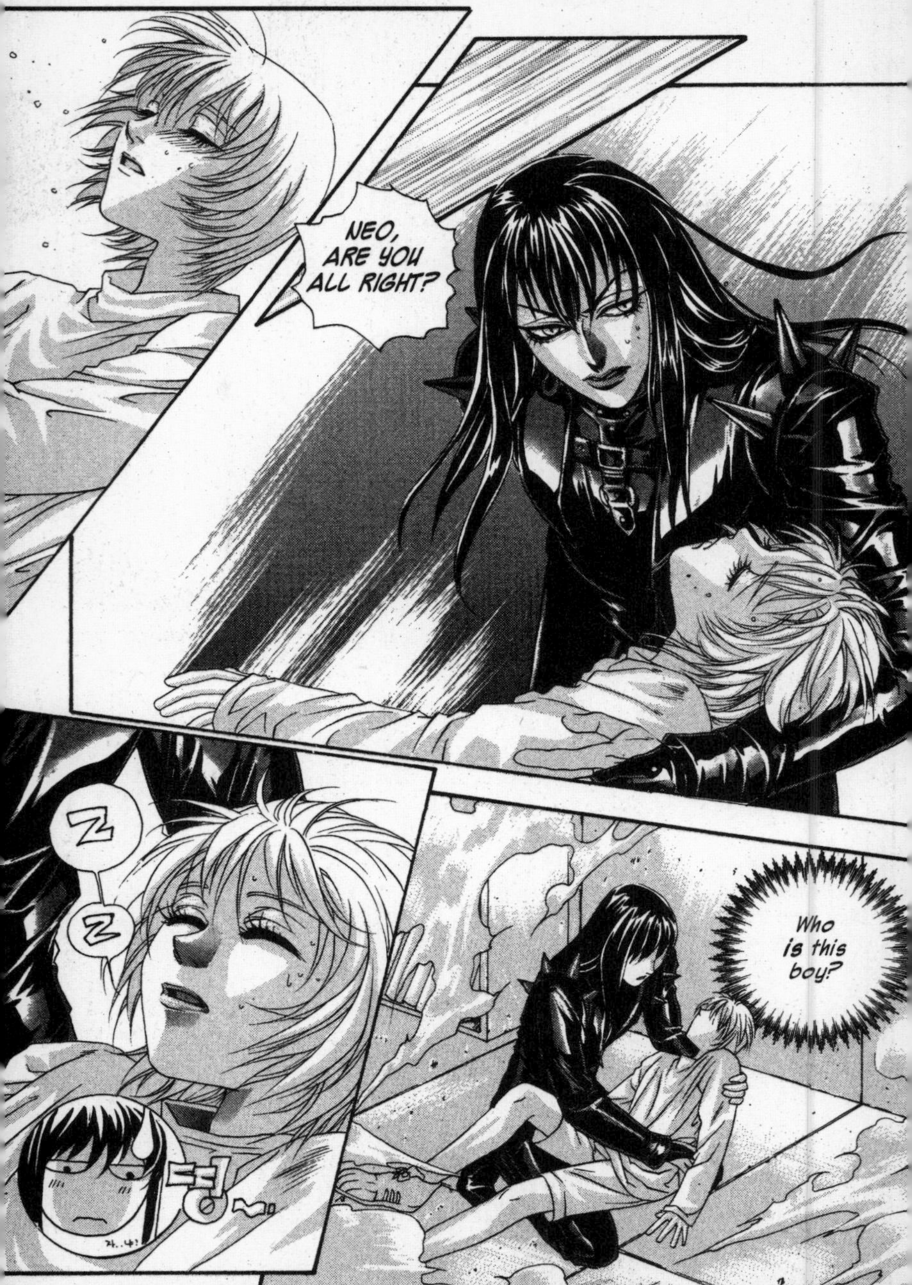
NEO, ARE YOU ALL RIGHT?
Z
Z
Who is this boy?

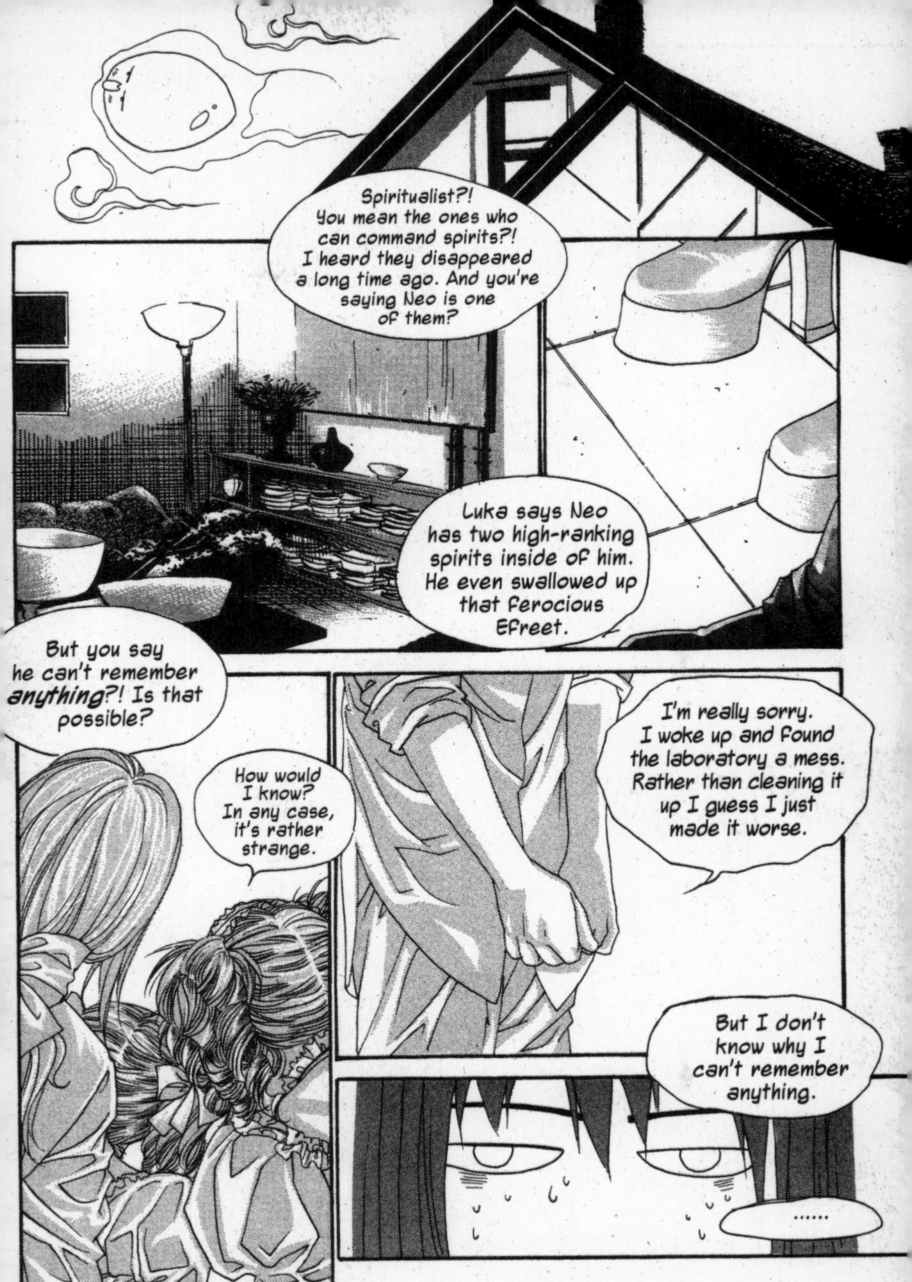
Spiritualist?! You mean the ones who can command spirits?! I heard they disappeared a long time ago. And you're saying Neo is one of them?
Luka says Neo has two high-ranking spirits inside of him. He even swallowed up that ferocious Efreet.
But you say he can't remember *anything*?! Is that possible?
How would I know? In any case, it's rather strange.
I'm really sorry. I woke up and found the laboratory a mess. Rather than cleaning it up I guess I just made it worse.
But I don't know why I can't remember anything.
......

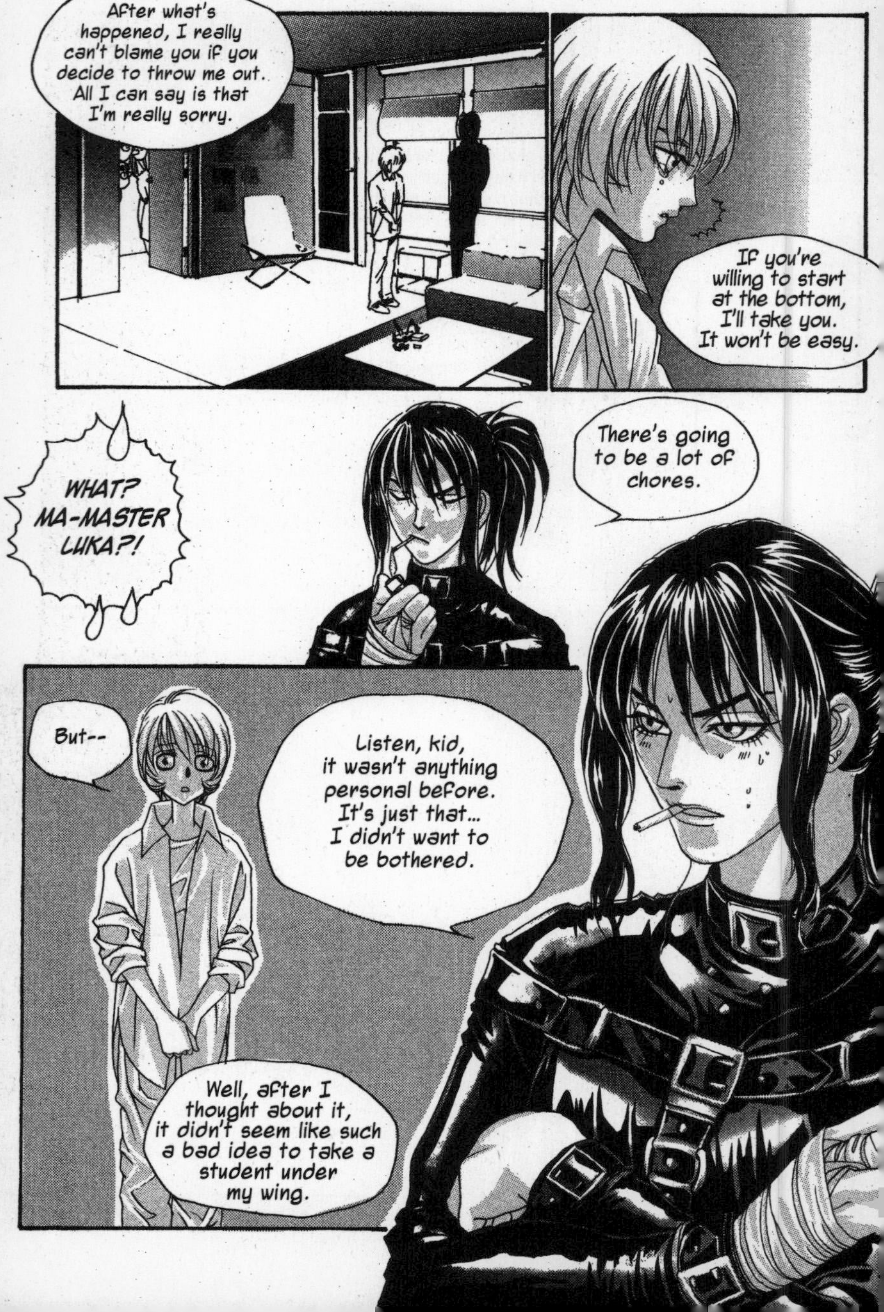
After what's happened, I really can't blame you if you decide to throw me out. All I can say is that I'm really sorry.
If you're willing to start at the bottom, I'll take you. It won't be easy.
WHAT? MA-MASTER LUKA?!
There's going to be a lot of chores.
But--
Listen, kid, it wasn't anything personal before. It's just that... I didn't want to be bothered.
Well, after I thought about it, it didn't seem like such a bad idea to take a student under my wing.

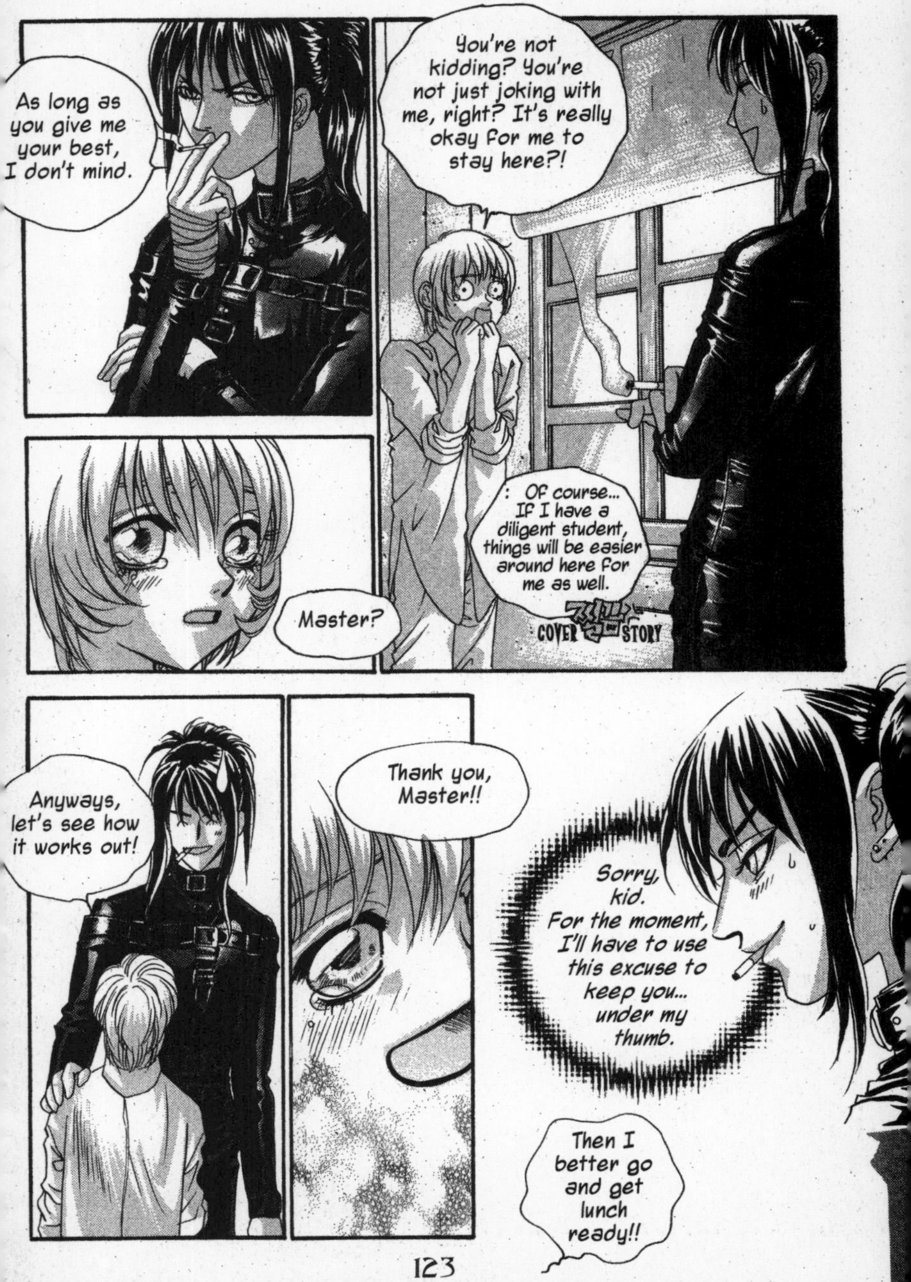
As long as you give me your best, I don't mind.
Master?
You're not kidding? You're not just joking with me, right? It's really okay for me to stay here?!
Of course... If I have a diligent student, things will be easier around here for me as well.
COVER STORY
Anyways, let's see how it works out!
Thank you, Master!!
Sorry, kid. For the moment, I'll have to use this excuse to keep you... under my thumb.
Then I better go and get lunch ready!!

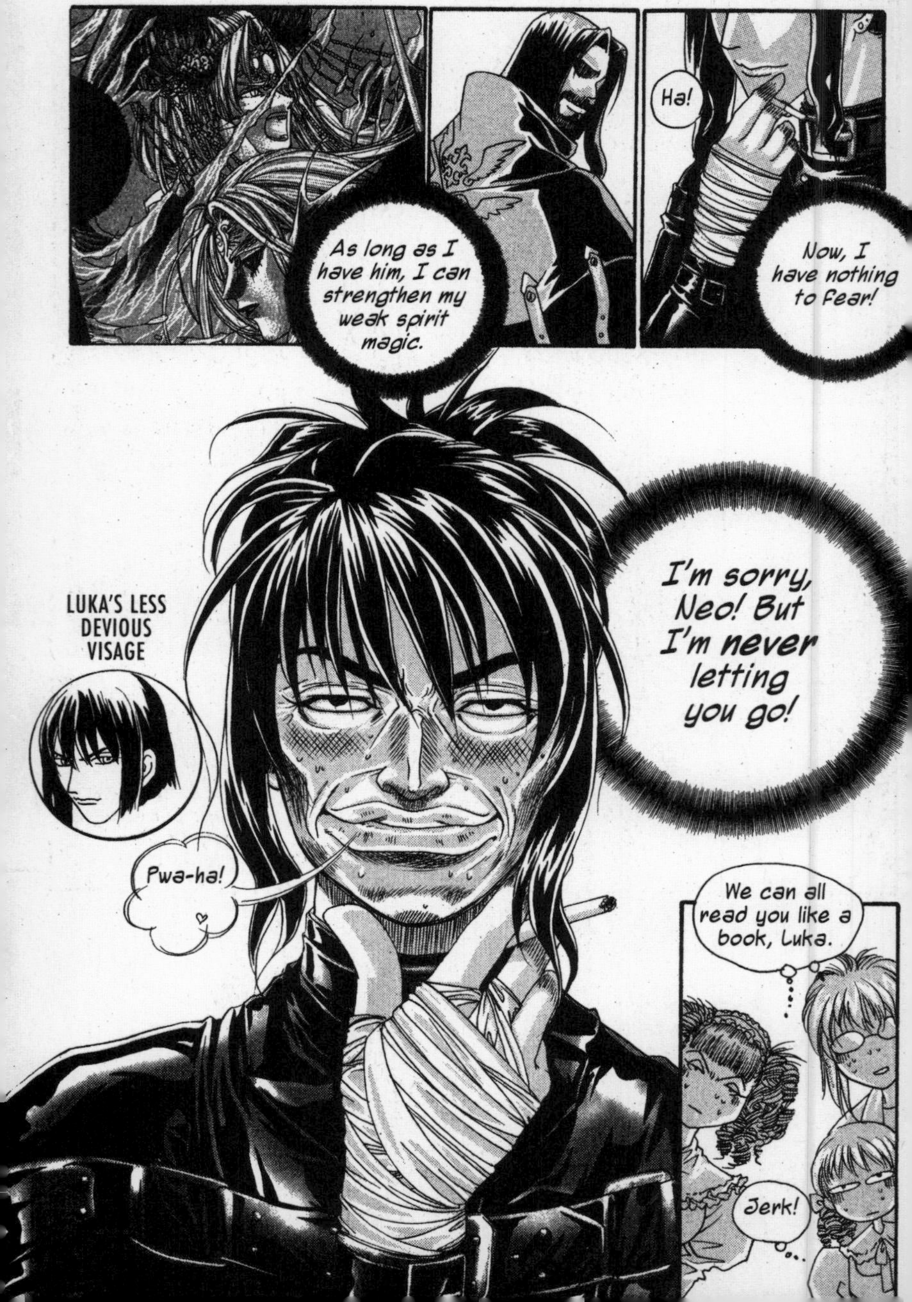
As long as I have him, I can strengthen my weak spirit magic.
Ha!
Now, I have nothing to fear!
LUKA'S LESS DEVIOUS VISAGE
Pwa-ha!
I'm sorry, Neo! But I'm **never** letting you go!
We can all read you like a book, Luka.
Jerk!

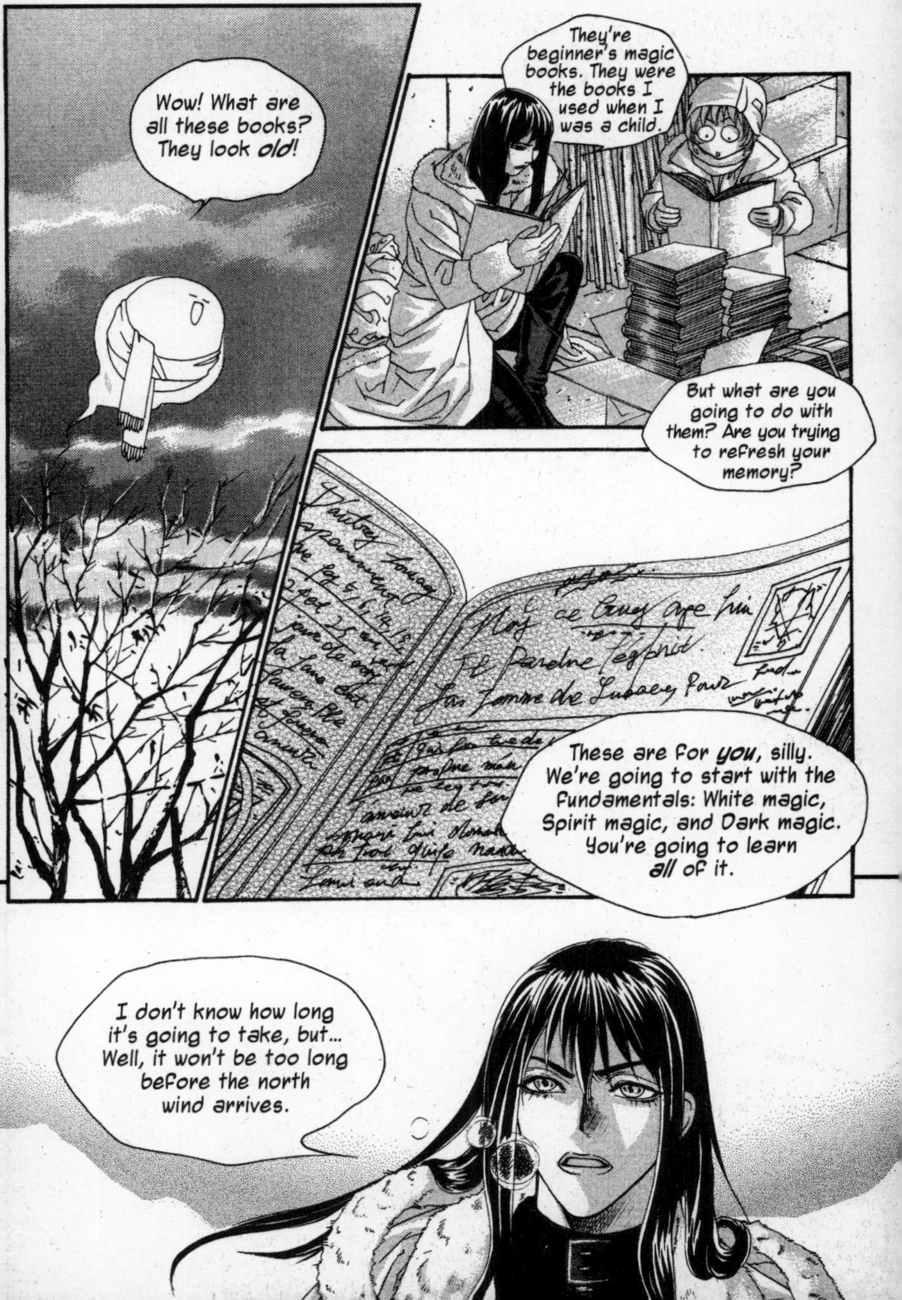
Wow! What are all these books? They look *old*!
They're beginner's magic books. They were the books I used when I was a child.
But what are you going to do with them? Are you trying to refresh your memory?
These are for **you**, silly. We're going to start with the fundamentals: White magic, Spirit magic, and Dark magic. You're going to learn *all* of it.
I don't know how long it's going to take, but... Well, it won't be too long before the north wind arrives.

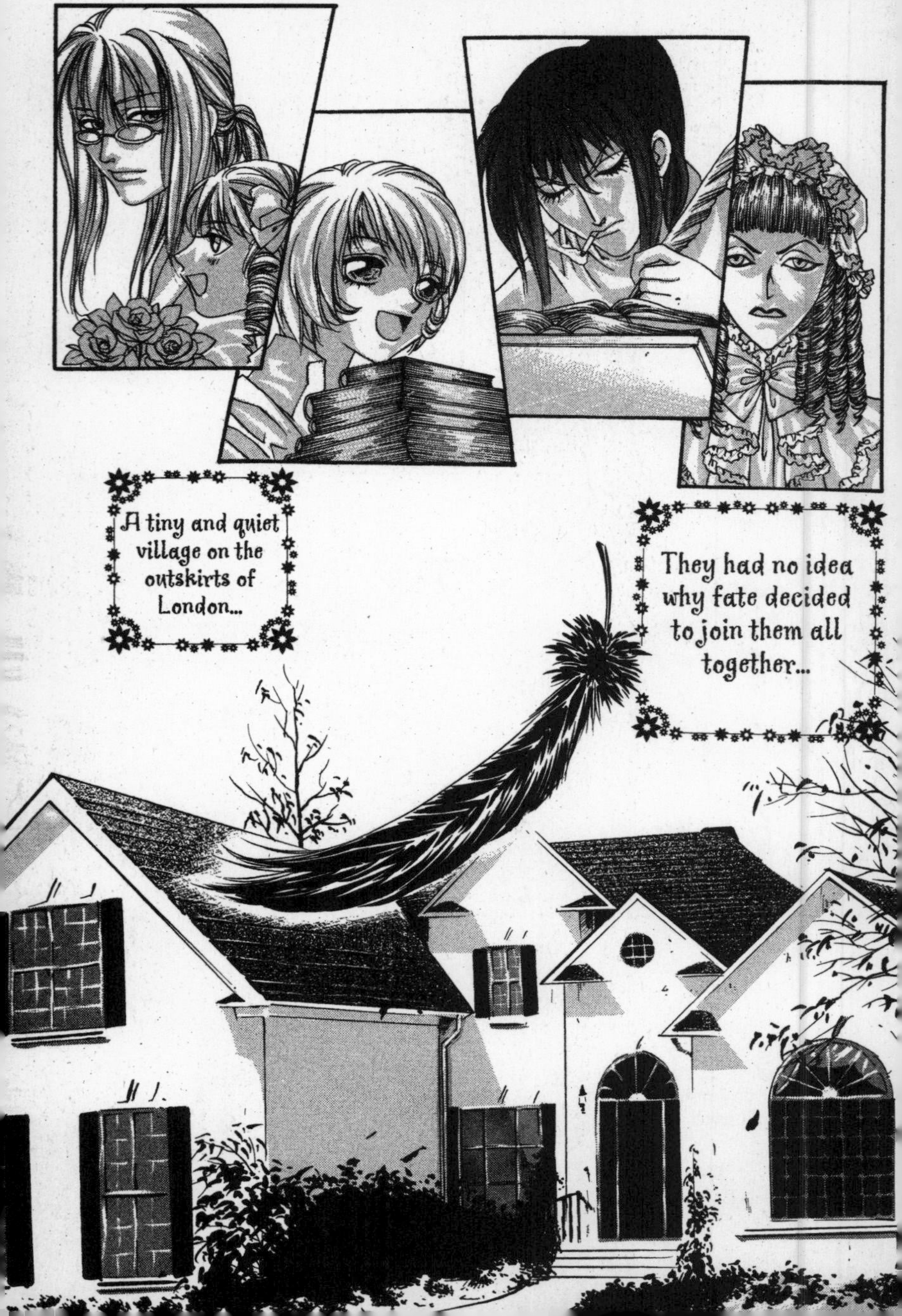
A tiny and quiet village on the outskirts of London...
They had no idea why fate decided to join them all together...

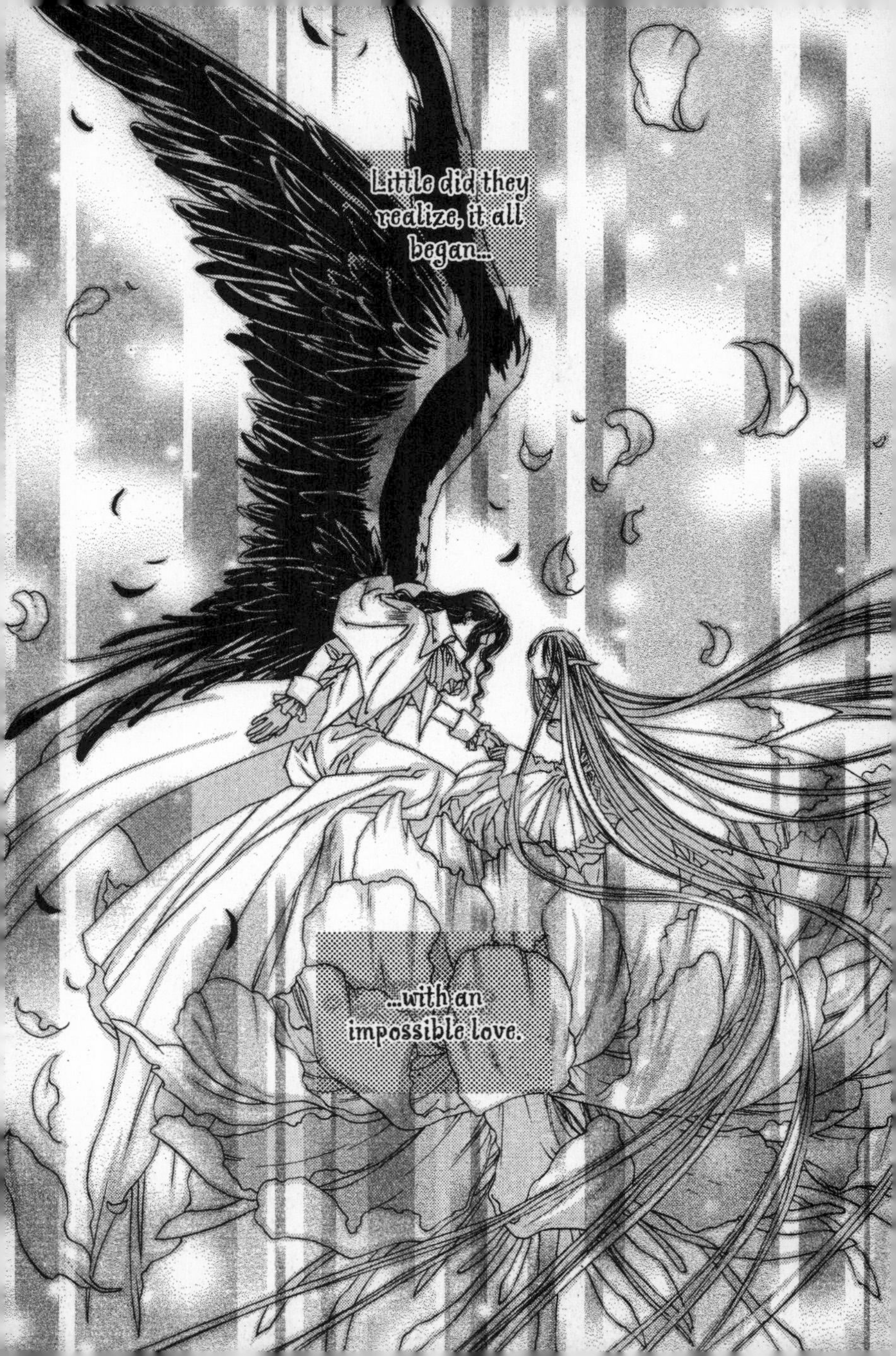
Little did they realize, it all began...
...with an impossible love.

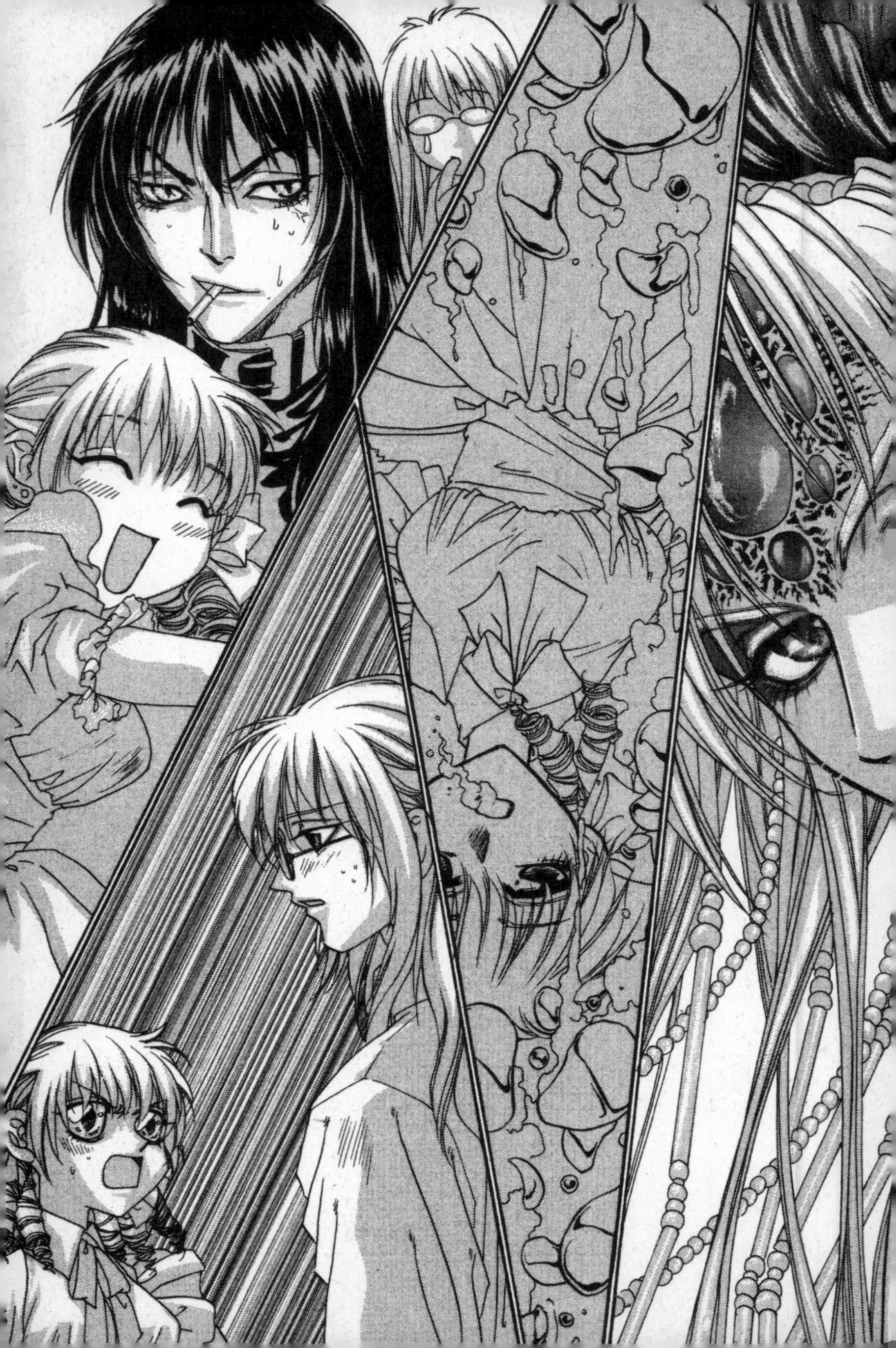

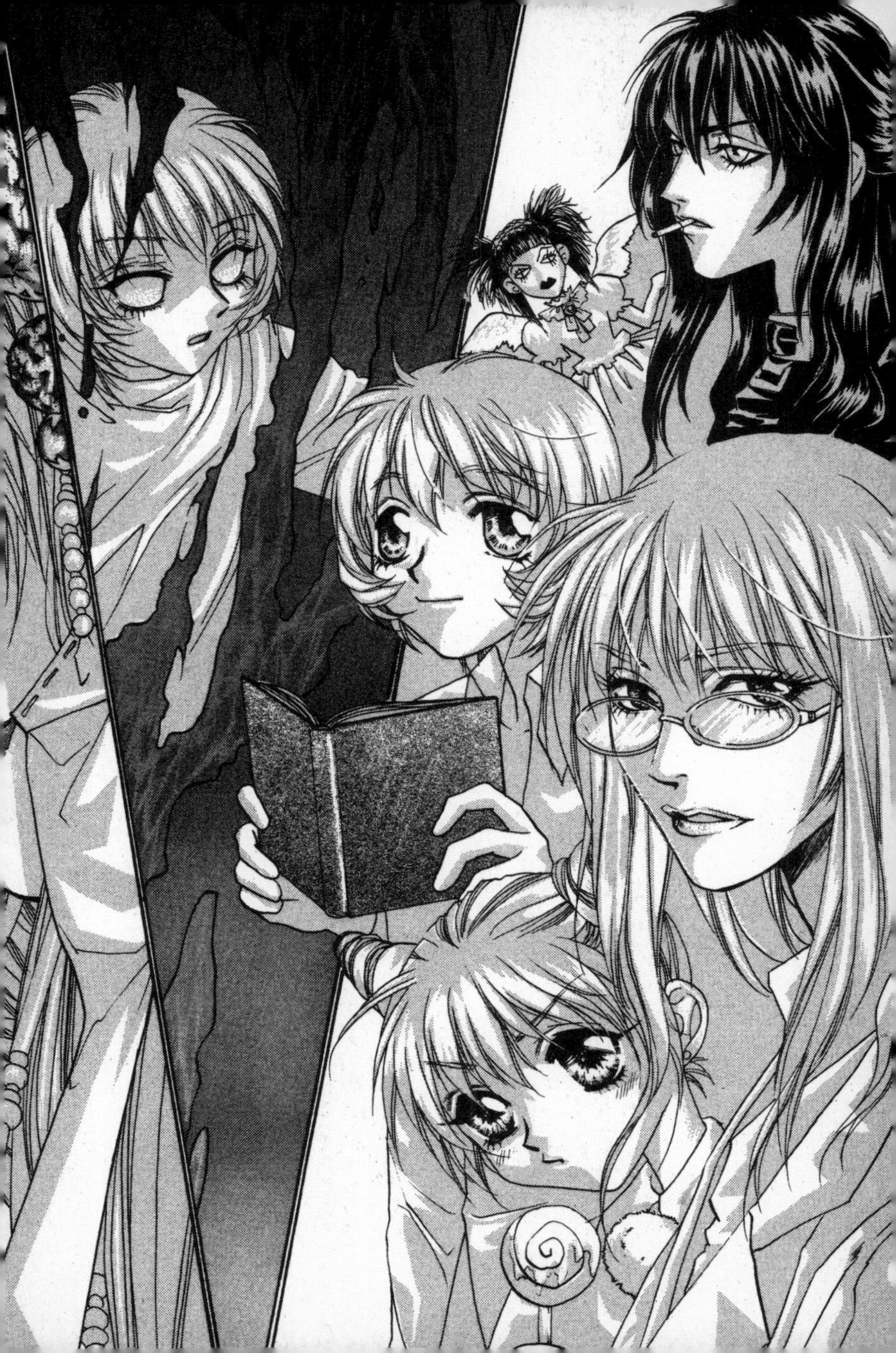

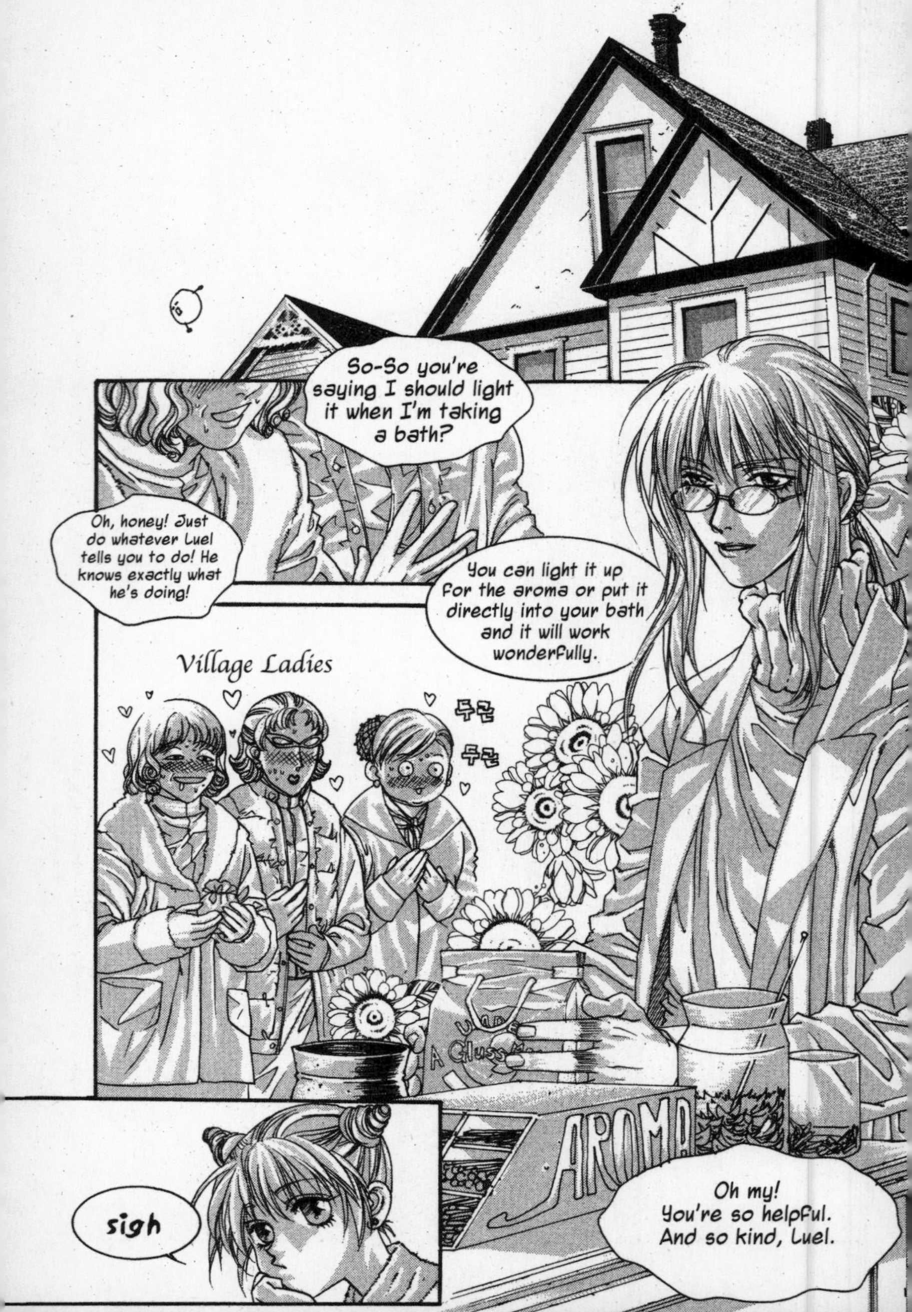
So-So you're saying I should light it when I'm taking a bath?
Oh, honey! Just do whatever Luel tells you to do! He knows exactly what he's doing!
Village Ladies
두근
두근
You can light it up for the aroma or put it directly into your bath and it will work wonderfully.
AROMA
sigh
Oh my! You're so helpful. And so kind, Luel.

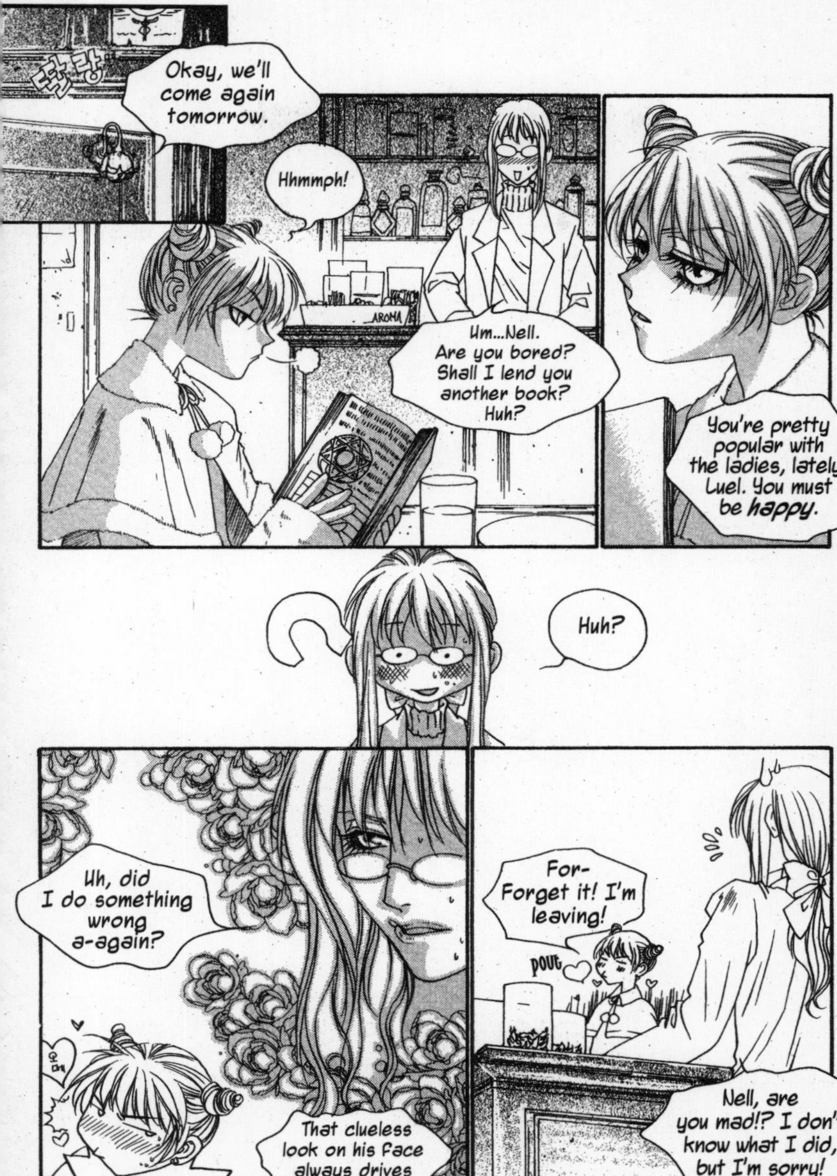

딸랑
Okay, we'll come again tomorrow.
Hhmmph!
AROMA
Um...Nell. Are you bored? Shall I lend you another book? Huh?
You're pretty popular with the ladies, lately, Luel. You must be *happy*.
Huh?
Uh, did I do something wrong a-again?
JEEZ!
That clueless look on his face always drives me crazy!
For- Forget it! I'm leaving!
pout
Nell, are you mad!? I don't know what I did, but I'm sorry!

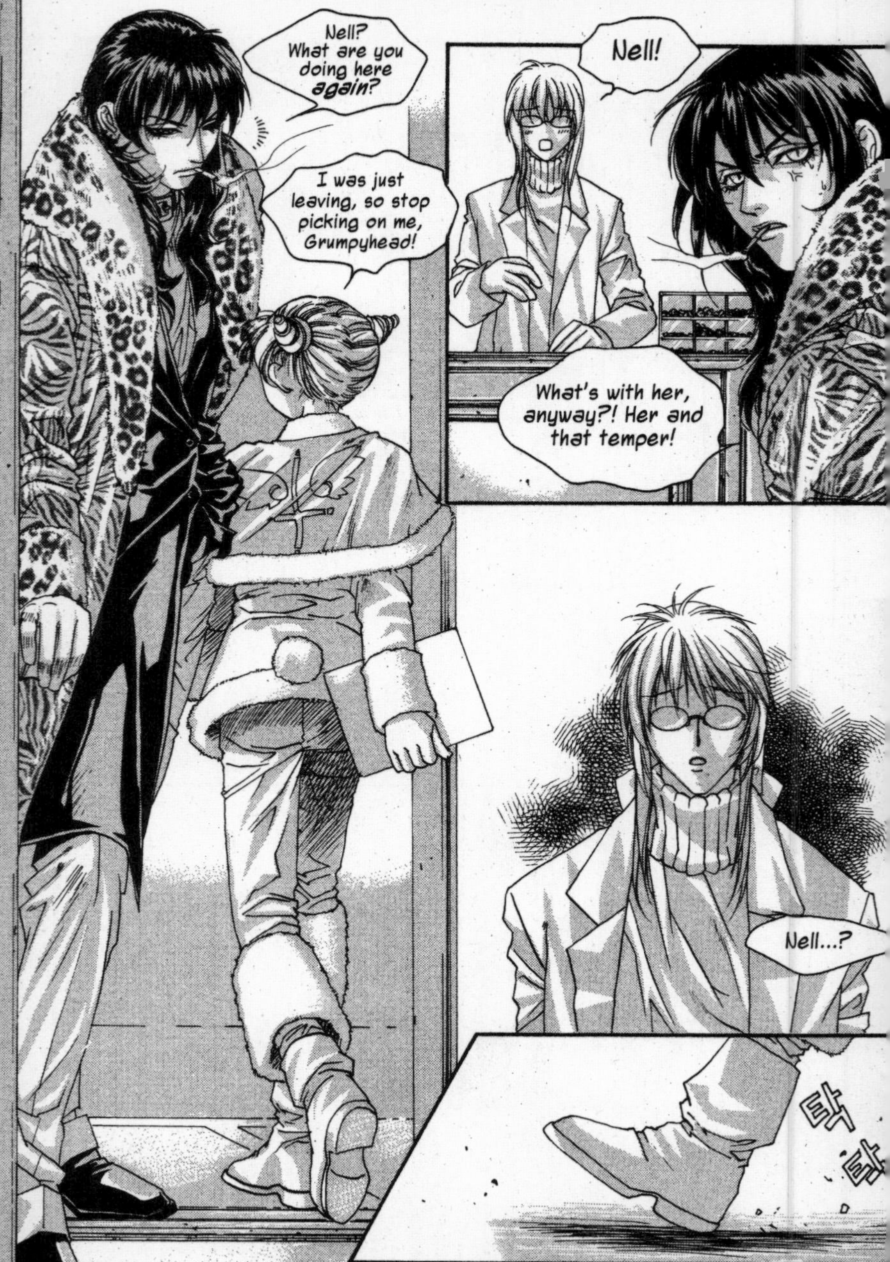

Nell? What are you doing here *again*?
I was just leaving, so stop picking on me, Grumpyhead!
Nell!
What's with her, anyway?! Her and that temper!
Nell...?

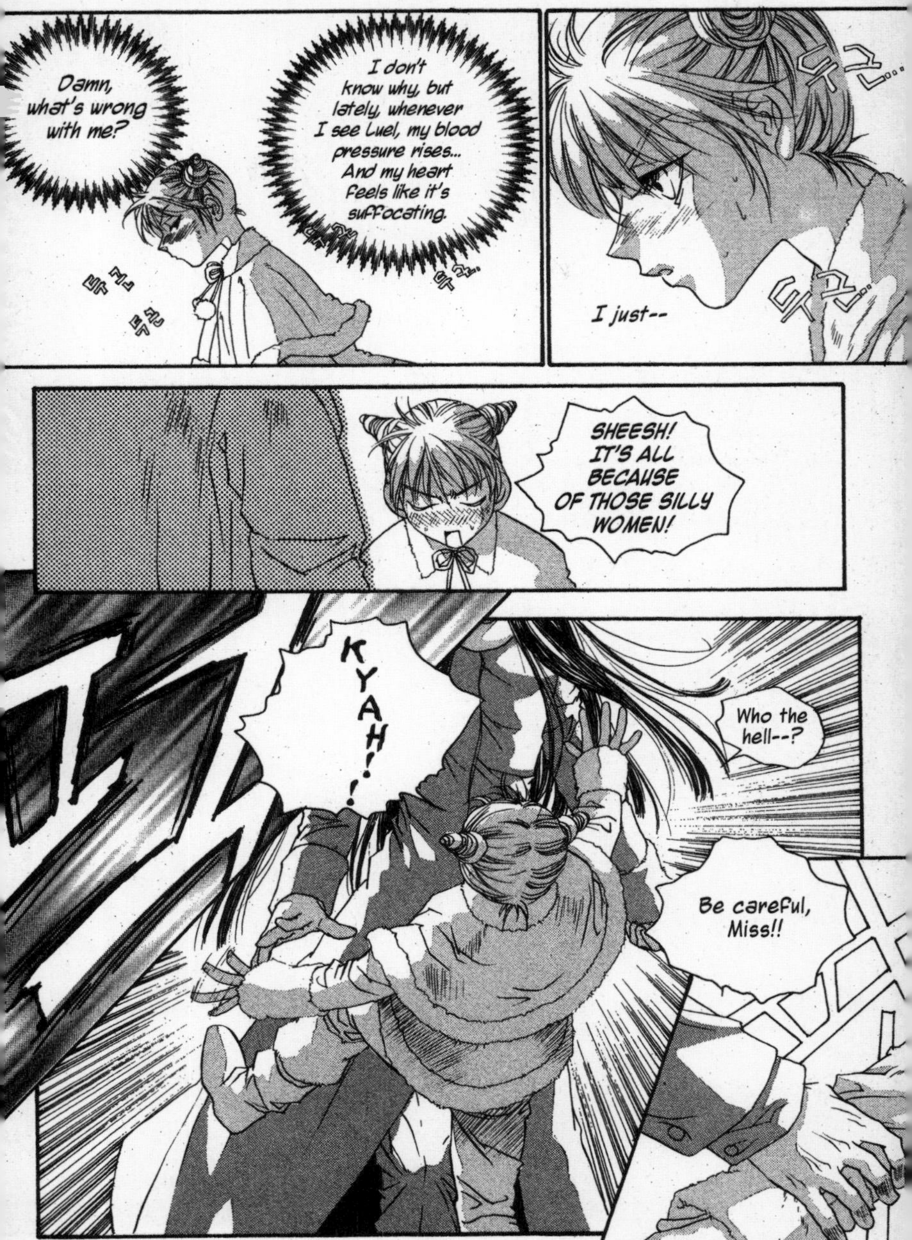
Damn, what's wrong with me?
I don't know why, but lately, whenever I see Luel, my blood pressure rises... And my heart feels like it's suffocating.
I just--
SHEESH! IT'S ALL BECAUSE OF THOSE SILLY WOMEN!
KYAH!!
Who the hell--?
Be careful, Miss!!

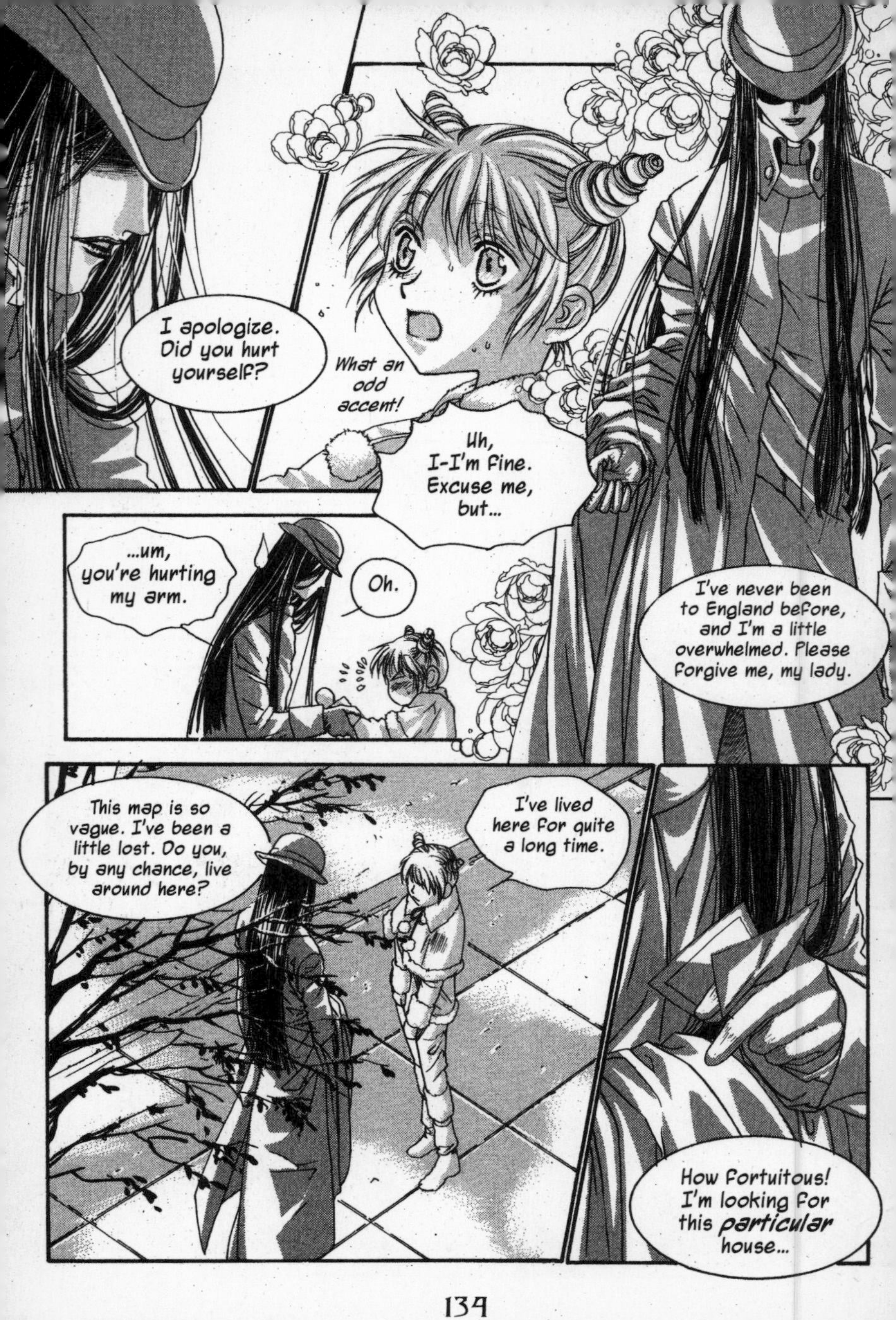
I apologize. Did you hurt yourself?
What an odd accent!
Uh, I-I'm fine. Excuse me, but...
...um, you're hurting my arm.
Oh.
I've never been to England before, and I'm a little overwhelmed. Please forgive me, my lady.
This map is so vague. I've been a little lost. Do you, by any chance, live around here?
I've lived here for quite a long time.
How fortuitous! I'm looking for this *particular* house...

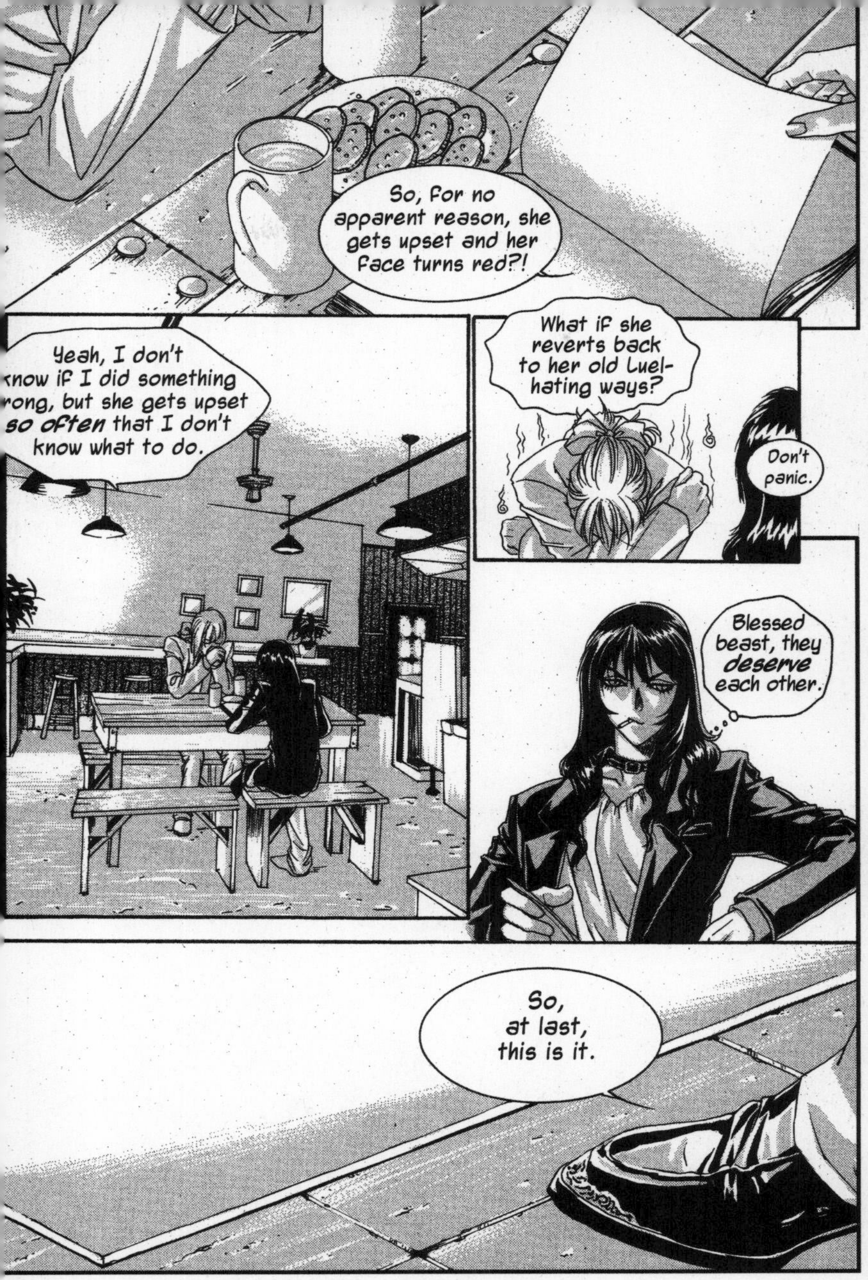

So, for no apparent reason, she gets upset and her face turns red?!
Yeah, I don't know if I did something rong, but she gets upset *so often* that I don't know what to do.
What if she reverts back to her old Luel-hating ways?
Don't panic.
Blessed beast, they ***deserve*** each other.
So, at last, this is it.

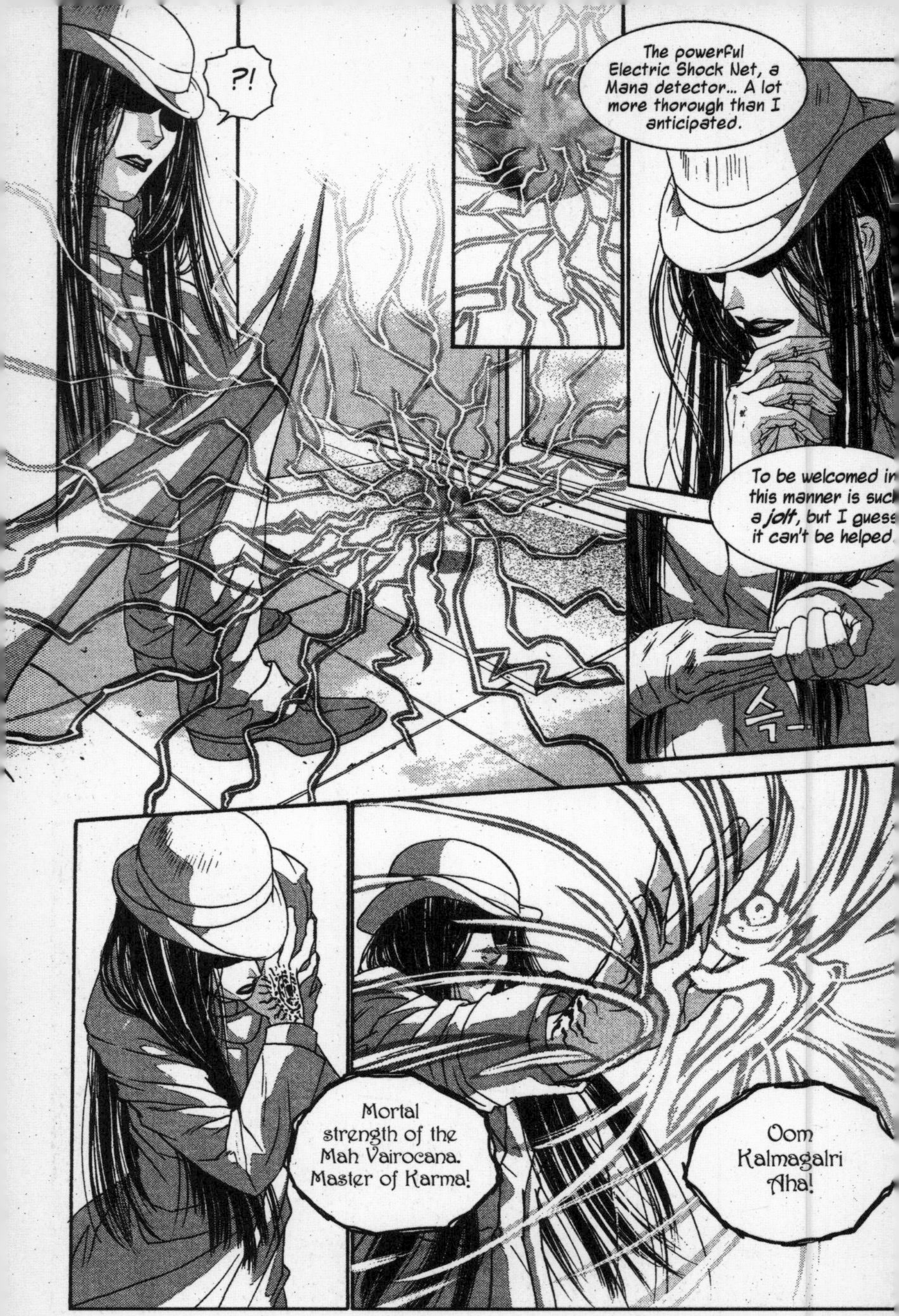
?!
The powerful Electric Shock Net, a Mana detector... A lot more thorough than I anticipated.
To be welcomed in this manner is suc a *jolt*, but I gues it can't be helped.
Mortal strength of the Mah Vairocana. Master of Karma!
Oom Kalmagalri Aha!

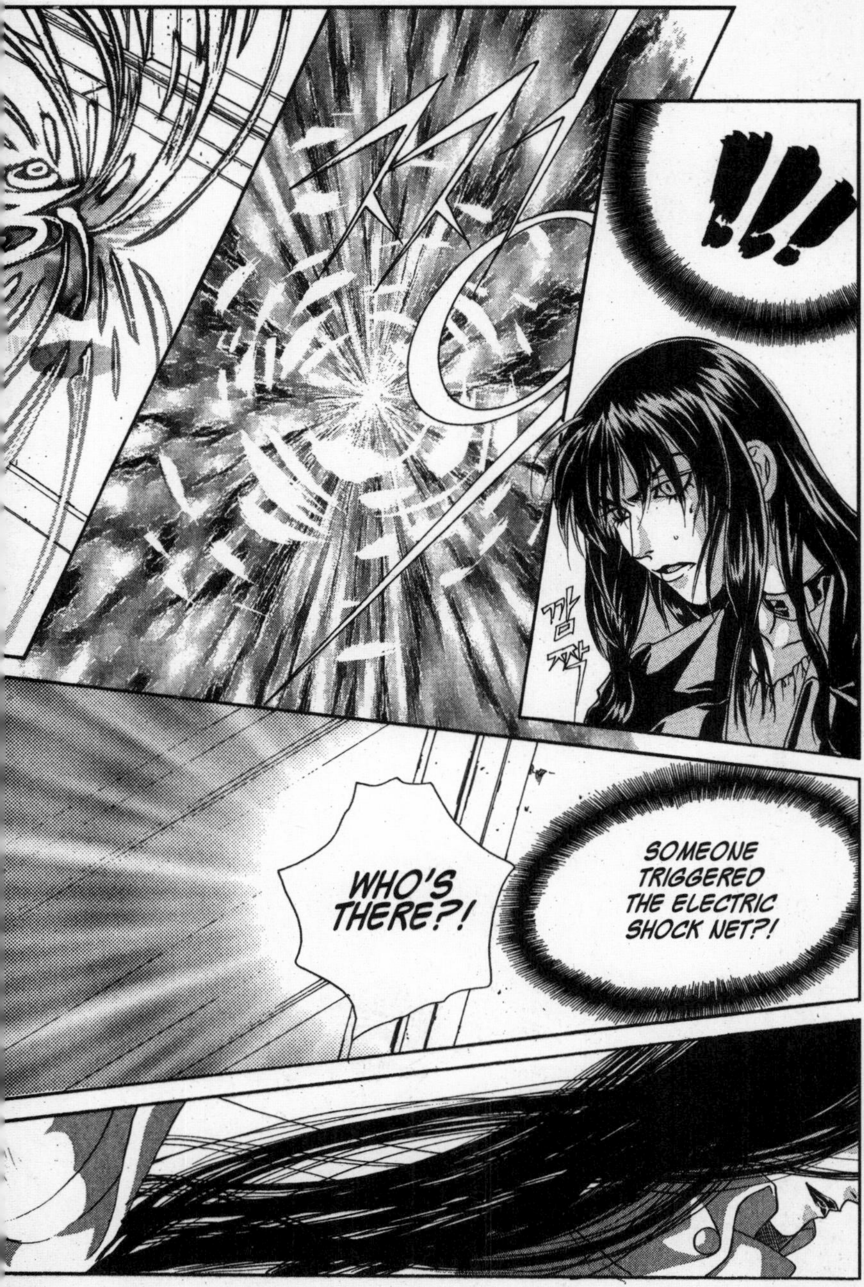
!!!
깜짝
WHO'S THERE?!
SOMEONE TRIGGERED THE ELECTRIC SHOCK NET?!

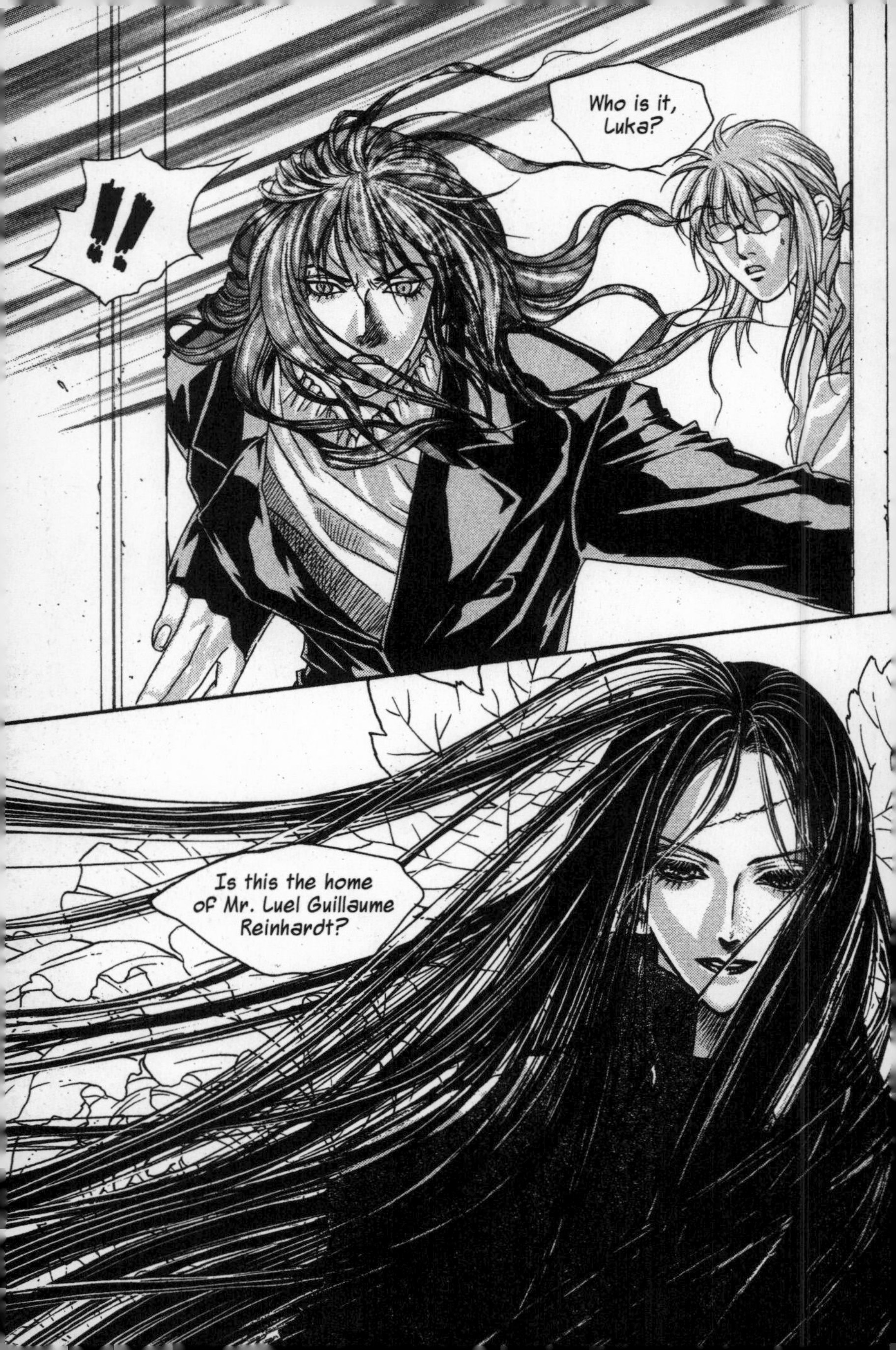
!!
Who is it, Luka?
Is this the home of Mr. Luel Guillaume Reinhardt?

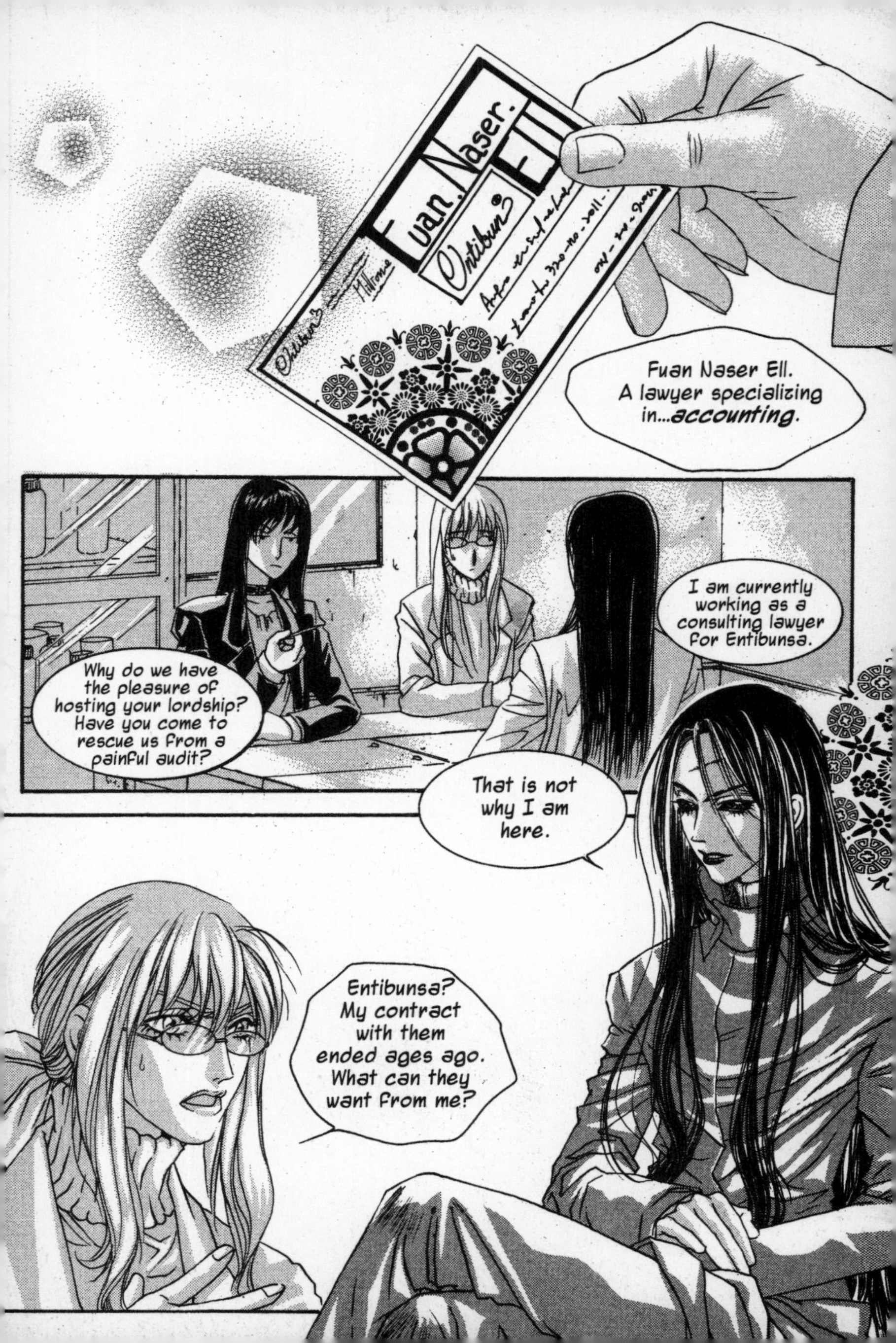

Fuan. Naser. Ell
Entibuns
Fuan Naser Ell. A lawyer specializing in...*accounting*.
I am currently working as a consulting lawyer for Entibunsa.
Why do we have the pleasure of hosting your lordship? Have you come to rescue us from a painful audit?
That is not why I am here.
Entibunsa? My contract with them ended ages ago. What can they want from me?

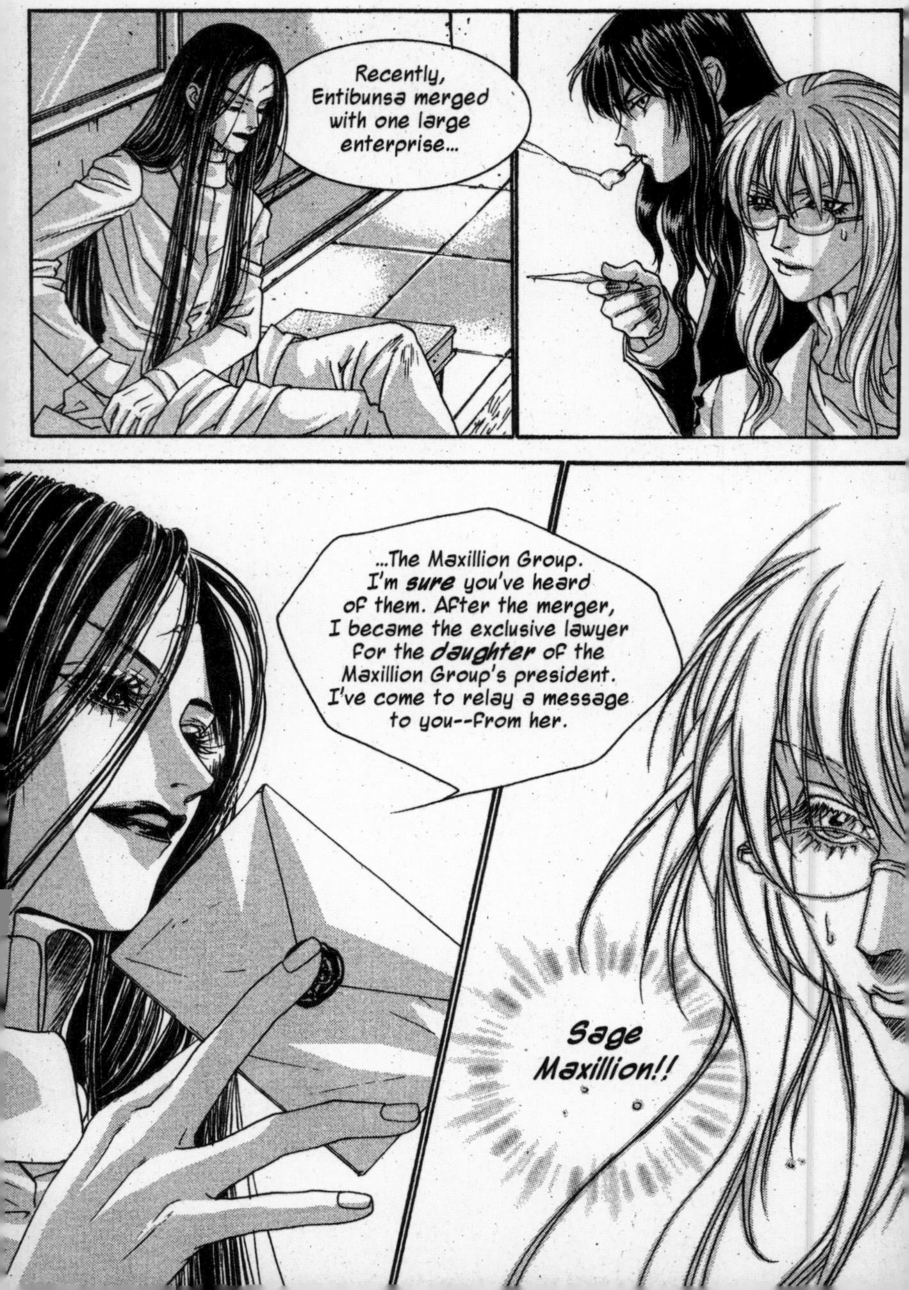
Recently, Entibunsa merged with one large enterprise...
...The Maxillion Group. I'm *sure* you've heard of them. After the merger, I became the exclusive lawyer for the *daughter* of the Maxillion Group's president. I've come to relay a message to you--from her.
Sage Maxillion!!

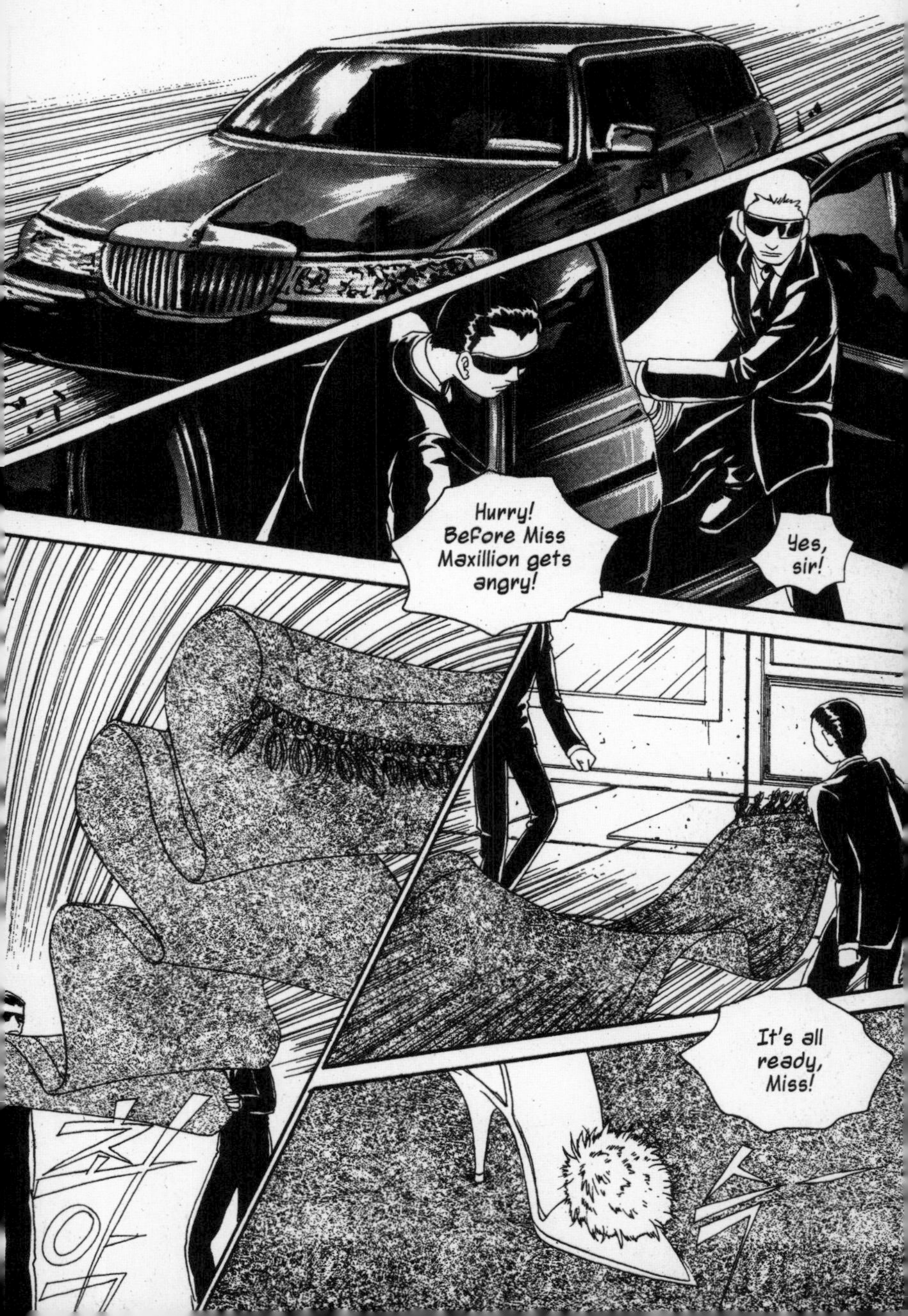
Hurry! Before Miss Maxillion gets angry!
Yes, sir!
It's all ready, Miss!

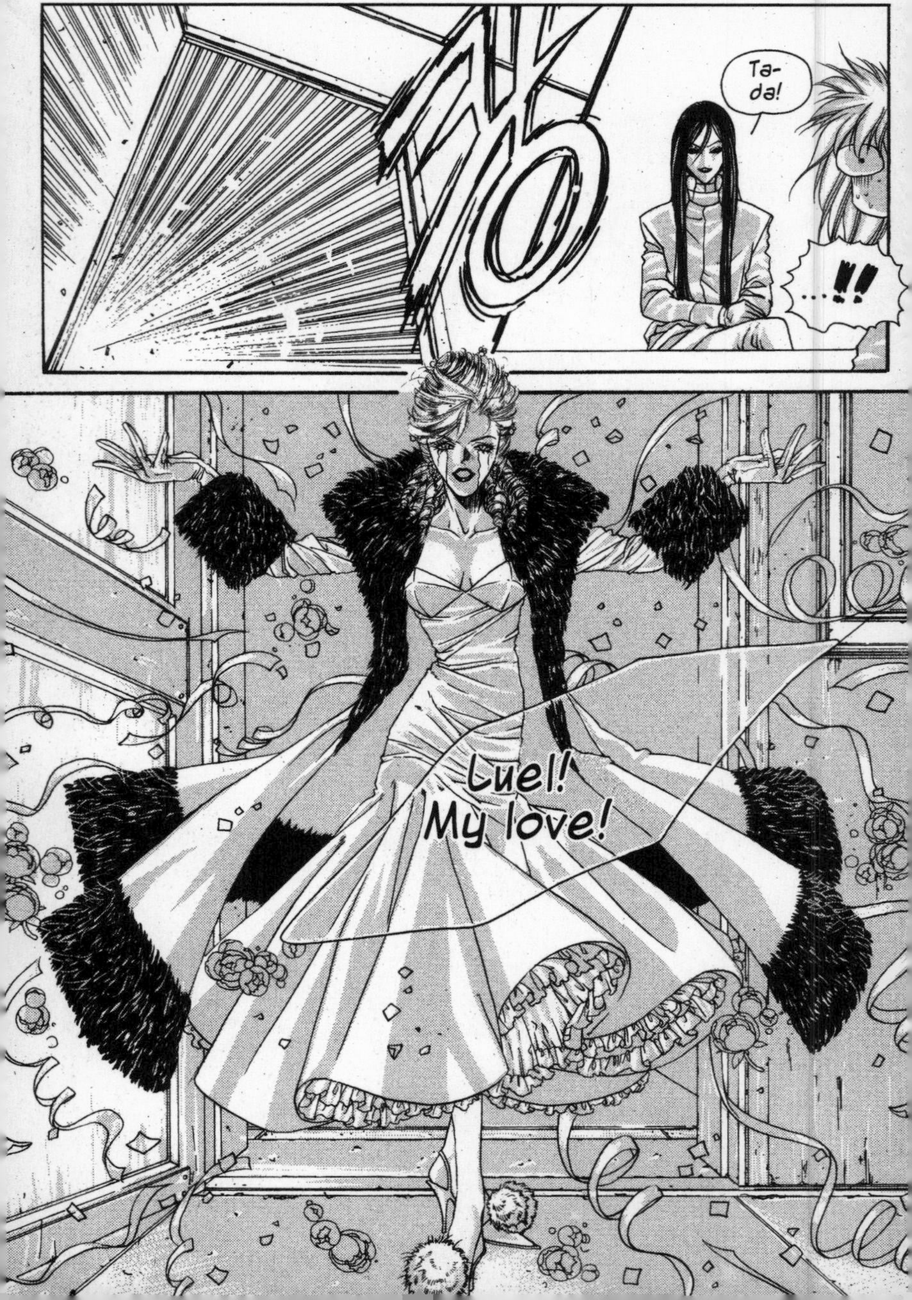
Ta-da!
...!!
Luel! My love!

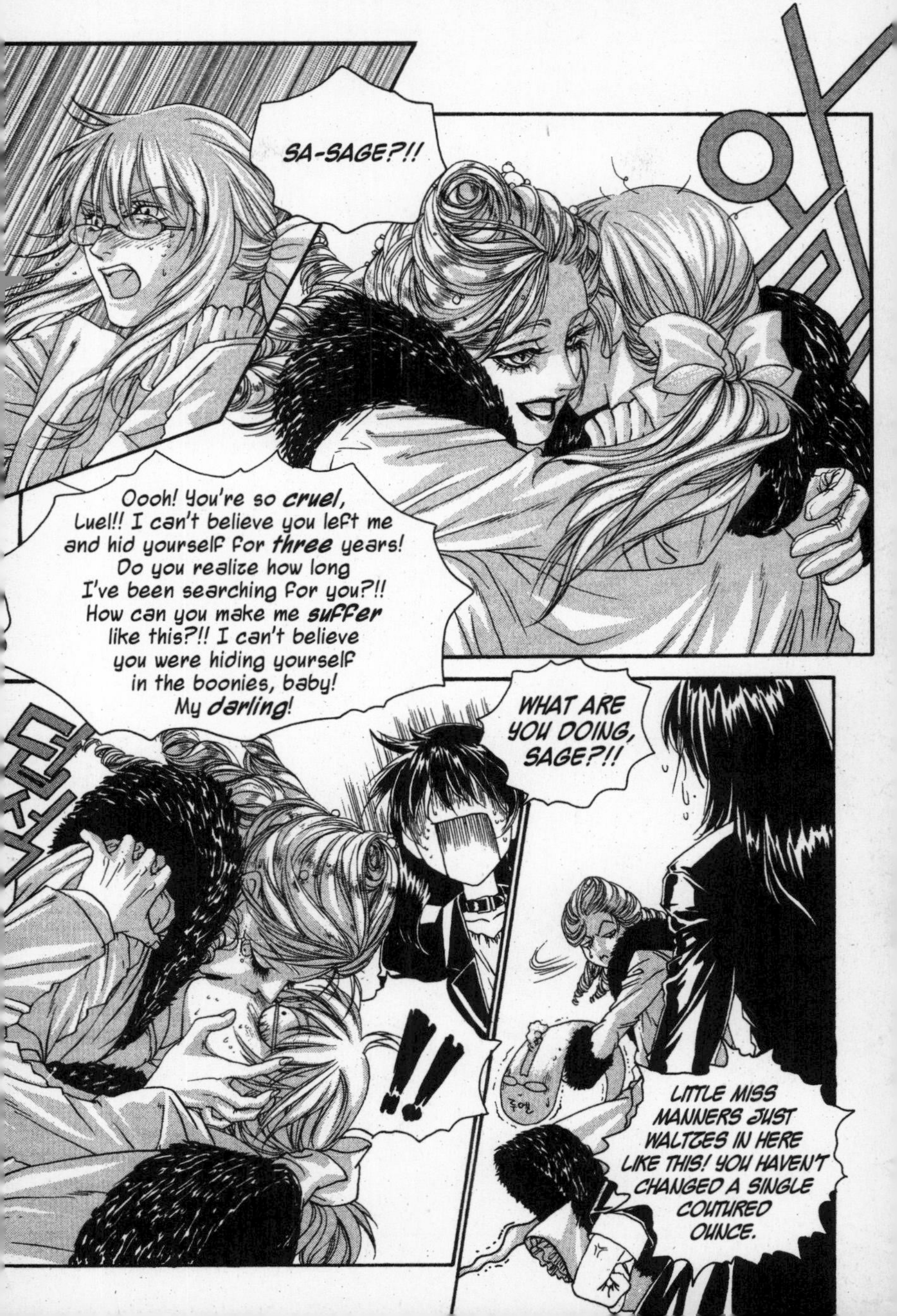
SA-SAGE?!!
Oooh! You're so cruel, Luel!! I can't believe you left me and hid yourself for three years! Do you realize how long I've been searching for you?!! How can you make me suffer like this?!! I can't believe you were hiding yourself in the boonies, baby! My darling!
WHAT ARE YOU DOING, SAGE?!!
LITTLE MISS MANNERS JUST WALTZES IN HERE LIKE THIS! YOU HAVEN'T CHANGED A SINGLE COUTURED OUNCE.

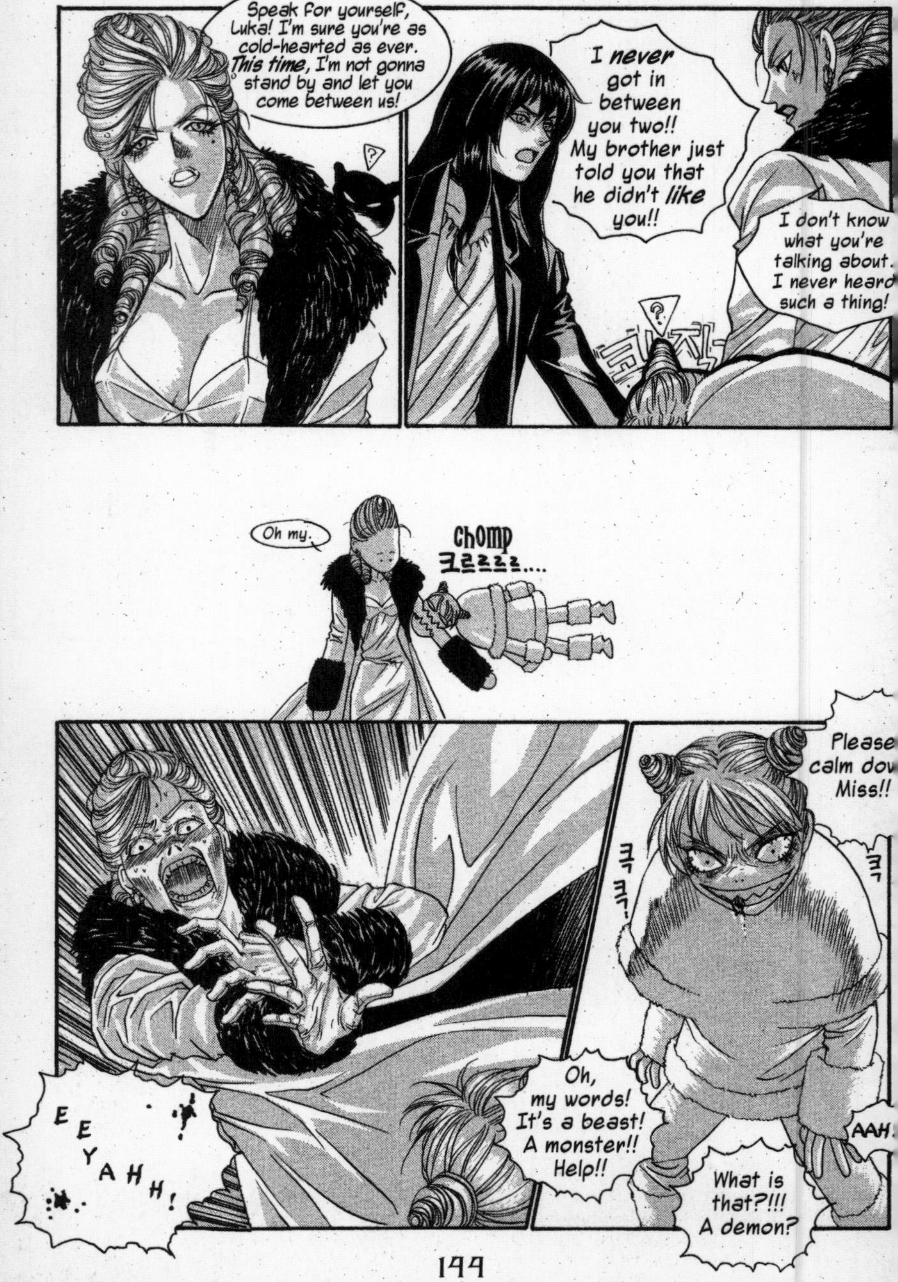
Speak for yourself, Luka! I'm sure you're as cold-hearted as ever. ***This time***, I'm not gonna stand by and let you come between us!
?
I ***never*** got in between you two!! My brother just told you that he didn't ***like*** you!!
I don't know what you're talking about. I never heard such a thing!
?
Oh my.
Chomp
EEYAHH!
Oh, my words! It's a beast! A monster!! Help!!
Please calm dow Miss!!
AAH
What is that?!!! A demon?

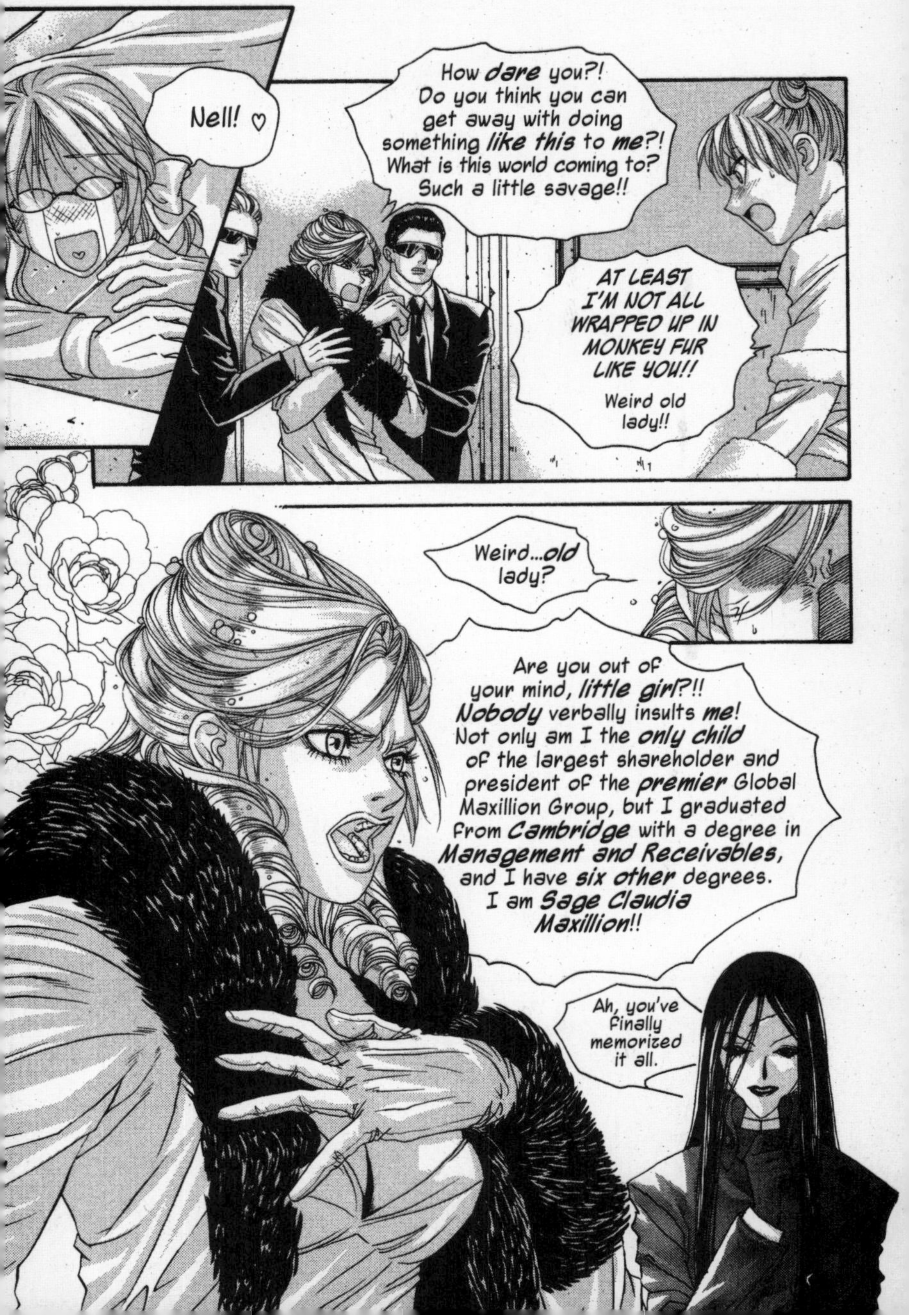
Nell! ♡
How dare you?! Do you think you can get away with doing something like this to me?! What is this world coming to? Such a little savage!!
AT LEAST I'M NOT ALL WRAPPED UP IN MONKEY FUR LIKE YOU!! Weird old lady!!
Weird...old lady?
Are you out of your mind, little girl?!! Nobody verbally insults me! Not only am I the only child of the largest shareholder and president of the premier Global Maxillion Group, but I graduated from Cambridge with a degree in Management and Receivables, and I have six other degrees. I am Sage Claudia Maxillion!!
Ah, you've finally memorized it all.

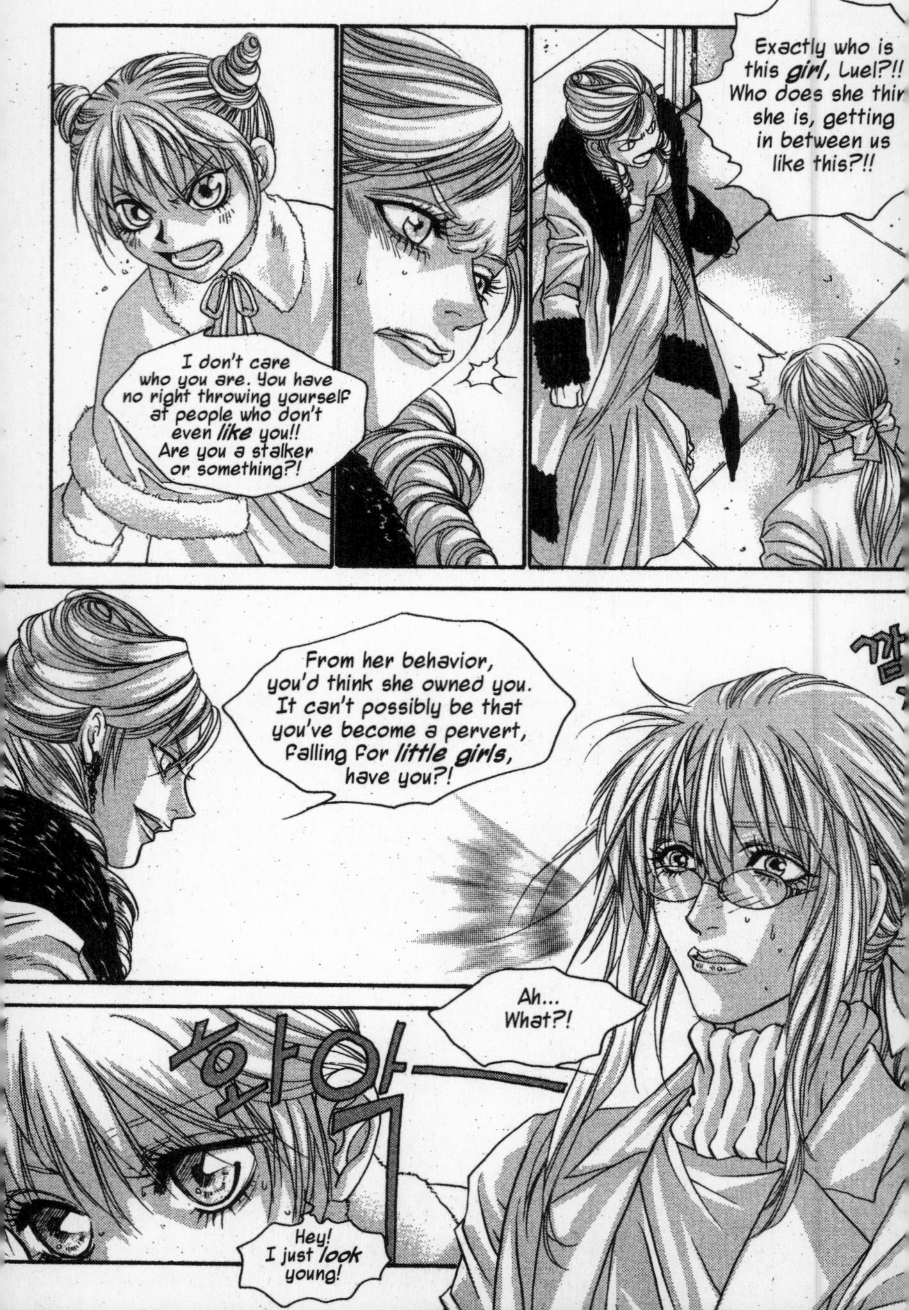
I don't care who you are. You have no right throwing yourself at people who don't even *like* you!! Are you a stalker or something?!
Exactly who is this *girl*, Luel?!! Who does she thir she is, getting in between us like this?!!
From her behavior, you'd think she owned you. It can't possibly be that you've become a pervert, falling for *little girls*, have you?!
Ah... What?!
Hey! I just *look* young!

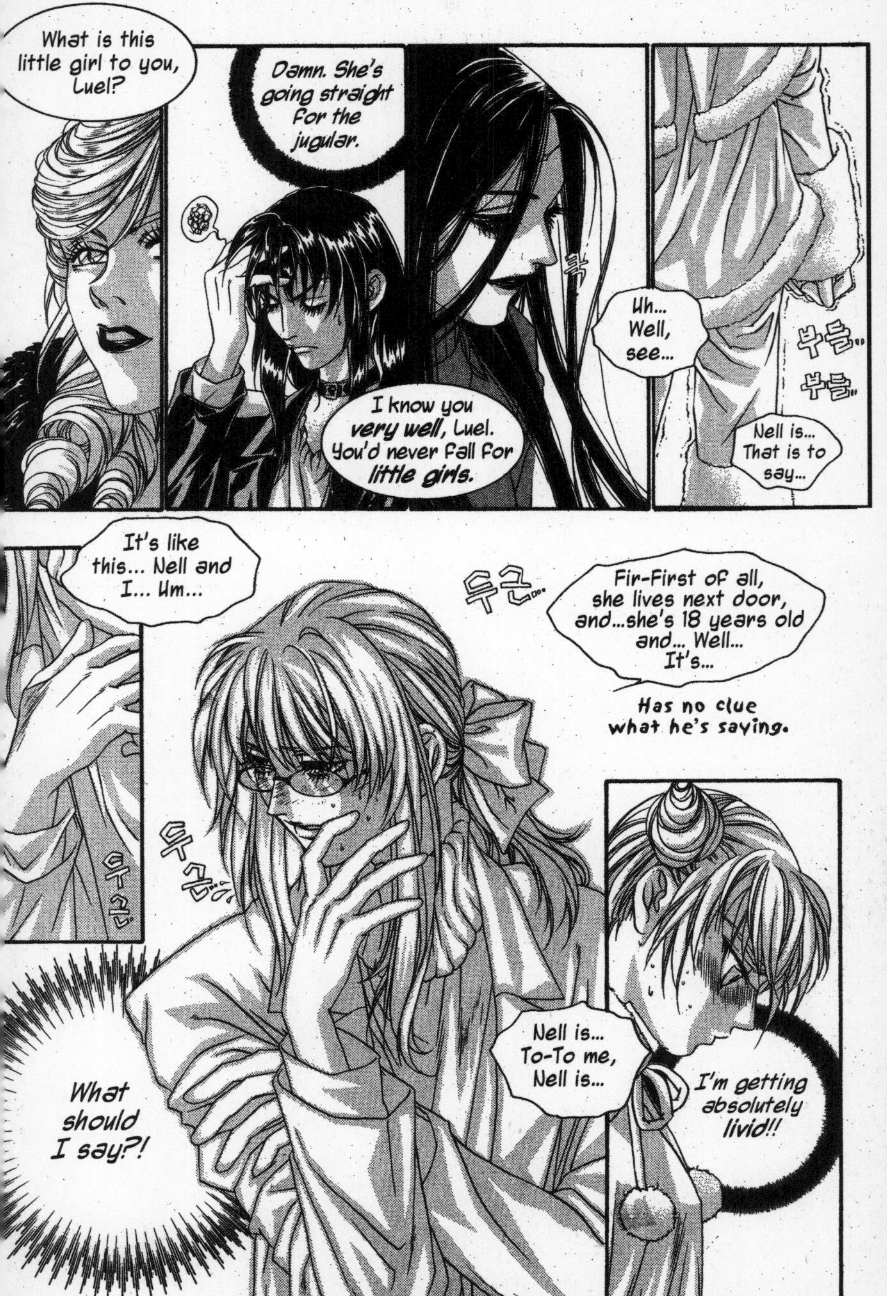

What is this little girl to you, Luel?
Damn. She's going straight for the jugular.
I know you *very well*, Luel. You'd never fall for *little girls.*
Uh... Well, see...
부들..
부들..
Nell is... That is to say...
It's like this... Nell and I... Um...
두근...
두근...
Fir-First of all, she lives next door, and...she's 18 years old and... Well... It's...
Has no clue what he's saying.
두근...
What should I say?!
Nell is... To-To me, Nell is...
I'm getting absolutely livid!!

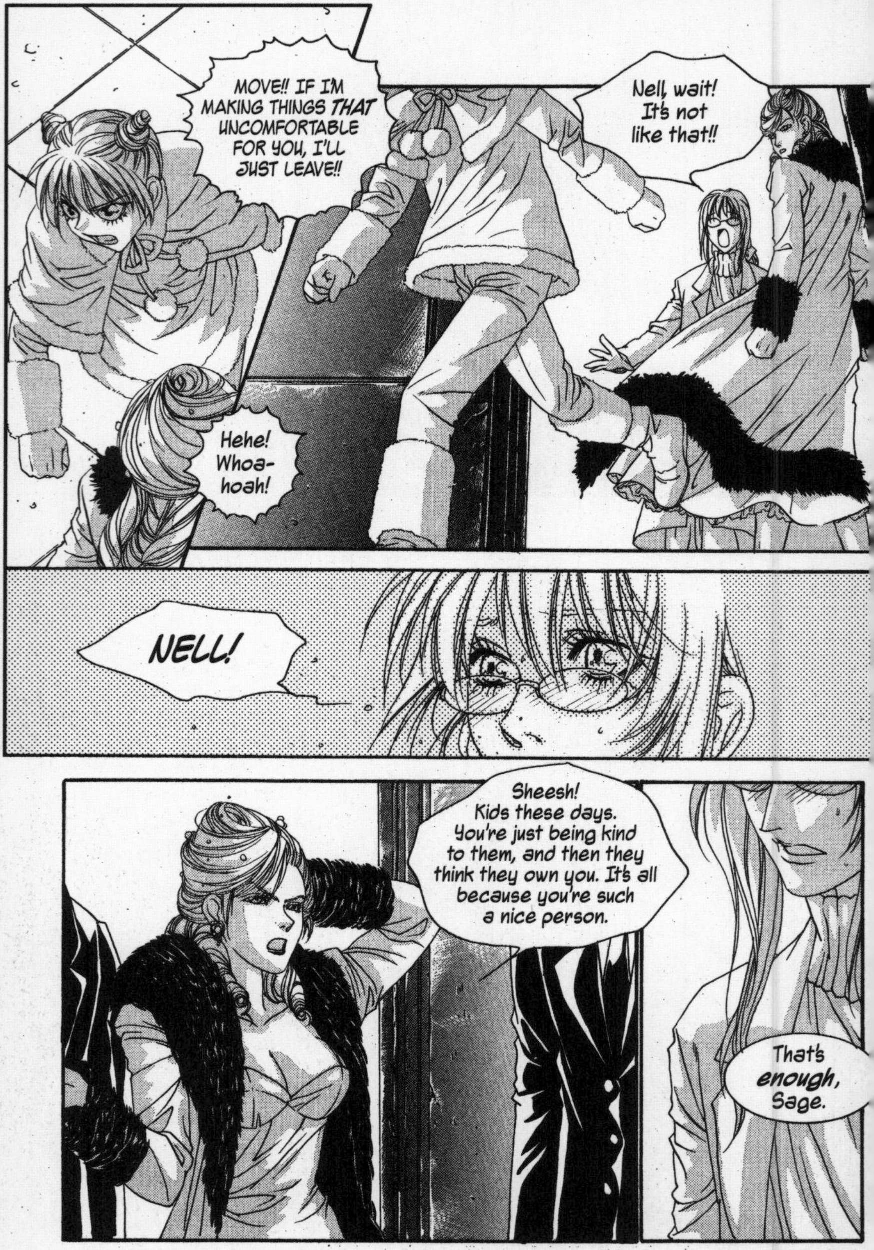
MOVE!! IF I'M MAKING THINGS *THAT* UNCOMFORTABLE FOR YOU, I'LL JUST LEAVE!!
Nell, wait! It's not like that!!
Hehe! Whoa-hoah!
NELL!
Sheesh! Kids these days. You're just being kind to them, and then they think they own you. It's all because you're such a nice person.
That's *enough*, Sage.

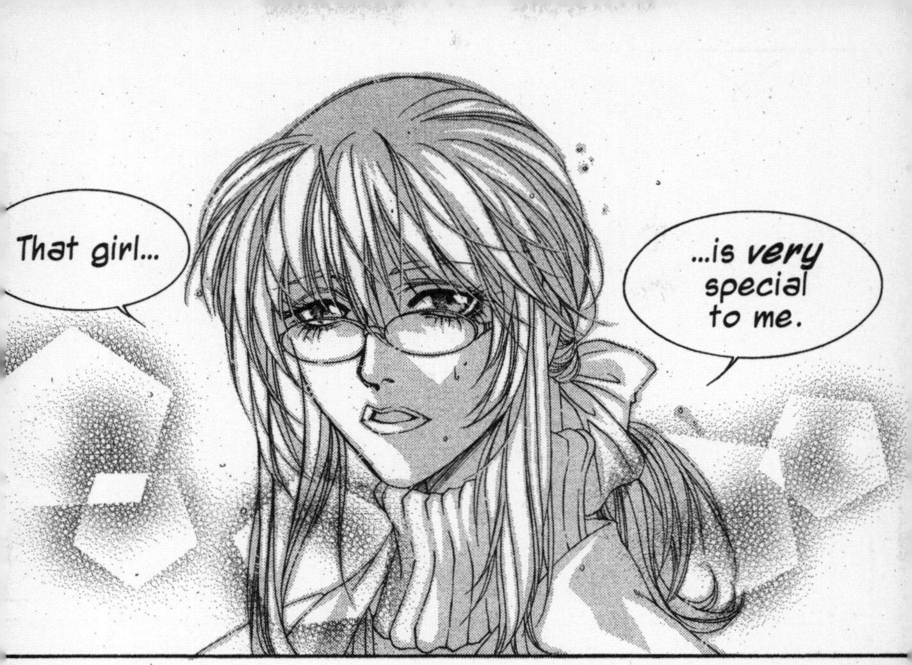
That girl...
...is *very* special to me.
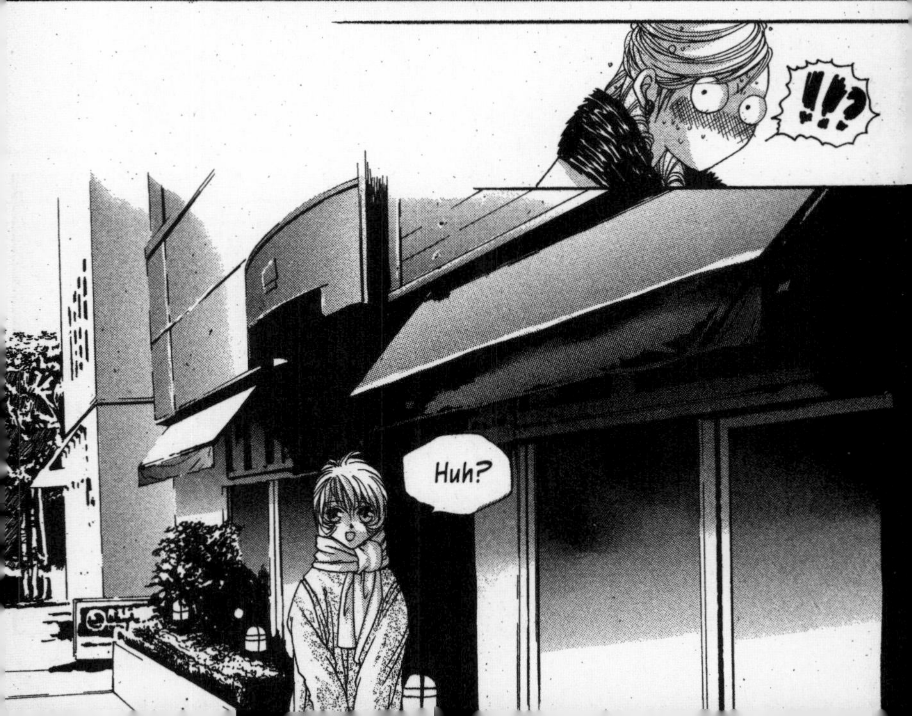
!!?
Huh?

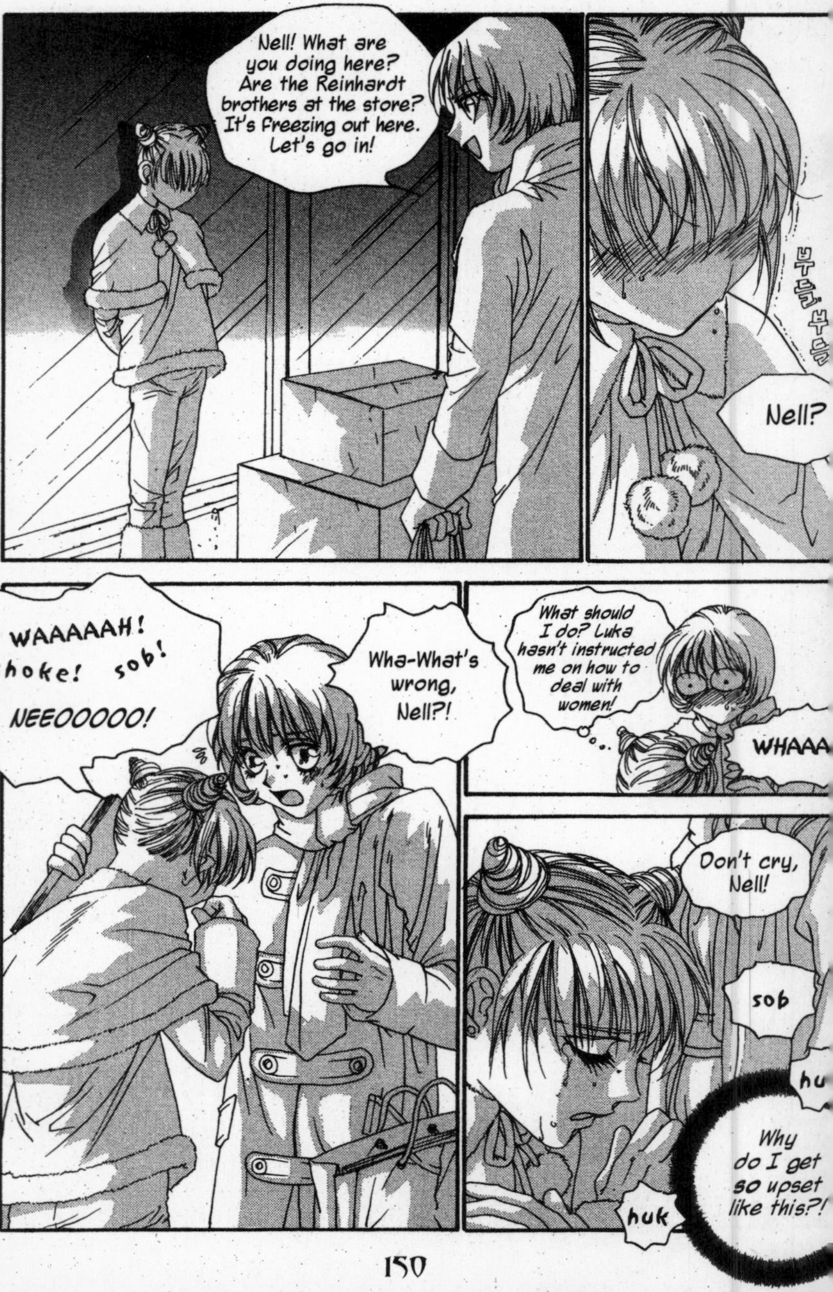
Nell! What are you doing here? Are the Reinhardt brothers at the store? It's freezing out here. Let's go in!
부들부들
Nell?
WAAAAAH!
choke! sob!
NEEOOOOO!
Wha-What's wrong, Nell?!
What should I do? Luka hasn't instructed me on how to deal with women!
WHAAA
Don't cry, Nell!
sob
hu
Why do I get so upset like this?!
huk

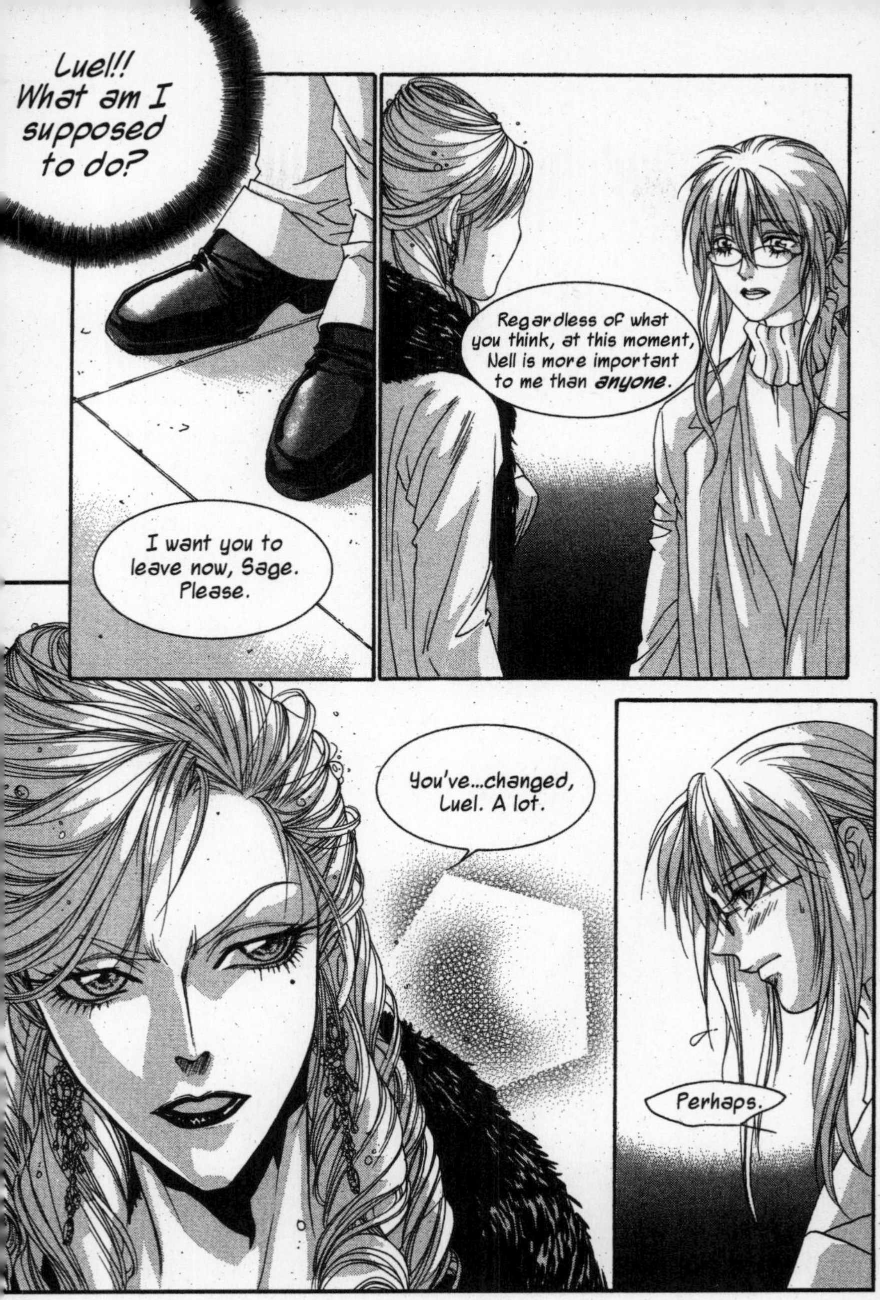
Luel!! What am I supposed to do?
I want you to leave now, Sage. Please.
Regardless of what you think, at this moment, Nell is more important to me than *anyone*.
You've...changed, Luel. A lot.
Perhaps.

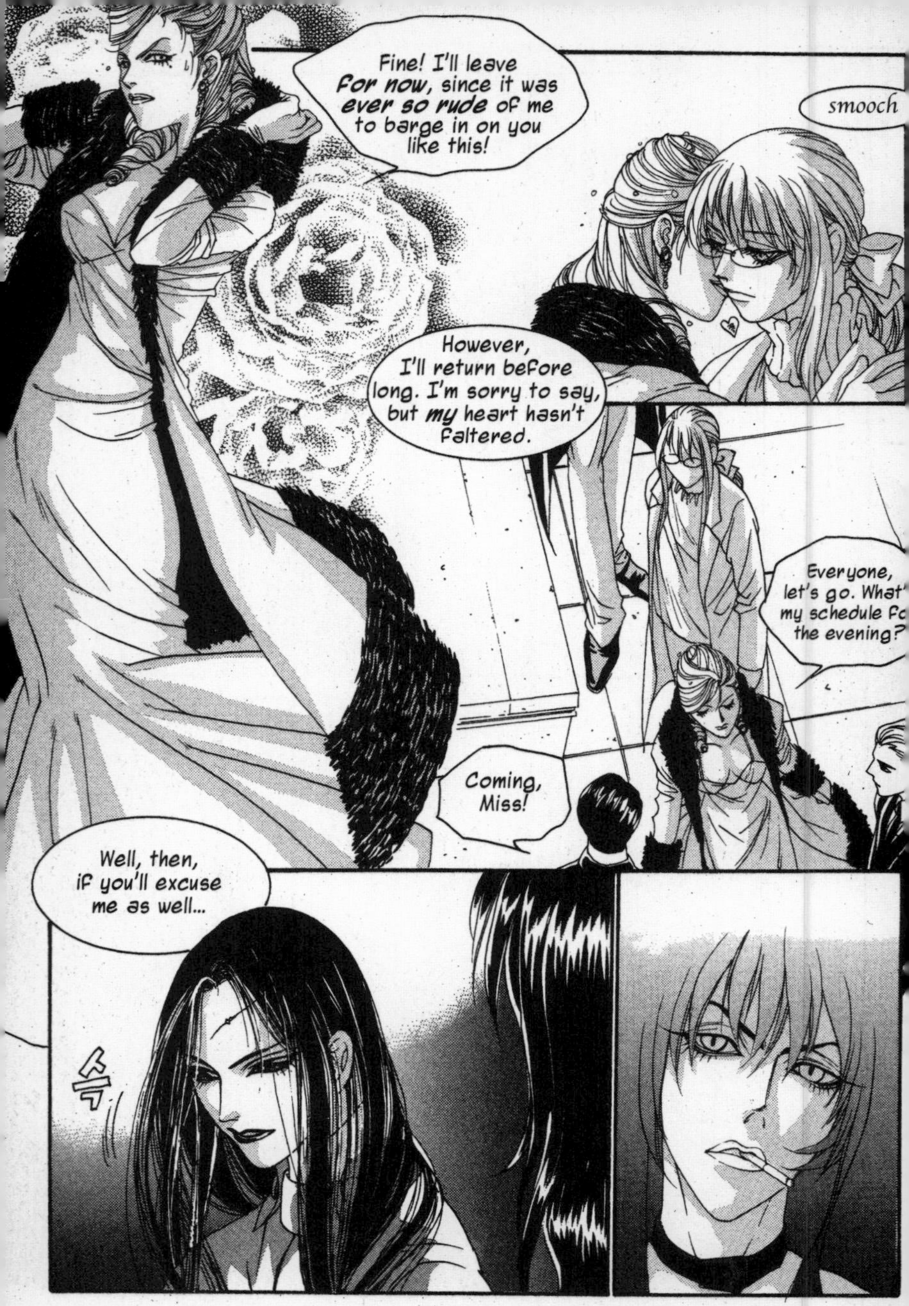
Fine! I'll leave *for now*, since it was *ever so rude* of me to barge in on you like this!
However, I'll return before long. I'm sorry to say, but *my* heart hasn't faltered.
smooch
Everyone, let's go. What' my schedule fo the evening?
Coming, Miss!
Well, then, if you'll excuse me as well...

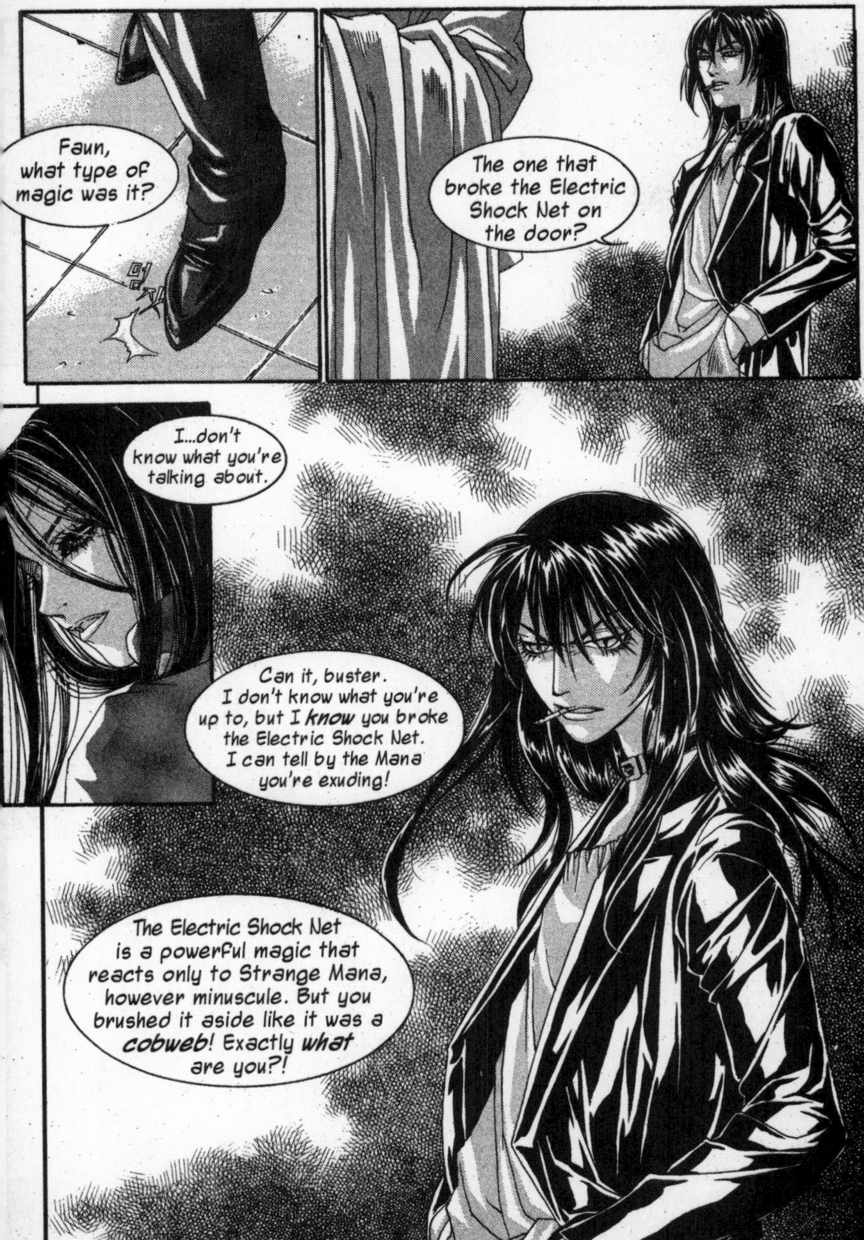

Faun, what type of magic was it?
The one that broke the Electric Shock Net on the door?
I...don't know what you're talking about.
Can it, buster. I don't know what you're up to, but I *know* you broke the Electric Shock Net. I can tell by the Mana you're exuding!
The Electric Shock Net is a powerful magic that reacts only to Strange Mana, however minuscule. But you brushed it aside like it was a *cobweb*! Exactly *what* are you?!

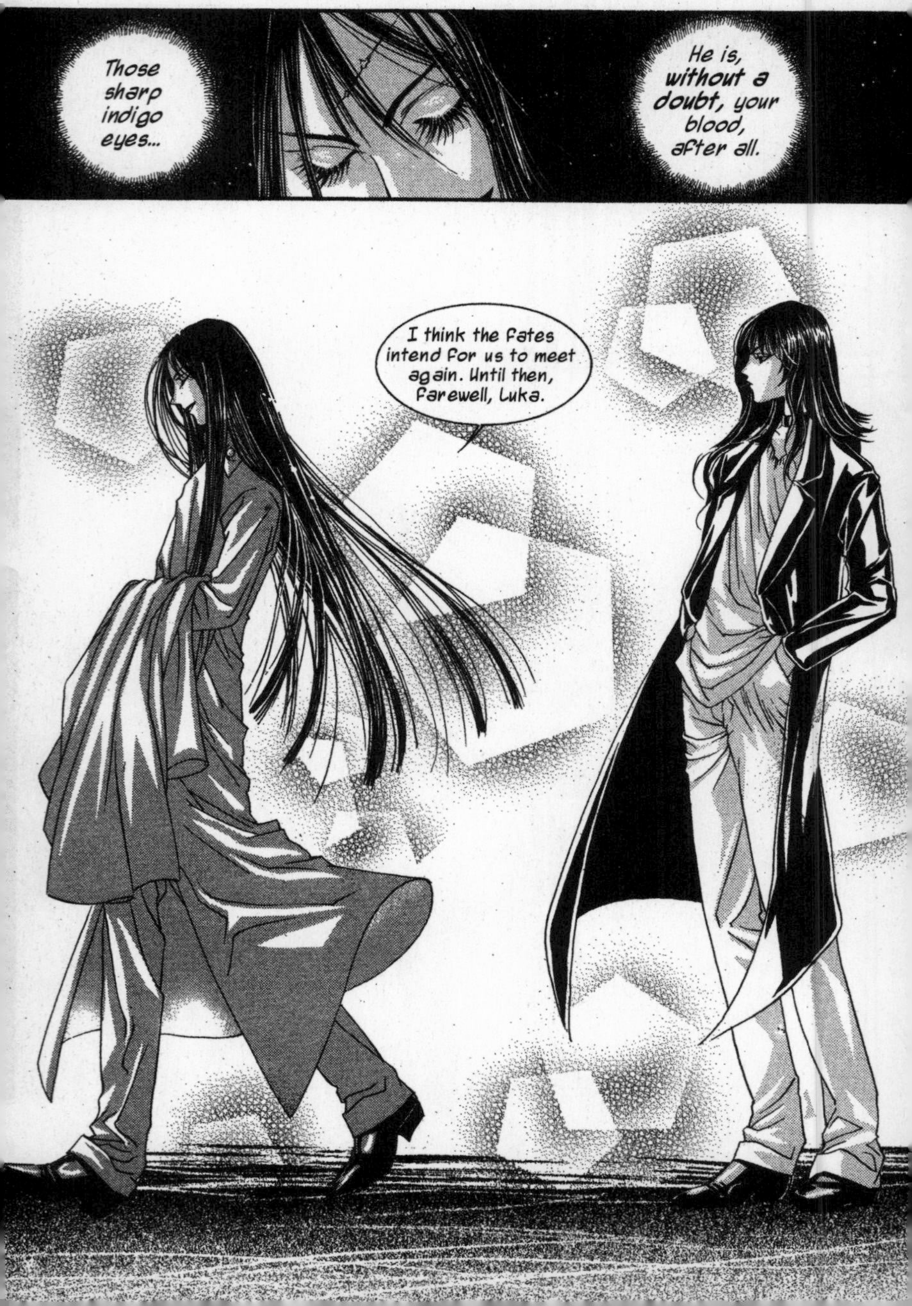
Those sharp indigo eyes...
He is, without a doubt, your blood, after all.
I think the fates intend for us to meet again. Until then, farewell, Luka.

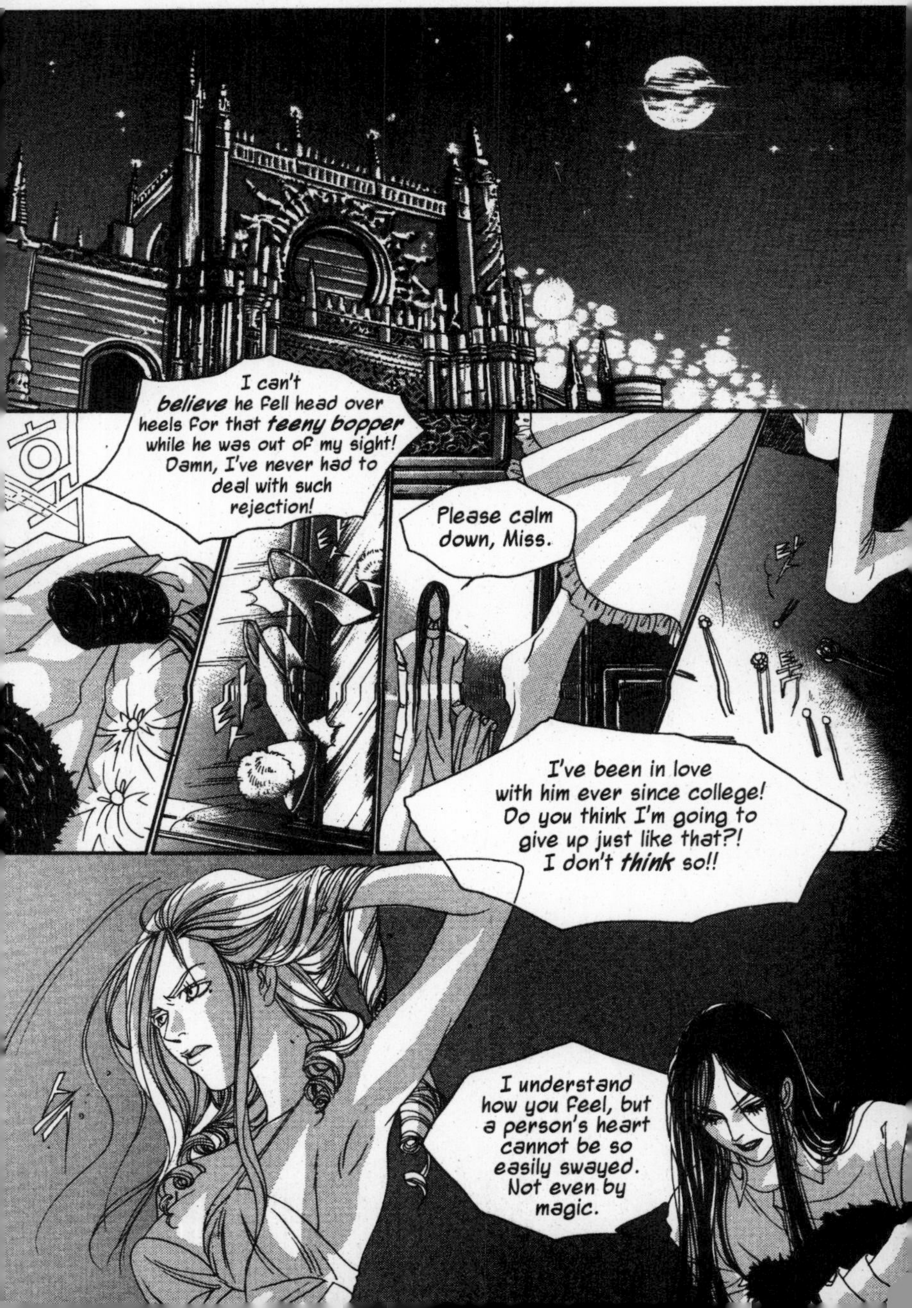
I can't ***believe*** he fell head over heels for that ***teeny bopper*** while he was out of my sight! Damn, I've never had to deal with such rejection!
Please calm down, Miss.
I've been in love with him ever since college! Do you think I'm going to give up just like that?! I don't ***think*** so!!
I understand how you feel, but a person's heart cannot be so easily swayed. Not even by magic.

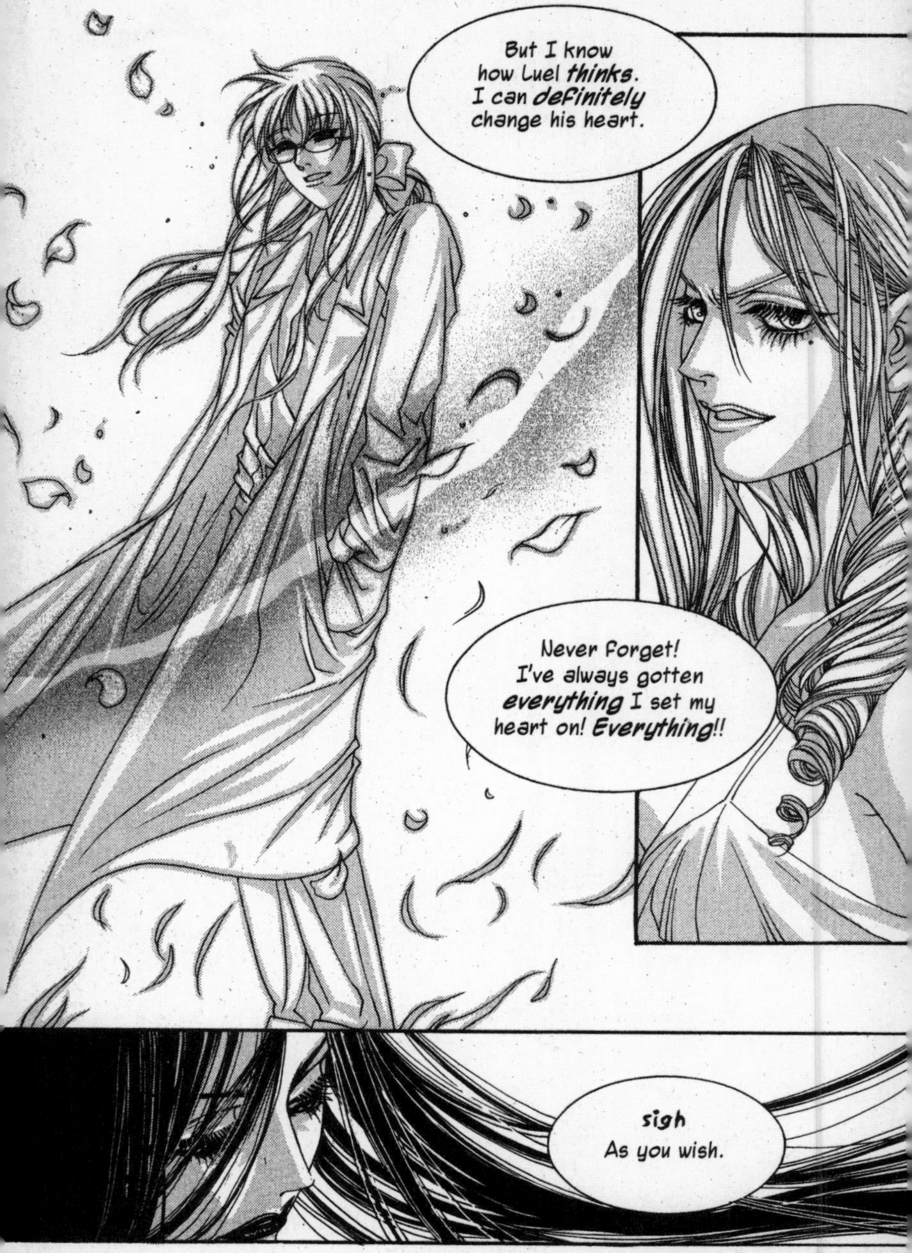
But I know how Luel *thinks*. I can *definitely* change his heart.
Never forget! I've always gotten *everything* I set my heart on! *Everything*!!
sigh As you wish.

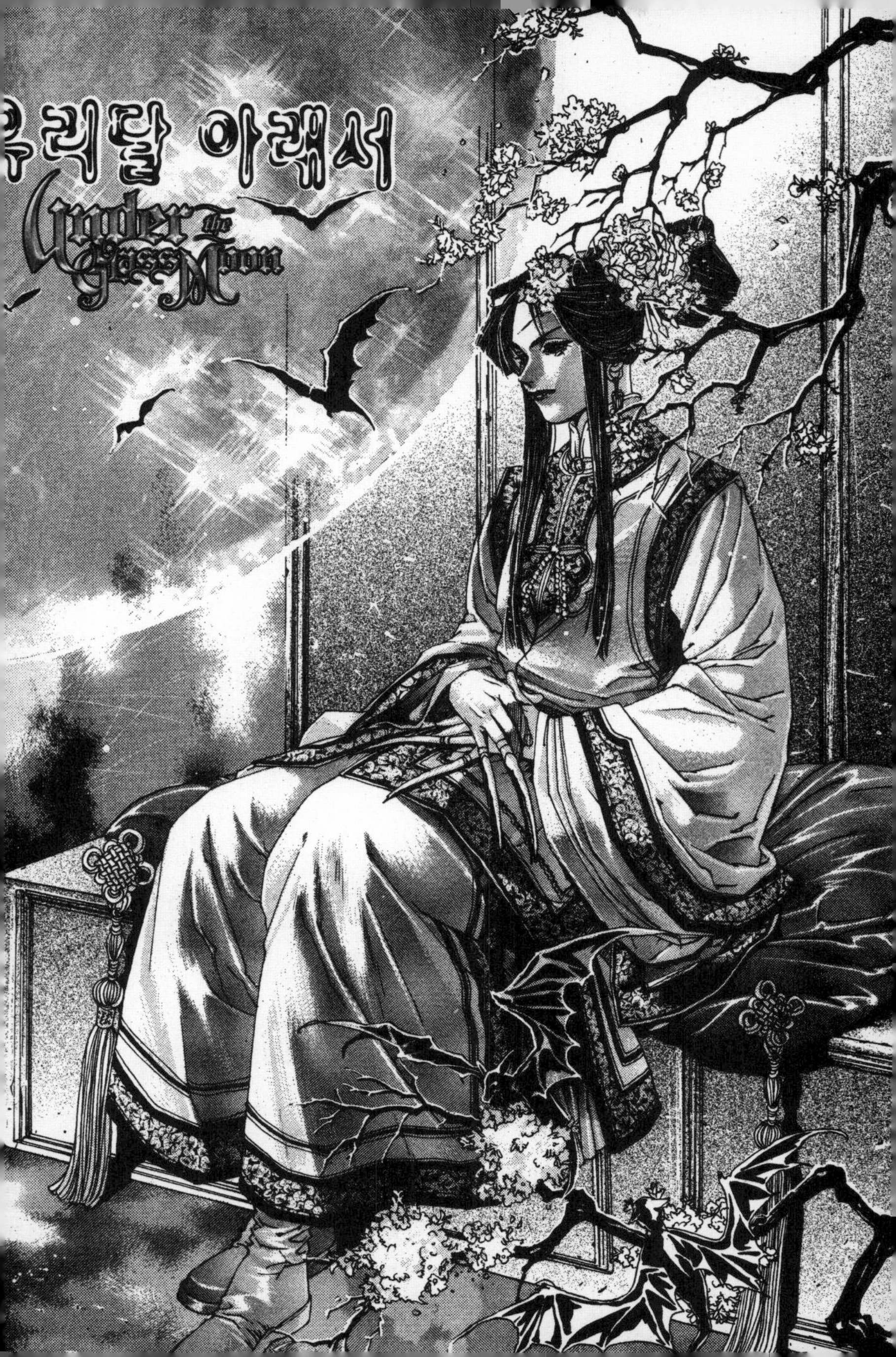
유리달 아래서
Under the Glass Moon

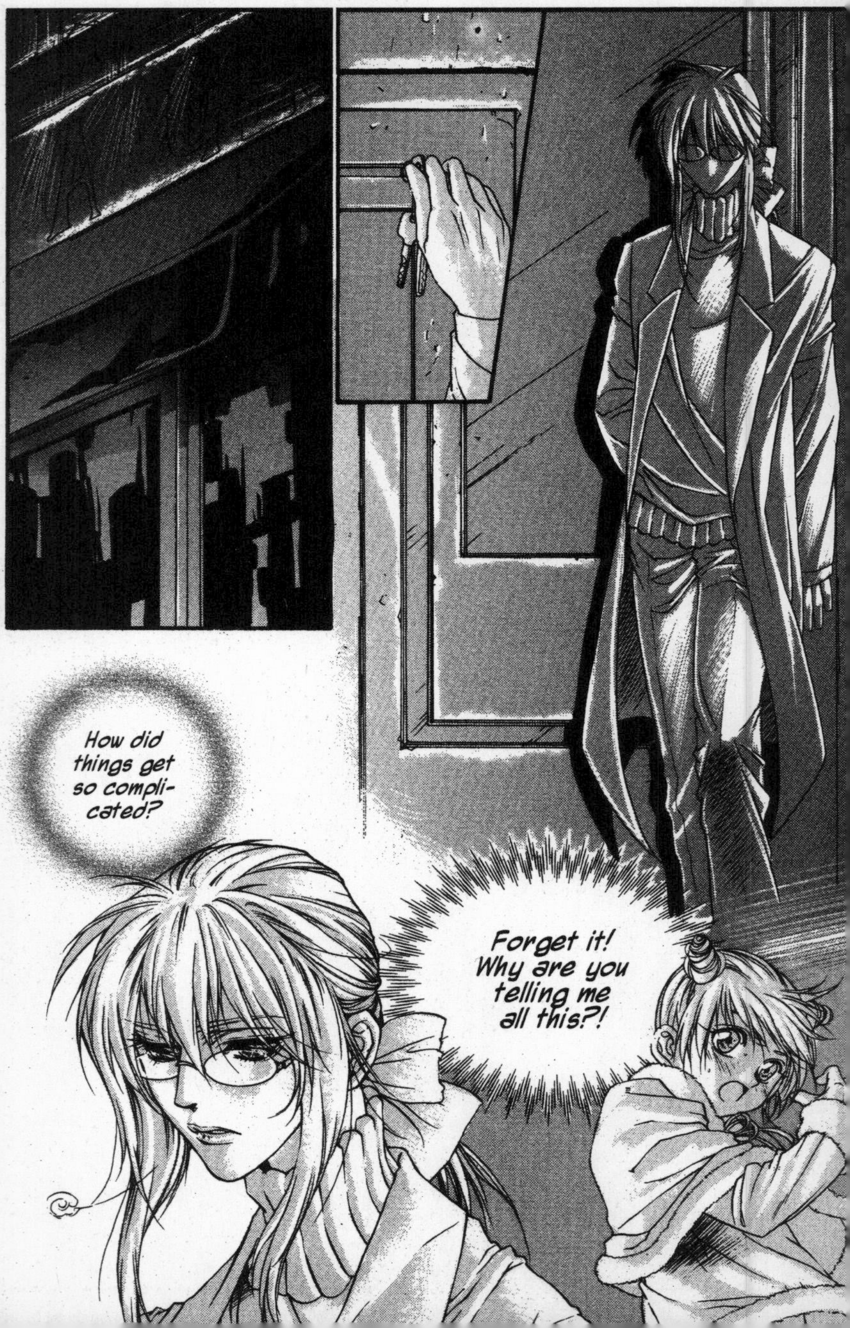
How did things get so compli-cated?
Forget it! Why are you telling me all this?!

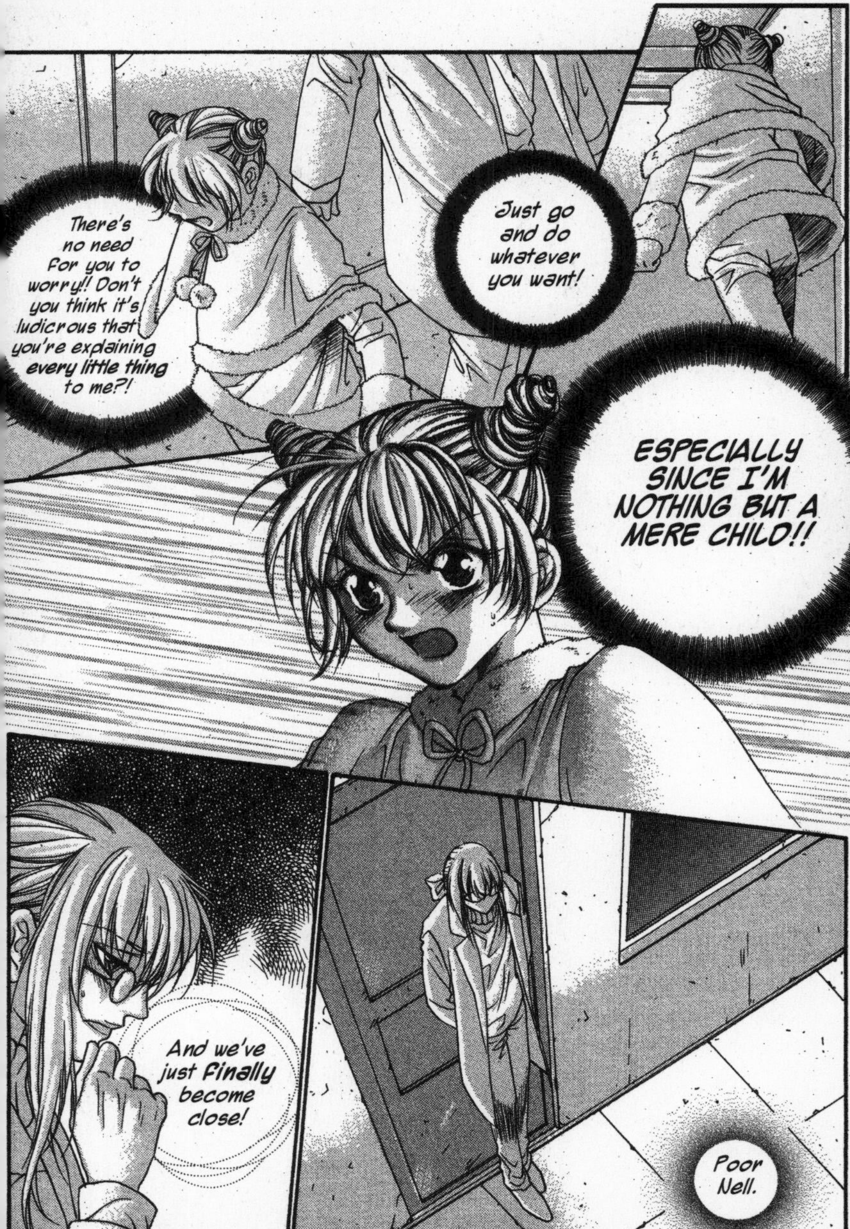
There's no need for you to worry!! Don't you think it's ludicrous that you're explaining every little thing to me?!
Just go and do whatever you want!
ESPECIALLY SINCE I'M NOTHING BUT A MERE CHILD!!
And we've just finally become close!
Poor Nell.

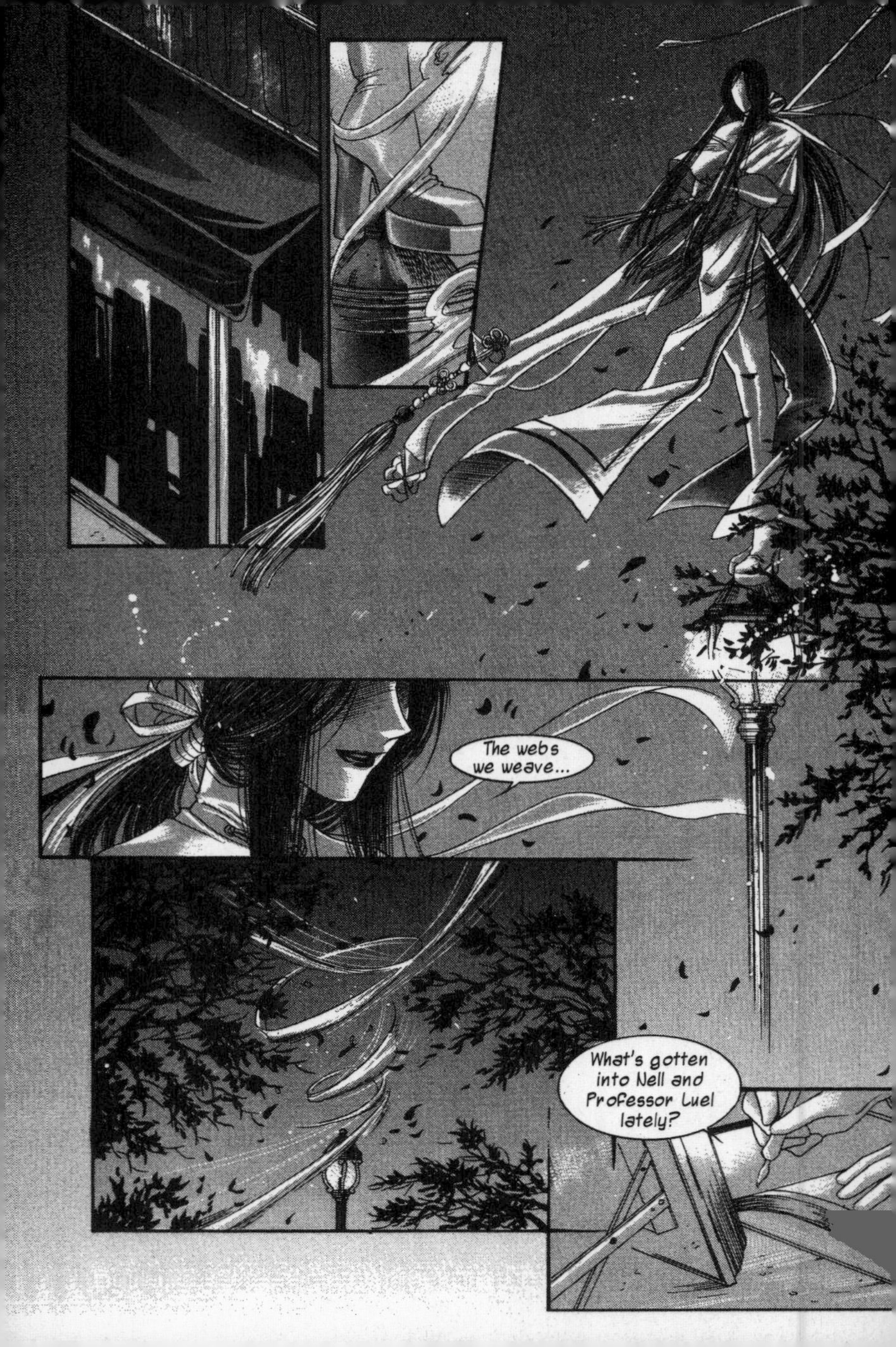
The webs we weave...
What's gotten into Nell and Professor Luel lately?

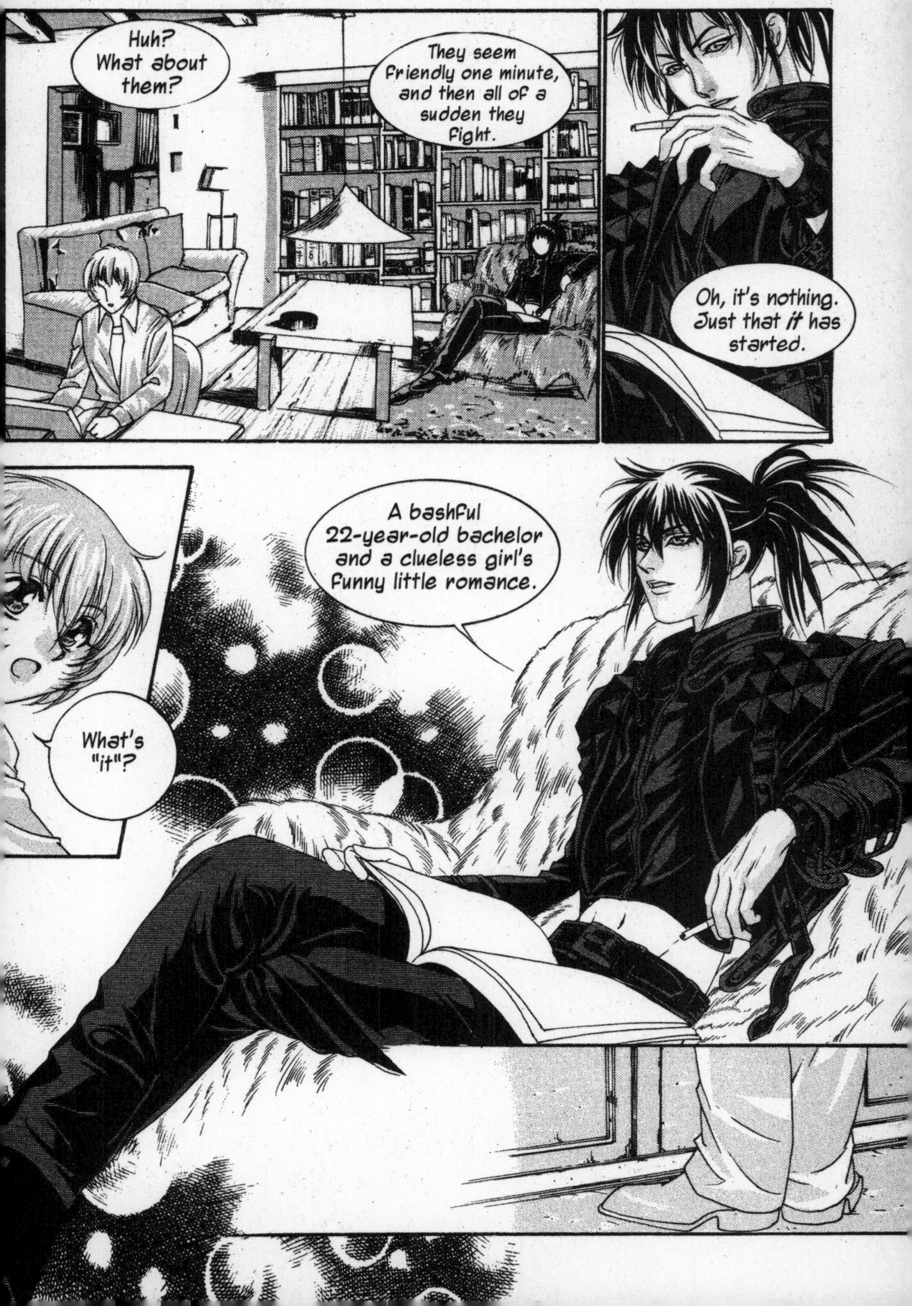
Huh? What about them?
They seem friendly one minute, and then all of a sudden they fight.
Oh, it's nothing. Just that *it* has started.
What's "it"?
A bashful 22-year-old bachelor and a clueless girl's funny little romance.

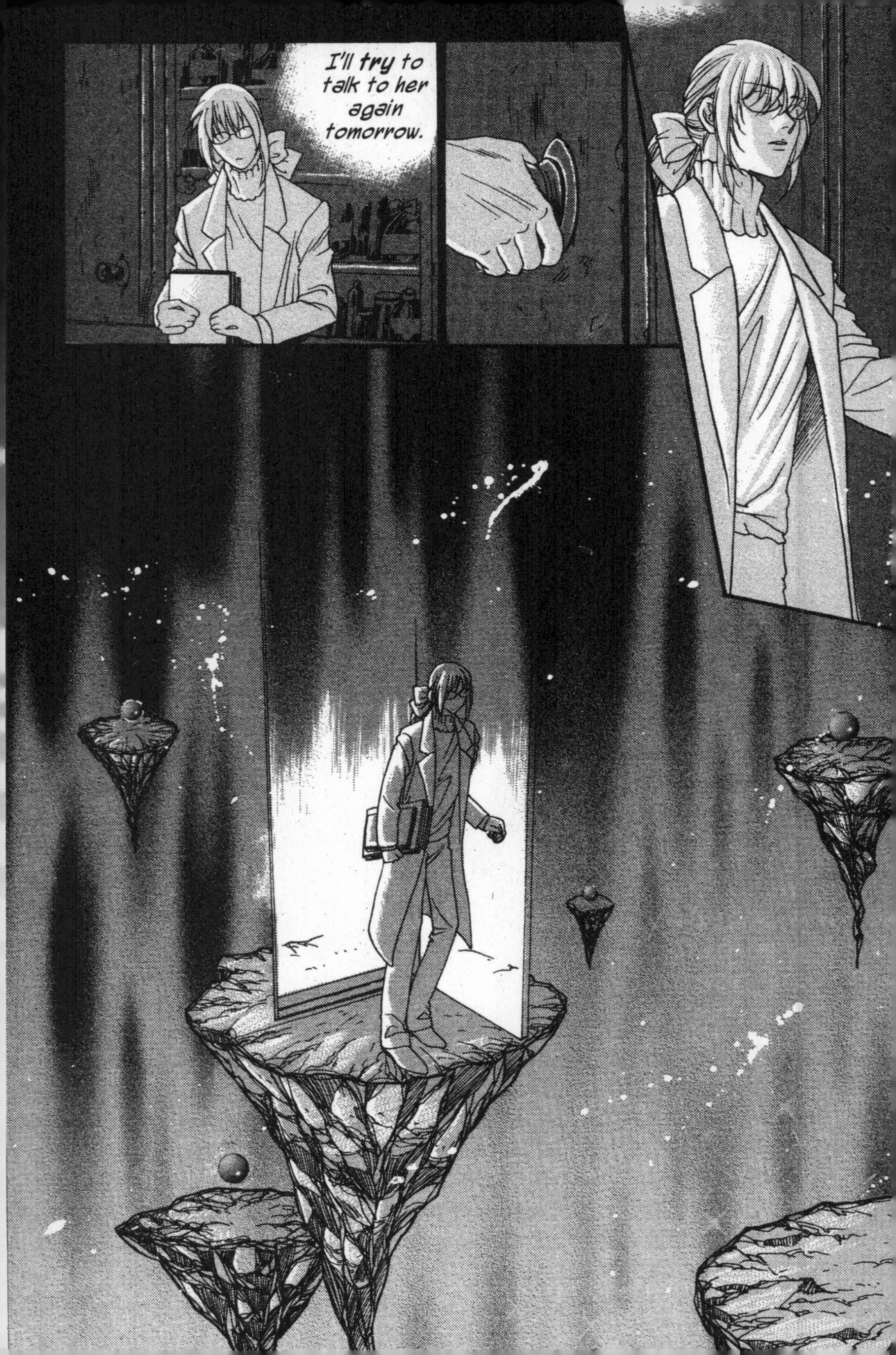
I'll try to talk to her again tomorrow.

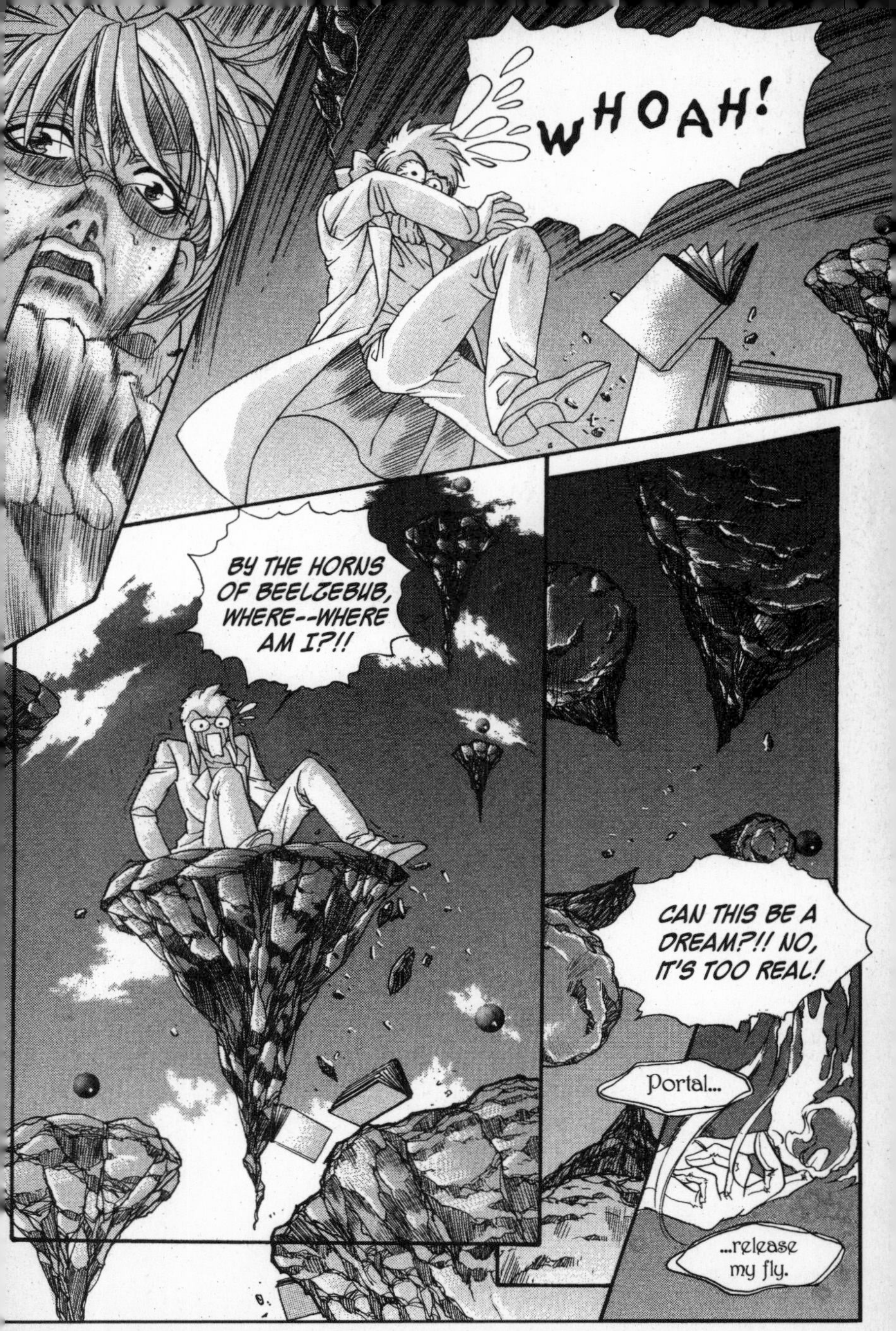
WHOAH!
BY THE HORNS OF BEELZEBUB, WHERE--WHERE AM I?!!
CAN THIS BE A DREAM?!! NO, IT'S TOO REAL!
Portal...
...release my fly.

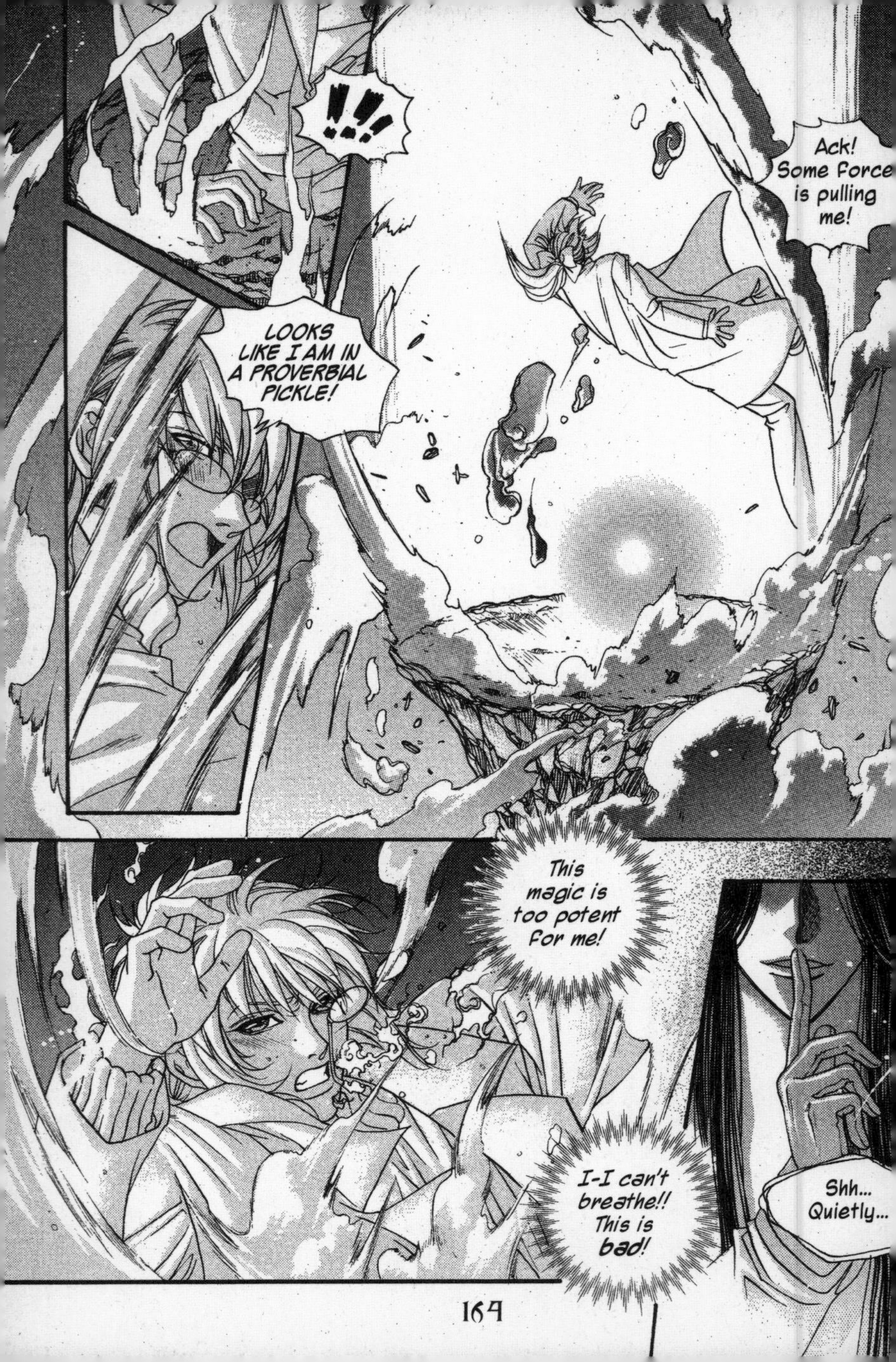
!!!
LOOKS LIKE I AM IN A PROVERBIAL PICKLE!
Ack! Some force is pulling me!
This magic is too potent for me!
I-I can't breathe!! This is bad!
Shh... Quietly...

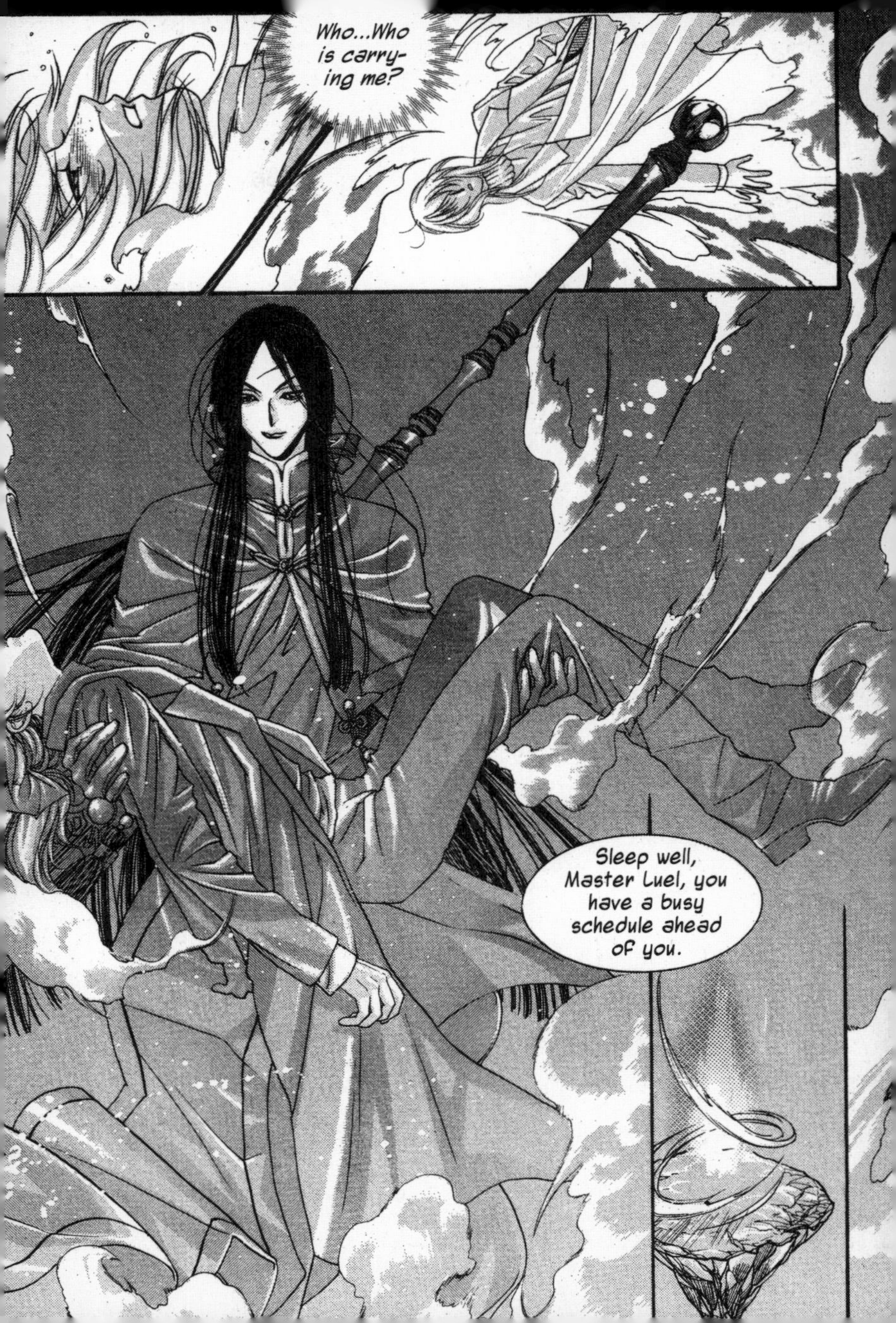
Who...Who is carrying me?
Sleep well, Master Luel, you have a busy schedule ahead of you.

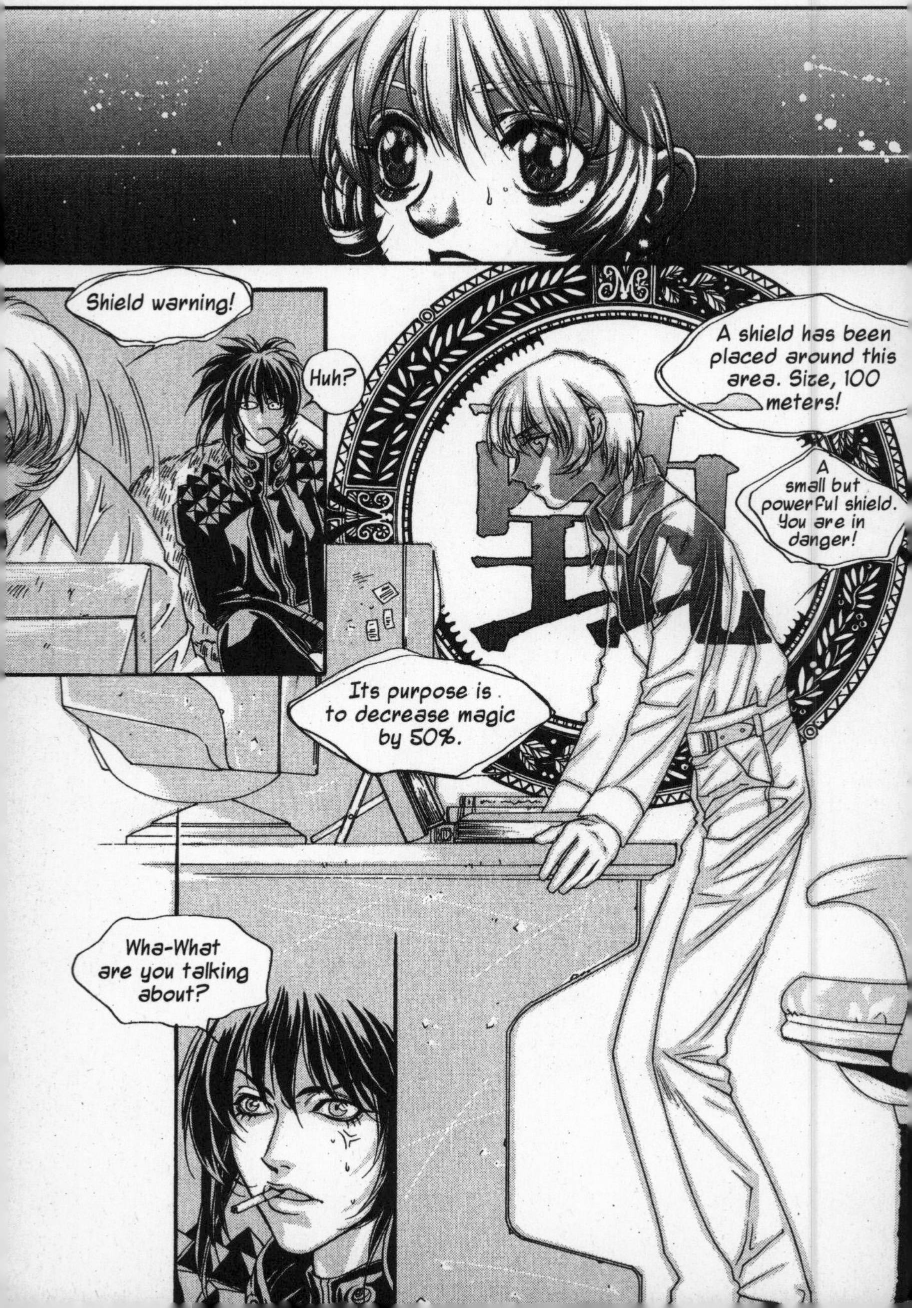
Shield warning!
Huh?
A shield has been placed around this area. Size, 100 meters!
A small but powerful shield. You are in danger!
Its purpose is to decrease magic by 50%.
Wha-What are you talking about?

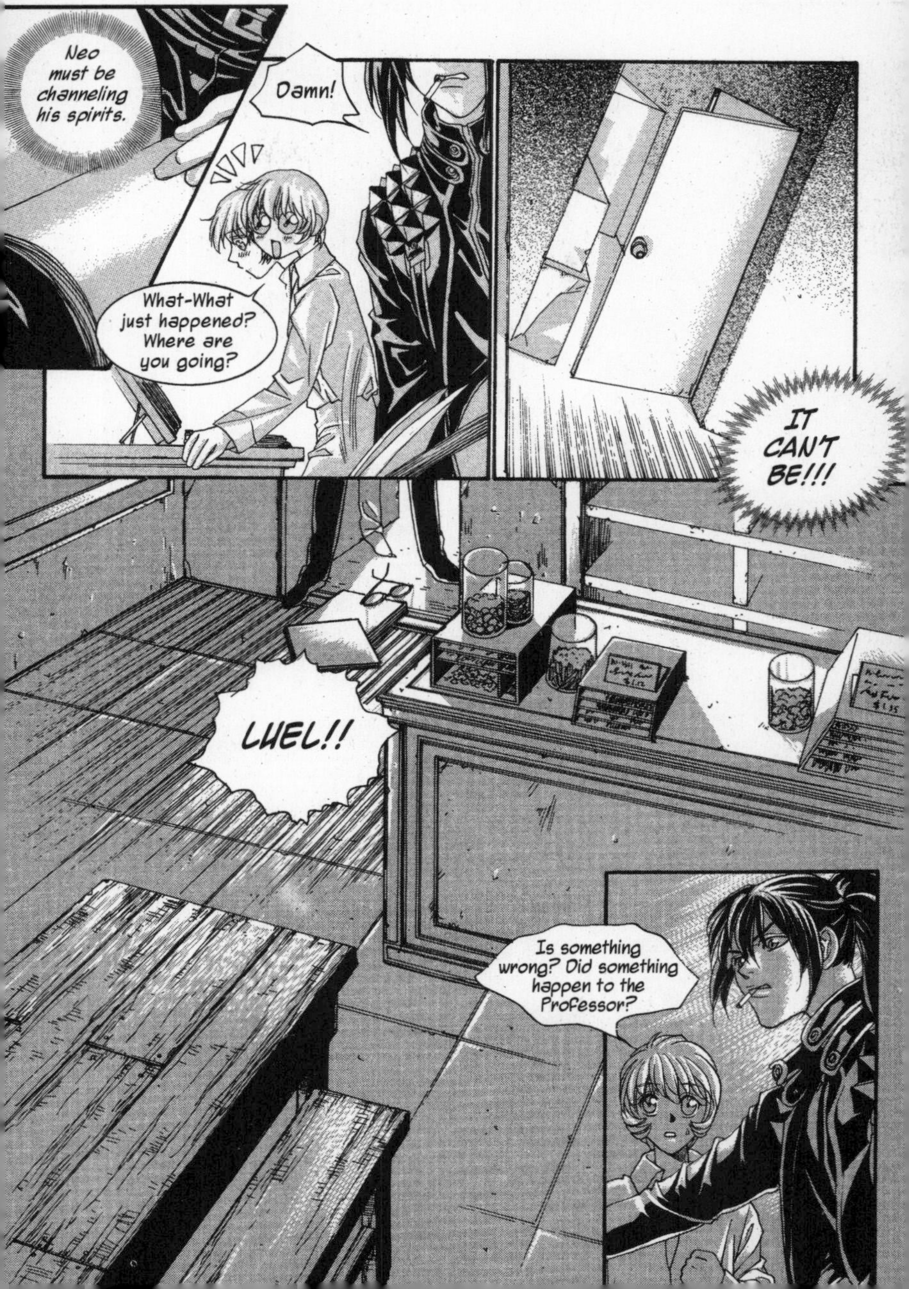
Neo must be channeling his spirits.
Damn!
What-What just happened? Where are you going?
IT CAN'T BE!!!
LUEL!!
Is something wrong? Did something happen to the Professor?

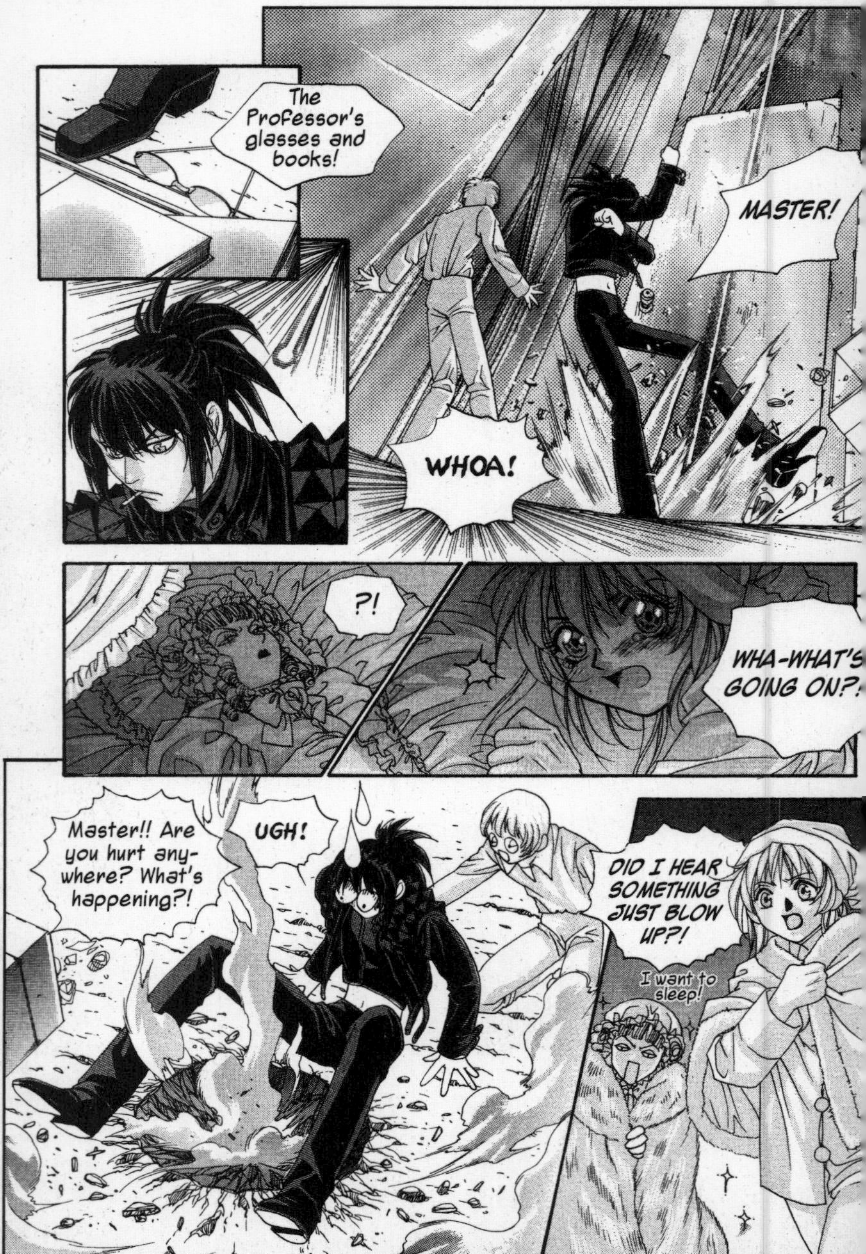

The Professor's glasses and books!
MASTER!
WHOA!
?!
WHA-WHAT'S GOING ON?!
Master!! Are you hurt anywhere? What's happening?!
UGH!
DID I HEAR SOMETHING JUST BLOW UP?!
I want to sleep!

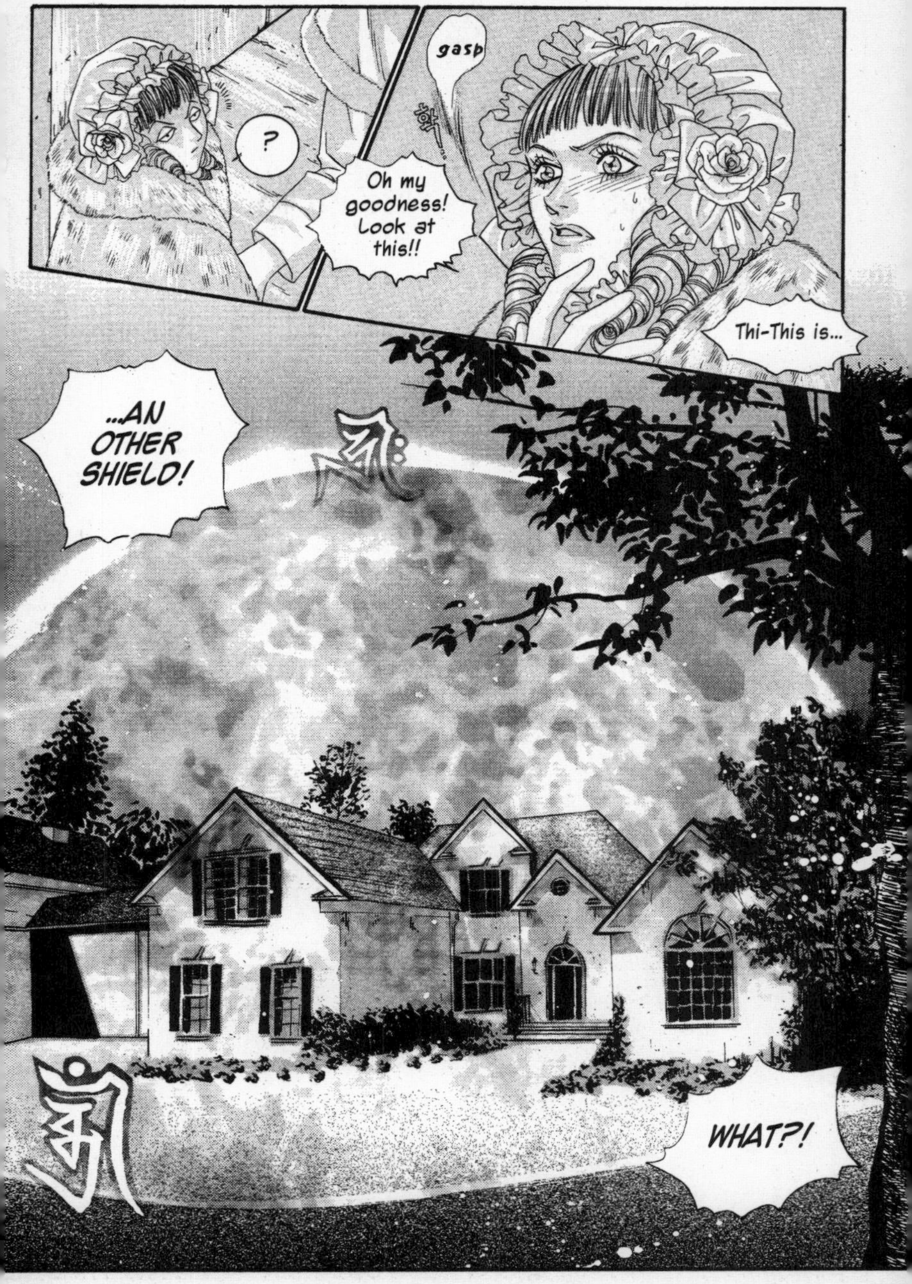
?
gasp
Oh my goodness! Look at this!!
Thi-This is...
...AN OTHER SHIELD!
WHAT?!

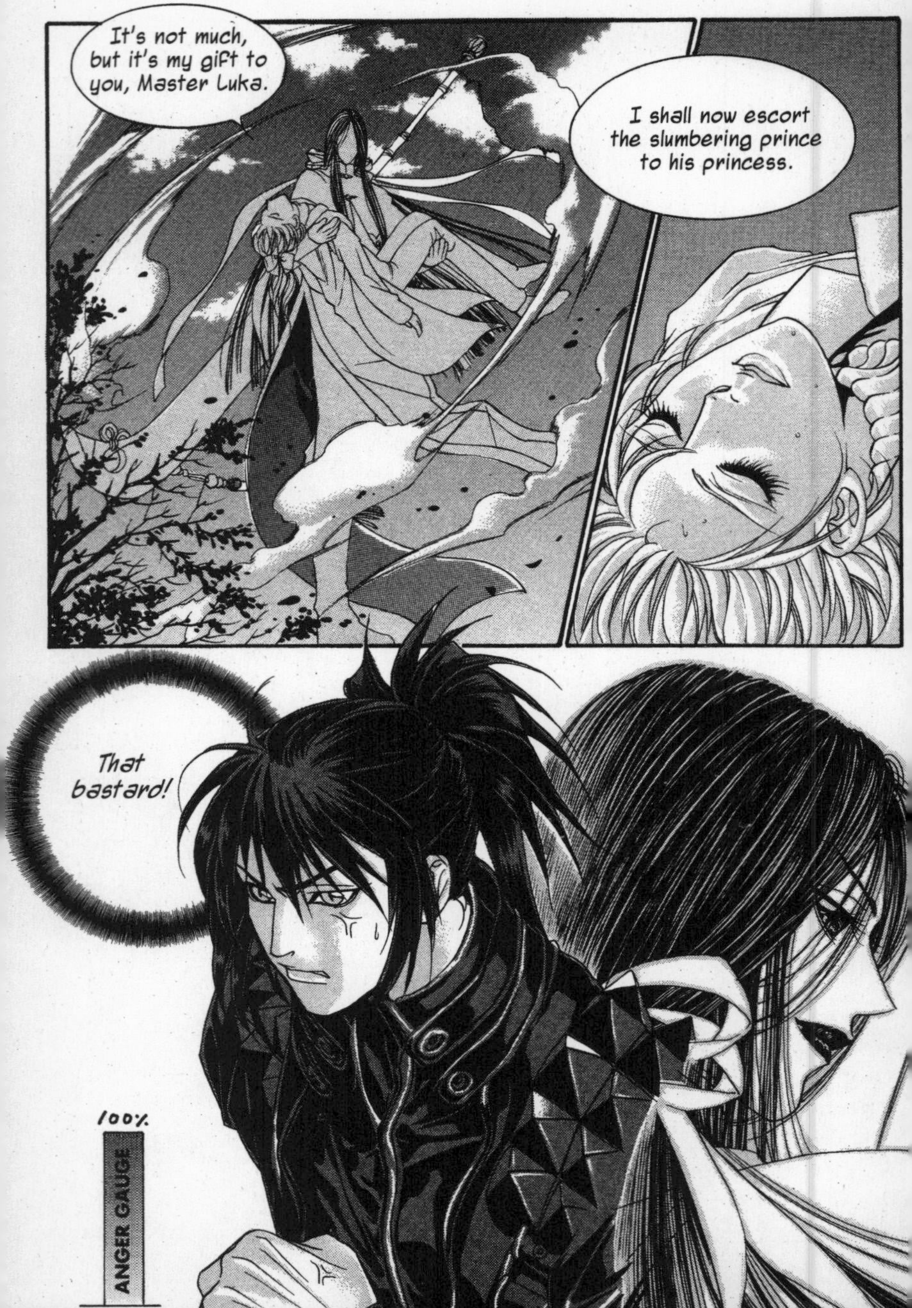
It's not much, but it's my gift to you, Master Luka.
I shall now escort the slumbering prince to his princess.
That bastard!
100%
ANGER GAUGE

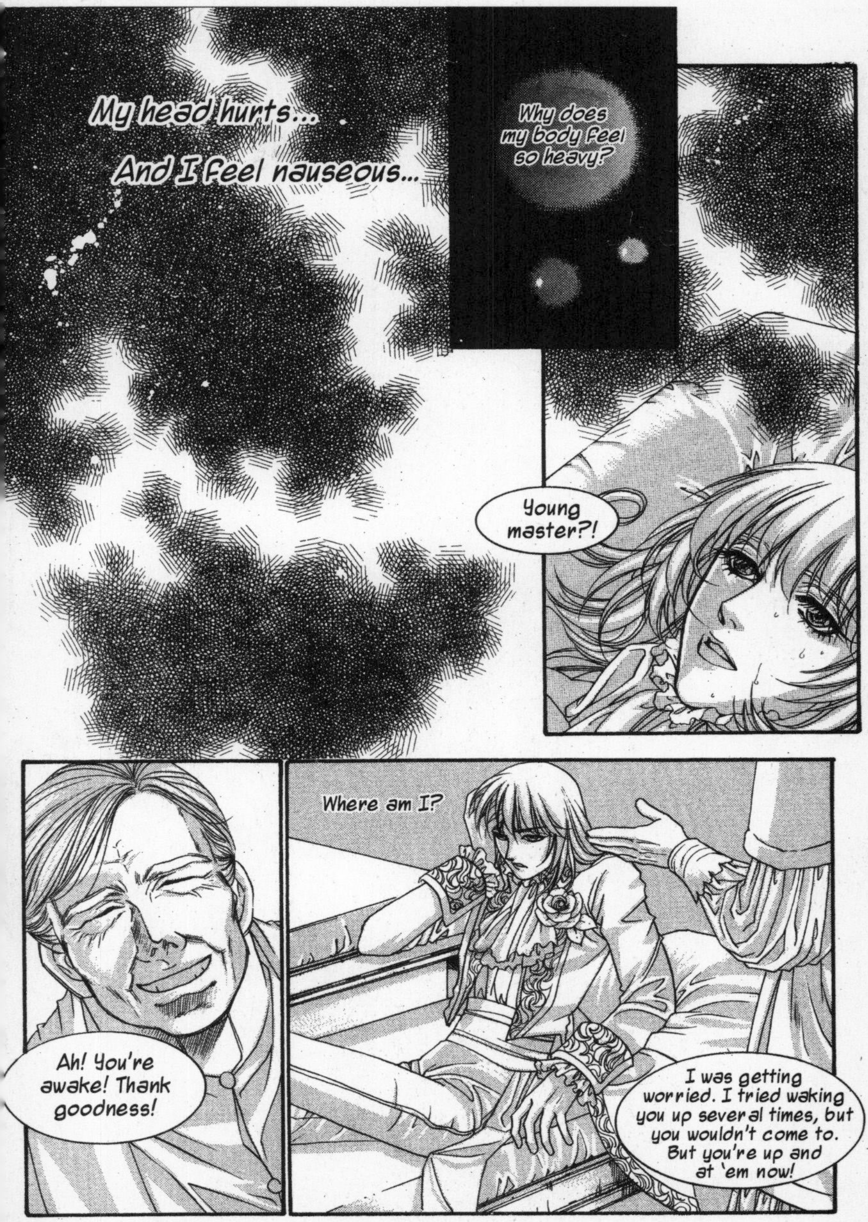
My head hurts...
And I feel nauseous...
Why does my body feel so heavy?
Young master?!
Ah! You're awake! Thank goodness!
Where am I?
I was getting worried. I tried waking you up several times, but you wouldn't come to. But you're up and at 'em now!

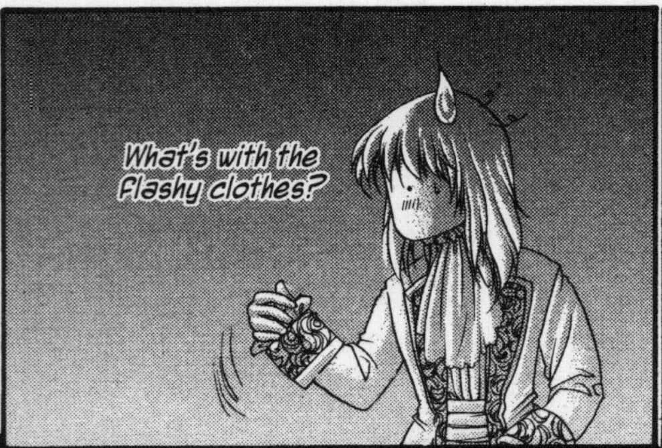
What's with the flashy clothes?
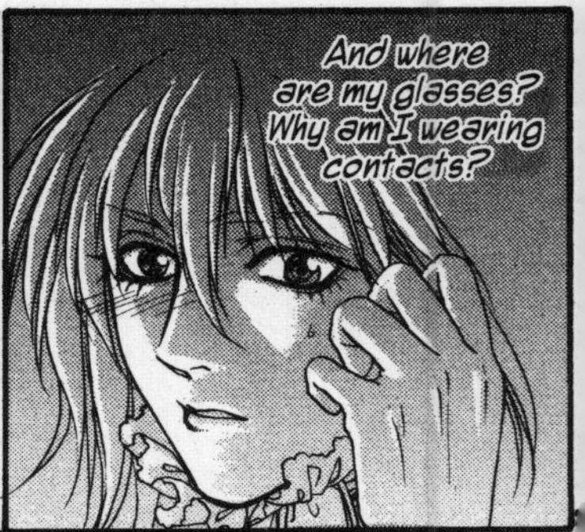
And where are my glasses? Why am I wearing contacts?
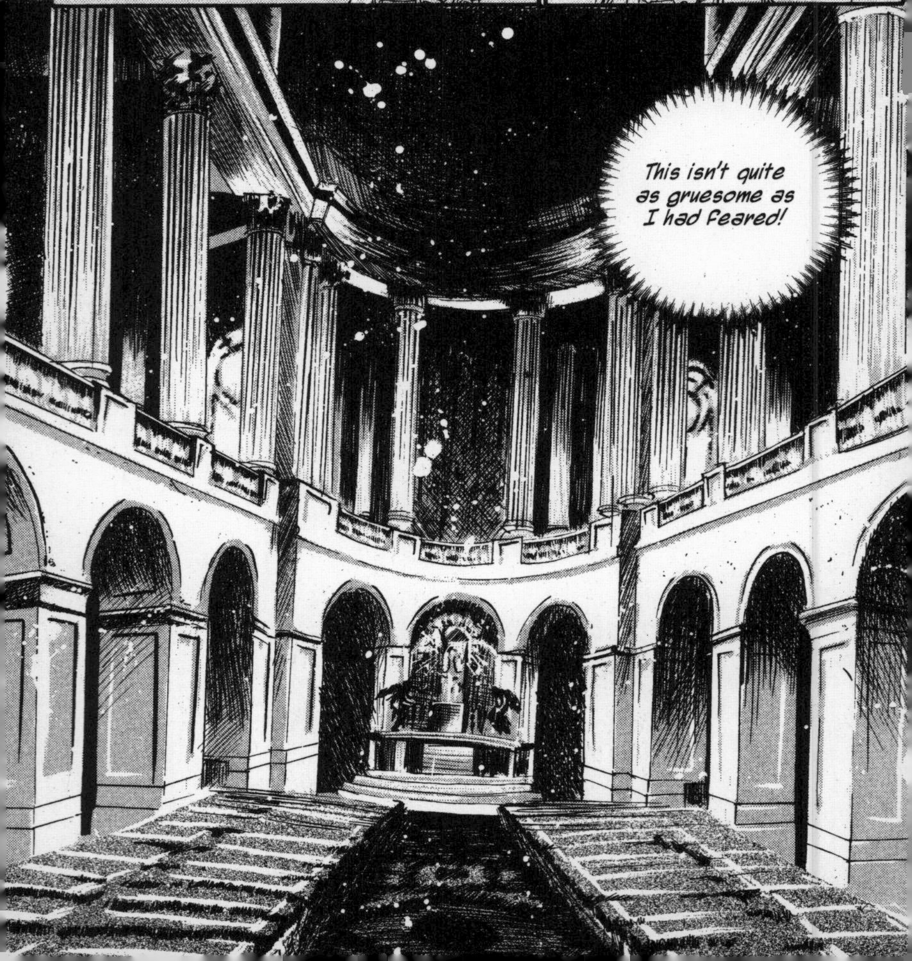
This isn't quite as gruesome as I had feared!

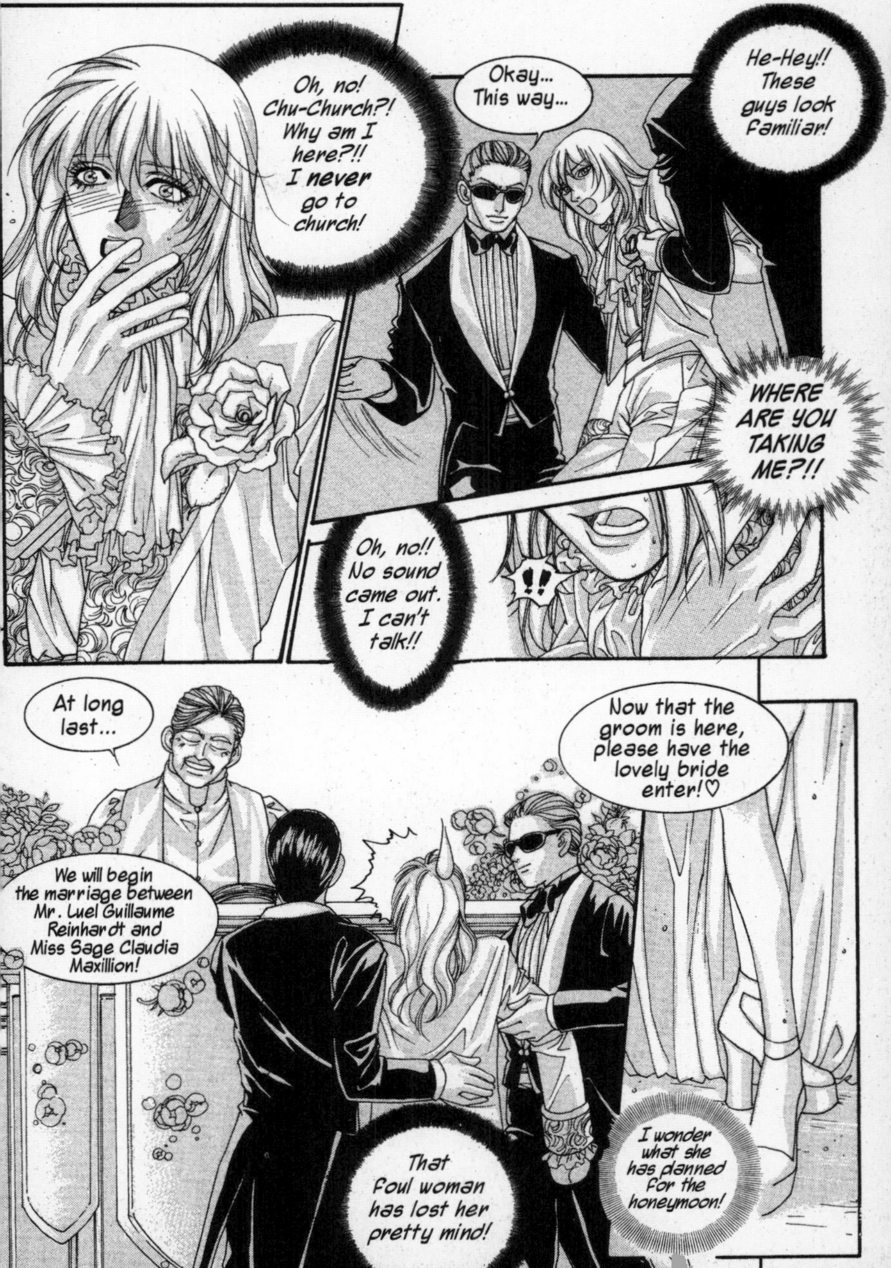
Oh, no! Chu-Church?! Why am I here?!! I never go to church!
Okay... This way...
He-Hey!! These guys look familiar!
WHERE ARE YOU TAKING ME?!!
Oh, no!! No sound came out. I can't talk!!
!!
At long last...
Now that the groom is here, please have the lovely bride enter!♡
We will begin the marriage between Mr. Luel Guillaume Reinhardt and Miss Sage Claudia Maxillion!
That foul woman has lost her pretty mind!
I wonder what she has planned for the honeymoon!

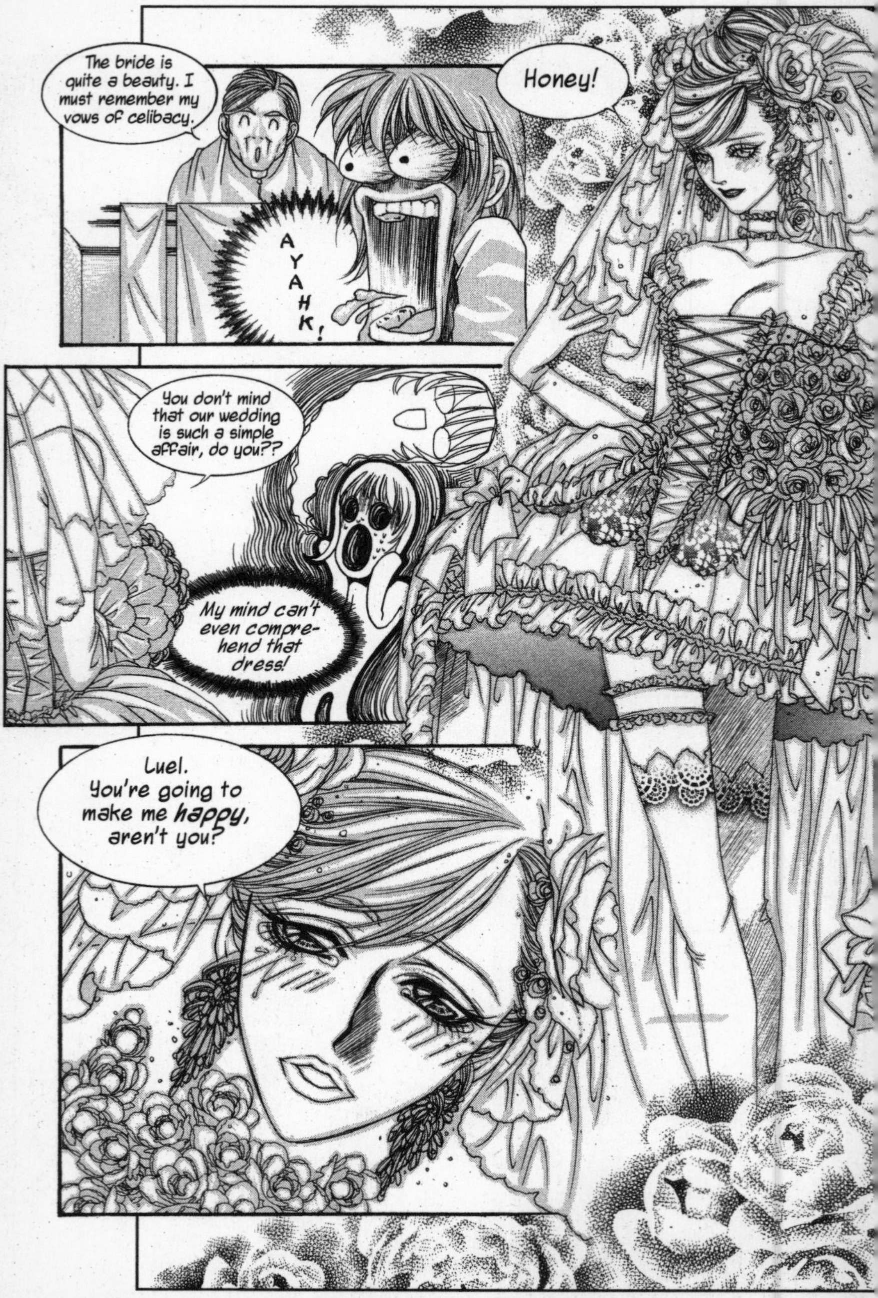

The bride is quite a beauty. I must remember my vows of celibacy.
AYAHK!
You don't mind that our wedding is such a simple affair, do you??
My mind can't even compre-hend that dress!
Luel. You're going to make me *happy*, aren't you?
Honey!

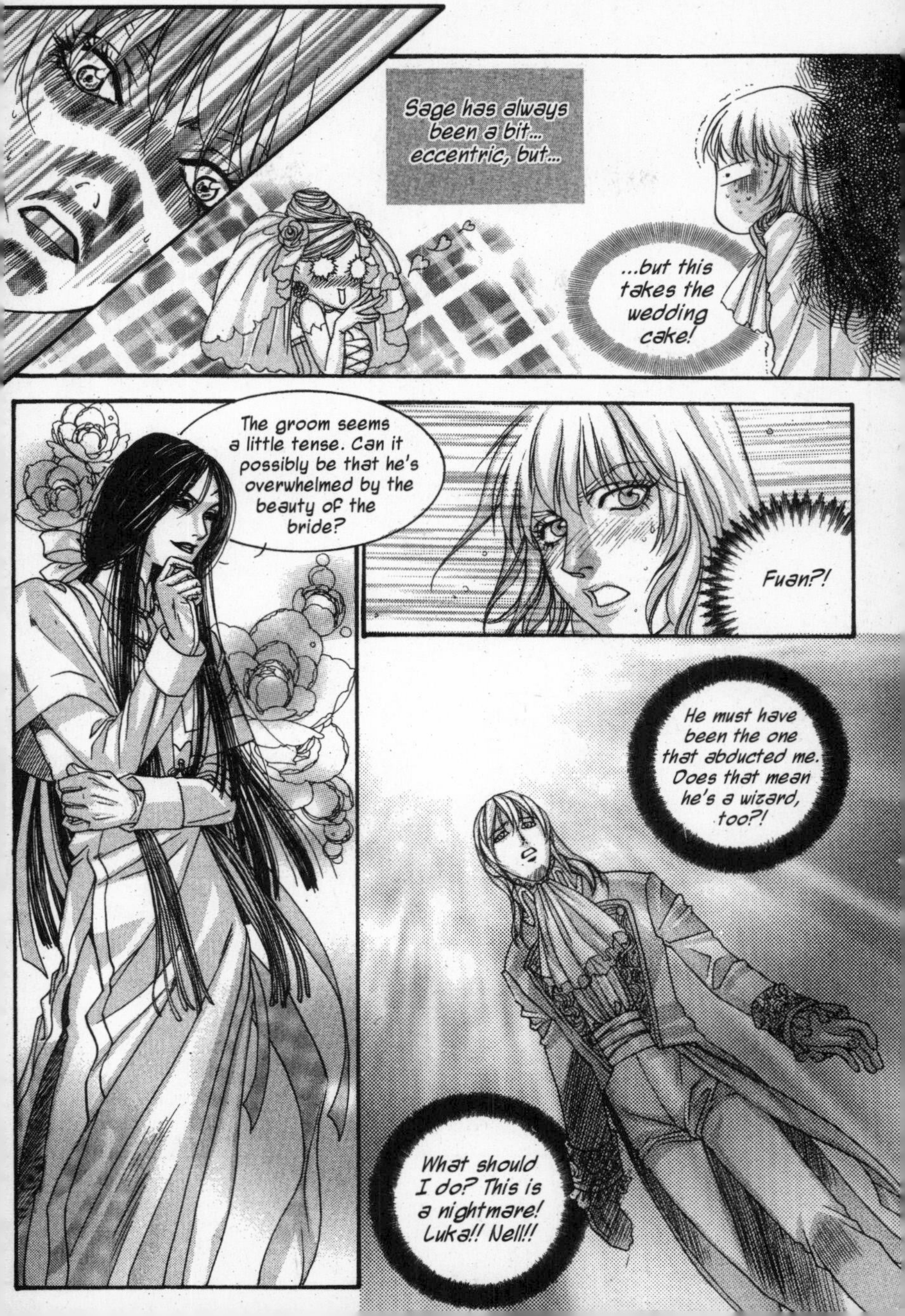
Sage has always been a bit... eccentric, but...
...but this takes the wedding cake!
The groom seems a little tense. Can it possibly be that he's overwhelmed by the beauty of the bride?
Fuan?!
He must have been the one that abducted me. Does that mean he's a wizard, too?!
What should I do? This is a nightmare! Luka!! Nell!!

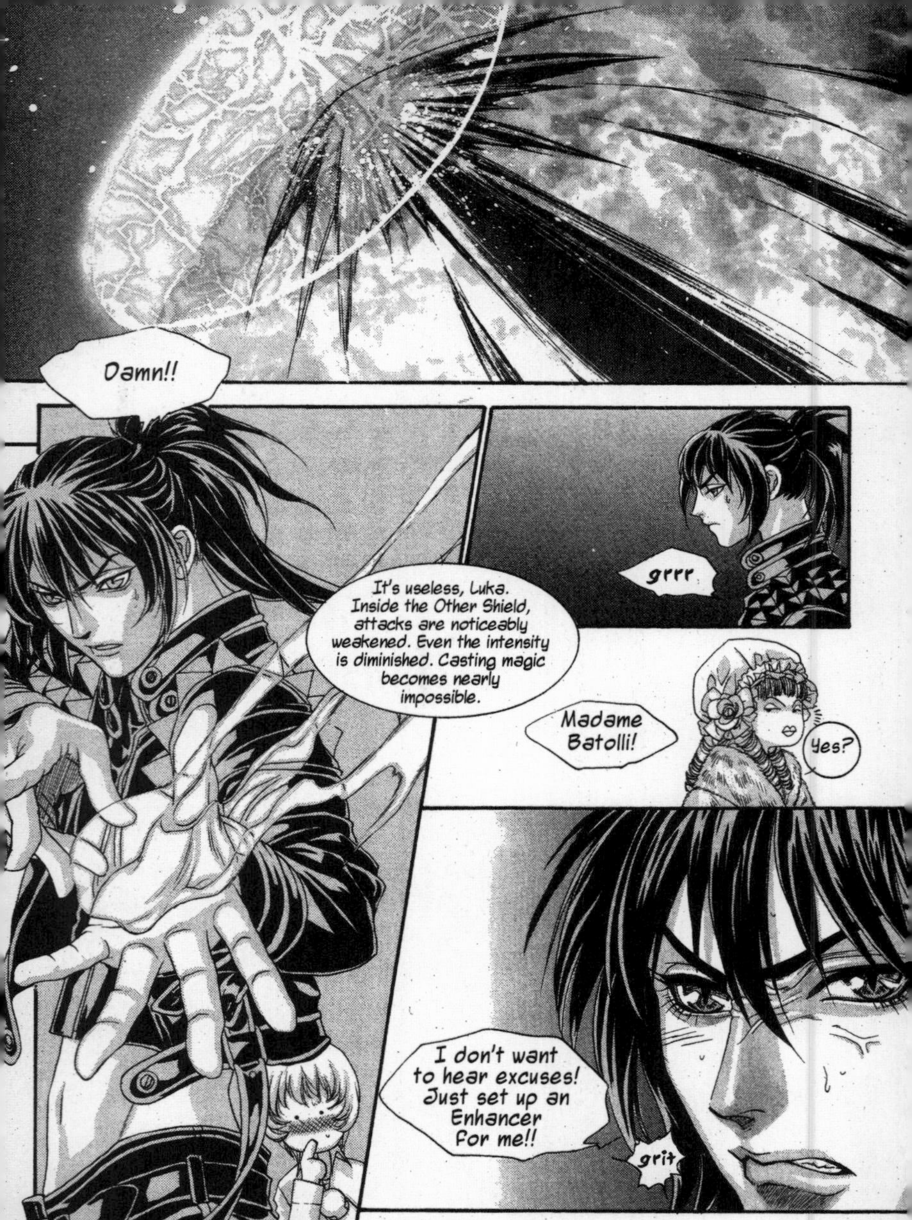
Damn!!
It's useless, Luka. Inside the Other Shield, attacks are noticeably weakened. Even the intensity is diminished. Casting magic becomes nearly impossible.
grrr
Madame Batolli!
Yes?
I don't want to hear excuses! Just set up an Enhancer for me!!
grit

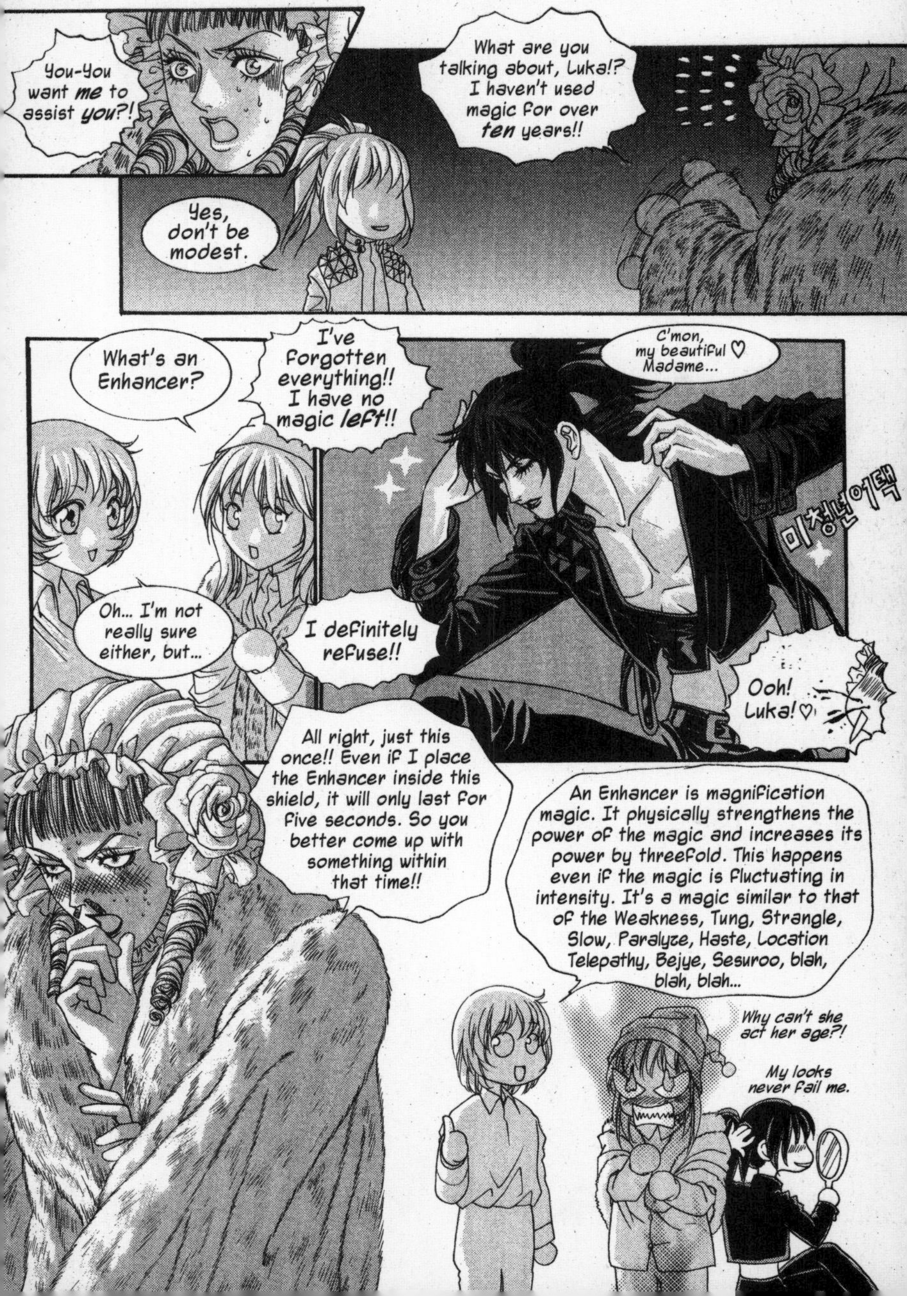
You-You want me to assist you?!
What are you talking about, Luka!? I haven't used magic for over ten years!!
Yes, don't be modest.
What's an Enhancer?
I've forgotten everything!! I have no magic left!!
Oh... I'm not really sure either, but...
I definitely refuse!!
C'mon, my beautiful ♡ Madame...
미청년어택
Ooh! Luka!♡
All right, just this once!! Even if I place the Enhancer inside this shield, it will only last for five seconds. So you better come up with something within that time!!
An Enhancer is magnification magic. It physically strengthens the power of the magic and increases its power by threefold. This happens even if the magic is fluctuating in intensity. It's a magic similar to that of the Weakness, Tung, Strangle, Slow, Paralyze, Haste, Location Telepathy, Bejye, Sesuroo, blah, blah, blah...
Why can't she act her age?!
My looks never fail me.

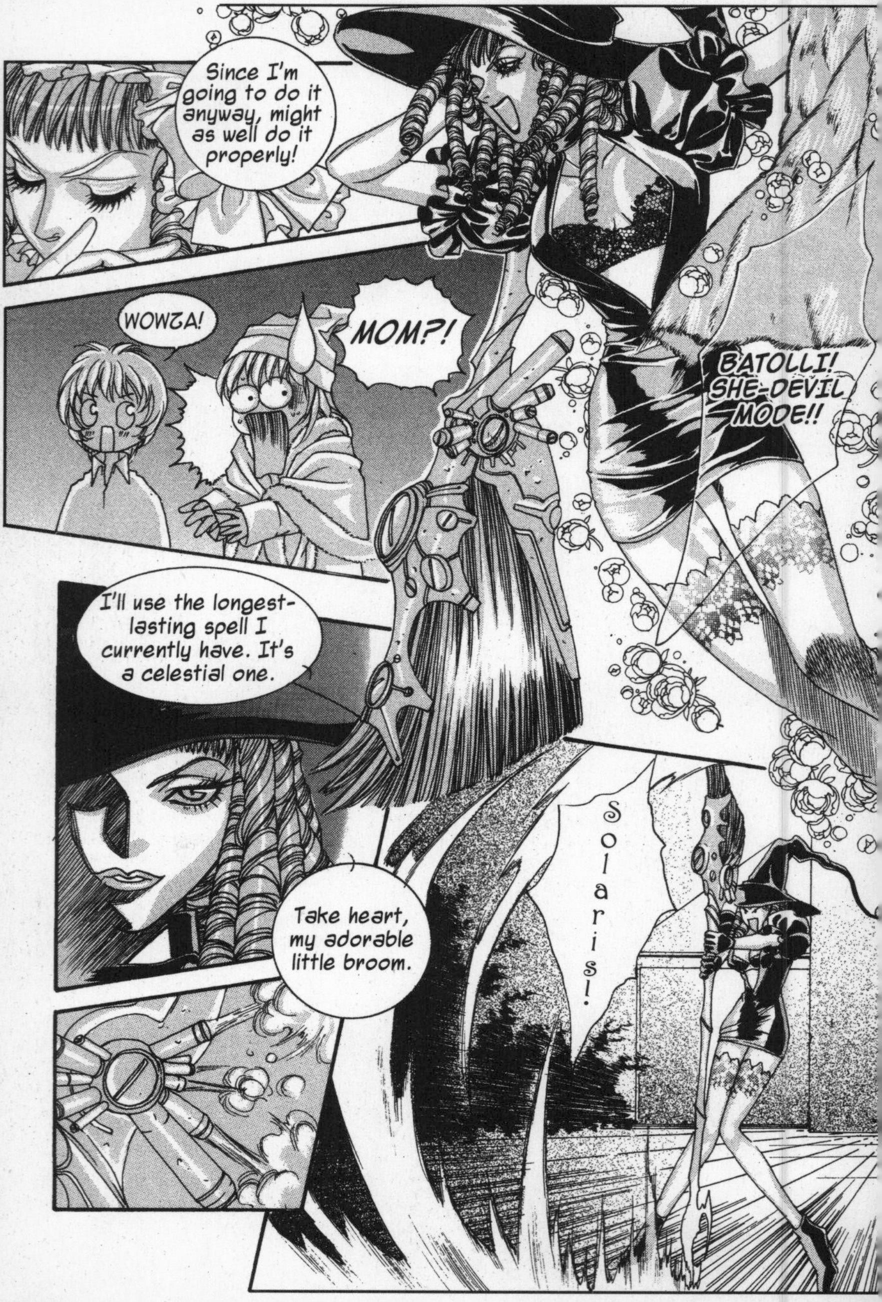
Since I'm going to do it anyway, might as well do it properly!
WOWZA!
MOM?!
BATOLLI! SHE-DEVIL MODE!!
I'll use the longest-lasting spell I currently have. It's a celestial one.
Take heart, my adorable little broom.
Solaris!

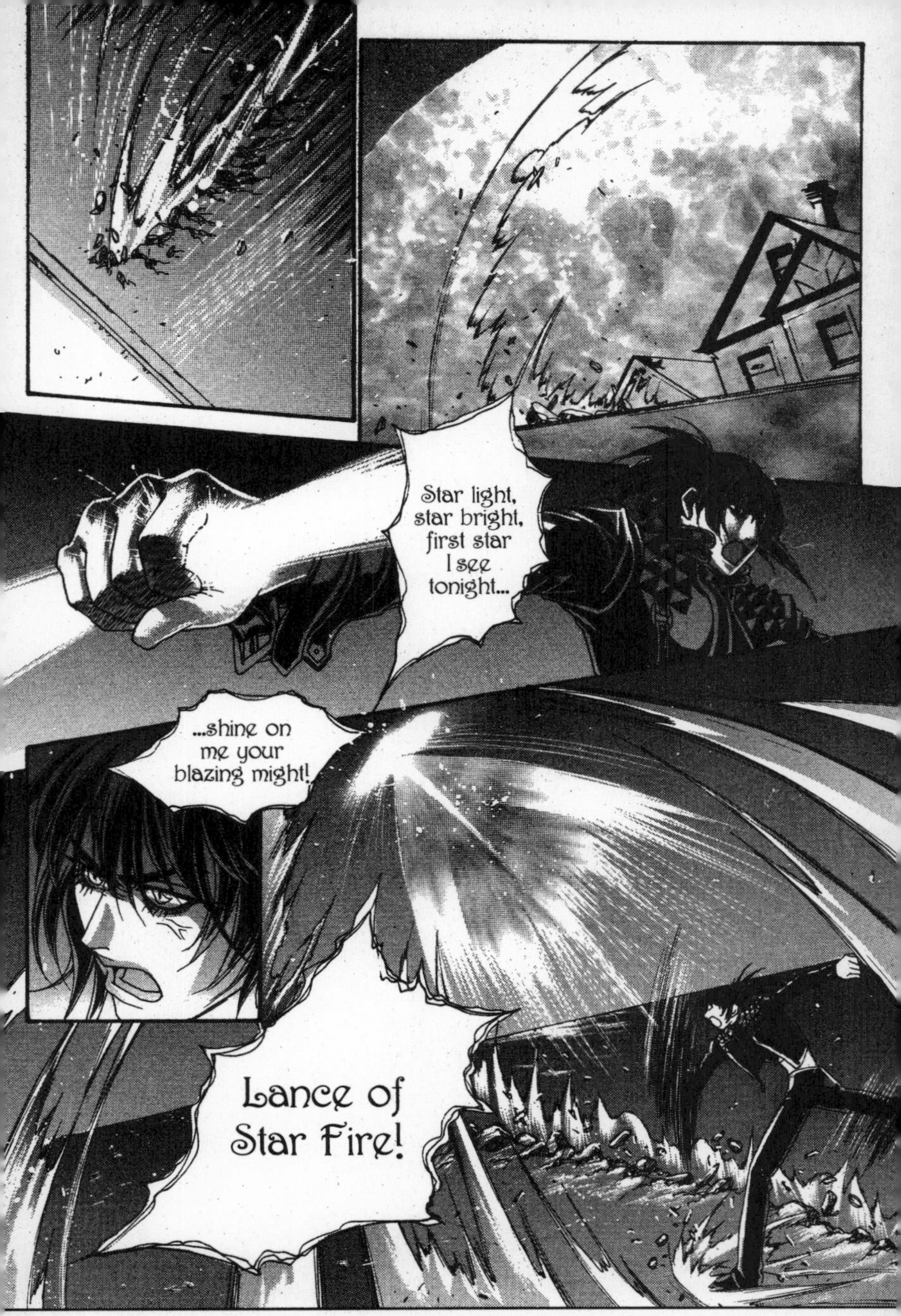

Star light, star bright, first star I see tonight...
...shine on me your blazing might!
Lance of Star Fire!

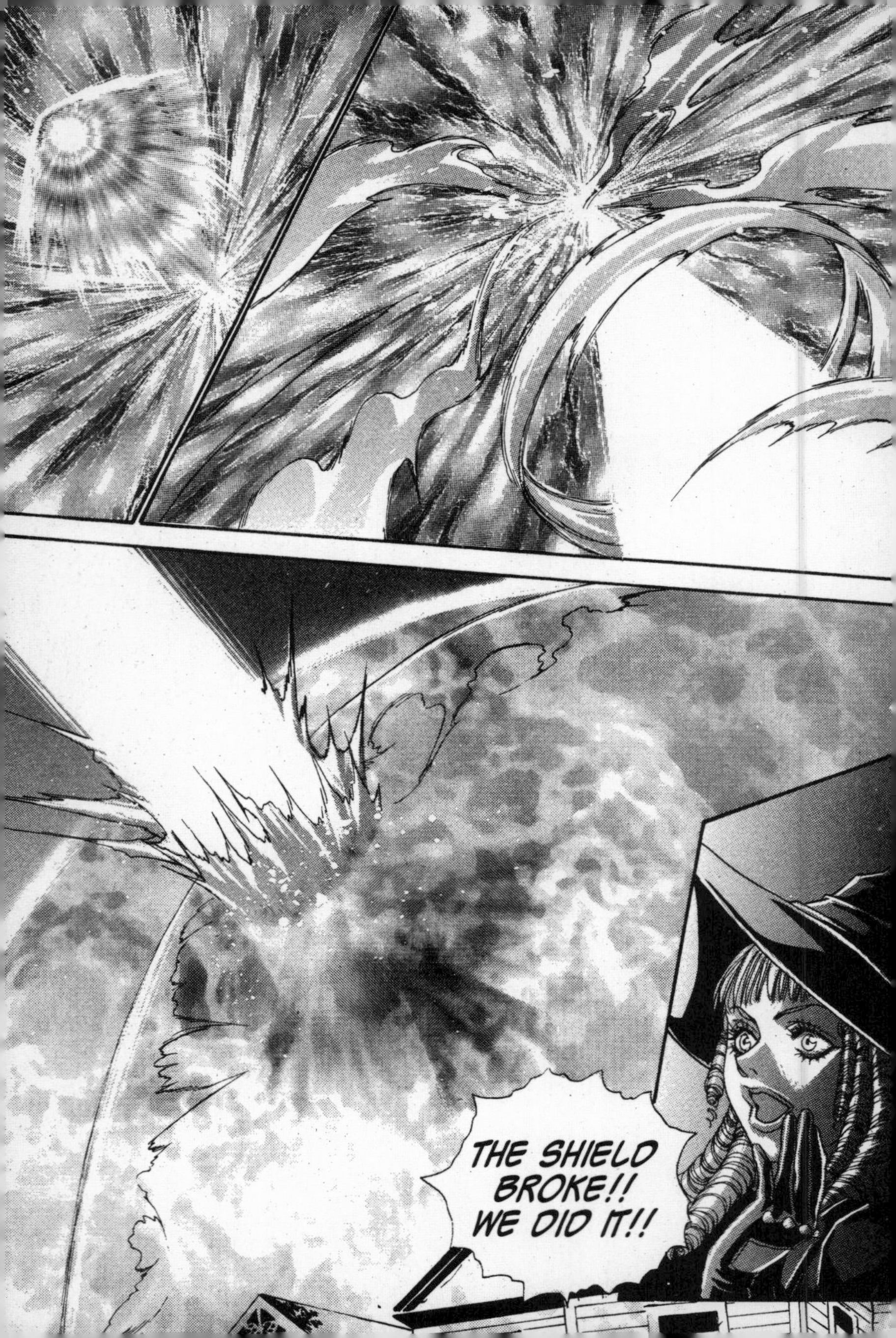
THE SHIELD BROKE!! WE DID IT!!

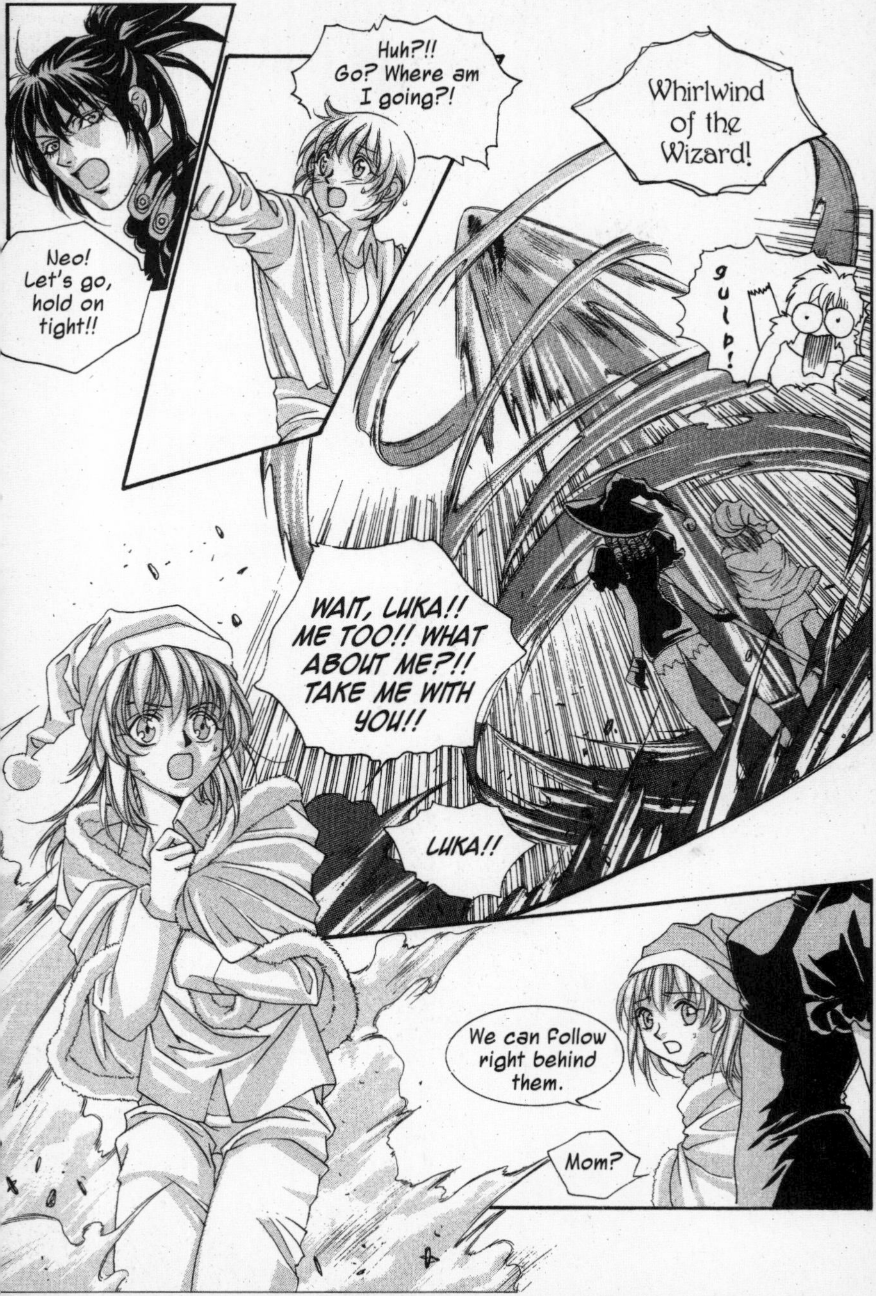
Neo! Let's go, hold on tight!!
Huh?!! Go? Where am I going?!
Whirlwind of the Wizard!
gulp!
WAIT, LUKA!! ME TOO!! WHAT ABOUT ME?!! TAKE ME WITH YOU!!
LUKA!!
We can follow right behind them.
Mom?

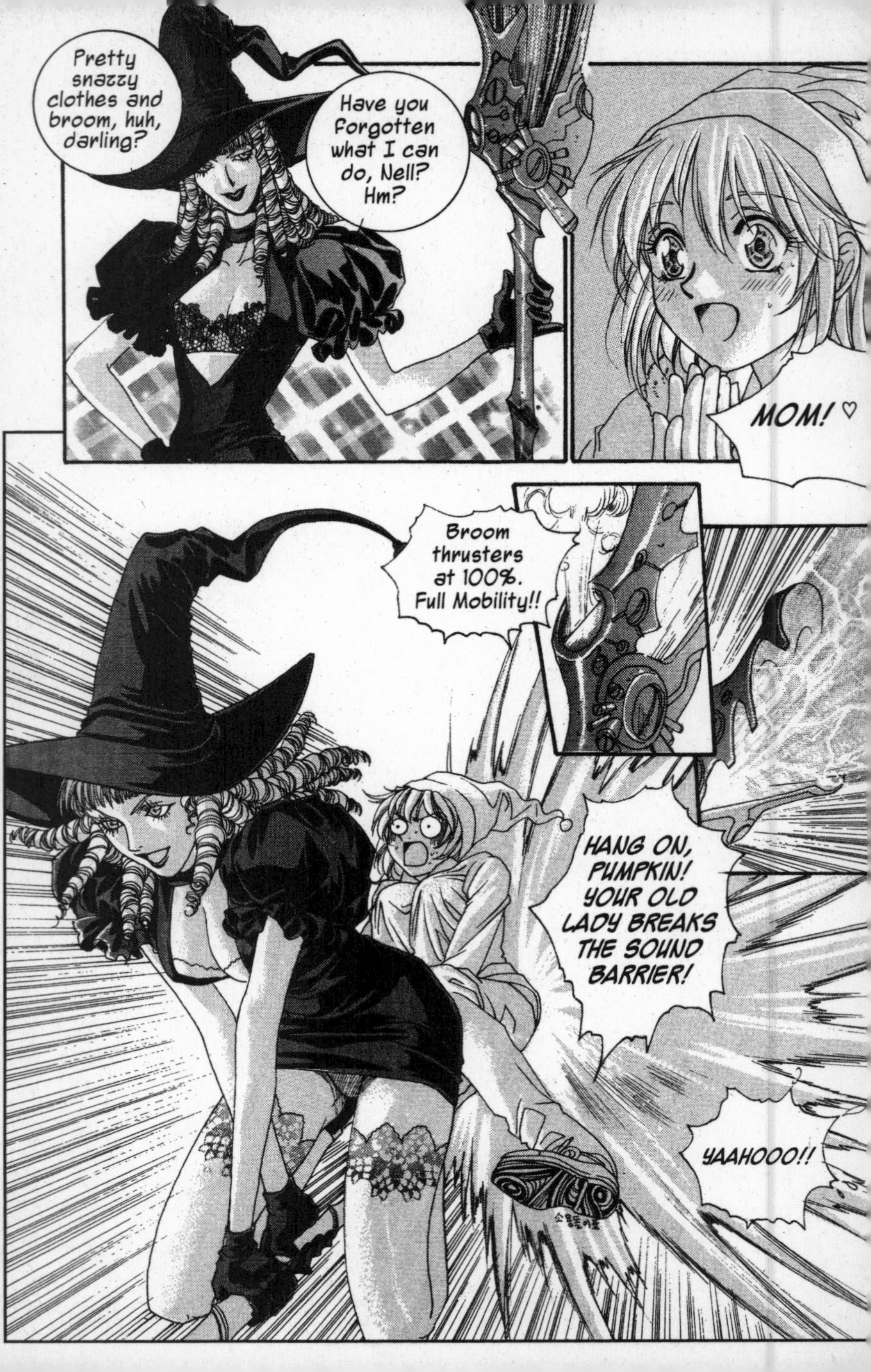
Pretty snazzy clothes and broom, huh, darling?
Have you forgotten what I can do, Nell? Hm?
MOM! ♡
Broom thrusters at 100%. Full Mobility!!
HANG ON, PUMPKIN! YOUR OLD LADY BREAKS THE SOUND BARRIER!
YAAHOOO!!

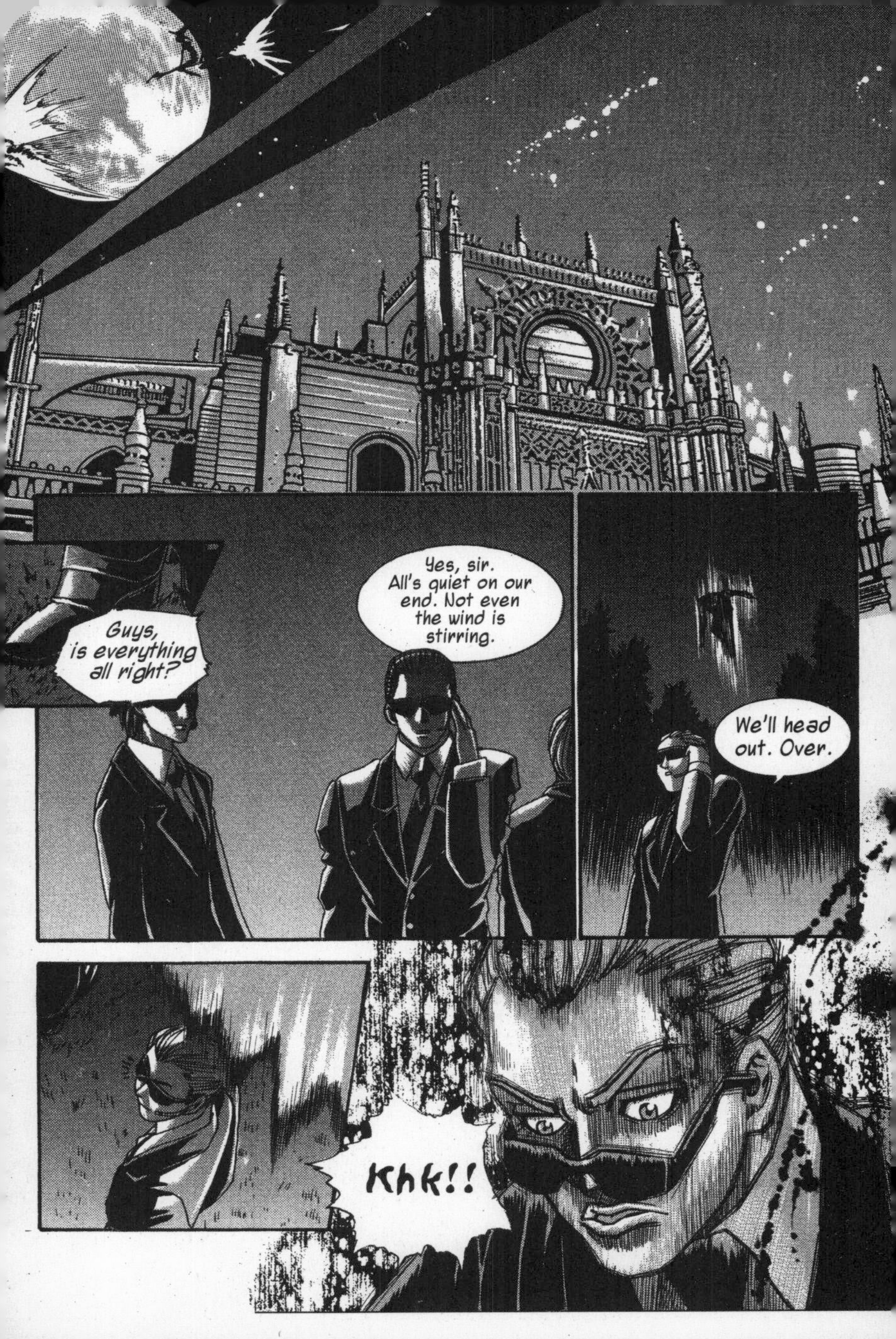
Guys, is everything all right?
Yes, sir. All's quiet on our end. Not even the wind is stirring.
We'll head out. Over.
Khk!!

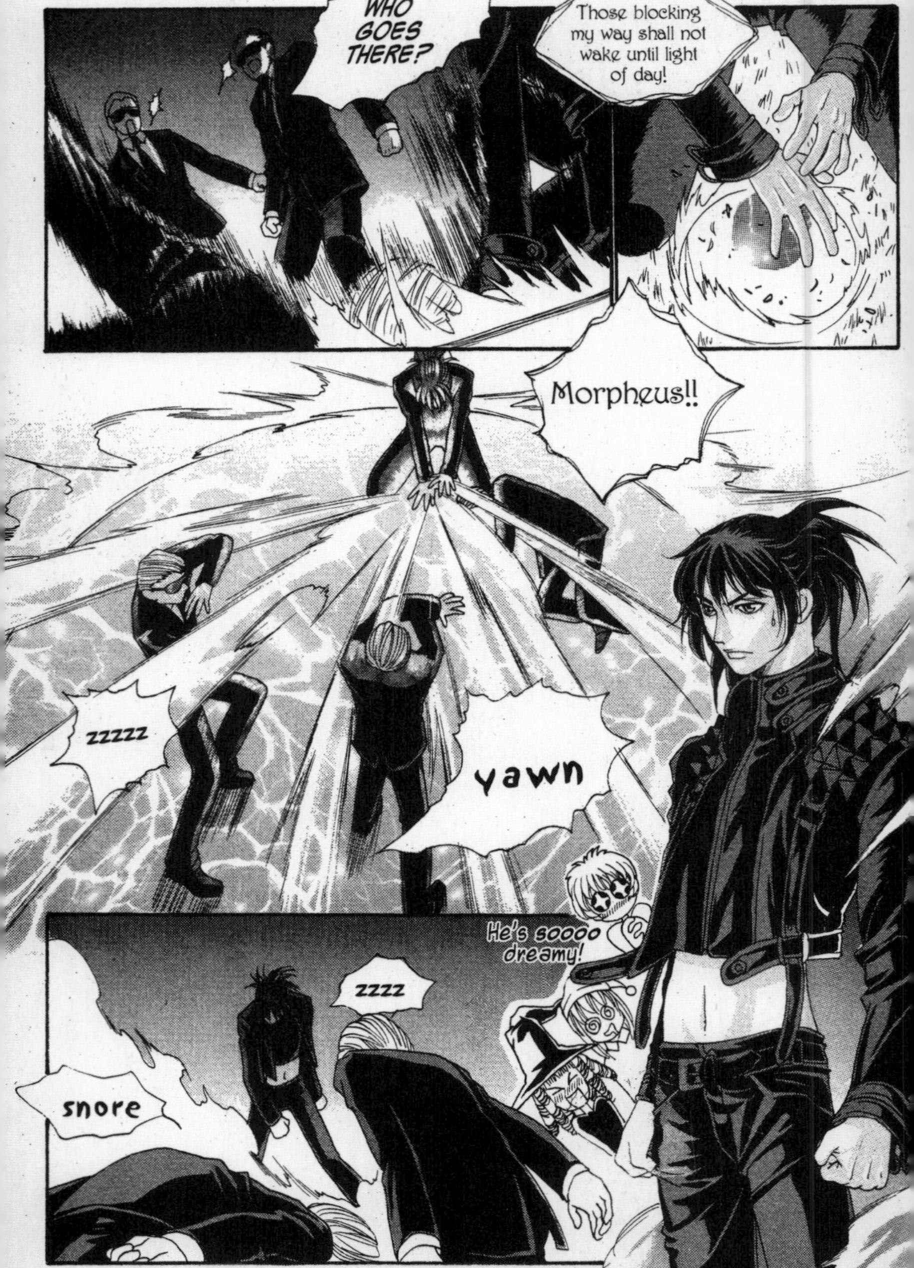

WHO GOES THERE?
Those blocking my way shall not wake until light of day!
Morpheus!!
zzzzz
yawn
He's soooo dreamy!
zzzz
snore

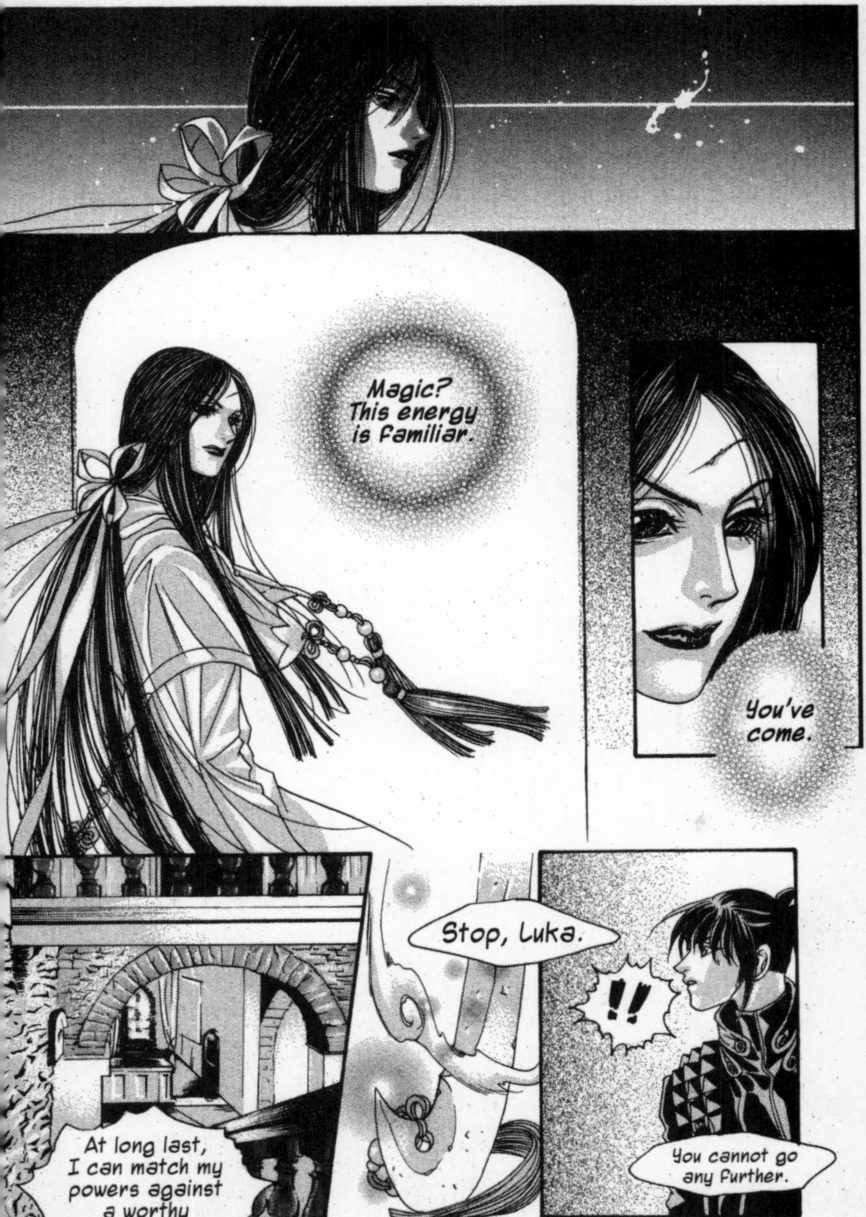

Magic? This energy is familiar.
You've come.
At long last, I can match my powers against a worthy adversary!
Stop, Luka.
!!
You cannot go any further.

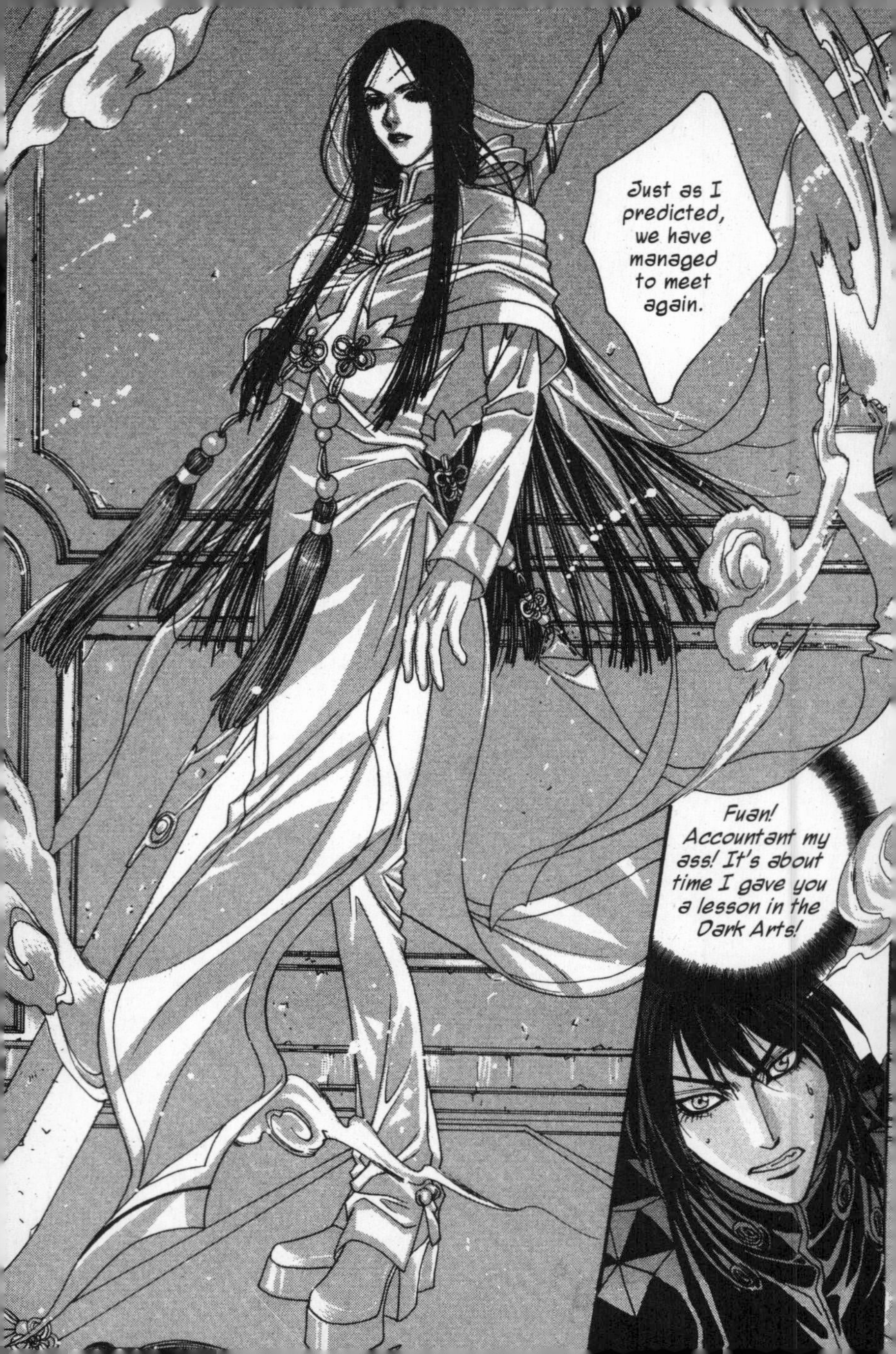
Just as I predicted, we have managed to meet again.
Fuan! Accountant my ass! It's about time I gave you a lesson in the Dark Arts!

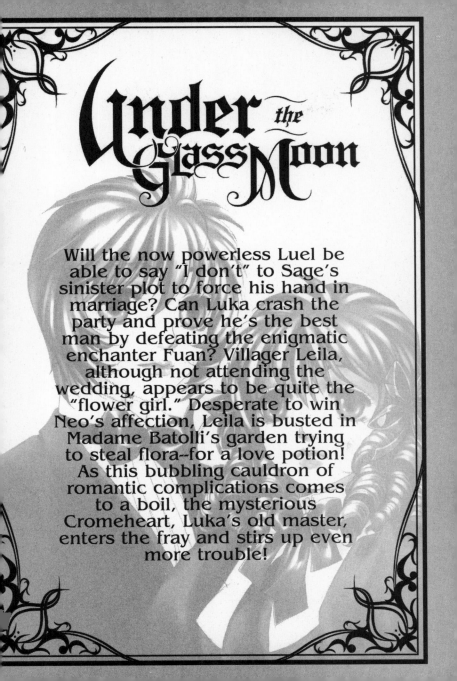

Under the Glass Moon

Will the now powerless Luel be able to say "I don't" to Sage's sinister plot to force his hand in marriage? Can Luka crash the party and prove he's the best man by defeating the enigmatic enchanter Fuan? Villager Leila, although not attending the wedding, appears to be quite the "flower girl." Desperate to win Neo's affection, Leila is busted in Madame Batolli's garden trying to steal flora--for a love potion! As this bubbling cauldron of romantic complications comes to a boil, the mysterious Cromeheart, Luka's old master, enters the fray and stirs up even more trouble!

BRIGADOON

TOKYOPOP

TWO UNLIKELY ALLIES IN ONE AMAZING ANIME.

BY SUNRISE:
*The Creator of
Gundam and
Cowboy Bebop*

*"Brigadoon is paving the
way for a new fan favourite in the
North American anime community.
...quite possibly, the perfect blend
of wacky humour and intense battles"*
—Otaku Aniverse

DVD Vol. 1 Available Everywhere Great Anime Is Sold!
Manga Coming to Your Favorite Book & Comic Stores August 2003!

T TEEN AGE 13+

www.**TOKYOPOP**.com

SAMURAI DEEPER

KYO

100% AUTHENTIC MANGA

BY: AKIMINE KAMIJYO

Slice the surface
to find the assassin within

The Action-Packed Samurai Drama that Spawned the Hit Anime!

SAMURAI DEEPER KYO, VOL. 1 BATTLING ITS WAY INTO YOUR FAVORITE BOOK & COMIC STORES JUNE 2003

OT OLDER TEEN AGE 16+

www.TOKYOPOP.com

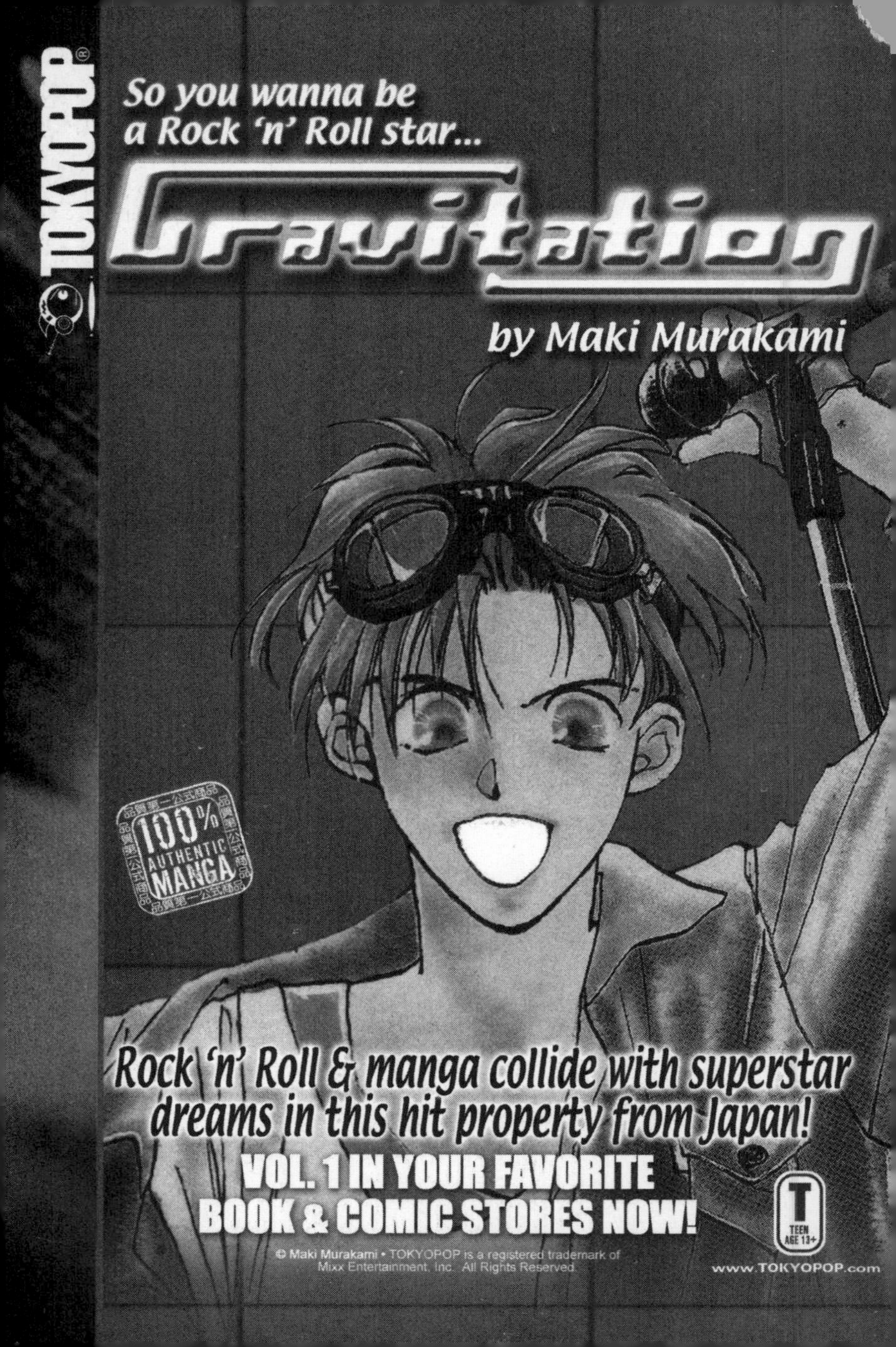
TOKYOPOP®
So you wanna be
a Rock 'n' Roll star...
Gravitation
by Maki Murakami
100% AUTHENTIC MANGA
Rock 'n' Roll & manga collide with superstar
dreams in this hit property from Japan!
VOL. 1 IN YOUR FAVORITE
BOOK & COMIC STORES NOW!
T TEEN AGE 13+
© Maki Murakami • TOKYOPOP is a registered trademark of
Mixx Entertainment, Inc. All Rights Reserved.
www.TOKYOPOP.com